ngJin Kim

Environmental interpretation and sustainable tourism

Aise KyoungJin Kim

Environmental interpretation and sustainable tourism

Promoting Visitors' Environmental Attitudes and Behaviour

LAP LAMBERT Academic Publishing

Impressum/Imprint (nur für Deutschland/only for Germany)
Bibliografische Information der Deutschen Nationalbibliothek: Die Deutsche Nationalbibliothek verzeichnet diese Publikation in der Deutschen Nationalbibliografie; detaillierte bibliografische Daten sind im Internet über http://dnb.d-nb.de abrufbar.
Alle in diesem Buch genannten Marken und Produktnamen unterliegen warenzeichen-, marken- oder patentrechtlichem Schutz bzw. sind Warenzeichen oder eingetragene Warenzeichen der jeweiligen Inhaber. Die Wiedergabe von Marken, Produktnamen, Gebrauchsnamen, Handelsnamen, Warenbezeichnungen u.s.w. in diesem Werk berechtigt auch ohne besondere Kennzeichnung nicht zu der Annahme, dass solche Namen im Sinne der Warenzeichen- und Markenschutzgesetzgebung als frei zu betrachten wären und daher von jedermann benutzt werden dürften.

Coverbild: www.ingimage.com

Verlag: LAP LAMBERT Academic Publishing GmbH & Co. KG
Dudweiler Landstr. 99, 66123 Saarbrücken, Deutschland
Telefon +49 681 3720-310, Telefax +49 681 3720-3109
Email: info@lap-publishing.com

Approved by: Guildford, Unversity of Surrey, 2007

Herstellung in Deutschland:
Schaltungsdienst Lange o.H.G., Berlin
Books on Demand GmbH, Norderstedt
Reha GmbH, Saarbrücken
Amazon Distribution GmbH, Leipzig
ISBN: 978-3-8454-2995-3

Imprint (only for USA, GB)
Bibliographic information published by the Deutsche Nationalbibliothek: The Deutsche Nationalbibliothek lists this publication in the Deutsche Nationalbibliografie; detailed bibliographic data are available in the Internet at http://dnb.d-nb.de.
Any brand names and product names mentioned in this book are subject to trademark, brand or patent protection and are trademarks or registered trademarks of their respective holders. The use of brand names, product names, common names, trade names, product descriptions etc. even without a particular marking in this works is in no way to be construed to mean that such names may be regarded as unrestricted in respect of trademark and brand protection legislation and could thus be used by anyone.

Cover image: www.ingimage.com

Publisher: LAP LAMBERT Academic Publishing GmbH & Co. KG
Dudweiler Landstr. 99, 66123 Saarbrücken, Germany
Phone +49 681 3720-310, Fax +49 681 3720-3109
Email: info@lap-publishing.com

Printed in the U.S.A.
Printed in the U.K. by (see last page)
ISBN: 978-3-8454-2995-3

Contents

CHAPTER 8 CASE STUDY 1: LULWORTH COASTAL AREA

CHAPTER 9 CASE STUDY 2: CHARMOUTH COASTAL AREA

List of Tables

CHAPTER 8

CHAPTER 9

List of Figures

List of Abbreviations

WCED – World Commission on Environment and Development

WTO – World Tourism Organisation

UNEP – United Nations Environmental Programme

AONB – Areas of Outstanding Natural Beauty

JCWHSSG – Jurassic Coast World Heritage Site Steering Groups

SSSI – Site of Special Scientific Interest

SAC – Special Areas for Conservation

SPA – Special Protection Areas

WWF – World Wildlife Fund

Acknowledgements

First of all I would sincerely like to express my deepest appreciation to my supervisor Professor David Airey. Throughout my research process, he has given me the valuable supervision, guidance, and especially, superb feedback in the final writing stage. I really appreciate his patience and encouragement, which has enabled me to move forward to the next step whenever I have struggled at each stage of the research process.

There are many academics who have helped me through the research process. I appreciate all of their suggestions and directions. I would especially like to mention the following researchers: The theoretical contribution of this research from Professor David Uzzell and Professor Michael Riley is greatly appreciated in providing me with a better understanding of psychological concepts, attitudes, and behaviour during the questionnaire development process at the early stages of the study. I appreciate all the Korean PhD students who have given me practical help and direction in the research methodology. The useful suggestions and encouragement from Dr. Yilmaz Guney are also greatly appreciated.

I would also like to thank Meirel Whaites who is from the Charmouth Heritage Coast Centre and Maddy Pfaff from the Lulworth Cove Heritage Centre. Their permission of the visitor surveys for this research and the initial interview during the data collection process. Throughout several pilot and main surveys, they have helped with collecting data from the visitors and given me special enjoyment and learning about the Jurassic fossils. I would like to thank all the visitors who had participated in the survey with their time and great interest into my research.

All my friends, Huseyin, Katherin, Jong-a, Seok, and Monica as research assistants have helped with the data collection. Especially, I really appreciate Simon and Nerea who have given me great emotional support along the way in following the research process. Their friendship and contributions to this research are immense.

Lastly, I would like to express the greatest appreciation to my parents, brother, and sister who have helped me with the financial and emotional support throughout this research. They have given me a great opportunity to follow my dream. Sadly, last year I lost two important people in my life, my brother-in-law and my good friend, Lui Ul-il Lee. I will always remember them and may they rest in peace.

CHAPTER

1

Chapter 1 Introduction

1.1 Background of the Research

As concern has grown about the negative impacts of tourism on the environment, sustainable tourism has become one of the most popular concepts in the tourism field (Tubb, 2003). As reviewed in the literature, the main principles of sustainable tourism management acknowledge that the potential conflict between tourism and its resources can be resolved by maintaining a balance between the needs and requirements of all stakeholders. This includes the quality of visitor experiences, the quality of life of the local community, the economic benefits for the tourism industry, and the protection of both the cultural and natural environments for both the present and future generations (Moscardo, 1997; Kuo, 2001). Although the potential significance of sustainable tourism has been recognised, the success of achieving different dimensions of sustainability has been debated in the context of the application of the principles into practice (Bramwell & Lane, 1993; Butler, 1998).

A key question is how best to achieve sustainable tourism by integrating tourism and conservation. Several management tools and strategies for sustainable tourism have been suggested including the participation and cooperation of local authorities, community involvement, local regulations, and interpretation/education (Barrow, 1995/96; Lane, 1994; Tubb, 2003). However, it is not easy to apply the integrated policy objectives for holistic goals of sustainable tourism to practical tourism contexts. Previous researchers have emphasised that it is important to employ appropriate management strategies and techniques for the implementation of sustainable initiatives in order to achieve the different dimensions of sustainability from different stakeholders' perspectives (Johnson, 2002).

In particular, in response to the increasing numbers of tourists visiting sensitive natural environments and their impact, visitor management has been considered as an important tool in achieving the goals of sustainable tourism development (Cooper et al., 1998, Kuo, 2002).

Several visitor management strategies have been identified including limiting activity to a site's capacity, adapting the resource and influencing visitor behaviour (Moscardo, 1996) as well as economic measures (Littlefair, 2002). Particularly, the objectives of visitor management can be achieved through two major approaches which include 'interpretation' and 'regulations' influencing visitor behaviour. Many researchers have supported the view that environmental interpretation can play an important role as an effective visitor management strategy in influencing visitor behaviour for effective management and conservation, as well as for sustainable tourism development, rather than regulations or rules (Cooper et al., 1998; Moscardo, 1998; Kuo, 2002; Tubb, 2003).

Tracking back to the role of interpretation in an early historical context, it is worth reviewing Tilden's definition of interpretation which has been widely used around the world. As defined by Tilden (1977:p.8), interpretation is 'an educational activity which aims to reveal meaning and relationships through the use of original objectives, by first-hand experiences, and by illustrative media, rather than simply to communicate factual information'. Recently, the educational role of interpretation emphasised by Tilden seems to have shifted to add management goals to the role of interpretation in natural areas or protected areas. It has been recognised that interpretation has become a widespread management tool in the park management field (Sharpe, 1976; Tubb, 2003).

Through a review of changes in the interpretation phase, it is also acknowledge that interpretation plays multi-functional roles in various ways according to in different tourism settings and different goals of the organisation involved it to be achieved. A number of the objectives of interpretation were identified as follows: promotional objectives; recreational objectives; educational objectives; management/conservation objectives. Many objectives of interpretation have been evaluated, but most of the research has focused on the recreational effectiveness of the programmes in holding the visitors' attention and enhancing visitors' enjoyment and satisfaction (Light, 1991). There has been less attention given to an evaluation of the management or educational objectives of interpretation. However, as the methodological approaches of the relationship between attitudes and behaviour have been developed in educational psychology, recently, the educational effectiveness of interpretation has been evaluated regarding increasing visitors' knowledge and understanding as well as changing attitudes and behaviour (Thom 1980; Cable et al., 1987; Orams 1997).

In order to achieve the goals of sustainable tourism development, the management/conservation objectives of interpretation should be emphasised and evaluated in the future. It is worth noting that there is a significant difference between educational objectives which are used mainly in the study of museums or heritage sites and management objectives of interpretation in protected areas or natural sites. In other words, educational objectives aim to increase visitors' knowledge and understanding of the environment and culture. Beyond encouraging greater levels of knowledge, management/conservation objectives of interpretation are to modify visitors' inappropriate behaviour and to encourage environmentally responsible behaviour toward the conservation of the site (Sharpe, 1976; Beckmann, 1991; Wearing & Neil, 1999).

16

Based on this line of research, several researchers support the premise that the evaluation of conservation objectives of interpretation can make a significant contribution to effective visitor management through influencing where visitors go and informing visitors about appropriate behaviour (Moscardo, 1998; Ham and Weiler, 2002). For example, inappropriate behaviour of visitors may cause negative environmental impacts and this may be due in some cases to visitors simply not being aware of the potentially negative environmental impacts of their activities (Tribe et al., 2000). In turn, successful interpretation leads to the achievement of the goals of sustainable tourism development for both the quality of the tourist experience and conservation of the environment (Moscardo, 1998; Ham and Weiler, 2002; Tubb, 2003).

Despite the widespread support for environmental interpretation as a solution to minimising tourists' impacts on the natural and cultural environment while encouraging their quality of experiences, there has been little empirical research or evaluation to determine whether and how interpretation helps to develop visitor understanding and modify their attitude and behaviour (McArthur and Hall, 1996; Kuo, 2002).

1.2 The Research Problem

In response to the need for research to evaluate the effectiveness of interpretation on attitude and behaviour change, this study aims to evaluate the effectiveness of interpretation in promoting responsible behaviour toward coastal conservation in particular tourism settings.

Due to the complexity and difficulty of measuring attitudes and behaviour, the effect of interpretation upon attitudes and consequent environmental behaviour has been a topic of much debate (Thom 1980; Cable et al., 1987; Orams 1997; Beaumont, 2001). Nevertheless, several efforts have been directed at determining the effect of interpretation programmes on attitudes and behaviour. Until now research findings suggest that interpretation programmes can help to enhance the quality of visitors' experience and knowledge of the features of the site. In turn, visitors may be influenced to be more environmentally aware and modify their previously inappropriate behaviour (Cooper et al., 1998; Moscardo, 1999; Kuo, 2002; Beaumont, 2001; Tubb, 2003).

However, the applied results of interpretation on knowledge, attitudes, and behaviour have been mixed (Cable et al., 1987; Orams, 1997; Kuo, 2002). The reasons for these unclear results may include a number of correlating factors regarding knowledge and attitudes, as well as the interpretive programmes themselves or the individual's attributes (Beaumont, 2001). It has been indicated that, in terms of attitudes and behavioural change, the application of interpretation in recreational sites is not always easy, and its effects may not occur immediately as a result of a single interpretive experience.

With regard to the inconsistent findings of the effectiveness of interpretation reviewed in the literature, research efforts now are focussing more on the question of 'when' and 'how' interpretation makes a positive contribution to changes in visitors' attitudes and behaviour rather than a simple question of 'if' interpretation influences visitors' attitudes and behaviour. While such research reviews are valuable, as Moscardo (1996) suggested, some integrative theoretical framework to guide both future visitor studies and the design of interpretation is clearly necessary to develop the effects of interpretation on attitude and behaviour change. Thus, for future research into the effectiveness of interpretation, it is worth assessing when and how visitors modify their behaviour after receiving that interpretation, considering a combination of correlated attitudinal components and other visitor variables (Kuo, 2002; Cottrell, 2003).

1.3   Purpose and Objectives of the Research

The main purpose of the research is to examine the role of interpretation in promoting the antecedents of responsible environmental behaviour toward conservation in order to achieve the environmental goal of sustainable tourism. In order to achieve this goal, this research includes two main research questions. The first aim of this study is to answer the question "is interpretation effective in promoting visitors' attitudes and behavioural intentions towards local environmental conservation issues?". The second research question aims to explore how interpretation influences visitors' specific responsible behavioural intentions along with the attributes of visitors and the attitude components.

(1) The specific objectives of the first research question are:
- To explore the profiles of visitors to the site
- To assess the visitor experiences on-site
- To explore the visitor attitudes and behavioural intentions toward conservation issues
- To identify the multi-dimensions of attitudes and behavioural intentions in the context of site-specific environmental conservation issues
- To examine the effects of interpretation on attitudes and behavioural intentions toward local environmental conservation issues and responsible behaviour

(2) The specific objectives of the second research question are:

- To investigate the relative contributions of interpretation methods, attitudes, and visitor characteristics to different types of specific responsible behavioural intentions
- To examine the inter-relationships between the most influential factors and different types of specific responsible behavioural intentions
- To identify which of the primary belief or feeling components of attitudes are the most significant contributors to different types of specific responsible behavioural intentions
- To assess which of the interpretation channel factors are the most significant contributors to different types of specific responsible behavioural intentions
- To identify which characteristics of the visitors are the most significant contributors to different types of specific responsible behavioural intentions.

1.4 Significance of the Research

Through its two main aims this study seeks to make several contributions to the emerging literature in the interpretation and tourism fields. It will examine the effects of interpretation upon visitors' attitudes and behavioural intentions from a number of perspectives. First, this research will provide evidence that will either support or reject the claims regarding the benefits of interpretation in fostering pro-environmental attitudes and behavioural intentions toward conservation. The evidence gained from the research may support the importance of the application of interpretation into various national and regional tourism plans and strategies as a key visitor management tool in achieving sustainability in protected areas.

In addition, based on the site-specific management policies regarding appropriate behaviour by visitors, this study will look at the strengths and weaknesses of interpretation in a variety of site-specific management issues, whereas previous research has focused mainly on one management issue. Empirical evidence from this study may help shifts and recommendations to be made regarding implications for local management policies and/or methods of improving interpretive programme design.

Finally, in terms of theoretical perspectives, the study will provide evidence regarding the relative contribution of interpretation along with attitudes and visitor characteristics to behavioural intentions. This information will make a contribution to the social and behavioural science literature in terms of those relationships. The research will also determine whether any particular types of individuals are more easily influenced in light of their environmental attitudes and behavioural intentions than others, and in particular, will reveal whether any specific aspects of the interpretation experience have a greater influence than others. These findings will enable decisions to be made in more appropriate and specific approaches in targeting visitors for effective interpretation in terms of integrated sustainable tourism and conservation.

1.5 The Structure of the Research

This research is organised on the basis of four main parts: literature review, methodology, the results of the field survey, and discussion and conclusions. The structure of this research is presented in Figure 1.1, consisting of eleven chapters. In the literature review, there are four main chapters, including sustainable tourism, interpretation, the theories of attitude and behaviour change and persuasion models, and interpretation in action.

Firstly, **Chapter 2** reviews the literature on the connection between sustainable tourism and interpretation. It starts with the concept of sustainable tourism, tourism impacts and the principles and policies of each dimension of sustainability are briefly explored in the following section. In addition, visitor management strategies including regulation and interpretation are reviewed at the end of the chapter.

Chapter 3, the definitions of interpretation are introduced along with a brief history of interpretation. Next, the role of interpretation as a visitor management tool is discussed. The principles of interpretation, the different types of interpretation methods, and effective techniques are also reviewed in the following section. Furthermore, the evaluation of interpretation is explored at the end of the chapter.

Chapter 4 provides an overview of numerous theories related to attitudes and behaviour change and persuasion models. The key factors identified by the theories, and measurement issues are also explored.

Chapter 5 summarises previous studies which have examined the effectiveness of interpretation upon visitors' knowledge, attitudes, behavioural intentions, and behaviour in the particular tourism fields.

The methodological approaches and the design for the research are described in Chapter 6 and Chapter 7. **Chapter 6** includes a discussion about the conceptual framework, specific research objectives, and the procedures for selecting the Dorset Heritage Coast, part of the Jurassic Coast, as the research site. It also gives a brief background of each heritage coast site, namely, the Lulworth Coastal Area and Charmouth Coastal Area.

Chapter 7 addresses the methodological approaches in terms of methods and techniques, and examines the strengths and weaknesses of the survey method as well as the sampling methods. The results from the pilot research helped design a questionnaire for the basis of the main survey. The modification of the questionnaire designs are discussed in the next sections respectively. Data collection and data analysis conducted for this study are also described.

The findings of the main visitor survey are presented in Chapters 8 and 9. The four stages in these chapters are organised around the research objectives and data analysis methods. **Chapter 8** presents the results relating to the Lulworth Coastal Area. Then the findings related to the Charmouth Coastal Area are described in **Chapter 9** in a similar format to Chapter 8.

After this, **Chapter 10** discusses the main outcomes of this study related to research objectives and the review of the literature. Finally, **Chapter 11** provides an overview of the main conclusions and significant contributions of this research, and presents implications, limitations and some recommendations for future research based on those findings.

Figure 1.1 Structure of the Research

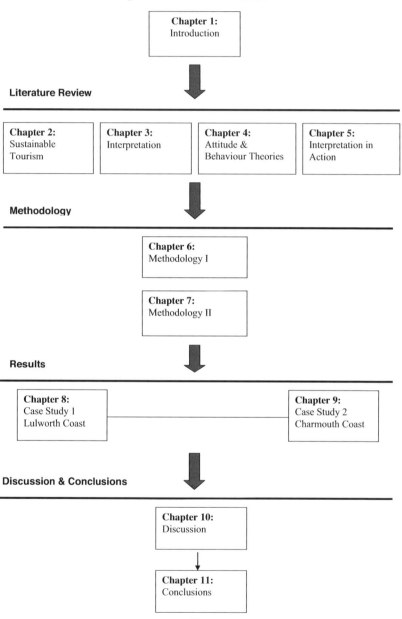

CHAPTER

2

Chapter 2 Sustainable Tourism

2.1 Introduction

This chapter explores the three main issues related to the concept of 'sustainable tourism' in the broader context: (1) the meanings of sustainable development and sustainable tourism; (2) the principles of sustainable tourism and detailed policies regarding specific goals of sustainability; (3) management approaches to sustainable tourism in the protected area context.

The first section discusses the key debates over how the concept of sustainable tourism is related to growth of and demand for sustainable development, its historical background, its definitions and its attainability. Then, the next section explores the key principles of sustainable tourism, the specific policies of different goals of sustainability in maximising the balance of benefits and costs of tourism on four main dimensions. Lastly, in response to lack of implementation of the goals of sustainable tourism in the context of a particular tourism destination, the essential attention in the present study is given to a focus on the role of visitor management strategies in implementing the objectives of environmental sustainability in protected areas.

2.2 The Concept of Sustainable Tourism

2.2.1 The Growth and Debate on 'Sustainable Development'

Over recent years, the phenomenon and growth of mass tourism has led to a range of problems such as environmental, social and cultural degradation and the unequal distribution of financial benefits (Mowforth and Munt, 2003). In response to the problems of the impacts of tourism and the global concern of sustainable development issues, sustainable tourism has become one of the most popular concepts in the tourism industry. Despite this high level of interest and the widespread acceptance of the term, there is an on-going debate over the concept of sustainability, sustainable tourism and the application of the principles of sustainable development in the context of tourism. Due to the uncertain, ambiguous, and ideological characteristics of the term 'sustainability' from a number of perspectives, the alternative viewpoints on sustainability and sustainable tourism might have a fundamental effect on altering the objectives and practice of tourism policy and management in different tourism situations (Bramwell *et al.*, 1996). However, the literature on sustainable tourism has tended to avoid the link with the sustainable development processes. Instead it concentrates on a more sector-specific approach to simplify and enhance the appeal of the concept for the commercial industry (Miller and Twining-Ward, 2006: 27). This section briefly discusses two main issues in how sustainable tourism needs to be understood in terms of a sustainable development perspective and how this is best approached in the application of sustainable development in tourism.

The Need for Sustainable Development to Be Seen in its Historical Context

The concept of sustainable tourism has evolved from its predecessor, the more general concept of 'sustainable development' (Hunter and Green, 1995; Hardy and Beeton, 2001). In the review of the historical background of sustainable development, it is acknowledged that the rise in environmental concerns for conservation and dissatisfaction with economic development, later combining with the importance of community concerns, has led to the development of the term 'sustainable development', and ultimately 'sustainable tourism' (Hardy, Beeton, and Pearson, 2002). With respect to this contradictory argument between environmental protection and economic development, one stressed that 'economic growth is essential and that its benefits can be available for all. The others argued that economic growth causes environmental degradation, which is damaging to all' (Jacob, 1994; Barrow, 1995, cited in Milne, 1998: 36). Through international attempts to solve the conflicts of earlier decades, the concept of sustainable development has been embraced by the need for the integration of economic and environmental issues and social equity (Miller and Twining-Ward, 2006).

In particular, the origins and international recognition of sustainable development can be traced back to two main conferences: the Brundtland Report and 'Rio Earth Summit' (Agenda 21). The first was the Brundtland Report entitled *'Our Common Future'* by the World Commission on Environment and Development (1987) where the term 'sustainable development' was first used to bring together the apparently disparate concepts of economic development and environmental conservation (Garrod & Fyall, 1998). In this report, sustainable development was defined as 'development that meets the needs of the present without compromising the ability of future generations to meet their own needs' (WCED, 1987: 8) and it was considered as the only effective method for protecting the environment, addressing economic progress, alleviating poverty and preserving human rights (WCED, 1987; McCool and Moisey, 2001). The core elements were identified: (i) the concept of needs and subjective well-being, particularly for the poor, to whom priority should be given; (ii) the idea of limitations imposed by the state of technology and social organisation on the environment's ability to meet the present and future needs' (WCED, 1987: 43).

It is argued that although the Brundtland Report has discussed the key idea of the future of human society and the equity of subjective well-being for both the present and future generations, there is a limitation with minimal guidance offered for making its ideas operational (McCool & Moisey, 2001;

Miller and Twining-Ward, 2006). In response to the main unanswered point, the second important international conference, the United Nations Conference on Environment and Development (1992), known as the 'Rio Earth Summit' has attempted to establish a basis for the practical implementation of sustainable development at the local, national and international level in Agenda 21.

However, there are on-going criticisms of the concept of sustainable development for unequal and uneven concentration on ecological and economic aspects depending on the relationships of power (Mowforth and Munt, 2003). Mowforth and Munt (2003: 299) argued that 'sustainability is used by a variety of interests in a variety of ways as a means of supporting and enhancing their basis of power'. From different interest groups' perspectives, in particular, these two contradictions between environmental conservation and economic development perspectives are inherent and most problematic. For example, 'environmentalists' are pushing for a greater consideration of ecological conservation as the most important element in sustainable thinking which reflects 'strong sustainability' or an 'ecocentric' approach. On the other hand, others who emphasise 'human progress' focus on the continuity of human well-being and development through the maximisation of economic benefits and technical innovation which reflects 'weak sustainability' or an 'anthropocentric' or 'technocentric' approach (Pearce et al., 1987, cited in Milne, 1998; Miller and Twining-Ward, 2006; Turner et al, 1994; Hunter, 1997; Bramwell et al., 1996). Therefore, the different viewpoints of the concept of 'sustainability' or 'sustainable development' by both different nations or regions (i.e. developing and developed countries) and different interest groups (i.e. developers, economists, politicians, communities and environmentalists) may lead to different priorities and policies in the decision-making processes and in turn might create an unfortunate barrier to its effective implementation (Mowforth and Munt, 2003; Miller and Twining-Ward, 2006).

Overall, it is clear that there is no consensus and there is continuing debate on the meanings and conceptualisations of 'sustainable development'. It is also acknowledged that the different approaches over the definitions of sustainable development by different interest groups and their power relationships at a global and local level are essential for an understanding of sustainability and especially the emergence of new forms of tourism (Mowforth and Munt, 2003). Based on the brief overview of the sustainable development debate in the historical context, the next section seeks to gain a better understanding of several debates over the concept of sustainable tourism in line with sustainable development.

2.2.2 Debates over Definitions of 'Sustainable Tourism'

In response to increasing international support for sustainable development since the Brundtland Report (WCED, 1987), considerable attention has been given to the need for the application of the concept of sustainable development in the tourism industry because of the growing importance of economic aspects and their potential impacts (positive or negative) on the environment and the host community (Sustainable Development, 1998). Since the late 1980s, the term 'sustainable tourism' began to be used with widespread acceptance (Swarbrooke, 1999:7), and the principles of sustainable development have been rapidly applied to the tourism sector (Butler, 1998). In particular, the World Conference on Sustainable Tourism (1995) held in Lanzarote has attempted to develop the principles and objectives for sustainable tourism within the basis of 'Agenda 21 for the Travel and Tourism Industry', developed by the World Travel and Tourism Council, World Tourism Organization and the Earth Council (1995).

Three Major Perspectives of Sustainable Tourism

However, there is a continuing debate over the definitions, operational concepts, and implementations of sustainable tourism within the context of the complex nature of 'sustainability' or 'sustainable development' (e.g. Butler, 1991; Bramwell & Lane, 1993; Hunter, 1995, 2002; Miller and Twining-Ward, 2006). The review of the literature shows that there are a large number of different definitions of the concept of sustainable tourism. Such definitions of sustainable tourism are divided primarily within three categories; i) 'tourism-centric' approach (Hunter, 1995), focusing on sustainable tourism as an economic activity; ii) the new 'alternative' forms of tourism; and iii) those which consider tourism as a tool to achieve wider sustainable development policies.

The first perspective of the concept of 'sustainable tourism' places the emphasis primarily on how to maintain tourism industry businesses over a long time period. The main concern of this view focuses on only the tourism industry, particularly firms, ensuring the constant increase of tourist numbers and their expenditure in the visited area (McCool and Moisey, 2001: 4). The problem with this perspective, however, is that it does not necessarily recognise tourism as a tool for the enhancement of economic opportunity, protecting a community's cultural and natural heritage and maintaining a desired quality of life (McCool and Moisey, 2001: 4). In this sense, arguably, it is considered that the tourism-centric approach fails to address many of the key principles of sustainable tourism development and may even relatively work against the general requirements of sustainable development (Hunter, 1995).

27

The second view of sustainable tourism has been introduced as a result of the need for a new form of tourism and awareness of the negative impacts of mass tourism. In other words, the application of sustainable tourism was approached by the emergence of the debate over alternative types of tourism which was considered as the solution to the problems of mass tourism (Boyd, 2000: 166). The concept of alternative tourism reflects several key aspects such as being small-scale, developed by local people, based on local nature and culture, and paying particular attention to functioning within an area's carrying capacity (cited in Boyd, 2000: 166). In this sense, sustainable tourism is viewed as a kinder, gentler form of tourism that is generally small in scale and is concerned itself with how the negative economic, environmental and socio-cultural impacts of tourism activity can be reduced (McCool and Moisey, 2001: 4). This approach places great emphasis on the benefits to the local communities and preserving natural and cultural resources because they are important elements for the continued growth of the tourism industry (McCool and Moisey, 2001: 4).

This second approach, however, also has a limitation for ensuring sustainable development in terms of considerable confusion regarding the term among the other forms of tourism. It appears that certain types of alternative tourism such as ecotourism, nature-based tourism, and small-scale rural 'agro-tourism' are viewed as being inherently more sustainable than others (Swarbrooke, 1999). In particular, the linkage between sustainable tourism and ecotourism was highlighted by some researchers because of coexistence and common characteristics (i.e. the desire of participants to learn more about their destination than the average tourist; the attempt to maximise contact with indigenous people; the small size of most groups) (cited in Page & Dowling, 2002:23). By contrast, others have argued that ecotourism as a form of alternative tourism should not be viewed as sustainable tourism (Boyd, 2000). Ecotourism could easily become as harmful as other forms if the growth of ecotourism is proceed without any regulation (Swarbrooke, 1999). Therefore, no matter which form of tourism is developed predominantly in the future, it is acknowledged that the contradictory distinctions between sustainable tourism as the form of alternative tourism and mass tourism are unnecessary as positive action could make mass tourism more sustainable (Clarke, 1997). Thus, an approach is needed to make all forms of tourism work in a sustainable way (Swarbrooke, 1999: 9).

With respect to the debate over the two perspectives above, the third perspective of sustainable tourism raised by several researchers such as Butler (1993), and Hunter (1997) has emphasised that sustainable tourism needs to be considered as a method to enhance sustainable development. Butler (1993: 29) describes tourism in a sustainable development context as:

"... tourism which is developed and maintained in an area in such a manner and at such a scale that it remains viable over an indefinite period and does not degrade or alter the environment (human and physical) in which it exists to such a degree that it prohibits the successful development and well-being of other activities and processes."

Hunter (1995: 155) also stated that 'the short and long term sustainable tourism development should be concerned with improving quality of life issues for hosts, meeting demands of the visitor and the tourism industry while correspondingly safeguarding human and natural resources in order to achieve both of the preceding aims' (Hunter, 1995: 155-156).

Based on the third perspective, the concept of sustainable tourism development is integrated into the broader economic and social development context. In addition, this view places greater emphasis on considering tourism as a tool and not an end in economic development (McCool and Moisey, 2001). As mentioned in the different perspectives of sustainable development by different interest groups in the previous section, sustainable tourism is also considered as part of a larger policy framework designed to achieve a sustainable society. Thus, the different demands and interests of stakeholders in sustainability can significantly lead to different implications for social and economic policy, selection of indicators, public participation and planning processes. In this sense, this requires highly sophisticated planning approaches as a key factor in implementing sustainability (McCool and Moisey, 2001: 6).

The Problems of Scale

Apart from the different perspectives of the definitions of sustainable tourism in terms of balance and equity aspects, another criticism involves the uncertainty and difficulty of operating sustainable tourism in terms of scale, which includes spatial and temporal scale (Miller and Twining-Ward, 2006). Given the lack of research on this issue, Butler (1998) stressed that the issue of scale is an important element in implementing and measuring sustainability in the tourism context. There are arguments on which level of scale is needed to be considered in the application of sustainability into the tourism sector. First, regarding spatial scale, although the importance of the global scale is emphasised in the sustainable development literature, in the context of tourism, it is recommended that a place-based scale is needed to approach sustainable development (Wall, 1997; Miller and Twining-Ward, 2006). This is explained in that there are different issues depending on the particular tourism setting and thus there is a need to ensure a fit between the problem and the response at a local level. Butler (1998: 34) suggested that 'thinking globally and acting locally will work only if local actions are part of an integrated holistic approach and include solutions to past problems'.

Regarding temporal scale, in the discussion of the equity of the present and future generations in the sustainable tourism context, Butler (1998) emphasised that it is necessary to research the needs of both present and future generations in terms of both local residents and tourists while much attention has been given to the long-term equity of environmental resources in the previous tourism research. It is also recommended that tourism should be approached as a dynamic system (Jennings, 2001: 67), so that the achievement of sustainability and sustainable tourism can be identified through an ever evolving process or further time rather than in a particular period time (Miller and Twining-Ward, 2006).

Overall, different approaches to the concept of sustainable tourism in the tourism literature regarding its definitions, attainability, and operational context are reviewed. Despite this debate, the key aspects of sustainable tourism are identified in line with the principles of sustainable development. It is clear that the main purpose of sustainable tourism is to resolve the problems and impacts of tourism on the environment and the host community in different situations and to achieve the long-term equity of human and environment aspects in a holistic and integrated basis. It is also suggested that the concept of sustainability should be approached as the ideal and guidance in the decision making process for policy and planning and continuing monitoring processes in order to make all kind of tourism more sustainable.

2.3 The Principles of Sustainable Tourism

2.3.1 The Principles of Sustainable Tourism

Although the concept of sustainable tourism has been applied in different ways, at both national and local levels, and in the public and private sectors in different settings, there is a common consensus of the key principles of sustainable tourism which has been identified by Bramwell *et al.* (1996:p.44); United Nations Environmental Programme (UNEP) and World Tourism Organization (WTO) (2005: 16-17); Mowforth and Munt, 2003: 107). There are:

1)   Emphasis on limitations to growth and that tourism must be managed within the limits of maximum use of tourism development resources regarding economic, social, cultural, and environmental dimensions

2)   The holistic and integrated approaches in terms of environmental, economic, social, cultural, political and managerial aspects

3)   Long-term rather than short-term thinking is necessary

4)   The importance of satisfying human needs and aspirations for equity and fairness

5)   The importance of appropriate policy, planning and management process in response to the problems of natural and human resource misuse in tourism

6)   The involvement and consultation of all stakeholders in tourism decision-making

7)   The importance of education and communication for both the community and tourists in relation to an understanding and awareness of the environmental issues and encouragement of appropriate attitude and behaviour toward the host community and the environment

8)   The importance of continuous monitoring using indicators regarding different impacts of tourism over time as well as the effects of sustainability aims and objectives

As with an understanding of the goals of sustainability and the principles of sustainable tourism management, again, it is reviewed that a holistic, integrated, long-term approach, equating the needs and interests of stakeholders are the main key issues in achieving the goals of sustainable tourism. However, when it comes to the complex and difficult aspects of the achievement of sustainable tourism, there is little guidance on the main issues such as 'how sustainable tourism might be achieved' and 'what the implications of sustainable tourism could be' (Swarbrooke, 1999; Bramwell *et al.*, 1996). In response to this, a number of measures of impacts, sustainability and planning frameworks have been developed in order to achieve the goals of sustainable tourism development (see Wright, 1998 for the review). Based on this point, this section focuses on the two major issues: (i) a brief overview of different aspects of the impact of tourism and the specific policies of different aspects of sustainability associated with each impact; (ii) a brief review of the key requirements in the appropriate policy and planning process and monitoring process.

2.3.2 The Impacts of Tourism and Different Goals of Sustainability (Economic, Socio-Cultural, Environmental and Political Dimensions)

For sustainable tourism to be achieved, as pointed out in the key principles of sustainable tourism above, a holistic approach is necessary to understand all impacts of tourism and its relationships with all stakeholders within the particular tourism destination in terms of economic, environmental, and socio-cultural aspects (see Figure 2.1). Although the impacts of tourism have been categorised in a number of ways by several researchers, in general, the impacts of tourism tend to depend on the economic diversity of the area, the number and type of visitors, and the social and cultural structure of the local community, as well as its geographical, physical and ecological capacity (Aronsson, 2000). In addition, tourism can influence both negatively and positively for most actors – destination communities, tourists, tourism businesses and the government (Milne, 1998; Bramwell *et al.*, 1996; Swarbrook, 1999). In this sense, as seen in Table 2.1, this section reviews briefly all

31

four main dimensions of the impacts of tourism categorised by Hall and Page (2006) based on the review of several researchers' categories.

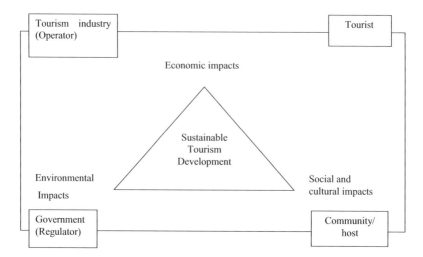

Figure 2.1 The Basic Impacts of Tourism on An Area and Stakeholders in Relation to Sustainable Tourism Development

(Source: Adapted from Aronsson, 2000 and Mason, 2003)

With regard to an understanding of different aspects of the benefits and costs of tourism above (see Table 2.1), the next step must be considered as how these impacts of tourism can be managed and implemented to achieve the different goals of sustainability associated with each of the impacts. As pointed out in one of the key principles of sustainable tourism above, it is important to understand appropriate policy, planning and management processes that address the problems of economic, social and environmental issues as well as political aspects to manage the potential of tourism in terms of both harm and benefit. In this section, as the current research focuses on environmental goals of sustainable tourism which is the primary policy in protected areas, this study reviews in more detail the environmental impacts of tourism and environmental sustainability than others.

Table 2.1 Positive and Negative Dimensions of the Impacts of Tourism

Type of Impact	Positive	Negative
Environmental Impacts (Physical/ Environmental)	• Conservation of heritage • Development of new facilities • Improvement of local infrastructure • Visitor management strategies	• Environmental damage • Changes in natural processes • Architectural pollution/destruction of heritage • Overcrowding • Changed feeding and breeding habits of wildlife
Economic Impacts (Economic)	• Increased expenditures • Creation of employment • Increase in labour supply • Increase in standard of living • Increase in investment	• Localised inflation • Real estate speculation • Failure to attract tourists • Better alternative investments • Capital outflows • Inadequate estimation of costs of tourism development • Undesirable opportunity costs including transfer of funds from health and education
Socio-Cultural Impacts (Social/Cultural)	• Increase in permanent level of local interest and participation in types of activity associated with event • Strengthening of regional values and traditions	• Commercialisation of activities which may be of a personal or private nature • Modification of nature of event or activity to accommodate tourism • Potential increase in crime • Changes in community structure • Social dislocation
Socio-Cultural Impacts (Psychological)	• Increased local pride and community spirit • Increased awareness of non-local perceptions	• Tendency toward defensive attitudes concerning host regions • High possibility of misunderstandings leading to varying degrees of host/visitor hostility •
Political impacts (Administrative)	• Enhanced international recognition of region and values • Development of skills among planners	• Economic exploitation of local population to satisfy ambitions of political elite • Distortion of true nature of event to reflect values of political system • Failure to cope • Inability to achieve aims • Increase in administrative costs • Use of tourism to legitimise unpopular decisions • Legitimisation of ideology of local elite

(Source: adopted from Hall and Page, 2006: p.145)

(1) Environmental Impacts of Tourism and Environmental Sustainability

Environmental Impacts

As seen in Table 2.1, there are both negative and positive aspects of environmental impacts on a destination environment and on the interaction between wildlife and tourists. A number of adverse environmental impacts caused by tourism include damage of ecological habitats and loss of flora and fauna due to overcrowding, overdevelopment of tourism infrastructure, and unregulated recreation activities; pollution (e.g. water, air, noise, architectural destruction of heritage); and changed feeding and breeding habits of wildlife caused by human behaviour (Mathieson and Wall, 1982; Holden, 2000; Hall and Page, 2006).

However, tourism such as natural-based tourism or ecotourism can influence the natural environment positively by providing a motivation for environmental conservation through raising tourist awareness of environmental issues (Swarbrooke, 1999). In addition, tourism can help protect the environment from other potentially more damaging forms of industrial and residential development (e.g. logging, farming, and mining) (Holden, 2000). In particular, it can provide new uses for abandoned buildings in towns and cities, through the development of new visitor attractions and improvement of local infrastructure (Swarbrooke, 1999; Hall and Page, 2006).

Environmental sustainability

Environmental sustainability means conserving and managing resources, especially those that are not renewable or are precious in terms of life support (UNEP and WTO, 2005:9). There are several key policies in achieving the environmental goals of sustainable tourism as follows:

- There is a need for the **designation and management of all types of protected area** for appropriate land use (e.g. national parks, areas of outstanding natural beauty (AONBs), sites of special scientific interest (SSSIs), wildlife reserves/refuges)
- There is a need for the **assessment of carrying capacities** in the planning process and in controlling visitor numbers. The concept of carrying capacity contains the idea of the maximum number of people who can use a site without causing negative effects on the resources and without reducing the quality of the experience gained by the visitors (i.e. the level of visitor satisfaction) (Mathieson and Wall, 1982: p.21; Butler, 1997). Recently, different elements in the concept of carrying capacity beyond physical considerations have been considered such as the social, cultural and economic capabilities of the destination (O'Reilly, 1986, cited in Butler, 1997; Holden, 2000). However, several researchers have argued that the concept of carrying capacity based on only the limit of maximum permissible visitor numbers is extremely problematical in its application in

tourist destination areas (Butler, 1997; Holden, 2000; UNEP and WTO, 2005). The different factors affecting the carrying capacity limit and the environmental impacts of tourism are quite both numerous and complex (UNEP and WTO, 2005). The influences of several factors include: the type of tourist and their behaviour; fragility of the landscape regarding development and change; existing levels of tourism development and supporting infrastructure; and the absence of responsibility for the quality of the resources and control for overuse and resource damage (Holden, 2000; Butler, 1997). Therefore, appropriate efforts at setting capacity limits should be considered in the planning process according to management objectives, expert judgement and broader public values rather than only limiting the number of visitors (Bramwell *et al.*, 1996; Wight, 1998; Holden, 2000).

- There is a need for **legislation and a system of resource-use planning** (land, water, energy, and other resources) **and development control** to reduce the negative impact of tourism on the environment. For example, these include ensuring the efficient use of land and raw materials in tourism development (e.g. zoning); promoting the use of more sustainable transport (e.g. the promotion of walking and cycling, trails and public transport services); the provision of environmentally sound infrastructure for the sewerage system and waste disposal; promoting a reduce, reuse, recycle mentality (e.g. purchasing of supplies from sustainable sources such as ecolabelling schemes for relevant consumer products, minimising use of unnecessary packaging)

- There is a need for **visitor education and communication**. This includes educational activity to change the inappropriate behaviour of tourists and development of codes of conduct for the tourism industry, local community and visitors in minimising the negative impacts of the environment

- There is a need for **environmental impact analysis and indicator monitoring**. Environmental impact assessment (EIA) can be used in decision-making in the development process through obtaining and evaluating environmental information about the potential impacts of a physical development (e.g. hotel complexes, visitor attractions, and infrastructure such as airports, roads, waste treatment and energy plants) (UNEP and WTO, 2005). In addition, regular monitoring of changes in environmental conditions using selected indicators (e.g. water and waste management, number of rare/endangered species, category of site protection) can allow for an adaptive management approach that is more flexible than the heavy use of regulations (UNEP and WTO, 2005: p.73)

(Source: Swarbrooke, 1999; Holden, 2000; Mowforth and Munt, 2003; UNEP and WTO, 2005)

(2) Economic Sustainability

35

The economic impacts of tourism have been mostly concentrated within tourism and recreation research. Previous research has emphasised the positive economic impacts of tourism rather than the negative economic impacts. In the sustainable tourism context, the goals of economic sustainability means 'generating prosperity at different levels of society and addressing the cost effectiveness of all economic activity' (UNEP and WTO, 2005:9). In order to achieve the goals of economic sustainability, it requires a number of key policies: 1) effective and ongoing market research to guide tourism development in the destination; delivering visitor satisfaction, to meet their expectations and the quality of the visitor experiences; 2) support for locally owned businesses and encouragement of employment of local labour; 3) strengthening networking between the local supply businesses including packaging of offers and the supply chain (e.g. between accommodation operators and suppliers of food or handicrafts) (UNEP and WTO, 2005).

(3) Socio-Cultural Sustainability

The social and cultural effects of tourism have been given less attention in the sustainable tourism debate than the environmental impact or the economic impact of tourism. This is because the socio-cultural impacts of tourism occur slowly over the long-term and are therefore more difficult to measure (Swarbrooke, 1999; Mowforth and Munt, 2003). However, in response to the integrated holistic approach to sustainable tourism, the attention to social-cultural aspects of sustainability has been increased in the recent literature (Bramwell *et al.*, 1996; Hardy *et al.*, 2002).

In order to overcome the negative effects of tourism on the local society and the conflicts between the host community and visitors, a more sustainable form of tourism in the context of socio-cultural dimensions can be achieved through several policies: 1) equity and fair distribution of economic and social benefits from tourism; 2) influencing the responsible behaviour of the tourists toward local communities; 3) encouragement of community participation in decision-making in the policy, planning and management process; 4) developing interpretation and education for both residents and visitors concerning the value of the historic heritage, authentic culture, traditions, and distinctiveness of host communities; 5) ensuring effective visitor management and conservation of cultural and historic heritage sites (Swarbrooke, 1999; UNEP and WTO, 2005)

(4) Political Sustainability

As discussed in the previous section, it is clear that different policies and approaches are considered in response to the different benefits and costs of tourism on each of the socio-cultural, economic, and environmental dimensions. Therefore, political aspects of sustainability are another important issue in achieving one of the key principles regarding the harmony and equity of these diverse elements for sustainable tourism (Bramwell *et al.,* 1996).

As seen in Table 2.1, there are both positive and negative impacts of tourism in terms of a political perspective. In order to achieve political sustainability, it requires establishment of appropriate goals and objectives in the process of policy, planning, and management within the local tourism context through two approaches: 1) ensuring effective coordination of policy and actions among the various government agencies at the national, regional, and local levels (e.g. collaboration between government agencies and other industry sectors); 2) engaging all stakeholders in the formation of a strategy and policies for sustainable tourism (e.g. community participation) (UNEP and WTO, 2005).

2.3.3 The Involvements of Stakeholders in the Policy and Planning Process

As pointed out above, stakeholder involvement has been recognised as a key step in shaping policies and actions of achieving sustainable tourism development (Bramwell *et al.,* 1996). Key stakeholders include the local community, the tourism industry, the tourists, and the government (Aronsson, 2000; Mason, 2003). Additional stakeholders are voluntary organizations/NGOs and the media (Swarbrooke, 1999). Among them, particularly, community participation is regarded as a central point of planning and management in the context of sustainable tourism (Bramwell *et al.,* 1996).

For a more sustainable outcome, the differences in perceptions and interests of stakeholders toward sustainability issues should be understood between groups through education and information provision. This helps the decision-makers to avoid any costs associated with poor planning and management and the consequential conflicts of interest over the use of resources between stakeholders (Hardy & Beeton, 2001; Bramwell *et al.,* 1996). Therefore, in practice, trade-offs and collaboration by stakeholders are necessary in the decision-making process on different courses of action in order to provide the equal distribution of the costs and benefits derived from tourism development between the stakeholders involved (Bramwell *et al.,* 1996).

2.3.4 The Importance of Monitoring Sustainability Indicators

Another related issue in the key requirement of sustainable tourism is the development and monitoring of sustainability indicators (McCool and Moisey, 2001). Monitoring sustainability indicators within a particular tourism destination is an important evaluation process in achieving the goals of sustainable tourism. This stage involves taking regular measurements of environmental,

37

social and economic conditions using selected indicators in order to assess their change over time (Twining-Ward and Butler, 2002; UNEP and WTO, 2005). This assessment can be used 'as an early warning of when a policy change or new action may be needed' and 'as a basis for the long term planning and review of tourism' (UNEP and WTO, 2005:p.72). The World Tourism Organisation has proposed a set of 11 core indicators for sustainable tourism management which are mainly macro-scale indicators without those indicators related to the micro-scale or site level. However, to be effective in practice, it is suggested that it is critical for local decision-makers to identify and select appropriate indicators through stakeholder involvement according to the priority issues identified in a specific tourism destination (Twining-Ward and Butler, 2002).

2.3.5 Problems of Implementation of Sustainable Tourism

Although sustainable tourism principles and requirements are well acknowledged, as pointed out in this section, there is lack of discussion on the issue of how the concept of sustainable tourism can be applied and implemented in practice (Garrod and Fyall, 1998). Garrod and Fyall (1998) suggested that now it is time to move on from defining sustainable tourism to begin to consider how best it may be implemented in practice. However, it is often argued that tourism may never be totally sustainable. Arguably, it is also difficult and still remains unclear which approaches and techniques for the application of the principles of sustainable tourism are needed to turn it into reality, and the required practical management actions needed in a specific tourism context. As mentioned earlier, the major reasons for the difficulty of the implementation of sustainable tourism lie in different environments and social circumstances as well as different value judgements and expectations of sustainability (ecological, economic, cultural, social and political) by different stakeholders (Wight, 1998; Bramwell *et al.*, 1996; Butler, 1998).

In implementing the goals of sustainable tourism, it is clear that the development of an appropriate management policy and planning is an important step based on the involvement of stakeholders. However, 'even the best planned management procedures will fail without public support' (Wearing and Neil, 1999: p.54). In this way, a strong base of public support is now regarded as one of the first prerequisites for recreation and tourism management (Wearing and Neil, 1999). The following section will discuss in more detail different management approaches of sustainable tourism, particularly visitor management strategies and actions which are the main subjects of this research.

2.4 Management Approaches of Sustainable Tourism

2.4.1 The Importance of Visitor Management Strategies in Achieving Sustainable Tourism

For the practical management actions applied in attempts to secure sustainable tourism, particular attention is given in the present study to the importance of visitor management strategies in the context of environmentally sensitive tourism destinations. In particular, recently, with regard to the continuing growth of nature-based tourism or ecotourism to the natural environment such as parks and protected areas, particular attention has been given and several attempts made to reduce the environmental impact of tourism, especially, that associated with visitor activities and behaviour (Leung *et al.*, 2001).

In the protected areas context, environmental sustainability is considered as the primary goal of sustainable tourism, although other goals of sustainability are needed to be integrated in the planning and management process. From the environmental sustainability perspective, the concept of sustainable tourism management places greater emphasis on two objectives (tourists' enjoyment and responsibility, and environmental protection) and proposes that the potential conflict between tourism activities and environmental protection can be managed by maintaining a balance between the needs of the environment and visitors (Kuo, 2002).

As reviewed briefly in terms of impacts of tourism in the previous section, the tourist is often considered as the cause of the 'problem', with respect to the environmental, economic and social impacts of their activities and behaviour (Swarbrooke, 1999). As most protected areas are fragile and the even the smallest human impacts can have significant environmental effects (Wearing and Neil, 1999), it is noted that the majority of the negative environmental consequences in environmentally sensitive areas are caused by the activities of the visitors rather than infrastructure and facility development (Leung *et al.*, 2001). Those negative impacts by tourist activities include soil and vegetation damage, water pollution, and wildlife harassment. For instance, overuse of sites by visitor activities influences the greater adverse impacts, particularly, on site damage along trails or campsites, and at attraction features such as waterfalls, coral reefs or wildlife viewing areas (Leung *et al.*, 2001). Another example by Deming (1996) indicated that migratory bird habits at Point Peele National Park in Ontario, Canada have been negatively influenced by birdwatchers and their inappropriate behaviour (e.g. walking off the footpaths for viewing and photographing species) during the spring migration (cited in Page and Dowling, 2002:178).

Therefore, visitor activity impacts are particularly important management concerns within the natural environment areas in managing the balance between nature-based tourism or ecotourism development and environmental protection (Ceballos-Lascurain, 1996, cited in Leung *et al.*, 2001). Without appropriate and effective visitor management, tourism can lead to adverse impacts on the fragile natural environments so that it might affect negatively on visitor satisfaction (Page and Dowling, 2002). In this way, visitor management strategy is considered to be a true tool of sustainable tourism management, encouraging visitors to adopt more appropriate behaviour to protect the resource-sensitive tourism destinations while ensuring that the visitor receives a high quality experience (Cooper *et al.*, 1998; Kuo, 2002).

In order to achieve the main objectives of visitor management, a wide variety of useful tools or techniques for visitor management have been developed and applied to ensure that use of the environment resources is more sustainable. To be effective, it is important to determine when selecting specific strategies and techniques what will be useful in a particular management situation (Eagles and McCool, 2002). The following section discusses in more detail the role and application of different tools and techniques in managing visitor impact.

2.4.2 Hard and Soft Visitor Management Strategy

There are two major approaches for visitor management strategies adopted in many tourism destinations, namely, 'hard' or 'direct' management (i.e. to regulate or restrict visitor activities and behaviour), and 'soft' or 'indirect' management (i.e. to influence visitor decision processes of the appropriate behaviour) (Orams, 1996b; Cooper *et al.*, 1998; Kuo, 2002; Eagles *et al.*, 2002).

Table 2.2 Functions of Hard and Soft Visitor Management Strategies

Hard visitor management strategies: aimed at regulating or restricting visitor activities	Soft visitor management strategies: aimed at educating visitors
• Resource hardening such as construction of boardwalks, reconstruction and repair of heritage buildings and monuments • Zoning • Restrictions on access and certain activities • Implementation of rules and regulations • Discriminated entrance and parking fee charges	• Provision of visitor information and environmental interpretation • Increasing visitor enjoyment and understanding • Minimising the inappropriate visitor behaviour

(Sources: Orams, 1999; Cooper *et al.*, 1998; Kuo, 2002)

40

Table 2.2 describes the different functions and purposes of hard and soft visitor management strategies. Hard management approaches restrict visitors' choice while soft management seeks to influence visitors, leaving them greater freedom to choose (Newsome *et al.*, 2002). The more detailed actions and tactics for each strategy are discussed in the following section.

2.4.2.1 Hard Visitor Management Strategies

Three broadly different management approaches for hard visitor management strategies are oriented towards: (1) physical management strategies; (2) regulatory management strategies; (3) economic management strategies (Orams, 1999).

(1) Physical Management Strategies

Physical management strategies focus on 'those human-made structures that control human activity by restricting the movement or type of activity which can be undertaken' (Orams, 1999: p.77). Physical structures can be utilised for several purposes including reducing negative environmental impacts by intensive use, discouraging use in sensitive areas, providing recreation needs better, and improving safety for tourists (Orams, 1999).

Such specific actions for physical controls involve:

• Site hardening such as building animal viewing platforms, boardwalks and pathways to prevent site deterioration from trampling, erosion, and disturbing flora and fauna.

• Building fences to stop visitors entering ecological sensitive areas;

(Source: Orams, 1999; Newsome, Moore, and Dowling, 2002)

These strategies have been used widely to manage visitors' interaction with sensitive resources in protected natural areas (Yale, 1991; McArthur and Hall, 1993; Orams, 1999). However, this approach is relatively expensive and can cause damage to vegetation if the wrong materials are used (Eagles *et al.*, 2002). Furthermore, this might influence increased crowding by restricting the flow of visitors (Hall and McArther, 1998).

(2) Regulatory Management Strategies

Regulatory management practices focus on managing visitors themselves through restricting access, group size and length of stay, times and numbers of visits as well as visitor activities or behaviour (Orams, 1999; Newsome *et al.*, 2002). The purposes for establishing rules and regulations include such as managing and operating the site; reducing conflicts between tourists or traffic congestion;

ensuring visitor safety at the site; and protecting wildlife and heritage from disturbance or inappropriate visitor behaviour (Kuo, 2002). Examples of specific actions involve:

• Closing a specific area for all use or for certain uses for a specified time. Area closures are used at environmentally sensitive sites, near wildlife concentrations, or in the habitat of endangered species in order to allow areas to recover and to reduce human impacts from certain activities (Orams, 1999; Eagles *et al.*, 2002)

• Spatial and temporal zoning: zoning is one of the key strategies for managing protected areas (Newsome *et al.*, 2002). It is designed to allocate specified areas for different types and levels of use of visitor activities, other land uses, and conservation (Hall and McArther, 1998; Orams, 1999; Eagles *et al.*, 2002). It involves a range of spatial zones from developed areas such as service centres or towns with a strong emphasis on tourist provision at one end to remote and wilderness areas with no development at all at the other end. Additionally, temporal zoning involves setting of different uses at different times, within the course of the day, over the week or seasonally (Eagles *et al.*, 2002).

• Restriction on visitation by numbers and group size: a limit on visitor numbers and restrictions regarding the size of groups entering a particular tourism setting can be commonly applied in camp-sites, wilderness hiking, canoeing situations and access to historic buildings and sites (Eagles *et al.*, 2002). This approach is useful in potentially controlling the biophysical and social impacts of excessive use levels (Eagles *et al.*, 2002).

• Restriction on access by transport: it can be applied in setting a limit on the size of car parks or other public transport (i.e. bus numbers, size of boats or frequency of trains) (Eagles *et al.*, 2002).

• Limits on times and locations: pre-registration or pre-booking allocates the specific sites to visitors or groups before entry into a recreation area such as camp-sites, trekking trails or historic sites. This approach is useful in minimising inter-party competition and spreading the number of visitors over time (Eagles et al., 2002). When the demands of visitors are higher than supply, length of stay limits can also be applied to provide increased accessibility to the area for more visitors (Eagles *et al.*, 2002).

• Restriction on types of visitor activity permitted: this approach prohibits visitors from certain types of activities which may be harmful or impact detrimentally on others (e.g. use of all motorised water craft within 100 metres of shore) in order to reduce conflict and harm between tourists (Orams, 1999)

• Requiring minimum skill level: only visitors with a certain training/ certification skill level (e.g. Scuba certification) are allowed to access the specific area (Orams, 1999).

• In addition, it includes restrictions on the types of equipment permitted such as off-road/highway vehicles as well as regulating visitor behaviour by codes of practice (Hall and McArther, 1998).

In general, physical construction and regulation management practices remain the most common management strategy in response to increasing recreational demand and in reducing visitor impacts on the natural environment (McArthur and Hall, 1993, cited in Orams, 1999; Orams, 1996b). However, there are several disadvantages of the enforcement of rules and regulations such as restricting the freedom of visitors, reducing enjoyment of the visitor experience, and increasing the cost of enforcing rules (Orams, 1999; Eagles *et al.*, 2002). Thus, the purposes of these restrictions and physical alterations of the resources should be explained to visitors so that they might be more supportive of the resource protection in the site (Kuo, 2002).

(3) Economic Management Strategies

Economic management approaches seek to use prices as incentives or disincentives to modify visitors' behaviour. An example of this type of strategy includes differential fees for certain groups, activities, times or locations (Orams, 1999). In other words, higher entry fees during peak use times or times when wildlife is more sensitive to disturbance can be utilised in an attempt to spread for off-time visiting. Another example of a regulation combined with an economic disincentive is imposing fines for littering or other inappropriate behaviour. On the other hand, it can be used for offering visitors a financial reward for undertaking the appropriate behaviour, such as reporting vandalism and a clean-up littering project (Orams, 1999). In a number of natural environment destinations, these techniques have been used for many years (Plimmer, 1992, cited in Orams, 1999) and in particular, may be useful to generate additional funds and accomplish management objectives when the public management agencies are under financial pressure (Orams, 1999).

2.4.2.2 Soft Visitor Management Strategies: Education and Interpretation

Another approach for visitor management is education and interpretation, namely 'soft visitor management strategies'. Education-based management strategies focus on two main functions: increasing visitor enjoyment and understanding of the site, and minimising the inappropriate visitor behaviour by encouraging a voluntary behaviour change (Orams, 1999). The purposes of education and interpretation help visitors to raise awareness of the local issues and leave the visitors the freedom to choose for themselves what to do or where to go rather than directly regulating or controlling visitors (Newsome *et al.*, 2002; Eagles *et al.*, 2002). In this way, the value of education and interpretation can be regarded as a longer-term, complementary strategy while the hard visitor management strategy is considered as more short term and immediate (Newsome *et al.*, 2002).

There are three types of visitor information identified: directorial, behavioural and educational.

- **Directorial information** contains a wide range of information, including direction, distance and approximate required time for travel, opening hours and emergency contacts.

- **Behavioural interpretive information** aims to provide a guideline of desired visitor behaviour and activities to carry out at a site, such as visitor code.

- **Educational interpretive information** includes essential interpretive information to provide visitors the opportunity to know about the site, and to further alter their inappropriate activities.

(Kuo, 2002)

Interpretation is widely applied in protected areas such as historical sites and national parks where a growing number of visitors causes severe pressure (Kuo, 2002). However, the effectiveness of providing education and information compared with other management actions is poorly known and is an on-going debate (Newsome *et al.*, 2002; Kuo, 2002). This might be because the immediate effects of interpretation provision are difficult to measure and the change of visitor behaviour may result not from the interpretation but from other factors such as the characteristics of visitors (e.g. different group size, age, social norms) (Orams, 1999; Kuo, 2002). As a result, education (or interpretation) has been little used as a management strategy while the use of physical or regulatory techniques has been predominant in some tourism situations (Orams, 1999; Kuo, 2002). In addition, it has rarely been incorporated fully into major planning frameworks (Roggenbuck, 1987, cited in Wearing and Neil, 2000). However, several researchers have argued that interpretation should be considered as a fundamental element for visitor management in managing nature area tourism (Roggenbuck, 1987; Bramwell and Lane, 1993 in Orams, 1999; Wearing and Neil, 1999; Newsome *et al.*, 2002). With regard to this point, the next chapter will explore the important role of interpretation in more detail for sustainable tourism management.

2.4.3 Selection of Appropriate Visitor Management Strategies and Actions

The previous section explores several strategies and techniques for visitor management in implementing and managing tourism in a more sustainable way. The next question asks how to select appropriate visitor strategies and actions in response to different visitor impacts in the specific tourism settings. A number of factors should be considered in selecting appropriate techniques by managers including 'the cause, location and extent of the impact of concern, the cost and ease of implementation of actions and their effectiveness, and the preferences of visitors and managers' (Newsome *et al.*, 2002:p.185).

In order to maximise the outcomes of visitor management strategies, the combination of two approaches (namely, 'hard' or 'soft' visitor management) is necessary and complementary. For example, if impact problems are widespread at particular locations or require immediate solution, then hard visitor management actions such as redistributing visitor use and regulating visitor number are required (Cole, 1995, cited in Newsome *et al.*, 2002). However, Kuo (2002) emphasises that hard visitor management is useful for a short-term effect in managing visitors' impacts but it cannot achieve long-term effect when applied alone due to their restrictive character. In order to maximise the outcomes of visitor management strategies, the soft management such as education (or interpretation) should be used to support the applications of hard visitor management strategies through explaining why the regulatory actions such as area closures or restriction of the visitor number are needed and the consequences of inappropriate behaviour (Newsome *et al.*, 2002; Eagles *et al.*, 2002; Kuo, 2002). In turn, it can help achieve a longer-term sustainability by encouraging tourists to engage in an environmentally responsible way for conservation goals as well as for enhancing the quality of the visitor experience (Newsome *et al.*, 2002; Kuo, 2002).

Overall, it can be concluded that successful visitor management can achieve a balance between the needs and requirements of the tourism resources and the visitors through implementing careful selection of appropriate visitor management strategies and actions. It is also emphasised that visitor management strategies should be an integral part of the tourism management plan (Kuo, 2002). In this way, effective visitor management can help to sustain the development of tourism in environmentally sensitive tourism sites (Kuo, 2002).

2.5 Summary

This chapter reviews the three major issues in the debate over the concept of sustainable development and sustainable tourism; the key principles and requirements of sustainable tourism; and visitor management issues in implementing the goals of sustainable tourism. Despite on-going debate over the definitions of sustainable tourism and its application in different tourism situations, overall definitions of sustainable tourism emphasise three main features: 'quality (quality of life for hosts, for environmental resources, for tourist experiences)', 'continuity (the present and the future generation)' and 'balance' (between the needs and interests of all stakeholders). Next, the main key principles and requirements for achieving sustainable tourism are discussed and the major issues reviewed: the holistic understanding of different impacts of tourism; identification of capacities and targets in the contexts of the goals of ecological, socio-cultural, economic, political sustainability associated with each aspect of impacts; involvement of all stakeholders in policy-decision making and planning process; the importance of community participation; government cooperation;

education; and continuous monitoring indicators of sustainability and assessment of impacts at a local or global level and at a present or future level. Lastly, two major approaches in managing the impacts of tourist activities on the environment include 'hard' visitor management strategies and 'soft' visitor management strategies. Despite the significant benefits of education and interpretation in achieving the goals of sustainability there was a lack of research on the effectiveness of interpretation on managing visitor behaviour. Therefore, the next chapter will discuss this issue, regarding the role of interpretation in visitor management.

CHAPTER

3

Chapter 3 Interpretation

3.1 Introduction

The previous chapter partly addressed the important role of interpretation as a visitor management technique in achieving the goals of sustainable tourism. This chapter will begin with the link between interpretation and sustainable tourism. Then, three main issues regarding interpretation will be discussed. First, it reviews the definitions of interpretation, the historical development of interpretation, different benefits of interpretation, and the management role of interpretation. Secondly, several principles and requirements for effective interpretation will be explored. These principles of interpretation will be useful in planning, implementation, and evaluation processes. Finally, the evaluation of interpretation will be addressed in terms of the purposes of evaluation, types of evaluation, different objectives and measurement techniques.

3.2. The Significant Contribution of Interpretation to Sustainable Tourism

Moscardo (1998) emphasised that 'interpretation has the potential to make significant and substantial contributions to the development of a more sustainable tourism industry (p.11).' As reviewed in the previous chapter, the use of interpretation is a key visitor management strategy in achieving the goals of sustainable tourism for a long-term effect, supporting the role of other hard strategies in reducing environmental impacts from visitor pressure (Wearing and Neil, 1999; Newsome et al., 2002; Eagles et al., 2002; Kuo, 2002). Indeed, many researchers have argued that interpretation can help to enhance the quality of visitors' experience and their understanding of management practices and the conservation value of the site, so that visitors may be influenced to be more environmentally aware and promote more responsible behaviour (Cooper et al., 1998; Bramwell & Lane, 1993; Orams, 1996a,b; Moscardo, 1999; Kuo, 2002).

With regard to increased recognition of the benefits of interpretation as a visitor management tool, the use of interpretation has become a widespread management technique in the park management profession (Sharpe, 1982) and is now a specialist subject within many natural resource management disciplines (Knudson, Cable & Beck, 1995; Ham, 1992; Tubb, 2003). Despite the widespread advocacy for education and interpretation as a solution to minimising tourists' impacts on the natural and cultural environment, there has been little empirical research or evaluation to determine 'if' and 'how' interpretation helps to develop visitor understanding and modify their attitude and behaviour (McArthur and Hall, 1996:103; Cottrell, 2003b; Kuo, 2002).

In order to have a better understanding of interpretation, the next section overviews briefly the fundamental issues regarding the definitions of interpretation, the historical background of interpretation, and the variety of the roles of interpretation.

3.3. Definitions of Interpretation

There is no single definition of interpretation that has been adopted by most practitioners (Hall and McArthur, 1998: 165). The most widely recognised definition of interpretation has been that coined by Freeman Tilden (1977). He defined interpretation as 'an educational activity which aims to reveal meaning and relationships through the use of original objectives, by first-hand experience, and by illustrative media, rather than simply to communicate factual information' (Tilden, 1977:8). Especially, Tilden recognised that interpretation had secondary aims and its own objectives, and has the potential, as a management tool, to contribute to the protection of the natural environment. This principle was originally emphasised in Tilden's oft-stated maxim:

'...through interpretation, understanding,

through understanding, appreciation,

through appreciation, protection.'   (Tilden, 1977: 38)

Based on Tilden's philosophy and definition, much debate continues on the definitions of interpretation, its limits, and how it overlaps with the meanings of education and information. A variety of other definitions have emerged reflecting the particular objectives of the organisations involved in serving their own needs (McArthur, 1998), resulting in developing simpler definitions which can be recognised and utilised more easily (Hall and McArthur, 1998: 165).

Nonetheless, several definitions by different organisations and researchers noted in Table 3.1 reflect similar main aims of interpretation including the importance of visitor enjoyment and appreciation, and communicating the idea, knowledge, and understanding of the objectives as well as encouraging conservation of the site.

In addition, the term of the type of interpretation has been used differently in different settings. There are useful distinctions between interpretation for historic sites, natural sites, environmental areas, and conservation education (Aldridge, 1975). At historic sites interpretation, in other words, 'heritage interpretation' is defined as 'the art of explaining the past, in relation to environmental and social conditions, to casual visitors by bringing it to life, usually in thematic or story form (p,4)'. At natural sites, environmental interpretation refers to 'the art of revealing the relationships between people and environments and of explaining the character of an area' to the general public. The target groups and basic method are the same at both sites. In contrast, conservation education is more explicitly the art of teaching with more in-depth methods to more committed students of heritage. Through all different situations, the same purpose in each type of interpretation includes increasing visitor awareness and the desire for environmental conservation (Aldridge, 1975; Herbert, 1989).

Table 3.1 Definitions of Interpretation

Tilden, 1977: 8	An education activity which aims to reveal meanings and relationships through the use of original objects, by first hand experience, and by illustrative media, rather than simply to communicate factual information
Society for Interpreting Britain's Heritage (quoted in Moscardo, 1998: 3)	The process of explaining to people the significance of the place or object they have come to see, so that they enjoy their visit more, understand their heritage and environment better, and develop a more caring attitude towards conservation
The American Association of Museums (Alderson & Low, 1985) (cited in Knudson et al., 1995: 4)	Interpretation is a planned effort to create for the visitor an understanding of the history and significance of events, people, and objects with which the site is associated
Interpretation Australia Association (1995) (quoted in Moscardo, 1999: 5)	Interpretation is a means of communicating ideas and feelings which helps people enrich their understanding and appreciation of their world, and their role within it
Moscardo, 2000, (quoted in Newsome et al., 2002:241)	Interpretation is any activity which seeks to explain to people the significance of an object, a culture or a place. Its three core functions are to enhance visitor experiences, to improve visitor knowledge or understanding, and to assist in the protection or conservation of places or cultures.

Moreover, there is some confusion between the terms 'information' and 'education' and the definitions of interpretation. First, 'information' refers to 'the knowledge derived from study, experience or instruction' (Knudson et al., 1995: 4). 'Interpretation' focuses on presenting 'information' in ways that attract, interest, and convey the meaning of something through exposition or explanation although it uses information as a raw material (Knudson et al., 1995).

Secondly, in terms of the meaning of education and interpretation, 'education' refers to 'a systematic version of instruction, training or study set up to help people to obtain knowledge, skills and awareness' (Hall & McArthur, 1998: 166).

As seen in Table 3.2, education is a more formalised form of interpretation with a 'captive audience' and can therefore develop facilities and programmes specifically designed for education while interpretation (environmental interpretation) tries to capture the attention of visitors,

50

especially a 'non-captive audience' (Wearing & Neil, 1999:58). In particular, 'environmental education' and the definitions of 'environmental interpretation' in natural setting contexts are so often used interchangeably, especially, in the field of ecotourism (Wearing & Neil, 1999).

Table 3.2. Environmental Education and Environmental Interpretation

	ENVIRONMENTAL EDUCATION	ENVIRONMENTAL INTERPRETATION
WHO?	School teachers; education officers; teacher educators	Interpreters; exhibition designers; scriptwriters; volunteers; archaeologists; education officers; academics; rangers; interpretive trainers
WHAT?	Understanding of environmental concepts; acquisition of environmental skills; integration of environmental knowledge, attitudes and behaviour	Information about people, places, activities and objects; interpretation of meanings
TO WHOM?	Educational conscripts; schoolchildren; student groups; adult/continuing education groups	Recreational volunteers; tourists; visitors; residents; wide age range
WHY?	Develop environmental literacy; fulfil curriculum objectives	Recreational entertainment; profit; site conservation
WHERE?	Schools; field study centres; interpretive centres	Interpretive centres; historic houses; archaeological sites; urban and countryside sites; national, state and regional parks
WHEN?	Timetabled periods; school trips; preparation and follow-up to visit	Whenever people engage in recreational or tourism activity; limited time involvement
HOW?	Instruction; heuristic and didactic techniques	Provocation; didactic and informal educational multi-media techniques

(Source: Ballantyne and Uzzell, 1995)

3.4 The Historical Development of Interpretation

Since the initial flourish of interpretation largely stimulated by Ernos Mills, a nature guide in Colorado's Rocky Mountains between 1889 and 1922, interpretation is now considered to have a much broader role to play within tourism industries. The most influential developments of interpretation occurred in the United States until the 1980s (Machlis and Field, 1992). In particular, Freeman Tilden (1977) attempted first to define the profession of interpretation and to develop the philosophy of interpretation through his book, *"Interpreting Our Heritage"*. Tilden's fundamental principles have been embraced in several definitions of interpretation by other organisations. His main philosophy, which emphasised provocation, revelation, and personal relevance has been widely used around the world.

In an early historical context in the UK, the concept of interpretation spread to the UK after the Second World War following the dissemination of Tilden's ideas. John Foster and Don Aldridge, the pioneers of countryside interpretation redefined the principles of interpretation in the 1950s and 1960s. Since the Countryside Commission for Scotland and the Countryside Commission were established in the late 1960s, the two Commissions came together to produce a guide to interpretive planning in the early 1970s. During the 1970s the second phase of interpretation in Britain began. As interpretation increasingly came to be recognised as a professional activity, the principles and practices of countryside interpretation began to be distributed to a wider range of sites (Light, 1991).

There are a number of important trends in the earlier development of interpretation in Britain: its wide acceptance as a practice; its extension into other areas, such as industrial social history; the growing professionalism and expertise in the area; and the wide range of bodies which engage in interpretation for the public (cited in Light, 1991). In response to these trends, from the 1980s to the 1990s, the growth of the heritage industry influenced the third phase of the development of interpretation in Britain (Light, 1991). The three main characteristics at the third phase in the case of the heritage industry included: 1) the changing aims of interpretation; 2) the development of the media technology used for interpreting an historic site; and 3) the creation of problems related to reliability and accuracy concerning the past or the site. First, the aims of interpretation within the historical tourism industry are separated from much earlier British interpretation concerning the conservation message (Light, 1991). As many modern heritage sites have been designed specifically to accommodate large numbers of visitors, the aim of interpretation has changed from the role of education to emphasising visitor enjoyment and satisfaction. This trend was pioneered by the independent museums (cited in Light, 1991). Consequently, the heritage boom focusing on entertainment has developed a variety of technology techniques of interpretive media. However, it has created several problems in terms of the reliability and accuracy of interpreting the past. In this response, the identifying of the problems and the technology development has led to two other main trends: (1) a move towards authenticity and (2) the use of sophisticated technology (Lumley, 1988; Light, 1991: 8).

Apart from the earlier development of interpretation in the heritage industry, because of the simultaneous growth of public interest in national parks, conservation, and heritage issues since the mid- to late 1980s, a small part of the market became interested in doing more than looking at natural areas (Hall and McArther, 1998: 167). As a result, the recent trend in nature-based heritage tourism began to redefine the definitions and objectives of interpretation based on the previous origins and meanings of countryside interpretation developed by Tilden and Aldridge. In this context, as seen in Table 3.1, the objectives of interpretation have shifted from enhancing visitors' enjoyment or entertainment to promoting pro-environmental attitudes and behaviour in order to contribute to the conservation of the natural environment (Knudson *et al*., 1995; Hall & McArthur, 1998; Beaumont, 2001; Tubb, 2003).

3.5 The Roles of Interpretation

3.5.1 Different Benefits of Interpretation

In reviewing different functions of interpretation in an historical context, a number of benefits of interpretation were identified in various ways and levels of detail as follows: promotional; recreational; economic; educational; management/conservation benefits. First, effective interpretive services can be useful in promoting the 'image' or 'visual identity' as well as promoting values, sites, management objectives and practices. Secondly, interpretation provides recreational benefits by enhancing a sense of meaning to recreational activity (e.g. sightseeing), and enjoyment and satisfaction for visitors. Thirdly, interpretation as a tourism attraction itself facilitates economic benefits in three main ways: contributing to the benefits and wealth of tourism businesses by utilising interpretation as facilities and services; creating local employment as interpreters and guides; and satisfying customer demand. Furthermore, the educational objectives are to increase visitors' knowledge and understanding of the environment and culture. Finally, the alternative purpose of interpretation can be utilised as a visitor management tool to reduce inappropriate behaviour by visitors and increase visitor support for the conservation of the site in the long-term (Sharpe 1976; Beckmann, 1991; Wearing and Neil, 1999).

3.5.2 The Management Role of Interpretation in Achieving Sustainable Tourism

With regard to several benefits of interpretation above, the particular attention of the present study is paid to how interpretation can contribute to the different goals of sustainable tourism. From a visitor perspective, interpretation can play a significant role as a visitor management strategy in achieving sustainable tourism, particularly, in two main goals: economic sustainability and environmental sustainability. First, interpretation can encourage the quality of the visitors' experiences and enhance continued visitor interest in the activity and revisits and staying longer to the site, thus contributing to economic sustainability. Secondly, it can also assist in managing visitors and their impacts on the environment and the host community, thus creating environmental sustainability (Moscardo, 1998).

3.5.2.1 Enhancing Visitor Experience

Interpretation can contribute to economic sustainability by enhancing the quality of the experience for visitors. This goal can be achieved through three types of interpretation activity:

- Providing information on recreation activity options and alternatives;
- Providing information to encourage safety and comfort;
- Creating the actual experience.

(Moscardo, 1999:8)

First, interpretation can provide visitors with good information and orientation about the available options of recreation activities and experiences, so that visitors can make the best choices about what they do and where they go (Moscardo, 1998/1999). For example, information and exhibits in the Kawuneeche Visitor Centre situated in the United States' Rocky Mountain National Park were presented to help visitors make the best choices about the activities they were interested in, and to match the time they had available (Mack and Thompson, 1991, see Moscardo, 1998/1999 for further review).

Secondly, simple information regarding comfort and safety issues, as the second function of interpretation, can also make significant differences in the quality of the visitor experience (Moscardo, 1999).

Finally, interpretation is either the experience itself or is an important component of the experience. For instance, interpretation is a major component of the experience provided in visitor activities such as guided walks and tours, self-guided trails, ecotours, fauna sanctuaries, zoos and art galleries (Moscardo, 1998). As visitors are increasingly seeking educational elements across all aspects of their travel, interpretation may become an integral part of the visitor experience at a variety of tourism sites (Moscardo, 1998). The study of Moscardo and Woods (1998) provided a good example of this. The Skyrail Rainforest Cableway, which takes visitors on a gondola trip above the canopy of the Wet Tropics World Heritage rainforests of North Eastern Australia, has developed and provided interpretation as integral parts of the visitor experience (Moscardo and Woods, 1998). The results of visitor surveys in their study indicated that visitors enjoyed their Skyrail experience, and the interpretation was an important component of satisfaction. In this case, interpretation was found to enhance visitors' experience and increase their satisfaction (Moscardo, 1998).

In this respect, Ham and Weiler (2002) also stressed that high-quality interpretation is the major contributor to the satisfaction of the visitor and this can contribute to economic sustainability because satisfied visitors create positive word-of-mouth advertising and repeat visitation in the long-term.

3.5.2.2 Managing Visitors and Their Impacts

Interpretation can also contribute to environmental sustainability by managing visitors and their impacts. These goals can be achieved by three main types of interpretation activity:

- influencing where visitors go;
- informing visitors about appropriate behaviours;
- influencing visitor's attitudes and behaviour toward long-term conservation.

(Moscardo, 1999:14; Ham and Weiler, 2002:39)

First, interpretation can provide visitors with information about alternative sites, routes, or activities as an attempt to move them away from heavily used sites, and thus it can help manage negative impacts at those sites under the most pressure (Moscardo, 1998). Huffman and Williams (1987, cited in Moscardo, 1998) provided a good example that a computer information display had a positive impact on change in the trail choices of back country hikers in the Rocky Mountains National Park. In their study, 60 percent of hikers who used the computer selected a new route while only 17 percent of those not using the computer chose an alternative trail to that which was heavily used.

Secondly, interpretation programmes can also help to encourage visitors engaging in environmentally responsible behaviour by influencing awareness of the potential negative environmental impacts of inappropriate visitor behaviour on-site (Cooper *et al.*, 1998; Moscardo, 1999; Kuo, 2002; Tribe *et al.*, 2000). For example, Orams and Hill (1998) studied the effectiveness of an educational programme for tourists who hand-feed wild dolphins at Tangalooma, Moreton Island in eastern Australia. The results of the study showed that interpretation was effective in reducing inappropriate behaviour of visitors such as touching dolphins through their increasing awareness of inappropriate visitor behaviour on causing potential stress for the dolphins.

In addition to influencing appropriate visitor behaviour on-site, ultimately, high quality interpretation can contribute to long-term conservation, which is the primary goal of environmental sustainability, by promoting positive visitor attitudes and conservational behavioural intentions (Ham and Weiler, 2002:40). However, simple information provided will not be enough in achieving these goals. Ham and Weiler (2002) provided evidence for success and failure of interpretation in the case of the Galapagos Islands and Yosemite National Park (USA). They indicated that a theme-driven communication campaign had led to significant increases in tourist donations to the Galapagos Conservation Fund. On the other hand, improper food storage problems remained in the black bear country although some of the messages regarding appropriate food storage behaviour were delivered to visitors to Yosemite National Park. One of the main reasons for the success or failure of interpretation to generate visitor attitudinal and behavioural change is dependent on the high-quality thematic interpretation which communicates specific belief-targeted messages about desired appropriate behavioural outcomes based on the theories of reasoned action and planned behaviour (Ham and Weiler, 2002).

In this respect, the following section explores the requirements for high-quality interpretation and how to make interpretation more successful in achieving its objectives in the planning, implementation, and evaluation processes.

3.6 The Principles for Effective Interpretation

The key principles of successful high-quality interpretation have been embraced by several researchers (Ham, 1992; Lewis, 1980; Newsome *et al.*, 2002; Moscardo; 1998). These reflect the three key principles of Tilden (1977) including provocation of ideas, revealing of meanings and emotions, and relevance to the personality or experience of the visitor.

Based on three key essences, several fundamental principles of effective interpretation are outlined as follows:

- Interpretation should centre on a theme and associated messages
- Interpretation entails active involvement and the engagement of first-hand experiences
- Interpretation facilitates maximum use of the senses
- Interpretation seeks to foster self-discovered insights
- Interpretation is of relevance to the visitor and he or she finds the imparted knowledge and insights useful.

(Source: Newsome *et al.*, 2002: 241-242)

3.6.1 Three Key Elements for Effective Interpretation

By utilising many of the principles identified above, three essential elements to be considered in the planning process for successful interpretation include 'a thorough understanding and integration of *audience*, *message* and *technique*' (Hall and McArthur, 1998:170). It is essential to ensure that interpretive information is delivered effectively to targeted visitors via a fluent communication channel. The overviews of those relationships are well explained in the mindful/mindless model developed by Moscardo (1999) although the criticism of this model has been made.

The model emphasises the flow of the relationship between visitor profile and interpretation technique to propose visitor cognition, satisfaction, and behaviour (Figure 3.1). In this model, effective interpretation depends on the relationship between two sets of factors: interpretation factors and visitor factors. Interpretation factors (setting factors) include interpretive content techniques and different forms of communication channels (e.g. exhibits, guided tours, signs, brochures, etc.). Visitor factors include familiarity with the place, motivation for the visit and interests in content. Targeted visitors can be divided into two groups as 'mindful' and 'mindless'.

As seen in the model (see Figure 3.1), the success or failure of interpretation to achieve its objectives (e.g. greater learning, satisfaction, and attitude and behaviour change) can be dependent on the different process of two sets of factors. In other words, it demonstrates that mindful visitors are more likely to learn from the interpretation and have a higher level of satisfaction from their visit to the site while mindless visitors have less interest in content, lack of learning and a lower level of satisfaction from the interpretation. More details of key elements for effective interpretation are as follows.

Figure 3.1 The Mindful/Mindless Model

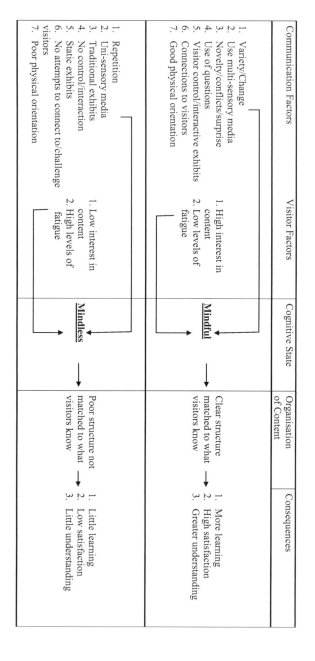

Communication Factors	Visitor Factors	Cognitive State	Organisation of Content	Consequences
1. Variety/Change 2. Use multi-sensory media 3. Novelty/conflicts/surprise 4. Use of questions 5. Visitor control/interactive exhibits 6. Connections to visitors 7. Good physical orientation	1. High interest in content 2. Low levels of fatigue	**Mindful**	Clear structure matched to what visitors know	1. More learning 2. High satisfaction 3. Greater understanding
1. Repetition 2. Uni-sensory media 3. Traditional exhibits 4. No control/interaction 5. Static exhibits 6. No attempts to connect to/challenge visitors 7. Poor physical orientation	1. Low interest in content 2. High levels of fatigue	**Mindless**	Poor structure not matched to what visitors know	1. Little learning 2. Low satisfaction 3. Little understanding

58

(Source: Moscardo, 1999:27)

3.6.1.1 To Whom? Targeting the Audience

Targeted interpretation must start with a detailed understanding of the audience, which is considered as the first step in planning interpretation (Hall and McArthur, 1998:170). Several researchers emphasise that visitors are different in a variety of ways (Hall and McArthur, 1998; Moscardo, 1998/99). Visitors are different in terms of demographics, previous experience, motivation, activity preferences, and social groups. These differences can influence visitors' responses to interpretation, the time spent in an interpretive place, the level of interpretation sought or expected, the amount of pre-existing attitudes and the content sought. For example, Fothergill *et al.* (1978, cited in Moscardo 1998) indicated that the expected substantial difference in knowledge gain was found with social class and years of education but not with the relevance of subjects studied at school. In addition, repeat visitors and holiday makers learned more than day trippers because they had more time and were more relaxed (Moscardo, 1998/99). Therefore, when identifying a target audience, it is important to ensure that interpreters provide interpretive experiences which are better suited to visitors' needs and interests (Hall and McArthur, 1998; Moscardo, 1998/99). To be effective, it is also necessary to provide different layers of interpretive experiences in order to tailor to a variety of visitors (Moscardo, 1998/99).

3.6.1.2 What? Targeting Clear and Thematic Content (Message)

In order to develop the content of interpretation for effective interpretation, there is a need to ensure a balance between resource-led messages which heritage organisations seek to communicate when managing the site and consumer-led messages that reflect the interests and needs of the visitor (Goodey, 1994).

From the heritage resource-led messages perspective, Moscardo (1998/99) emphasise that using themes and telling stories are much more effective methods than listing facts. In particular, it is important to develop a theme that contains concepts and messages, because the use of a theme allows interpretive ideas and information to be organised and easy to follow (Newsome *et al.*, 2002). Themes embrace a single focus or core idea to which all other information or concepts are linked (Ham, 1992; Moscardo, 1998/99). Themes reflect the characteristics of the region's natural or cultural heritage being interpreted. Concepts refer to 'a strong idea underlying a group of common messages' while messages refer to 'what is actually planned to be said' based on themes and concepts (Hall and McArthur, 1996:96). For example, Hall and McArthur (1998) explain how these are organised. In the example of forests, several themes can be drawn from forests including management through community values, ecology of rainforests, and the natural disturbance of forests by fire. When focused on specific themes regarding natural disturbance of fire on forests, the concept of naturally changing forests which can be subsequently developed from this theme can contain fire-adapted plants as a specific example. Then, the interpretive messages can target the changed diversity, structure, and complexity of forests in response to fire. In this way, as mentioned in the previous section, thematic-based interpretation can lead to the achievement of the objectives of interpretation including greater visitor understanding and attitude and behavioural change (Ham and Weiler, 2002).

From a visitor perspective, the content of interpretation requires to be organised in such a way that visitors can both access and follow it (Moscardo, 1998: 10). To be effective, first, it is important for interpreters to provide the visitor with the introduction or orientation of the overview of the interpretive activity. Another important skill is providing personal connections for presenting information to visitors, using personal interpretation (guides or interpreters) (Moscardo, 1998). Moreover, it is necessary to target the different level of messages relevant to visitor's interests, capabilities, and pre-existing knowledge (Moscardo, 1998; Hall and McArthur, 1998). Finally, several other techniques in the development of links between the interpretive content and visitors' experiences include the use of humour, analogies and metaphors, giving visitors opportunities to interact, ask questions, participate, and make choices about their interpretive experiences or about what to do in their everyday lives (Moscardo, 1998). This will attract visitor attention more easily, and allow visitors to memorise the information for longer (Kuo, 2002).

3.6.1.3 How? Determining Appropriate Techniques

Techniques for effective interpretation can be summarised in two main ways: designing different interpretive experiences and providing opportunities for visitor participation.

(1) Designing differences into interpretive experiences

It is important to provide variety in the interpretive experiences to visitors or a change of pace to other activities because any repetition will quickly lose visitor attention and without attention it is difficult to create successful communication (Moscardo, 1998). For example, Schänzel and McIntoch (2000) studied how effective different methods are in enhancing visitors' enjoyment, knowledge and awareness about the endangered penguins at Otago Peninsula, New Zealand. The result showed that a wildlife viewing tour with a trained guide had a positive impact on the memorable and authentic experiences of the visitors because the tour provided visitors with the opportunity to experience seeing and photographing penguins without disturbing them. However, the extra interpretive media provided, such as video, were not favoured by most of the visitors. They suggested that it would be useful to have an information leaflet about penguins at the site to take home.

(2) Practising participation

Providing opportunities for visitor participation or interaction in an interpretive experience has several benefits. Opportunities for interaction or participation can encourage a sense of control over their experiences as most activities require decisions and choices as well as build personal connections (Moscardo, 1998). In addition, personal contact with a guided tour or talking with staff offers opportunities for visitors to ask personally relevant questions and allows staff to immediately tailor information to the individual needs of the visitors (Moscardo, 1998).

In order to make interpretation effective it is thus important to determine when interpreters can apply different types of interpretive techniques in order to attract visitor's attention and deliver effective information to target visitor groups at the right time and place. This requires identifying the strengths and weaknesses of each type of interpretive technique, which will be discussed in the following section.

3.7 Methods of Interpretation

In general, there are two different types of interpretation: non-personal and personal techniques. Despite the great variety of interpretive channels, this section focuses on the most common and the most important media as follows.

3.7.1 Personal Interpretation Techniques

In the literature of interpretive practice, personal interpretation such as face-to-face communication is generally recognised to be far more powerful and highly effective than non-personal methods because the interpreter can respond to changing conditions, particularly the various needs and interests of visitors (Hall & McArthur, 1998). It is acknowledged that interpreters or guides can also facilitate active visitor involvement (Newsome *et al.*, 2002). Several empirical studies indicated that personal contact with visitors has more influence on the knowledge and behaviour of the visitor than non-personal techniques such as brochures, signs and media (Martin and Taylor, 1981), although some of the studies found there were no differences between interpreters and the visitor centre in changing visitor knowledge toward National Park Service fire management in the USA (Nielsen and Buchanan, 1986).

In the context of ecotourism, Wearing and Neil (1999:62) indicate that guided tours might be the most widely used method as a means of controlling where visitors go and what they do. In particular, personal interpretation is useful with school children and formal tour groups.

Although personal interpretation has several benefits (see Table 3.3), the problems can occur when tourism staff fail to meet the information needs of the visitors (cited in Aiello, 1998). Aiello (1998) reviewed one of previous studies of tourist-guide interaction in natural tourism areas and indicated that the major source of tourist dissatisfaction was the guides' lack of environmental knowledge. In his case study of the interpretive training approach adopted by marine tourism operator, Great Adventures, in Australia, he provided the empirical evidence of this view and showed that their interpretation training programme has been successful in increasing the staff's environmental knowledge and awareness and the quality of their presentations (Aiello, 1998). Therefore, for successful personal interpretation through various techniques, interpreters can help to achieve successful interpretive strategies, creating an informal atmosphere. They include the use of humour, stories, metaphors, analogies, comparisons and examples, as well as presenting interpretation in a logical sequence (Ham, 1992).

However, there are limitations to personal interpretation including the requirement for many human resources and the high cost of guide training programmes (Newsome et al., 2002). In addition, some visitors prefer self-guided programmes rather than guided tours because they may find guides an interference that impinges upon their desired sense of freedom (Wearing and Neil, 1999).

3.7.2 Non-Personal Interpretation Techniques

Non-personal interpretation techniques are utilised far more because of their lower short-term costs (Hall and McArthur, 1998). In addition, they provide the visitor with more freedom. Visitors can participate in their own schedule and they can spend as much time as they want Non-personal interpretation methods include exhibits and displays, visitor centres, signs, self-guided trails, brochures and other publications (Hall and McArthur, 1998; Newsome et al., 2002; Wearing and Neil, 1999).

Visitor Centres

Visitor centres like galleries and museums are special buildings or rooms to house not only exhibits and displays but also audio-visual presentations in relative comfort and in controlled surroundings. They also contain other media such as site maps, brochures, and books (Wearing and Neil, 1999; Hall and McArthur, 1998; Newsome et al., 2002). Visitor centres serve a variety of primary functions: offering the tourist information such as access, accommodation, recreation activities and guided tour services; providing toilets, gift shops, and restaurant services; enhancing the quality of visitor experiences and enjoyment; and improving visitors' understanding of the site and management issues (Newsome *et al.*, 2002; Wearing and Neil, 2000; Fallon and Kriwonken, 2003). Although visitor centres have several different functions, they can be expensive to set up and a central focus of visitor centres may be entirely on school groups instead of reaching a broad range of different audiences (Newsome *et al.*, 2002).

Exhibits and Displays

Exhibits and display are one of the most common forms of communication media within visitor centres or outdoors areas (Wearing and Neil, 1999). Exhibits can serve as a means to display original objects, such as the object of discovery, an artefact of human history, or a specimen of natural science. Thus, the exhibit can protect the valuable culture and natural resources with certain safety precautions. Also the exhibit provides visitors the freedom to move through an interpretive experience at their own pace (Sharp, 1976). In addition, displays and exhibits are useful because they are cost-effective and can be located indoors or outdoors (Wearning and Neil, 1999). There are several types of exhibits including photographs arranged in wall or panel displays, map models, mounted specimens, or diagrams (Wearing and Neil, 1999). Each exhibit type performs different functions and involves the audience in a different manner so that these types are widely used to provide the attracting, holding, and teaching power of different messages (Marsh, 1986:32). However, exhibits and displays have the limitations that they can not explain policy nor present detailed information or abstract ideas so well as a publication (Sharp, 1976).

Audio-Visual Programs

Audio-visual programmes are widely used within visitor centres and museums. The most common types of audio-visual interpretation include tape-slide presentations and video films (Herbert, 1989). They can be applied in several situations: appealing to at least two of people's senses at the same time, sound and sight; providing immediate responses to demands of the visitors; offering repeated functions of those type of media over and over; and adapting to various sizes of visitor groups (Hall and McArthur, 1998).

Table 3.3 Summary of Major Interpretation Techniques

Technique	Application	Strengths/advantages	Weaknesses/Disadvantages
Guided touring	• Wide application in all environments. • Especially important in forests, wildflower tourism and during wildlife observation. • Time frames can be from only 1 hour up to 2 weeks duration.	• Very powerful and highly effective if applied properly. • Interpreter can respond to client needs and deal with various levels of complexity. • Information can be constantly updated. • Interpreter can facilitate active involvement.	• Requires the availability of well-trained and effective interpreters. • Requirement of audience attention and commitment to be entirely successful.
Visitor centres	• Information on landscape, fauna, flora and management. • Opportunity for face-to-face contracts with staff. • Located at the entrance gates to national parks and within popular nature-based recreation areas.	• Recognisable sites where visitors can obtain information. • Scope for the application of a wide range of techniques (e.g. audiovisual, verbal interpretation, interactive displays and original objects).	• Can be expensive to set up. • May not be designed to cater for different audiences (e.g. focus may be entirely on school groups).
Self-guided trails	• Focus of attention for visitors in various natural settings. • Opportunities to provide messages through signage.	• Always available and visitors can explore trails at their own pace.	• Signs and displays subject to vandalism. • Signage may contain too much information. • Generally not suitable for children.
Publications and websites	• Supply of pre-contact information. • Visitor orientation and trip planning support for visitor centres and self-guided trails. • Information on landscape, fauna and flora.	• Cost effective and portable information. • Many possible distribution/access points with wide dissemination.	• There is no active visitor involvement. • Does not necessarily cater for different visitor needs. • Can be expensive if subject to frequent updates and alterations.

(Source: Adopted from Newsome, Moore, & Dowling, 2002: p.251)

Self-guided trails

A self-guided trail usually involves a series of designated stops along a route that visitors can follow. Each stop along the trail interprets the integrated features of the site or attractions such as specific plants, geological characteristics and plant-animal interactions via a brochure, a sign or an audio facility such as radio or cassette (Newsome *et al.*, 2002; Wearing & Neil, 1999). A self-guided trail provides the visitor with freedom to explore at their own pace and is a cost-effective way of reaching a lot of people (Wearing & Neil, 1999). However, some of the disadvantages of a self-guided trail are that this is not suitable for children and that signs and displays may be easily exposed to vandalism by visitors (Newsome *et al.*, 2002).

Signs

Two types of signs are commonly used in interpretive programmes: interpretive signs and administrative signs (McIntosh, 1976). Interpretive signs are to interpret historic or environmental sites thus increasing understanding and appreciation of the resources (Sharpe, 1976). Administrative signs which are the most basic form of sign or label provide an orientation or some strategic information (Sharpe, 1976; Hall and McArthur, 1998). Orientation information usually includes directions, distances and names. Strategic information includes all basic information for access of a heritage site, safety and comfort experiences. These signs, particularly administrative signs, have advantages including being relatively cheap to produce and maintain and being long-lasting. However, they have several limitations including the limited presentation of the amount of information, and lack of adaptability to different audiences (Hall & McArthur, 1998).

Brochures and Other Publications

Publications include brochures, leaflets, note-sheets, maps, books, posters, postcards, calendars and stickers (Wearing and Neil, 1999). Publications can play different roles such as promotion/information-based and interpretation-based. For example, the standard brochures or site maps tend to provide orientation information regarding access, available services and infrastructure, major site characteristics and wildlife. They can also promote the options of recreational activities available in the site (Wearing & Neil, 1999; Newsome *et al.*, 2002; Hall and McArthur, 1998). Interpretive based publications can provide the specific management objectives, visitor impact minimisation, and wider environmental conservation messages for educational purposes (Newsome *et al.*, 2002). In particular, previous researchers show that interpretive brochures are as effective as personal contact methods if the purpose of the brochure is to educate and influence visitors' behaviour (Roggenbuck and Berrier, 1982;

McAvoy and Hamborg, 1984). For example, McAvoy and Hamborg (1984) assessed the effectiveness of a brochure on visitors' knowledge of regulations within the Boundary Waters Canoe Area Wilderness. They found that the brochure and the distribution method employed by the Forest Service were highly successful in raising visitors' knowledge of area regulations.

As with the strengths and weaknesses of signs, publications are a cost-effective way of reaching different range of visitors. However, publications have limited ability to satisfy different visitor needs. They also can be expensive to distribute and frequent updates and there is no active visitor involvement (Wearing and Neil, 1999; Newsome *et al.*, 2002).

3.8 Evaluation of the Effectiveness of Interpretation

The previous section provided a brief overview of the different objectives of interpretation and important principles and requirements for effective interpretation in terms of audience, message, and technique. As the final step for developing a higher quality of effective interpretation in planning and implementing process, evaluation is required to determine whether site-based interpretation has achieved its objectives as well as to provide feedback on its effectiveness and efficiency for the future improvement of interpretation. "Evaluation of interpretation is a multidimensional process used to determine the qualities of interpretation and is an integral part of all interpretive operations. The process includes input and feedback and considers the interrelationships among people, organisations, environments, and technologies" (National Association for Interpretation, 1990, cited in Knudson *et al.*, 1995:441). Considerable attention of the present study is given to explore why, when, what, and how interpreters evaluate.

Why:

Evaluation can play an important role in stimulating improved interpretive programmes to the visitor as well as demonstrating the value of interpretation and its effectiveness (Knudson *et al.*, 1995). Several key purposes of evaluation are:

- to determine the educational and recreational impact of interpretation;
- to assess cost effectiveness of various methods;
- to provide accountability and public responsibility;
- to convince others of the value of interpretation, providing proof that interpretation addresses and achieves important public goals

- to help make policy and planning decisions
- to provide the public with a way to indicate their response to interpretive services, beyond simple attendance data. (Source: Marsh, 1986)

In assessing those purposes of evaluation, the results of the evaluation process can contribute to better achievement of an organisation's aims and objectives so that it will help interpretive managers to develop and modify a higher quality of interpretation in the future. Therefore, it is clear that the evaluation process should be considered as an integral part of the visitor management process (National Association for Interpretation, 1990; Knudson *et al.*, 1995).

When:

Evaluation requires an on-going process, demanding regular assessment and modification of interpretation where appropriate. Evaluation can be implemented at all phases of the interpretive effort – before, during and after the preparation and development of interpretation (Knudson *et al.*, 1995; Uzzell, 1998). It consists of three forms of evaluation as follows: front-end (before), formative (during) and summative (after) (Uzzell, 1998). First, front-end evaluation is undertaken at the earliest stage of the interpretative planning process. It aims to identify errors and problems of interpretation before they begin or develop. This may involve market research about visitors' pre-existing knowledge of the interpretive themes, perceptions and interests of new interpretive stories or techniques, preferences for types of interpretive programmes, and their attitude toward conservation (Uzzell, 1998). Additionally, formative evaluation can occur during the implementation of an interpretive plan to test the efficacy of the trial version of the interpretation (Uzzell, 1998). It can test visitors' reactions to the particular programmes by examining visitor's attention to interpretation and their understanding of the messages which the interpretation tries to communicate to the visitors. This allows for interpretive planners to change the design or content to make sure it is effective (cited in Light, 1991). Finally, summative evaluation is generally more widespread than the other two forms. It is carried out after completing exhibition and interpretive programmes to assess their success or failure with regard to their objectives (e.g. learning, preferences for types of media, knowledge gain, enjoyment, attitude and behaviour change) (Light, 1991; Uzzell, 1998).

What:

It is critical to formulate clear objectives or goals for the effectiveness of interpretation. The research questions of the evaluation of interpretation require us to determine exactly what should be evaluated and how to measure it, we can then explore the potential outcomes of the evaluation in relation to its objectives of interpretation (Thome, 1980; Knudson *et al.*, 1995).

Table 3.4 illustrates different aspects of evaluating the effectiveness of interpretation according to the interrelationships between different objectives, the required information associated with its objectives, the potential application of various techniques, and desired outcomes as reviewed the studies by Thom (1980) and Knudson *et al.*, (1995).

Evaluation of interpretation has four major categories:

• Evaluating *visitors* to examine their attentiveness and reactions to interpretation, as well as their responses to learning, attitude and behaviour change objectives;

• Evaluating *interpretive programmes* to determine which types of interpretation have achieved their objectives and to modify them for greater effectiveness or timeliness;

• Evaluating *the performances of interpreters* and helping them to improve their delivery methods, messages, and their interpretive approach in future presentations;

• Evaluating *overall productivity* of the programme mix and facilities to determine whether money and effort are managed efficiently. (Knudson *et al.*, 1995).

How:
Evaluation can use various measurement methods according to its objectives of interpretation and the type of information required. They include questionnaires, interviews, focus groups, observation studies, and behavioural mapping (Uzzell, 1998; Lee, 1998; Knudson *et al.*, 1995). Single or multiple methods can be applied when evaluating different objectives or research questions as seen in Table 3.4. More details will be discussed in Chapter 7: Methods and Techniques.

Table 3.4 The Evaluation of Different Aspects of Effectiveness and Techniques

Evaluation Objectives	Type of Information Required	Evaluation Technique	Desired Outcomes
Visitor Their openness to interpretation Their attention to interpretation	Comparison between numbers using the provision and numbers in a situation of use; Comparison between time visitors spend looking at interpretation and minimum time needed for exposure to full message	Value judgements/ Behavioural mapping/ Observation/ Questionnaire/ Focus group	Improvement of media and design techniques; Visual impact of interpretation provision; Appropriateness of interpretive content
The Impacts of interpretation on visitors' enjoyment	Comparison of visitor's enjoyment and satisfaction before and after visit	Interview/ Questionnaire	Satisfaction & enjoyment
on visitor learning	Comparison of visitors' understanding of site/topic interpreted before and after visit	Questionnaire/ Interview	Knowledge/ awareness gain
on visitor concerns	Changes in attitude resulting from visit; Needs to examine visitor profiles	Questionnaire/ Interview	Attitudes change
on visitor behaviour	Changes in behaviour Needs to examine sub-indicators (enjoyment, knowledge, attitudes, and visitor profiles)	Questionnaire/ Observation/ Interview	Behaviour change
Interpreter Performance	Evaluation criteria of interpreter performance by supervisor, peers or outside experts, self-evaluation, and audience responses	Individual or group critique	Improved presentation skills
Operator Cost-effectiveness	Capital or establishment costs Annual running and maintenance costs Staffing requirements and costs Visitor numbers in attendance of a certain programme	Record keeping/ Observation/ Interview/	Cost-effectiveness in operating the provision of interpretation
Functional efficiency	Records of operational problems encountered such as accidents Visitor behaviour observations Visitor and staff comments	Record keeping/ Operator experience	Functional efficiency in relation to maintenance and visitor management

(Source: Developed from Thom, 1980; Knudson *et al*., 1995)

The Need for Evaluation of the Effectiveness of Interpretation on Attitude and Behaviour Change

Although many objectives of interpretation are identified above, particular attention is paid by previous studies to visitors' reactions to the interpretation programmes or their responses to the key objectives of interpretation. In other words, visitor evaluation of interpretation can be tested to determine the extent to which types of interpretive programmes can achieve each of the key objectives of interpretation (visitors' enjoyment, learning, attitude and behaviour change). From a visitor perspective, research has shown that most previous studies have focused on the effectiveness of interpretive programmes on visitors' attention and satisfaction in relation to the museum study (Light, 1991).

Recently, as the methodological approaches of the relationship between attitudes and behaviour have been developed in the psychological field, the educational effectiveness of interpretation has been evaluated with relation to the topic to increase visitors' knowledge and understanding as well as attitudes and behaviour. However, due to the complexity and difficulty of measurement of attitude and behaviour (Beaumont, 2001; Cottrell, 2003a,b), the management effectiveness of interpretation upon attitudes and consequent environmental behaviour has been a topic of much debate, and produced mixed results (Thom 1980; Cable *et al.*, 1987; Orams 1997; Kuo, 2002).

In response to the needs of the research to evaluate the effectiveness of interpretation in enhancing visitors' attitudes and behaviour, which is one of the main management objectives of interpretation for achieving the goals of sustainable tourism, it is worth assessing whether and how visitors modify their behaviour after receiving that interpretation, when considering a combination of visitor variables and other correlated attitudinal components for future research into the effectiveness of interpretation (McArthur and Hall, 1996; Kuo, 2002; Cottrell, 2003).

3.9 Summary

This chapter explores three main issues regarding interpretation. First, it reviews the definitions of interpretation, different benefits of interpretation, and the management role of interpretation in achieving the goals of sustainable tourism. It is clear that interpretation plays an important role as a visitor management strategy in two main ways: enhancing the quality of the visitor experience and managing visitor behaviour.

Secondly, to achieve these goals of sustainable tourism through interpretation, effective interpretation requires several key principles and requirements in terms of a thorough and integrated understanding of audience, thematic message, and technique. It is suggested that a clear and thematic message is needed to deliver effective communication to the targeted audience.

Finally, this chapter addresses the importance of evaluation of interpretation in determining whether interpretation achieves effectively its objectives or goals. The different aspects of evaluation of interpretation include visitor evaluation, interpreter performance evaluation, the effectiveness of interpretation, cost-effectiveness evaluation, and functional efficiency evaluation. The different objectives of the effectiveness of interpretation from a visitor perspective are identified including visitors' attendance of and reactions to interpretation, satisfaction, learning, and attitudinal and behavioural change.

It is suggested that the effectiveness of interpretation upon attitudes and consequent environmental behaviour might be a challenge topic. Pre-existing empirical studies on this matter have been much debated and produced mixed results due to its complexity and the difficulty in achieving attitude and behavioural change. To design effective interpretation on the attitude and behaviour change, this in turn requires an understanding of 'what attitude and behaviour are'; 'how are they measured' 'what kinds of cognitive processes are involved in their change'; and 'how persuasive interpretation processes are involved in their change'. The following chapter will discuss in more detail theories of attitude and behaviour change in the context of persuasion.

CHAPTER

4

Chapter 4 Attitude and Behaviour Theories

4.1 Introduction

The third topic of the current research focuses on a review of literature relevant to the concepts of attitude and behaviour change which are the core management objectives of interpretation for environmental conservation. As discussed in Chapter 3, the beneficial effects of interpretation in the context of sustainable tourism have been recognised as an effective visitor management tool in promoting pro-environmental attitudes and modifying visitor behaviour. Therefore, a practical question arising from this situation is how can interpretation influence visitor attitude and behaviour in an environmentally responsible way? The answer is not likely to be simple because the process of attitude and behaviour change is quite complex and it involves a number of factors that may influence visitor behaviour.

On this point, in order to understand the process of a person's attitude and behaviour change through his or her interpretation experience, it is important to understand the three important lines of research as follows: (1) the conceptualisation and measurement of attitude and behaviour in the context of environmental domains; (2) understanding of key theoretical frameworks in the link between attitude and behaviour in both a broader context of general attitude-related theories and a more specific context of persuasive interpretation related theories; (3) the relationships between various underlying core antecedents (e.g. knowledge, beliefs, attitudes) and behaviour based on both attitude-related and persuasion-related theoretical frameworks.

The first section reviews the main debates over the concepts and measurement issues in relation to both attitudes and behaviour in the environmental domains. Several key issues are focused on as follows:

- what environmental attitudes are (see 4.2.1);
- how to conceptualise and measure environmental attitudes (see 4.3);
- what environmental behaviours are (4.4) ;
- what types of environmental behaviours are present in tourism settings (4.4.3) ;

In particular, this chapter provides an insight into the two main lines of the literature reviewed moving from a general attitude-related perspective to a specific persuasion-related perspective. For a better understanding of the attitude-behavioural change process, the key selected theoretical frameworks for the current study are summarised in Table 4.2.

The second section explores attitude-related theories and models. This puts greater emphasis on how attitude as one of the important determinants are associated with environmental behaviour in the social psychology fields. The two major issues were identified as follows: the measurement correspondence (4.5.2.1) and the influences of other determinants on the attitude-behaviour link (4.5.2.2).

After reviewing the theoretical process of attitudes and behaviour change in a broad and general perspectives of social and psychological fields, the following section narrowed down into the particular perspective of persuasion-related theorists in order to provide a better understanding of how interpretation as another important determinant are related with the attitude and behaviour change process. The practical questions include as follows:
- what kind of persuasion processes influence the visitor's attitude and behaviour change (4.5.3);
- what are the main persuasion factors to influence the persuasion process and target variables (4.5.3.2).

4.2 The Nature of Attitudes

As mentioned above, one way of changing human behaviour is through changing the attitudes that may underlie their behaviour. Primarily, attitude measurement has been used to understand the reasons why people behave the way they do (Newhouse, 1990). However, defining attitudes is problematic and they have been defined in many different ways. This section explores several definitions of attitudes from a number of perspectives in both the general nature of attitudes and the specific nature of attitudes in the environmental context.

In general, the debate over the definitions of attitudes in nature falls into two major perspectives: those who believe attitude is a unidimensional structure and those who believe it is multidimensional. This is based on the collection of a large number of literature related to the concepts of attitudes reviewed by Beaumont (1999).

In terms of the unidimensional view, it consists of only an evaluative (or affective) component. In general, the common definitions of attitudes accepted by most researchers refer to the enduring positive or negative, or favourable or unfavourable feelings about some person, object, or issue (Petty & Cacioppo, 1981; Ajzen, 1988; McDougall & Munro, 1994; Newhouse, 1990). In other words, attitude is a psychological tendency that is expressed by evaluating a particular entity with some degree of favour or disfavour (Eagly & Chaiken, 1993: 1).

On the other hand, the definitions of attitude from the multidimensional view are considered as a mental system of three dimensions: cognitive (beliefs, facts, principles, knowledge), affective (emotions, feelings) and conative (behavioural tendencies or intent) components, directed towards a person, object, or idea (McDougall & Munro, 1994; for the review, see Beaumont, 1999).

In more detail, the cognitive component reflects the individual's beliefs and knowledge about a particular object, or the manner in which the object is perceived (McDougall & Munro, 1994). Beliefs may be factual information or based on personal opinion (Petty and Cacioppo, 1981, Newhouse, 1990). An individual's feelings of like or dislike for a particular person, object or issue comprise the affective component of an attitude (McDougall & Munro, 1994). The conative (or 'behavioural') component of an attitude refers to the action taken or the expressed intent to act with respect to a particular object or place (McDougall & Munro, 1994). The conative element is more easily separated and measured as a behavioural modification variable (Newhouse, 1990).

As reviewed in several definitions of attitudes above, generally, attitudes are considered as the process of three types of evaluative response that underlie all three components, cognitive, affective, and conative. Most attitude theorists now agree that attitudes are characterised predominantly by an evaluative dimension and the three dimensional components. However, there is some confusion of the terms, 'affect' and 'evaluation' with regards to the differentiation between evaluative and affective dimensions. McGuire (1969, cited in Beaumont, 1999) stated that many theorists agree that evaluation takes place only in the affective domain. In contrast, Ajzen (1988:4) argued that 'the characteristic attribute of attitude is its evaluative nature' and does not refer specifically to the affective component. Similarly, other researchers also supported the idea that 'evaluation is the core of the attitude concept' and 'evaluation and affect (or 'emotion') are not the same concept' in relation to attitudes (Eagly and Chaiken, 1993: p.666; Zanna and Rempel, 1988:p.320). That is, 'affect' refers to the feelings or emotions that people experience in relation to the attitude objects. Therefore, the concept of 'affect' should not be equated with the concept of evaluative aspects of attitude (Eagly and Chaiken, 1993; Beaumont, 1999).

Another debate is considered in terms of formation and response levels. According to McGuire (1969, cited in Beaumont, 1999), the cognitive, affective and behavioural components of attitude are so highly interrelated that it is not meaningful to make distinctions between them. On the other hand, attitudes can be formed 'primarily or exclusively' on any one of them even though the three components tend to impinge upon and interact with one other (Eagly and Chaiken, 1993; Beaumont, 1999). For example, although people may hold strong beliefs about an issue, they may not engage in relevant behaviours or experience emotional reactions. Therefore, attitudes would be formed on the basis of cognitive beliefs alone, or may be primarily formed by affective or behavioural processes or a combination of two or all three of the components (Beaumont, 1999).

With regard to the debate on the various definitions of attitude by several researchers, the major consensus points are as follows: an attitude is evaluative in nature; it consists of one dimension or a combination of two or all three of the components (Eagly and Chaiken, 1993; Beaumont, 1999); it is learnt; it is relatively lasting; it always involves an objective and it is predisposes a person to act in a specific manner towards a given object (cited in Adams, 2003).

4.2.1 Definitions of Environmental Attitudes

As the attitude object for this research is on the environmental conservation domain, this section reflects the particular debate over the definitions of environmental attitudes. It is addressed that they may not be readily apparent in terms of the distinctions between these concepts 'concerns', 'attitudes', 'value', and 'worldview'. Indeed, many researchers often used these terms as interchangeable or synonymous in the literature of environmental research (for the review, see Van Liere & Dunlap, 1981; Dunlap & Jones, 2003; Milfont and Duckitt, 2004; Schultz, Shriver, Tabanico, & Khazian, 2004).

'Environmental concern' commonly refers to a general attitude towards the environment or some particular aspects of the environment and is used either as a multiple or a single component approach (Kaiser *et al.,* 1999). Similarly, Schultz et al. (2004) defined the term 'environmental concern' as 'the affect (i.e. worry) associated with beliefs about environmental problems. For example, 'a person may be concerned about the harmful consequences of air pollution for his or her health, or concerned about the long-term consequences of improper disposal of hazardous household waste' (Schultz *et al.*, 2004: p.31). Now, most researchers view environmental concern as a general attitude, which focuses on the cognitive and affective evaluation of environmental protection (e.g. Dunlap & Van Liere, 1978; Weigel & Weigel, 1978, cited in Bamberg, 2003; Kaiser *et al.*, 1999).

'Environmental attitude' is defined as 'a learned belief which develops from an individual's knowledge and values about the environment and governs action to support or sustain the environment' (Unitto *et al.*, 2004:p.82). Similarly, Schultz *et al.*, (2004: p.31) defined environmental attitudes as 'the collection of beliefs, affect, and behavioural intentions a person holds regarding environmentally related activities or issues.'

The term, 'worldview' represents a person's belief system or cognitive paradigm about the relationships between human and nature (Schultz *et al.*, 2004). On the other hand, the term 'values' refers to important life goals or standards which serve as guiding principles in a person's life (Rokeach, 1973, cited in Schultz & Zelezny, 1999) and are distinct from attitudes or beliefs (Olson & Zanna, 1993). Another view of 'environmental attitudes' is conceptualised as a person's more general set of values comprising multidimensional beliefs according to a value-basis theory (Stern and Dietz, 1994). Both a worldview and values are viewed as determinants of a wide range of environmental attitudes or behaviour (Schultz *et al.*, 2004; Olson & Zanna, 1993).

In the above review, an inclusive definition of 'environmental concern' or 'environmental attitudes' seems to range from both a more broadly general attitude or value orientation to a specific environmental attitude toward environmentally related behaviours or issues. More recently, research of attitudes toward environmental objects has begun to differentiate between different types of environmental attitudes, such as 'worldview' or 'value-based environmental attitudes' or 'specific attitudes towards issues or actions' as well as moving away from an examination of general environmental concern and toward a more differentiated conceptualisation of environmental attitude formations (Schultz and Zelezny, 1999; Schultz *et al.*, 2004). Some researchers have focused on their relationships either at a general or specific level (Schultz *et al.*, 2004). In the following subsection, the different conceptualisations or measurement of environmental attitudes is addressed in more detail.

4.3 Conceptualisation and Measurement of Environment Attitudes

Environmental attitude has been conceptualised and measured in a variety of ways. Many of these ways of conceptualising environmental attitudes have been determined on the basis of three types of attitude to predict ecological behaviour as follows: (1) attitudes toward the environment or issues such as recycling, pollution, conservation, wilderness or nature preserve management; (2) attitudes toward ecological behaviour or specific responsible behaviour; (3) environmental worldview or value orientation. In examining various conceptualisations of environmental attitudes, another problem arises regarding how to measure environmental attitudes. Since the 1970s, environmental sociologists have been developing scales that measure a person's attitude toward the environment in order to predict ecological behaviour (Dunlap and Van Liere 1978; Weigel and Weigel 1978; Stern *et al.*, 1995). Many different methods have been used to measure environmental attitudes, even where they have been conceptualised in a similar way (Beaumont, 1999).

(1) General Environmental Attitudes toward the Environment or Environmental Issues

Starting from the conceptualisation of environmental concern as a general attitude towards the environment and related issues, there are a variety of measurement approaches used in previous attitude research. Many studies have been designed to determine attitudes towards the natural environment itself, or some aspects of the environment. Several measuring instruments have been developed in both the multiple and single dimension approaches within the context of different substantive issues (Kaiser *et al.*, 1999; Van Liere and Dunlap, 1981). In other words, some studies have measured a single dimension of the environmental attitude construct (mainly beliefs or opinion statements) with the different substantive issues while other studies have measured the multiple dimensions of the environment attitude construct with a single substantive issue (Beaumont, 1999).

This research tradition of environmental attitude measurement can be traced back to the Ecological Attitude Scale (EAS) (Maloney & Ward, 1973; Maloney *et al.*, 1975) which has been frequently used in previous attitude research. The Ecological Attitude Scales were developed by Maloney and Ward (1973), and later refined and shortened by Maloney, Ward and Braucht (1975). The shorter version of the EA scale contain 45 items focusing on various substantive issues such as pollution, recycling, litter, pesticides, food contamination and the environment in general (cited in Beaumont, 1999). They consist of four scales based on separate conceptualisations of knowledge (i.e. specific factual knowledge related to ecological issues), affect (i.e. the degree of emotionality related to such issues), verbal commitment (i.e. the degree to which a person states he is willing to protect the environment) and actual commitment (i.e. the degree to which a person actually does protect the environment) (Fransson and Gärling, 1999). For example, the EAS measurement was adopted and tested by several researchers (for the reviews, see Borden and Francis (1978), Gifford et al (1982/83), Schahn and Holzer (1990) and Kuhlemeier *et al.*, (1999). In particular, Schahn and Holzer (1990) included specified domains, such as residential energy conservation, environmentally responsible purchasing, and water conservation using four scales. They found positive correlations between all scales with the exception of knowledge (K) scale.

Regardless of using the EAS scale, in addressing an attitude-object, many studies have been particularly specific in assessing attitudes towards specific environmental issues using a number of theoretical conceptualisations. The major substantive issues have been included such as pollution, state of the environment, science, technology, natural resources, recycling, resource management, and conservation (Beaumont, 1999). Many empirical studies of specific attitudes have been used across a number of different populations and to explore a range of environmental topics. For example, visitors' environmental attitudes toward nuclear power technology have been measured by Lee and Balchin (1995) for their study of Sellafield Visitor Centre using cognitive/belief-type and emotional components. Holden (2003) has examined trekkers' environmental attitudes toward specific aspects of a particular environment site in Annapurna, Nepal. He investigated substantive issues of appreciation of the environment, views on the impacts of trekking, the level of knowledge of trekkers about the environment of Annapurna, and their experiences and behaviour using three separate components of the attitude construct. Others have studied the general public's attitude towards conservation of the natural environment and a respect for nature across seven nationalities (Hayes, 2001); children's attitudes toward sea turtle conservation, in Greece (Dimitrios and Pantis, 2003); the general public's attitudes towards sustainable forest management in Canada (McFarlane and Boxall, 2003); and residents' attitudes towards negative impacts of tourism on the forest environment in Turkey (Kuvan & Akan, 2004).

(2) Attitudes toward Environmental Behaviour

Attitudes toward environmental behaviour have been best conceptualised and measured based on the theory of reasoned action (Ajzen and Fishbein, 1980) and the theory of planned behaviour (Ajzen, 1991). Those theories provide clear theoretical and operational definitions of the attitude constructs and show the causal processes of the main components in the way in which they affect behaviour (Bamberg, 2002).

According to them, to predict ecological behaviour, several main domains have been measured such as actual behaviour, intentions, attitudes toward a particular behaviour, beliefs toward the outcomes or evaluations of a particular behaviour, and social normative beliefs. The Theory of Reasoned Action (TRA) and the Theory of Planned Behaviour (TPB) have demonstrated good empirical support in applications to a wide variety of different domains including the interpretation and tourism fields. The reviews of empirical studies examining specific attitudes towards environmental behaviour based on those theories will be discussed in more details in the following section, the review of the Theory of Reasoned Action and/or Planned Behaviour.

With regards to the measurement of specific attitudes toward the issues or actions, several researchers have argued that specific environmental attitude measures are better determinants of specific rather than general environmental behaviour measures (c.f. Kaiser *et al.*, 1999). In contrast, specific measures seem to be more strongly affected by situational influences than general ones. In addition, as several studies of attitudes towards specific issues or a particular behaviour are limited in overall generalisability beyond the environmental issues (Cottrell, 2003a), specific measures make empirical findings from different domains hardly comparable (Kaiser *et al.*, 1999).

(3) Environmental Worldview or Value-Based Orientation

As reviewed in the previous section, most of the attitude research has focused on attitudes about environmental issues or activities based on cognitive, affective, and behavioural dimensions. Rather than measuring specific attitudes, some authors have argued that general environmental worldview or different value-orientations will ultimately shape different attitudes towards the environment/issues and environmental behaviour (Schultz, 2001; Schultz *et al.*, 2004; Schultz and Zelezny, 2002; Bamberg, 2003).

First, the most frequently used instrument for measuring general environmental attitudes or concern is the New Environmental Paradigm (NEP) Scale which is called an 'environmental worldview' developed by Dunlap and Van Liere (1978) and revised by Dunlap, Van Liere, Mertig, & Jones (2000). The original NEP scale consists of 12 items which were designed to measure the pro-ecological worldview in terms of the relationships between humans and nature while the revised one is reduced to 10 items. There are three distinct bases: beliefs about the limits to growth, humanity's ability to upset the balance of nature, and humanity's right to rule over nature (*see* Fransson and Garling, 1999; Schultz *et al.*, 2004). Several researchers have found that the original and revised NEP scale has a unidimensional construct and a high degree of internal consistency and predictive, construct, and content validity (Dunlap and Van Liere, 1978; Lee & Moscardo, 2005). In tourism settings, the measure of NEP scale has been used to understand the visitor's environmental attitudes by several researchers: environmental attitudes of visitors to the US Virgin Islands (Uysal *et al.*, 1994); ecotourism resort tourists' attitudes in Australia (Lee & Moscardo, 2005); environmental attitudes of the visitors to Wickanninish Visitor Centre in Canada (Alessa *et al.*, 2003). The NEP scale used in these studies has been found to have good reliability and validity.

However, others have argued that the NEP scale only measures general environmental concern rather than specific beliefs (Stern *et al.*, 1995). Empirical studies have found a weak relationship between environmental attitudes measured by the NEP scale and environmental behaviour (Dunlap and Van Liere 1978; Kaiser *et al.*, 1999).

Apart from the NEP scale for general environmental attitudes, other researchers have approached measuring environmental attitudes with respect to multi-dimensional value-based orientations, which are another alternative measure of environmental attitudes. Using a somewhat different terminology with two motives/values of Thompson and Barton (1994, cited in Milfont & Duckitt, 2004) such as Ecocentric (or a concern for all living things) and Anthropocentric (or a concern for humans), Stern and his associates (e.g. Stern and Dietz, 1994; Stern *et al.*, 1995) have designed three sets of values associated with environmental attitudes. This is divided into three categories: egoistic (it refers to 'self' or self-oriented goals such as social power, wealth, personal success), altruistic (it refers to all people such as family, community, humanity, friends), and biospheric (it refers to all living things such as plants, animals, trees) (for a review of this, see Schultz *et al.*, 2004). For example, Schultz (2000, 2001) developed the Environmental Motives Scale which contained 12 items to measure three sets of value orientations across 14 countries. In the results of this study, the clear structure of three value-based environmental attitudes including egoistic, altruistic, and biospheric values has been shown across 14 countries.

From a natural-based tourism perspective, the empirical measurement of values and their causal influence on attitudes toward resource management has been rarely examined in natural resource settings (Borrie *et al.*, 2002). Based on the review of previous empirical studies by Borrie et al. (2002), some researchers have investigated different types of value-orientation measures in national resource settings and different objects: four categories of benefits and values of forests and forest ecosystems (e.g. recreation, commodity, ecological, and moral/spiritual values) in the study of U.S. media by Bengston *et al.*, (1999); ten major typologies of values of parks (e.g. aesthetic, recreation, scientific/education, moral/ethical, ecologic, therapeutic, economic, intellectual, historic/cultural, and spiritual) in the study of visitors to the Vermont State Parks, U.S.A by Gilbert *et al.*, (1996). For example, in the study of the visitors to Yellowstone National Park, U.S.A by Borrie *et al.*, (2002), they constructed four broad categories of the perceived values of Yellowstone National Park. They include protection of nature; the symbolic and historic role of Yellowstone park; the recreation and tourism resource values as a tourism destination; and personal growth and development values. The results of this study also found that groups of visitors with different value orientations demonstrated correspondingly different levels of support for management actions related to winter snowmobile access issues.

Furthermore, another theoretical approach to environmental attitudes has been developed in terms of the measurement of primary attitude factors (c.f. Wiseman & Bogner, 2003) through factor analysis of established or modified measures of a broader range of items drawn from previous attitude research (Milfont and Duckitt, 2004). In turn, this has emerged a large number of environmental attitude measures, probably at least 700 (see Dunlap & Jones, 2002 for the review)

Summary of Conceptualisations of Environmental Attitudes and their Relevance to Interpretation

To sum up, the major distinct conceptualisations of 'environmental concern' or 'environmental attitudes' seem to range from a more broadly general attitude toward the environment through value orientations to a specific attitude toward environmentally related behaviours (Fransson and Gärling, 1999). The reviews of previous attitude research have indicated that there is no consensus about the structure of environmental attitude and its measurements. On this point, in the context of interpretation and tourism fields, the various scales have been used in a variety of studies designed to measure environmental attitudes or concern of visitors or residents across different settings and issues. The majority of recent studies using a sample of the visitors to natural-based settings have focused on site-specific issues based on the multidimensional aspects of the attitudes constructs (e.g. Tubb, 2003; Orams, 1997; Madin and Fenton, 2004; Littlefair, 2003). For example, Tubb (2003) has studied the effects of the visitor centre on the key measures for behavioural modification in Dartmoor national park,

UK. The substantive issues in measuring the visitor's environmental attitudes include the purpose and nature of values of national parks, the consequences of feeding the Dartmoor ponies, farming, tourism impact, and the role of the Dartmoor national park authority. Some have measured environmental attitudes and behaviour based on the theory of reasoned action (e.g. Bright *et al.*, 1993; Chandool, 1997; Aipanjiguly *et al.*, 2003). Others have used general environmental attitudes using the NEP scale (e.g. Lee and Moscardo, 2005). Moreover, Cottrell (2003a) measured both general attitudes using the NEP scale and specific attitudes towards issues or activities based on multidimensional structure (e.g. knowledge, attitudes, intentions, and behaviour).

As reviewed above, some criticisms of the measurement of environmental attitudes in nature-based tourism settings have been made arguing that various scales have been used and modified to measure environmental attitudes and some of them have not been tested for reliability, validity and internal consistency (Beaumont, 1999). Therefore, it is more difficult to compare results of the various studies using different measurement methods and theoretical conceptualisations across different settings or issues. Recently, some researchers have focused on analysing the different types of environmental attitudes and the relationship between worldview, values and environmental attitudes and specific pro-environmental behaviours. The important agreements of the new perspective research have suggested that both narrowly defined and more generally defined environmental attitudes or concerns are important determinants of pro-environmental behaviour.

4.4 Environmental Behaviour

The previous section discussed in more detail regarding the conceptualisations and measurements of environmental attitudes which are one of the management goals of interpretation. Another ultimate management objective of interpretation is to promote conservation behaviour for the long-term as well as to minimise inappropriate behaviour on-site in achieving the environmental goals of sustainable tourism. As human behaviours have been classified in various ways, it is important to understand different definitions and types of environmental behaviour that might be targeted by site-based interpretation programmes (Ham and Krumpe, 1996; Monroe, 2003). Therefore, this section explores the definitions of environmentally responsible behaviour and typology of visitor behaviour in natural tourism settings.

4.4.1. Definitions of Environmental Behaviour

Human behaviour refers to any of the actions engaged in by people (cited in Brown, 2001:43). Among human behaviour in environmental domains, there is no consensus to define a clear concept of environmental behaviour and there is use of several different terms of environmental behaviour by different researchers. For example, Monroe (2003: p.114) stated that conservation behaviours represent those activities that support a sustainable society. Some researchers used the term "environmentally responsible behaviour" in a broad sense. According to Hines *et al.*, (1986/87), Hungerford and Volk (1990) and Cottrell (2003a,b), 'general responsible environmental behaviour' is defined as any individual or group action aimed at doing what is right to help protect the environment in general daily practice – e.g. recycling or household water conservation (Sivek & Hungerford, 1989-1990, cited in Cottrell, 2003b). Others used the term 'specific responsible environmental behaviour' which represents any behaviour that is more activity-specific in nature (e.g. not littering or climbing in the designated areas) as related to rule compliance or illegal, inappropriate, or non-sustainable behaviour (Cottrell, 2003a:p.1) in a particular setting.

4.4.2 Types of Environmental Behaviour

Environmentally relevant behaviours may differ in many ways. There are several ways to categorise behaviours in terms of the specific physical actions performed or indirect actions, where and when they are performed, the amount of effort and/or resources expended, and/or the specific outcomes obtained. (Thøgersen, 2004: p94). Clearly, all types of behaviour have different motives and rewards that draw people to engage in different aspects of environmental opportunities. Therefore, it is rarely possible to change conservation behaviour with one strategy (Monroe, 2003).

Some researchers have identified different categories of environmental behaviours based on similarities in motives or opportunities of that behaviour that could make it easier to encourage behaviour by interpretation (or information programmes) (cited in Monroe, 2003). From an interpretation perspective, the targeted behavioural outcomes by site-based interpretive programmes are classified either in terms of whether the behaviours should occur on-site (within the protected area) or off-site (in general daily practice in a person's life) or in terms of the time period in which given behaviours may be changed in the short-term or in the long-term (Ham & Krumpe, 1996).The reviews of the classifications of environmental behaviour identified by several authors are summarised in Table 4.1.

As reviewed above, within the context of interpretation and natural tourism areas, some empirical research of environmental behaviour have studied mostly 'environmental activism' category and 'site-specific appropriate behaviour' (Orams, 1997; Beaumont, 2001; Roggenbuck, 1992).

Table 4.1. Typology of Target Behaviours

(On-site Behaviours vs Off-site Behaviours)

On-site Visitor Behaviour	Off-site Behavioiur
1) Illegal actions	1) Environmental activism
2) Careless actions	(e.g. actively participating in or leading
3) Unskilled actions	environmental initiatives)
4) Uninformed actions	2) Non-activist political behaviours
5) Unavoidable actions	(e.g. joining an organisation, voting, and
	signing a petition)
(Source: Roggenbuck, 1992)	3) Consumer behaviours
	(e.g. purchasing 'green' products, recycling,
6) Consumer behaviours	reducing energy use, and altering consumption
(e.g. not buying products made	habits)
from threatened species or	4) Ecosystem behaviours
protected artefacts; purchasing	(e.g. putting up bird boxes, planting sea oats,
'green' products)	counting wildlife populations, promoting
	prescribed fire)
(Ham and Krumpe, 1996)	5) Specific behaviours which are performed in
	specific settings
	(e.g. reducing waste in the production process,
	establishing mortgage criteria for energy
	efficient houses, suing a polluter, etc.)
	(Monroe, 2003: p. 115)

4.4.3 Categories of Visitors' Problem Behaviour

Since visitor behaviour in tourism settings is the object of the present study, it focuses on the visitors' problem behaviour or responsible environmental behaviour at site-specific level. Hendee et al. (1990, cited in Roggenbuck, 1992) have identified and categorised five types of undesirable visitor actions which is based on apparent motives for each behaviour: illegal, careless, unskilled, uninformed and unavoidable. Similarly, another typology of depreciative behaviour (or inappropriate behaviour) in park settings provides six classifications (namely unintentional, releasor-cue, uninformed, responsibility-denial, status-conforming, and wilful violations) identified by Gramann and Vander Stoep (1987, cited in Roggenbuck, 1992).

85

The following typology of problem behaviours based on Hendee et al.' classifications (1990) are described in more detail.

1) ***Illegal behaviours*** refers to wilful violations of park laws and rules categorised in Grammann and Vander Stoep (1987) typology, and persuasion is likely to achieve only limited effectiveness. The examples include theft of Indian artefacts, off-road vehicles, and invasion of wilderness by motorists.

2) ***Careless actions*** involve behaviours such as littering, shouting or playing radios at night, which the recreationist knows is wrong or inconsiderate, but which he or she does without thinking. This action represents 'responsibility-denial violations' in another typology of Gramann and Vander Stope's (1987). In their terms, responsibility-denial violations are defined as an inappropriate behaviour when people generally believe an action is wrong, but don't assume moral responsibility for the problem behaviour in a specific situation (e.g. littering, failing to pick up other's litter, failing to pay self-registration camping fee).

3) ***Unskilled actions*** occur when recreationists want to do the right thing, but lack the skill to carry it out (e.g. selecting an improper camping spot, building improper campfire). This can be referred as 'unintentional behaviours' in Gramann and Vander Stoep (1987) typology such as 'entering a wildlife sensitive zone', and 'camping too close to a trail'.

4) ***Uninformed actions*** results from ignorance of the rules, and of the negative consequences of the action in question (e.g. selecting a lightly used campsite in the wilderness, using dead snags for firewood). Uninformed actions that degrade the environment or cause visitor conflict are common in unfamiliar park settings, and here persuasion has an extremely high potential for reducing problems.

5) ***Unavoidable actions*** involve any behaviours which people can not avoid such as urinating or defecating while in a park setting and trampling ground cover vegetation. (Source: Roggenbuck, 1992: p.163-164)

The conclusions drawn from the literature are that there are many types of problem behaviours which each have different motives. Also, it is reviewed that the effectiveness of persuasive communication (or interpretation) can vary according to the types of behaviour. The review of the empirical studies of the effects of information on the typology of the visitor behaviour has provided that information/education may have limited effectiveness on illegal and unavoidable actions. However, the other three types of problem behaviours (e.g. careless actions or responsibility-denial violations), unskilled actions (or unintentional behaviours), and uninformed actions may be considerably altered by the successful influences of information/education programmes ranging from moderate levels to high levels of effectiveness (Roggenbuck, 1992; Manning, 2003).

This would suggest that simply providing visitors with information and education about environmental conservation would not be the most effective means of control. We might need to approach more effective strategies to help visitors to minimise the problem actions, particularly undesirable or uninformed behaviour based on understanding a theoretical process of attitude and behaviour change through persuasion.

4.5 Theories of Attitude and Behaviour Change in the Context of Environmental Behaviour

The previous section reviewed the overview of the debates on the definitions, conceptualisations and measurement of environmental attitudes and behaviour. This section addresses the key theoretical frameworks related to the attitude and behaviour change process in both a broader context of attitude-related perspective and more specific persuasion-related perspective in the field of environmental behaviour.

Numerous theoretical frameworks have been developed rooted in different areas, psychology, education, and tourism. Table 4.2 summarises the key theories of attitude and behavioural change which will be discussed in more detail in this section. These selected key theories provide the basis for the theoretical understanding of the process on how the key determinant variables (e.g. attitudes, interpretation) are related to behaviour and the gap between the independent variables and behaviour. This section explores the two main line of research reviewed moving from general attitude-related perspective to narrowly specific persuasion-related perspective. The several key models of environmental behaviour were first reviewed based on both attitude-related theories which have been mostly used within the interpretation fields. In addition, the persuasion communication theories which also appear to have the greatest application to the interpretation field were discussed in the following section. These are: traditional behaviour change system (4.5.1); attitude-related behaviour theories (4.5.2); and finally, persuasion-related models (4.5.3). Each of the theoretical models relevant to the research topic, attitude and behaviour change in an interpretation context is discussed in more detail. Several factors in two lines of key theories and models of the attitude and behaviour change were also described in the following sub-sections.

Table 4.2 Selected Key Theories of Attitude and Behavioural Change

Theory or Model	Authors	Key Concepts

Traditional Behaviour Change System (see 4.5.1)	Hungerford & Volk, 1990: p.9	A linear link between knowledge, attitudes and behaviour.

The Attitude-related Perspectives (see 4.5.2)

Theory of Reasoned Action Theory of Planned Behaviour See 4.5.2.(1)	Ajzen & Fishbein, 1980 Ajzen, 1991	Human behaviour or behavioural intention is consistent with attitudes. Behavioural intention is affected by attitudes towards behaviour, subjective norm, and perceived behavioural control. These attitudes are consistent with beliefs.
Model of Responsible Environmental Behaviour See 4.5.2.(2)	Hines et al. (1986/87)	Responsible behaviour is influence by intention to act and situational factor. Intention to act is influenced by action skills, knowledge of action strategies, knowledge of issues and personality factors (including attitudes, locus of control and personal responsibility)
Conceptual framework of Responsible Environmental behaviour See 4.5.3.(3)	Cottrell & Gaefel, 1997; Cottrell, 2003a	In order to influence both general environmental behaviour and specific environmental behaviour in different levels, general environmental attitudinal variables affect specific environmental attitudinal variables which then lead to specific behaviour. Socio-demographic and situational variables are also linked to different levels of the behavioural process

The Persuasion-related Perspectives (see 4.5.3)

The tradition persuasion communication theory See 4.5.3.1	The Hovland group(1953); Petty & Cacioppo, 1981	The four main contextual factors (e.g. source, message, channel, receiver) influence three target variables (e.g. change in belief, attitude, behaviour) through the integrated process of the mediating process variables (e.g. attention, comprehension, acceptance, integration)
Three routes to persuasion See 4.5.3.2	Roggenbuck, 1992; Petty & Cacioppo, 1981	There are three routes to persuasion to influence attitude and behaviour change to different target receivers in different situations. 1) The applied behavioural analysis 2) Central route to persuasion 3) Peripheral Route to Persuasion

4.5.1 Traditional Behaviour Change System

Earlier studies of environmental behaviour have focused on the assumption that knowledge is linked to attitudes, and attitudes to behaviour in a linear model (Cottrell & Graefe, 1997). As seen in Figure 4.1, this proposes that if individuals become more knowledgeable about the environment and its associated issues, they will, in turn, become more aware of the environment and its problems that would in turn lead to pro-environmental attitudes and thus, be more motivated to act toward the environment in more responsible ways (Hungerford & Volk, 1990: p.9). In the context of visitor management situation in tourism settings, this assumption is widely accepted throughout the park visitor management and interpretation fields (Beckamann, 1999). In other words, if visitors are taught about a place and the values of the site, they become more concerned about the environment and become motivated to sustain the place by altering their behaviour during their visit (Bramwell & Lane, 1993).

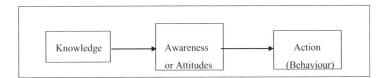

Figure 4.1 Traditional Behavioral Change System
(Source: Hungerford & Volk, 1990: p.9)

However, the linear model of environmental behaviour has not been seen as valid or true. Prior research has shown that increases in knowledge and awareness did not lead to pro-environmental behaviour in most cases (Kollmuss & Agyeman, 2002) and there was an inconsistent and weak relationship between attitude and behaviour (Fransson and Gärling, 1999; Newhouse, 1990). In particular, 'if the attitude is not measured closely in time and at the same level of specificity as the behaviour, there is seldom a strong relationship' (Fransson and Garling, 1999: p.379). Instead of a simple linear model, several efforts to predict human behaviour have been made through both identifying a variety of other determinants of such behaviour and examining the potential for practical application in terms of methodological and measurement approach. To date, it has become apparent that the interrelationships between knowledge, attitudes and behaviour is a far more complex one (Beckmann, 1999; Hines *et al.*, 1986/87; Cottrell, 2003b).

4.5.2 Attitudes and Behaviour Theories

This section focuses on key attitude-based theories as follows: (1) Theory of Reasoned Action and Theory of Planned Behaviour; (2) Model of Responsible Environmental Behaviour; and (3) Conceptual framework of responsible environmental behaviour.

(1) Theory of Reasoned Action and Theory of Planned Behaviour

The 'Theory of Reasoned Action' (Ajzen & Fishbein, 1980) is a general theory of human behaviour that deals with the relationships among beliefs, social norms, attitudes, intentions and behaviour (Fishbein & Manfredo, 1992). This model has been the most influential attitude-behaviour model in social psychology (Kolimuss & Agyeman, 2002).

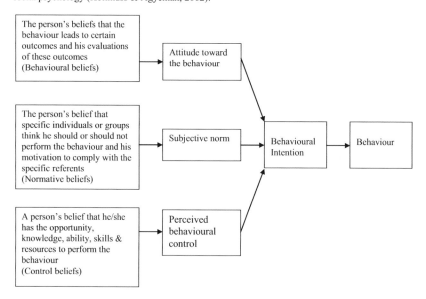

Figure 4.2 The 'Theory of Planned Behaviour'
(Source from: Ajzen, 1991)

The theory of reasoned action was subsequently modified to its revision version, the Theory of Planned Behaviour. The Theory of Planned Behaviour is extended by its inclusion of influences of beliefs about the perceived control behaviour on behavioural intention (Ajzen, 1991) (see Figure 4.2).

One great advantage of these theories is that they provide clear theoretical and operational definitions of the model constructs and organise these constructs with respect to the causal processes by which they affect behaviour (Bamberg, 2002). Both the Theory of Reasoned Action and the Theory of Planned Behaviour postulate that a specific behaviour can be predicted from the behavioural intention that corresponds directly to the target behaviour. In particular, according to the Theory of Planned Behaviour, behavioural intention (it refers to 'a person's motivation, conscious plan or decision to exert effort to perform the behaviour') can be predicted by three major components. They are: attitudinal influences (it refers to the individual's positive or negative feelings about performing the behaviour); the subjective norms regarding the behaviour that may be defined as the extent to which others influence the person's decision (Fishbein & Manfredo, 1992); and the perceived behavioural control (it refers to the perceived ease or difficulty of performing the behaviour, and it is assumed to reflect past experience as well as anticipated impediments and obstacles) (Ajzen & Driver, 1992). Three constructs of beliefs (behavioural beliefs, normative beliefs, and control beliefs) are related to each of corresponding components (attitude about the behaviour, subjective norm, and perceived behavioural control) (Ham and Krumpe, 1996). Figure 4.2 shows the relationships of these factors determining a person's behaviour.

The theory of reasoned action (TRA) or the theory of planned behaviour (TPB) has been used extensively as a theoretical framework to predict and explain why people have or have not engaged in a wide variety of behaviours related to the environment (Fishbein & Manfredo, 1992; Kaiser *et al.*, 1999; Bamberg, 2002) in different settings. It has been considered especially useful in predicting ecological behaviour (Kaiser *et al.*, 1999).

In tourism settings, several studies have used TRA or TPB theory as a theoretical framework to examine the site-specific environmental behaviour but limited application to investigate a variety of tourists or visitor behaviours (Lee & Balchin, 1995). They are as follows: Climbing the Uluru rock in Australia (Brown, 1999); hunting (Rossi & Armstrong, 1999; Hurbes *et al.*, 2001); vandalising petrified wood fossils (Chandool, 1997); following speed zones for manatee conservation (Aipanjiguly *et al.*, 2003); support for controlled burn policy in the US National Park Service (Manfredo *et al.*, 1990, see Fishbein and Manfredo, 1992; Bright *et al.*, 1993). For example, the study of the visitors' climbing of the Uluru rock in Australia conducted by Brown (1999) indicated that the Theory of Reasoned Action was useful as a guided framework to explain and predict why the visitors engage in the culturally inappropriate behaviour of climbing Uluru. The findings of this study provided the empirical evidence of the relationships between all components (beliefs, social norms, attitudes) and behavioural intentions and behaviour regarding climbing Uluru. In general, the results of many other studies emphasise the usefulness of these theories in terms of identifying primary beliefs to predict target audiences' behaviour (Aipanjiguly *et al.*, 2003). In particular, Ham and Krumpe (1996) stressed that both theories provide a useful guide in evaluating the effectiveness of interpretation on attitude and behaviour change as well as developing the effective programmes tailoring the primary beliefs-targeted messages.

However, these reviews of the empirical studies have also showed that there are major criticisms of the TRA or TPB models. One of the major criticisms is that the associations between the main components in the model are limited in terms of explained variance (Bamberg, 2002). Another criticism of the TRA or TPB model is limited to apply to measuring and predicting only volitional behaviour (Fabrigar *et al.*, 1999) than actions in all situations. These theories propose the assumption that all behaviour is intentional, planned, rational and consistent with their beliefs, and so does not apply to behaviours that are spontaneous, impulsive, addictive, or wilfully destructive (Fishbain & Manfredo, 1992; Ham & Weiler, 2002). Then, the question lies in how much of human behaviour is rational or under volitional control. In fact, several researchers have argued that much behaviour is spontaneous (Petty *et al.*, 1992) and that some of the given spontaneous behaviours might be influenced by other factors, such as personal norms (Schwartz, 1977; Stern & Oskamp, 1987), prior behaviour (Bentler & Speckart, 1979; Triandis, 1977), and the accessibility of attitudes (Vincent and Fazio, 1992; Bamberg, 2002). For example, indeed, everyday behaviours frequently performed in stable contexts might be more controlled by habits than intentions (Verplanken and Aarts, 1999, cited in Bamberg, 2002). This can be explained in Triandis's model (1977), the Theory of Interpersonal Behaviour (TIB). He suggested that actual behaviour is directly determined by the three major factors: intentions, habit strength and facilitating conditions. In another model, the Attitude-to-Behaviour Process Model focuses upon the issues of spontaneous behaviour and the accessibility of attitudes from memory which is influenced by such factors as level of direct experience or degree of the mere presence of the attitude object (e.g. the environment) (Vincent and Fazio, 1992; Bamberg, 2002). In this situation, a general attitude guides the perception of a situation in a way that is congruent with this attitude and so the behavioural response to a trigger situation would be automatically prompted without deliberative reflection or the need of behavioural or social norm beliefs (Bamberg, 2002, 2003; Manfredo *et al.*, 1992).

The other criticisms of the TRA or TPB models are that the framework has no mechanism to account for situations where resources and opportunities necessary for performing a particular behaviour are limited by a range of other factors and not directly under the individual's volitional control (Liska 1984, cited in Brown, 2001). Such factors might be internal to the individual (e.g. demographic, skills, abilities, and knowledge) and/or external (e.g. time, access or dependence on others (Ajzen, 1988). Thus, as ecological behaviour (or environmental behaviour) appears to be susceptible to a wide range of influences beyond volitional control (Hines *et al.*, 1986/87; Kaiser *et al.*, 1999), it is important to acknowledge that the Theory of Planned Behaviour or Theory of Reasoned Action may have limited application to managing visitor behaviour in park settings, unless all behaviours of visitors are rational (or intentional) behaviours (Littelfair, 2003).

(2) Model of Responsible Environmental Behaviour

Hines et al's Model of Responsible Environmental Behaviour (1986/87) is another framework for promoting pro-environmental behaviour. This model was based on the Theory of Planned Behaviour (Hines *et al.*, 1986/87; Hungerford & Volk, 1990; Sia *et al.*, 1985-86). According to Hines, Hungerford, and Tomera (1986/87), predicting responsible behaviour is not a simple process. Hines et al. (1986/87) reviewed their meta-analysis of 128 pro-environmental behaviour research studies and found that several variables associated with responsible environmental behaviour were in four categories: (1) cognitive factor (knowledge of issues, knowledge of action strategies, action skills); (2) socio-psychological factor (locus of control, attitudes, an individual's sense of responsibility); (3) verbal commitment; and (4) situation factors.

As seen in Figure 4.4, first, the knowledge factors are associated with behavioural intentions (verbal commitment) and divided more specific variables (i.e. action skills; action strategies; and knowledge of issues) related to environmental problems and issues (Hines *et al.*, 1987). In addition, the personality factors seem to be the important influential factor to the behavioural intention and it includes specific elements such as locus of control, attitudes toward environment and behaviour, and personal responsibility toward the environment (Hines *et al.*, 1986/1987). These variables were defined as follows:

- 'Locus of control' represents an individual's perception of whether or not he or she has the ability to bring about change through his or her own behaviour. Individuals with an internal locus of control were more likely to have reported engaging in responsible environmental behaviours.

- 'Attitudes' refers to positive or negative feelings of the object (i.e. the environment or responsible environmental behaviour).

- 'Personal responsibility' represents an individual's feelings of duty or obligation. This obligation was either expressed in reference to the environment as a whole, or in reference to only one facet of the environment.

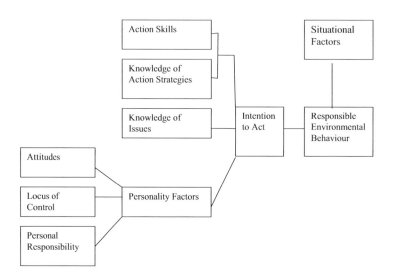

Figure 4.3 The Model of Responsible Environmental Behaviour

(Source: Hines, Hungerford, and Tomera, 1986/1987: p.7)

Moreover, 'intention to act' is associated with two main components: knowledge and personality factors. Hines *et al.* (1986/87) suggest that 'intention to act' is the most important variable related to responsible environmental behaviour (r=.49). Many other studies have also found that environmental behavioural intentions is strongly related to environmental behaviour, or at worst moderately related (Kaiser *et al.*, 1999).

In the final stage, it is assumed that situational factors might also influence behaviour, either counteracting or strengthening the variables in the model. The examples of situational factors include economic constraints, social pressures and opportunities to choose alternative actions.

The model is more sophisticated and identified other factors to explain pro-environmental behaviour than Ajzen and Fishbein's (1980), the Theory of Reasoned Action. In addition, the model views that both knowledge of the issues, action strategies and action skills and psychological factors have relative impacts on environmental behaviour. This model has been tested by Hwang *et al.*, (2000) who studied in the case of the forest national park, Korea. The results of the study by Hwang *et al.*, (2000) provided the empirical evidence of the relationships between selected components (knowledge, attitudes, locus of control, responsibility) and behavioural intention proposed in Hines *et al.*'s model of Responsible Environmental Behaviour (1986/87).

Although Hines *et al.*'s (1986/87) the model provides a better understanding of people's responsible environmental behaviour, the weak relationship between knowledge and attitudes, attitudes and intentions, and intentions and actual responsible behaviour has been examined in the results of empirical studies. It might be assumed that there are many more factors that influence pro-environmental behaviour (Kollmuss & Agyeman, 2002).

(3) Conceptual Framework of Responsible Environmental Behaviour
Subsequently, a conceptual framework of Responsible Environmental Behaviour model developed by Cottrell and Graefe (1997) and Cottrell (2003a,b) was adopted from the REB model developed by Hines *et al.*, (1986/87) and the review of prior research (Hungerford & Volk, 1990; Sivek & Hungerford, 1989/90). Cottrell and Graefe (1997) have developed a more detailed model to identify determinants of both General Responsible Environmental Behaviour (GREB, 'pro-environmental action on a general level') and Specific Responsible Environmental Behaviour (SREB, 'raw sewage discharged from recreational vessels in a sewage pump-out station') in the case study of boat owners in the Chesapeake Bay, USA (Cottrell and Graefe, 1997: p.17). The model is clearly explained using the different levels of the variables that influence both GREB and SREB including the main categorised variables (1) socio-demographic variables and boating experiences; (2) both general and specific attitudinal variables; and (3) situational factors. In particular, both issue-specific and general attitudes are integrated in terms of environmental concern defined in a general way (i.e. attitudes towards the environment, verbal commitment, and perceived knowledge of ecology) and specific environmental

attitude defined more narrowly (i.e. awareness of consequences of specific behaviours, knowledge of issues, personal commitment to issue resolution). Furthermore, the socio-demographic variables (i.e. income, age, education, and political ideology), boating background experiences variables, and situational factors are also included.

Although this model is quite complex, compared to previous theories presented above (TPB: Ajzen, 1991; REB: Hines *et al.*, 1986/87), it demonstrates the inclusion of some additional measures and explain different predictive strength of independent factors on both general environmental behaviour and specific environmental behaviour. Another important point is that it proposes an extended theoretical model for the relationships between general environmental attitudes (e.g. worldview using the NEP scale) and issue-specific attitude variables. In accordance with the value-attitude-behaviour theory (Stern *et al.*, 1995), this framework provides a new perspective that general environmental concern (i.e. value orientations or worldview) influences indirectly specific environmental behaviour through its direct impact on specific attitudes toward specific behaviours (Eagly and Chaiken, 1993; Bamberg, 2003). In this way, this model proposed that the more specific the indicator of behaviour was, the better predictive ability that indicator had of specific behaviour.

It is suggested that a predictive model of responsible environmental behaviour is a useful tool for monitoring visitor behaviour in order to help a greater understanding of the interrelation between variables pertinent to inappropriate or non-sustainable behaviour, then leading to better visitor management planning (Cottrell, 2003a). It is suitable to apply this model to predict visitor behaviour related to environmental protection as it consists of the specific-issue variables.

The Application of Attitude-based Theories to the Interpretation Field
All of these theories can be applied to the interpretation and tourism fields and are useful as a theoretical framework to affect an attitude and behavioural change. As reviewed, the theories and models of attitude and behaviour change above suggest that the core influential variables for pro-environmental behaviour should be considered, such as knowledge of action strategies and issues, beliefs about outcomes of a given behaviour, attitudes toward a particular behaviour and behavioural intentions. Based on this point, those key factors have been most consistently considered as antecedents of environmental behaviour in the adopted process models for behavioural change in the interpretation field (Orams, 1996/97; Cable *et al.*, 1986; Ham and Krump, 1996; Ballantyne and Packer, 1996/2005). For example, in order to accomplish lasting, meaningful and effective change in environmental

conceptions (e.g. beliefs, attitudes, behaviour) through the interpretation experiences, it is necessary to address the incorporated process involving personal knowledge of sustainability issues; changes in awareness, appreciation and concern for wildlife; development of intentions to take or refrain from specific personal actions that have an impact on the environment; and enactment of lifestyle changes designed to support environmental sustainability (Ballantyne and Packer, 1996).

4.5.2.1 The Main Issues of Relationships between Attitude and Behaviour

Overall, the previous section explored attitude-related theories of the behaviour change process and examined the relationships between several antecedent variables and environmental behaviour in a general psychological perspective. Different approaches to the attitudinal and behavioural change process emphasis different predictive ability of antecedent variables on the different behavioural processes. Recent researches have demonstrated that the relationships between variables are far more complex (Hungerfod & Volk, 1991; Cottrell, 2003b).

As seen in the review of attitude-related theories, it has been assumed that environmental attitude is one of the most influential factors in predicting environmentally responsible behaviour. However, several empirical studies based on traditional attitude theory have provided disappointing evidence for the predictive ability of attitudes on environmental behaviour (Kaiser et al., 1999; Kollmuss & Agyeman, 2002). Prediction was low to moderate with respect to types and aspects of behaviour (Bamberg, 2003, cited in Milfont and Duckitt, 2004). Although people's attitudes toward the environment or environmental protection increase through increased knowledge or direct experiences in the nature, their positive attitude will not automatically lead to pro-environmental behaviour.

The major reasons for the inconsistent and low correlations between attitude and behaviour have been explained in two main issues. These are the lack of measurement correspondence and the lack of consideration of situational influences on a given behaviour (Kaiser et al., 1999; Kllmuss & Agyeman, 2002; Olli et al., 2001).

Measurement Correspondence

From the measurement perspective, this inconsistency between attitude and behaviour has been explained as being caused by: (i) the use of inadequate measures of the environmental attitude (Weigel,

1983, cited in Costarelli and Colloca, 2004), (ii) the lack of measures at the same level of specificity (Ajzen, 1988; Kaiser *et al.*, 1999), and (iii) the effects of the constraints beyond people's control (Kaiser *et al.*, 1999). This methodological issue addresses how difficult it is to design valid studies that measure and compare attitude and behaviour (Kollmuss & Agyeman, 2002).

First, the use of inadequate measures of the environmental attitudes might lead to the inconsistency between attitude and behaviour as the dimensionality of environmental attitudes have not yet been clarified adequately in the literature of attitude research (Costarelli & Colloca, 2004). From a theoretical point of view, there are at least three main research traditions that use quite different attitude concepts: attitudes toward the environment (e.g. value orientations or New Environmental Paradigm); attitudes toward specific issues; attitudes toward specific environmental behaviour (Frasson and Gärling, 1999; Kaiser *et al.*, 1999). The different conceptualisations of environmental attitude confuse the comparison of research results in the ecological domain.

Secondly, the inconsistency between attitude and behaviour can be explained through measurement correspondence. Measurement correspondence refers to measurement of attitude and behaviour on the same level of specificity (e.g. Ajzen & Fishbein, 1977/80; Kaiser *et al.*, 1999; Fransson and Gärling, 1999). For example, it is suggested that if a person's environmental attitude is assessed generally, the behavioural measurement should be equally general or comprehensive (e.g.Weigel et al. 1974; Kaiser *et al.*, 1999). On the other hand, there is consensus that specific environmental attitude measures to a given behaviour are better predictors of specific environmental behaviour measures than are more general measures (e.g.Weigel *et al.*, 1974; Kaiser *et al.*, 1999; Cottrell & Graefe, 1997). Measurement correspondence at the same level of specificity has been addressed in the Theory of Reasoned Action and the Theory of Planned Behaviour by Ajzen and Fishbein (1977/80) and Ajzen (1991).

With respects to the relationships between general measure and specific measure, research has also shown that general environmental concern (e.g. Dunlap & Van Liere, 1984; Black *et al.*, 1985) affects more specific attitudes and personal norms concerning environmental issues (Schultz *et al.*, 2004; Schultz, 2001). Some studies have shown that general attitudes can be good predictors of specific behaviour, if one uses a "multiple act" criteria. For example, if a multitude of behaviours, such as using public transport, signing environmental petitions, contributing to conservation organisations, and so on, are assessed, there is generally a higher consistency between attitude and behaviour (Rajecki, 1982). Recently, research efforts have used more multiple-item measures of environmental behaviour versus single-item measures to improve the reliability of those measures and to increase the application of advanced statistical methods (e.g.Van Liere & Dunlap, 1981). As seen, the model of Cottrell and Graefe (1997/2003) has provided the premise that general environmental concern (e.g. New Environmental Paradigm) is differently related to both general environmental behaviour and specific environmental behaviour. Therefore, both narrowly defined and more generally defined environmental attitudes need to be measured to predict the multiple act behaviour as both are important determinants of pro-environmental behaviour (Fransson and Gärling, 1999).

Furthermore, the effects of the constraints beyond people's control may mediate the gap between attitude and behaviour. One of the constraints beyond people's control is behavioural difficulty (a person's perceived level of difficulty in carrying out a certain behaviour). In other words, each of the general environmental behaviours has a given difficulty in being carried out beyond individuals' control (Kaiser *et al.*, 1998). In the typology of visitor behaviour in a tourism setting (See the section 4.4), for instance, some of behaviours (e.g. uninformed or undesired behaviour) seem to be easier to carry out than others (e.g. responsibility and moral behaviours such as picking up litter). Therefore, the easier a behaviour is to carry out, the less constraints have to be assumed (Kaiser *et al.*, 1999). In other words, positive attitudes toward the environmental protection or the environment will easily lead to pro-environmental behaviour if the behaviour is easy to perform (Stern and Oskamp, 1987).

Finally, although previous tradition attitude related theories assume that attitude and behavioural intention play a key role in promoting pro-environmental behaviour, an alternative reaction to the low intention-behaviour relation leads to the search for additional psychological processes that might mediate the effect of intention on behaviour as well as other external variables to mediate the attitude-behaviour gap. The following section will discuss in more detail the other influential factors of environmental behaviour.

4.5.2.2 The Influence of Other Factors on the Link between Environmental Attitude and Environmental Behaviour

Apart from the key theories of attitude and behaviour change in the previous section, other theorists in different line of behavioural research also have identified several other intervening factors to mediate the consistency between attitudes and behaviour relationship in the process of attitude and behaviour change. In addition, the types of factors and the extent to which each factor influences the relationship between attitude and behaviour and the process of behavioural change can be different from one another in terms of types and aspects of behaviour and situations. Therefore, it cannot be visualised to integrate all factors into one single framework or diagram due to the complexity of behaviour change. It would be too complicated and lose its practicality and probably even its meaning if the single framework is developed to integrate all factors that shape and influence behaviour (Kollmuss & Agyeman, 2002).

Therefore, it needs to acknowledge the limitations in identifying proper factors for successful behavioural change that are applicable to a wide range of situations. In particular, this section reviews the main factors that are supposed to be common to each case and specifically relevant to tourism and interpretation. These factors are categorised into five levels: key internal personal factors, socio-demographic factors, previous or direct experiences, external situational factors, and information factors. There is no consensus of the distinctions and categories of the different influential factors due to difficulty of definitions of factors and their interrelations with each other (Kollmuss & Agyeman, 2002).

Key Internal Factors

Knowledge: lack of knowledge is one of the factors that can explain the weak relationship between general environmental attitudes and environmental behaviour (Fransson and Garling, 1999). However, most researchers agree that there is a weak relationship between pro-environmental behaviour and knowledge (Kaiser *et al.*, 1999; Kollmuss & Agyeman, 2002; Hwang *et al.*, 2000). As mentioned in Hines et al's model (1986/87) and Cottrell and Gaefe (1997), when knowledge is assessed by different types of knowledge, knowledge of issues and action strategies appear to be stronger relationships with environmental behaviour rather than factual knowledge about the environment (Kaiser *et al.*, 1999).

Value: values are defined as beliefs pertaining to desirable end states or modes of conduct that transcend specific situations and guide choices of actions (Schwartz, 1992, cited in Fransson and Garling, 1999). Values are responsible for the formation of attitudes and influence specific attitudes toward the environmental issues or toward specific environmentally related behaviours (Schultz, 2001;

Bamberg, 2003;Schultz, 2004). Three types of value orientations (See 4.3 in this chapter) are indirectly related to environmentally related behavioural intention (Fransson & Garling, 1999; Kaiser *et al.,* 1999).

Emotional involvement: emotional involvement is defined as the extent to which we have an affective relationship to the natural world (Kollmuss & Agyeman, 2002). In other words, emotional involvement reflects people's ability to have an emotional reaction when confronted with environmental degradation or problems. Such an emotional connection appears to be very important in shaping people's beliefs, values, and attitudes towards the environment (Chawla, 1999, cited in Kollmuss & Agyeman, 2002). The emotional reaction such as feelings of fear, sadness, pain, anger, and guilt is stronger when a person experiences environmental degradation or problems through direct life experiences (Newhouse, 1990; Chawla, 1999). Such feelings of fear, sadness, pain and anger are more likely to promote pro-environmental behaviours than guilt or a sense of helplessness (Kollmuss & Agyeman, 2002).

Norms: A norm refers to an expectation held by an individual about how he or she ought to act in a particular social situation (Schwartz, 1977). Social norms, cultural traditions, personal norms and family customs influence and shape people's attitudes (Rajecki, 1982, cited in Kollmuss & Agyeman, 2002). In particular, social norms may play an important role in the low correlations between general environmental attitude and behaviour (Fransson and Gärling, 1999:374). In other words, social norms prevent people from acting in accordance with their attitudes (Newhouse, 1990). According to Ajzen and Fishbein (1977), they have found that attitudes predict behaviour better when no strong norms exist dictating how to behave. Therefore, a social norm needs to be enforced by the threat of punishment or promise of reward (Fransson and Garling, 1999).

Locus of control: As seen in Hines et al's model (ERB) above, locus of control refers to a person's perception of whether he or she has the ability to bring about change through his or her own behaviour (Newhouse, 1990; Hines *et al.,* (1986/87) in terms of environmental conservation. The internal locus of control (individuals who perceive that their own behaviour makes a difference) is also similar with other terms, self efficacy (Kaiser *et al.,* 1999). It is also one of the important determinants of environmentally responsible behaviour, but an inconsistent relationship between perceived control (locus of control or self efficacy) and environmental behaviour has been found in previous research (Kaiser *et al.,* 1999).

Responsibility: Environmental responsibility is shaped by values and attitudes and are influenced by locus of control (Kollmuss & Agyeman, 2002). This is strongly related to environmental behaviour (Hines *et al.*, 1986/87; Kollmuss & Agyeman, 2002).

Socio-Demographic Factors

Socio-demographic factors include gender, socio-economic status (e.g. education, income), group membership (environmentalists vs nonenvironmentalists: Hines *et al.*, 1986/87), age, residence, political-ideology (Fransson and Garling, 1999), and family type (Barr, 2003). In the review of the empirical studies of the impact of each socio-demographic factor on a given environmental behaviour, inconsistent and contradictory findings have been produced (Fansson and Garling, 1999). Although such generalisation drawn from previous empirical studies must be made with great caution, there is consensus that younger, female, wealthy individuals in nuclear families, and more educated individuals with liberal political ideologies living in urban areas are the most environmentally concerned and likely to engage in pro-environmental behaviour (Fransson and Garling, 1999; Hines *et al.*, 1986/87). For example, women usually have a less extensive environmental knowledge and believe less in technological solutions than men. However, they are more emotionally engaged, show more concern about environmental destruction, and are more willing to change than men (Lehmann, 1999, cited in Kollmuss & Agyeman, 2002). The longer the education, the more extensive is the knowledge about environmental issues. However, more education does not necessarily mean increased pro-environmental behaviour (Kollmuss & Agyeman, 2002). Since the late 1980s, the influence of age has been found to be contradictory in that older people have changed their attitudes and are showing more environmental concern because they have been exposed to the increased environmental campaigns or media effects related to environmental issues (Fransson and Garling, 1999).

Moreover, environmental group membership is also an important determinant influencing pro-environmental behaviour (Hines *et al.*, 1986/87), particularly, in the context of nature-based tourism. Several studies have shown that most nature-based tourists and ecotourists tend to be members of conservation organisations. For instance, Ballantine and Eagles (1994) studied that just over 40 percent of the Canadian ecotourists were members of conservation or wildlife organisations. Beckman (1993) also found that participants in interpretive programs in 28 Victorian national park sites considered themselves very interested in the environment and were active as members of conservation groups or other environmental organisations.

However, the results concerning relationships with socio-demographic factors are generally weak and partly contradictory (Hines et al., 1987; Fransson and Garling, 1999). From the perspective of nature-based tourism and interpretation, individual differences according to socio-demographic factors mediate the educational impact of interpretation and learning experiences. Therefore, this high degree of heterogeneous group of the visitors at tourism settings has made it more difficult to measure the outcomes and impact of interpretation experiences (Falk & Adelman, 2003; Ballantyne and Packer, 2005).

Previous Experiences

The impact of a person's past experiences play an important role in the environmental behaviour change process. Previous research has supported the premise that most environmental attitudes are formed as a result of various life experiences involving nature and the outdoors activities (Newhouse, 1990; Palmer, 1993, cited in Beaumont, 1999). In addition, several prior empirical studies have shown a close relationship between significant life experiences and a person's current environmental behaviour, as well as between childhood experiences and adult environmental behaviour.

With regards to the relationship between childhood experiences in the outdoors activities (e.g. environmental educational programmes) and in natural environments and environmental concern, Kellert's (1985, cited in Beaumont, 1999) study found that children who participated in recreational activities were more knowledgeable, appreciative and concerned about animals. Other youth life experiences, such as a person's place of residence, also have been found to be associated with environmental attitudes (Newhouse, 1990). For example, Kostka (1976, in Newhouse, 1990) found that urban children in the US scored much lower on an environmental attitude assessment than did children who lived in a suburban environment. Kostka suggests that this may be due to various combinations of factors, for example, the influence of peers and family and the physical environment (e.g. little exposure to the natural environment).

Moreover, attitudes formed on the basis of past behaviour or prior experiences would be more predictive of future behaviour (Beaumont, 1999) in some situations. However, previous environmental experience seems to lessen attitude and behavioural change as a result of the following new experiences (Dresner and Gill, 1994). Beaumont (1999) reviewed several studies (e.g. Gillett et al., (1991) and Asfeldt (1992)) and indicated that they found that participants in wilderness activities had more positive attitudes than the control group who did not attend the wilderness experience. However, these studies have shown that trip experiences of the visitors did not significantly change attitudes in a more positive way. This may have been due to a ceiling effect that prevented already well-defined attitudes from increasing (Beaumont, 1999). According to some theorists (e.g. the attitude-process model by Vincent and Fazio, 1992), when attitudes may be irrelevant to predict behaviour in some situations, the person's attitude drawn from previous experience or social norms will influence immediate or spontaneous behaviour or habitual behaviour (Petty & Cacioppo, 1981) than reflecting or evaluating the outcomes of performing the behaviour through the process models such as the Theory of Reasoned Action or the model of Responsible Environmental Behaviour.

Direct Experiences and Attitude Accessibility

Direct experiences based on wilderness experiences or outdoor recreational activities are also one of the major influential factors on individuals' development of environmental concern and the future pro-environmental behaviour (Palmer, 1993, cited in Beaumont, 1999). In the context of nature-based tourism or ecotourism, several studies have shown that ecotourists have a greater tendency to be interested in the environment and/or to be involved in environmental matters (Blamey, 1995). Those participating in outdoor education or wilderness experiences have already strong pro-environmental attitudes (Beaumont, 1999). In other words, as individuals who have been involved in wilderness experiences are likely to have a greater interest in the environment and tend to be more interested in learning about nature, and in turn, their direct experiences in the nature and in the interpretive programmes promote positive environmental attitudes and responsible environmental behaviour.

Therefore, attitudes formed by direct experience tend to be stronger and predict behaviour better than other attitudes drawn from indirect experiences (learning in school) (Bell *et al.*, 2001; Newhouse, 1990; Petty *et al.*, 1992). Moreover, attitudes based on direct experience are more stable over time while attitudes based on indirect experience are more likely to change when an individual actually encounters the attitude object (e.g. the environment, the issues, or the particular behaviour). In this sense, attitudes formed by direct experience may be more accessible from memory than those formed by indirect means (e.g. learning in school) (Fazio & Zanna, 1981, cited in Beaumont, 1999) and this premise has been supported by several empirical studies (Eagle & Chaiken, 1993). Therefore, like previous experience, in some situations, attitude accessibility (it refers to how readily an attitude comes to mind) from memory is another important factor in explaining the attitude and behaviour gap as well as in predicting subsequent behaviour.

External Situation Factors

External situation factors serve as intervening variables to manipulate the gap between attitude and behaviour and the process of behavioural change (Hines *et al.*, 1986/87). These include three categories: infrastructural factors; economic and political factors; and social and cultural factors. For example, the effect of a given infrastructural service differs according to the behaviour in question (Barr, 2003) but in general research has shown that people who have greater access to services, such as recycling schemes, taking public transportation if provided, or the opportunity to purchase 'greener' produce, are likely to be pro-environmental in behaviour (Barr, 2003; Kollmuss & Agyeman, 2002). Another external factor, economic and political variables have a strong influence on individuals' decisions and behaviours. Finally, social and cultural factors (or cultural norms) are also important in shaping people's behaviour (Kollmuss & Agyeman, 2002).

Information

Finally, although direct or previous experiences influence the shaping of a person's environmental attitude and behaviour, information or education plays another important role to strengthen and alter environmental conceptions during his or her life experiences (Monroe, 2003). Several researchers have indicated that a lack of information can be a barrier to changing behaviour (Schultz, 2002; Monroe, 2003). However, empirical studies have provided inconsistent findings of the influence of information on environmental attitudes and behaviour (Newhouse, 1990; Beaumont, 1999). The empirical studies of this will be discussed in more detail in the next Chapter 5. In reviews of several studies, there has been considerable debate about whether providing environmental education or interpretation can lead to a change in attitudes and behaviour toward the use of natural and cultural resources, particularly by the intervention of a short interpretive programme (Tilden, 1977; Sharpe, 1976; Orams, 1997; Beaumont, 2001). Therefore, it is important to acknowledge that information alone will not motivate people to adopt a new behaviour (Monroe, 2003).

Considering a greater impact of information (persuasion or interpretation) on the behavioural change process which is the essential interest in the current study, the following section provides an insight into how persuasion theorists process the attitude and behavioural change in different ways. Different approaches to the behavioural process in the context of persuasion related models emphasis different antecedent variables and its relationships between them.

4.5.3 Persuasive Communication Theories

Three key persuasion theories and models in the context of attitude and behaviour change are addressed as follows: (1) traditional persuasion communication theory; (2) three distinct routes to persuasion (e.g. applied behaviour analysis; central route of persuasion; and peripheral route to persuasion).

4.5.3.1 Traditional Persuasion Communication Theory

Persuasive communication theory was developed in the 1950s by Carl Hovland (1953) and his colleagues at Yale University and became known as the Yale approach to attitude change with behavioural consequences. It is one of the most common techniques used in everyday life or in the interpretation field for attempting to influence people and change their attitudes (Petty & Cacioppo, 1981; Ajzen, 1992).

In order to induce people to change their attitudes in a desired direction, there is a sequence of steps in this model. First, it is simply necessary to expose people to messages that change their underlying beliefs. Secondly, the person must attend to the information presented. A third issue reflects reception, or retention (it refers to what part of the information presented enters long-term memory). Once the information is received and processed by the receiver through three steps, received new information may influence beliefs, attitudes, and behaviour (Petty *et al.*, 1992).

While these conditions are important, the conceptual framework developed by the Hovland group (1953) proposes the persuasion process of context factors (source, message, channel, and receiver factors) and mediating processes variables (attention, comprehension, acceptance, and integration or retention) in influencing target variables (immediate attitude change, retention, behaviour change) (Ajzen, 1992; Cable *et al.*, 1986). Figure 4.4 shows the interrelationships between persuasion context factors and mediating process variables and each of targeted outcomes of the persuasion.

According to this theory, it was assumed that exposure to an effective communication or interpretation raises the new response to the attitude object and provides answers that support the appropriate belief and an opportunity to practice the new response. The various contextual factors were assumed to facilitate learning and attitude and behaviour change as seen in Figure 4.4 (Ajzen, 1992). In application of the Hovland approach to interpretation, it can serve to organise thinking about the persuasion process (Ajzen, 1992) and also provide a better understanding of how and why the visitors can be persuaded to adopt more positive attitudes towards the environmental conservation and ultimately appropriate behaviours in different situations.

However, there are several criticisms of this model. First, much of the empirical research focused on the impact of contextual factors and a recall or recognition test to measure attention and comprehension among the mediating process variables. The inconsistent findings of those earlier studies have been produced in the light of the effects of contextual variables (Ajzen, 1992). Thus, the impact of contextual factors on persuasion has produced few generalisable conclusions, leading to widespread disappointment with the Hovland approach by the late 1960s (Ajzen, 1992).

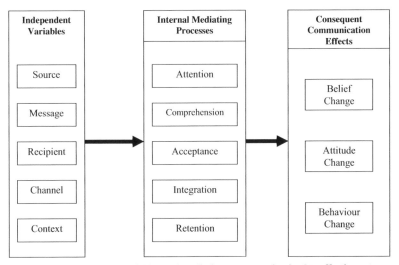

Figure 4.4 Independent variables and mediating processes that lead to effective outcomes in persuasive communications (Source: Petty & Cacioppo, 1981)

Secondly, the complexity of the persuasion process has been considered as one of the major reasons for the failure of the Hovland approach. As persuasion is influenced by so many different factors interacting with each other, only complicated, multidimensional research strategies can cope with the complexities (Ajzen, 1992).

Thirdly, the model paid little attention to the content of persuasive communication and its role in the persuasion process or to the role of the receiver. These two issues also led to the failure of the Hovland tradition in empirical research (Ajzen, 1992). In the light of the role of the receiver, the Hovland group tended to view the receivers of a persuasive communication as passively learning the information presented and then changing their beliefs and attitudes accordingly. This view led to a concern with contextual factors, and neglect of the contents of the communication and its processing by the receiver (Ajzen, 1992). In contrast to the passive role of the receiver in the persuasion process, Ajzen (1992) argued that recipients exposed to a persuasive message in the communication may engage in an active process of deliberation that involves reviewing the information presented, accepting some arguments, rejecting others, and drawing inferences about issues addressed that go beyond what was mentioned in the original message. Therefore, it is suggested that the active role of the receiver should be emphasised in the persuasion process. In this sense, theoretical and empirical progress of the persuasion theory was extended to three distinct routes to persuasion which are addressed in the following section.

4.5.3.2 Three Distinct Routes to Persuasion

Roggenbuck (1992) suggested three distinct routes to persuasion and learning: 1) applied behaviour analysis, 2) the central route to persuasion, and 3) the peripheral route to persuasion. Three basic approaches which include both applied behaviour analysis and the Elaboration Likelihood Model of two distinct routes to persuasion (Petty & Cacioppo, 1981) explain the persuasive influences of interpretation or information through different means in different situations.

(1)   Applied Behaviour Analysis

The applied behaviour analysis approach to persuasion focuses directly on overt behaviour rather than antecedent variables such as beliefs, attitudes, thoughts or values (Roggenbuck, 1992; Manning, 2003). It attempts to accomplish behavioural changes through manipulation of the environment, behaviour prompts, punishing inappropriate behaviour or rewarding appropriate behaviour (Geller, 1987). The behaviour change strategies of applied behaviour analysis are the simplest and most direct theoretical models of interpretation/education (Manning, 2003). For example, it may be useful in influencing some types of behavioural change, such as reducing littering and increasing voluntary litter clean-up behaviours through written, oral and environmental prompts, incentives such as rewards and punishments, petition signing and role modelling of appropriate behaviour (Roggenbuck, 1992). However, since it does not address attitudes, beliefs, norms, and values, its effectiveness might not produce long-term behaviour change (Roggenbuck, 1992; Manning, 2003). There is the need for continual promise of reward or punishment for behavioural change in the applied behavioural analysis approach (Roggenbuck, 1992). Thus, this strategy is much better suited to solving on-site specific behaviour problems rather than to teaching an attitude or a low-impact ethic (Roggenbuck, 1992).

(2)   Central Route of Persuasion

The central route of persuasion involves effortful cognitive activity where an individual thinks about, processes and evaluates the arguments presented in the persuasive communication or interpretation (Petty *et al.*, 1992, cited in Littlefair, 2003). The central route to persuasion reflects one of the Elaboration Likelihood Models developed by Petty and Cacioppo (Petty and Cacioppo, 1981/86) and the two theories (Theory of the Reasoned Actions and Theory of Planned Behaviour) developed by Ajzen and Fishbein (1980) and Ajzen (1991) which address voluntary behaviour. Persuasion via the central route occurs when the individual is motivated and capable of processing the issue-relevant arguments in the message through their careful thought or elaboration of the message content and integration of the message content into existing belief systems (Roggenbuck, 1992; Petty *et al.*, 1992). Such elaboration and integration results in new beliefs or changes in old beliefs, and this in turn leads to desired changes in behaviour (Roggenbuck, 1992). Any learned behaviour change that does occur as a result of the central route to persuasion appears to be enduring, because the beliefs and attitudes that support the behaviour have been internalised (Roggenbuck, 1992; Bright *et al.*, 1993; Petty *et al.*, 1992).

The success of persuasion via the central route is dependent upon the many characteristics of the message (e.g., personal relevance of content, strength of argument, message complexity and repetition), of the medium or channel of message transfer (e.g., the written word, audio or video presentations), of the recipient (e.g., personal involvement with the park, prior experience, prior knowledge and the amount of personal responsibility for actions in the park), and of the situation (e.g., timing of message transfer and distractions of the communication setting) (Roggenbuck, 1992).

(3)   Peripheral Route to Persuasion

In contrast to the central route to persuasion, the peripheral route to persuasion which is another approach of the Elaboration Likelihood Model developed by Petty and Cacioppo (Petty and Cacioppo, 1981/86) occurs when a person is either unmotivated or incapable of processing a logical argument in the message (Petty *et al.*, 1992). This route for the passive/nondeliberative recipients reflects the attitude-to behaviour process model developed by Fazio and his groups (Vincent and Fazio, 1992) which addresses spontaneous attitude and behaviour (McCarville *et al.*, 1992). In this peripheral route to persuasion, when people cannot internally process all the information, simply characteristics of the source, message (other than content) and communication channels (Roggenbuck, 1992). For example, some of messages may be ignored by visitors while other messages from sources considered by visitors to be expert, attractive or powerful may influence behaviour (Roggenbuck, 1992; Manning, 2003). This model may be useful in situations where it is difficult to attract and maintain the attention of visitors, such as at very noisy and active visitor centres, entrance/ranger stations, and bulletin boards, all of which may offer multiple and competing information/education messages (Manning, 2003). However, like applied behaviour analysis, the peripheral approach can be expected to prompt spontaneous behaviour and reduce or solve specific problems only temporarily, because this approach fails to consider issue-relevant reasons for behaviour (Roggenbuck, 1992; Manning, 2003).

The Application of Persuasion-based Theories to the Interpretation Field

Overall, in the reviews of both theories and models of persuasion communication above for attitude and behaviour change, characteristics of each of five main persuasion factors (e.g. source, message, recipient, channel, and situational factors) can affect the mediating processes variables in the persuasion process (Petty & Cacioppo, 1981). Subsequently, the main components of mediating processes (e.g. attention, comprehension, acceptance, integration, and retention) in the persuasion process also contribute to the effectiveness of persuasive communication. This mediating process involves the individual's motivation and ability to process a communicated message which may lead to different outcomes of the persuasion effects through different routes, namely, the central route to persuasion (the active/deliberative route) or the peripheral route to persuasion (passive/nondeliberative route) (Petty *et al.*, 1992; McCarville *et al.*, 1992) as well as the applied behavioural analysis (Roggenbuck, 1992) in different situations.

Although the various theoretical approaches to the behavioural change process differ in many ways, the three different strategies of persuasive interpretation on behavioural change can be applied to tourism settings. It is worth noting that they provide a better understanding of why and how interpretation influences behavioural change to a range of visitors through different means in different situations. This also helps to explain why pervious research on the effects of interpretation in the context of tourism has sometimes failed to influence attitude and behaviour change through increased knowledge change or learning.

In order to change a receiver's attitude or behaviour, first, the information needs to be received by the visitor through attention, comprehension, and memory process (Cable *et al.*, 1986). However, individual differences in their motivation and ability to process the persuasive communication will have different results and in turn lead to different outcomes in the effectiveness of persuasion (e.g. persistent behaviour change, short-term behaviour change or no change in beliefs, attitudes, and behaviours). For example, if the visitor does not have any motivation to attend the communication programmes, or does not perceive any relevance in the message. No matter how logical or well-organised the programme is, they will not be persuaded to change their attitudes or behaviour. In addition, if the receiver does not have any ability to process the message through comprehending the message, then no matter what the level of attention paid to it the communication will not be effective in changing attitude or behaviour (Beaumont, 1999). In this case, the visitor will be influenced by the peripheral route or the applied behavioural analysis. Thus, the source factors, incentives (punishment or rewards), language and style of message may be important to attract the target audience's attention and their comprehension.

On the other hand, other visitors will come to a national park with a high degree of environmental knowledge and desire to learn more about protecting and managing the national park. In this case, once the information or message is received by the active visitor with high level of motivation and ability to process information, the recipient will then elaborate the message through active thought processes (the central route to persuasion) as mentioned in the previous section, 4.5.3.2 (McCarville *et al.*, 1992; Petty *et al.*, 1992). In this elaboration process, the receiver reflects the received arguments presented in the messages and then they accept or reject arguments through several other variables such as the message content, the contextual features of the message or the communicator attributes (Cable *et al.*, 1986). Finally, after the information is received, the recipients integrate the information through developing counterarguments, forming new beliefs or altering old beliefs and store them in their memory. This process is affected by the perceiver's valuation of the importance of the information, prior attitudes, and prior knowledge (Cable *et al.*, 1986). Thus, behavioural change for the active visitors can be influenced by the central route to persuasion.

In short, there are three main issues in the review of theories and models related to the influence of persuasion on attitude and behaviour change. In order to produce long lasting changes in attitudes with behavioural consequences and a sensitive and low-impact ethic among park visitors, the central route to persuasion is likely to be the preferred influence strategy. On the other hand, the peripheral route may be acceptable when the goal is immediate on-site formation of a new attitude or spontaneous behaviour (Petty *et al.*, 1992; McCarville *et al.*, 1992). Another important issue is that recipient characteristics have a powerful influence over the relative success of the various routes to persuasion (Roggenbuck, 1992). For example, with the central route approach to persuasion and behavioural change, it emphasises that the recipients need to have the motivation and ability to process the message which are drawn from their amount of prior experience and knowledge, and their response to persuasive message (Manfredo and Bright, 1991; Roggenbuck, 1992).

According to the emphasis of the role of individual differences (e.g. the first-time or low-knowledge visitor vs experienced users), Cable et al. (1986) have developed the conceptual model which integrates the characteristics of the recipient and persuasion process variables into the Theory of Reasoned Action developed by Fishbein & Ajzen (1980). This expanded model assumes that individual differences which include external variables (e.g. demographic variables, extant attitudes, and personality traits) and persuasion process variables (e.g. reception, acceptance, integration) can influence behaviour indirectly by affecting the attitudinal and normative considerations (Cable *et al.*, 1986). Thus, in the review of theories and models of persuasion, it is suggested that attention must be paid to the characteristics of the visitors to the site in different settings in order to develop and design effective influences of interpretation on attitude and behavioural change through different strategies.

4.5.3.2 Factors Influencing the Success of Persuasion Communication

Much theoretical and empirical research suggests that many persuasion factors influence the success of persuasive interventions or interpretation. Table 4.3 shows the key factors influencing the success of persuasion. From the review of a persuasive communication theory, there are five main components: a message source, the message, the channel, the recipient, and the context (or the situation) which are all important influences on persuasion (Ajzen, 1992).

Source Factors

The influence of interpretation and education programmes depends in part on who or what originates the programmes (Knopf and Dustin, 1992; Ajzen, 1992). The message source refers to observed or inferred characteristics of the person communicating the message (e.g. attractiveness, likeability, credibility, age, and sex) (McCarville *et al.*, 1992, cited in Beaumont, 1999), the local management authorities that created the message, or the broader institution or agency that framed the management context for the locale in question (Knopf and Dustin, 1992). Research has found that the source of a message has a significant influence on attitude change as people can accept or reject a persuasive communication on the basis of source cues rather than on the content of the message itself (Ajzen, 1992; Petty & Cacioppo, 1981; Knopf and Dustin, 1992).

In addressing the issue of promoting voluntary change in recreation behaviour through information and interpretation programmes, three points for source effects are discussed including credibility, attractiveness, and the basis of personal style (when the message is delivered by interpreters or tour guiders) (Knopf and Dustin, 1992). First, the credibility of the source or communicator is a major determinant of the source's effects. The two major components of credible sources are generally seen as expertise and trustworthiness (Ajzen, 1992). Previous research showed that high credibility sources have been found to be more effective in persuading attitude change than low credibility sources (Ajzen, 1992; Petty & Cacioppo, 1981; Widner and Roggenbuck, 2000).

Secondly, attractiveness of the source includes a recipient's likeability and familiarity with the source, or the perceived common needs and goals of the source. Third, various other attributes of a communicator can contribute to his or her persuasiveness. These include the communicator's physical attractiveness and style, age, race, gender, and height as well as behavioural characteristics (e.g. body movements and dress) and personality traits (self-confidence and extroversion) (Ajzen, 1992; Knopf and Dustin, 1992).

Table 4.3 Factors Influencing the Success of Persuasion

Persuasion Factors	Sub-variables of each factor
Source Factors	Credibility, attractiveness, various attributes of the communicators or interpreters
Message Factors	the actual content of the communication, the structure, style or order of presentation of the arguments, and emotional versus non-emotional appeals
Channel Factors	video, personal guides, or print media
Receiver Factors	gender, age, initial attitudes, prior knowledge, involvement and commitment, social status, traits intelligence, self-esteem, and various other personality
Contextual Factors	mood, distractions, forewarning, affective reactions
Processing Factors	Attention, comprehension, acceptance, integration, and retention

Message Factors

The impact of interpretation and education programmes is also influenced by the message characteristics and content. Message factors concern the ways in which information is presented to a recipient and can relate to the actual content of the communication, the structure, style or order of presentation of the arguments, and emotional versus non-emotional appeals (Ajzen, 1992; Knopf and Dustin, 1992). In order to maximise the persuasive impact of the message itself, first, the content of message's object must be relevant to recipients' existing attitudes, experience and level of knowledge (Knopf and Dustin, 1992; Ballantyne and Packer, 2005).

With regards to presentation of clear reasoning and argument presented in the messages, more persuasive messages appear to have stronger supporting arguments and a greater number of arguments. Presentation of both sides of an issue is more effective than a message supporting only the advocated position (Ajzen, 1992). In addition, a few convincing arguments would be more influential than a large number of weaker arguments (Petty and Cacioppo, 1981). The order of presentation of a message may also be a factor in persuasion. The message should build from what is known to recipients to what is unknown; from the least complex concepts to the most complex; from the concepts that recipients most likely would find agreeable to those that most likely would be disagreeable; and from the strongest arguments to the weaker arguments; and presenting the conclusions at the end of the message rather than summarising them at the beginning (Knopf and Dustin, 1992).

Finally, the other factor of an effective message is addressing emotional versus neutral appeals such as fear and concern or joy and pleasure. However, inconsistent findings have been shown when examining the effects of a humorous style of presentation and fear message. It appears that a humorous style may work in some circumstances but not where a more serious topic is being presented (Petty and Cacioppo, 1981). Similarly, inconsistent findings have emerged with respect to the effects of a fear message in persuasive communication (Ajzen, 1992).

Channel Factors

Channel factors refer to the medium through which the persuasive message is communicated. Information can be communicated by such as video, face to face, or print media (Ajzen, 1992; Knopf and Dustin, 1992). Persuasion theorists have conducted relatively little basic research on the effectiveness of the various media because basic theories might not have been developed in a way that makes them interesting (McGuire, 1969, cited in Knopf and Dustin, 1992; Pearce, 1988; Beaumont, 1999). From the perspective of persuasive impact, the most consistent finding is that face-to-face communications were far more effective than mass media (Petty and Cacioppo, 1981; Knopf and Dustin, 1992).

However, inconsistent findings of the effects of different channel factors have been produced in empirical research. One of the reasons is that it is often difficult to determine whether the channel is the cause of the differentiation in persuasion or whether source or message factors are responsible since the different channels provide information in different ways via source and message factors (Ajzen, 1992). With regard to this point, recent researchers have emphasised that use of multiple media to deliver messages can be more effective than use of a single medium in influencing visitors' attitude and behaviour change (Manning, 2003; Roggenbucks, 1992; Madin and Fenton, 2004).

Receiver Factors

The recipient factors reflect certain characteristics of the receiver or the audience to whom the message is addressed (Ajzen, 1992). Previous research has suggested that the characteristics of the individual receiving the message may manipulate the impact of a message (Knopf and Dusting, 1992; Ajzen, 1992). In other words, some individuals will be persuaded by a message and others will not, and various characteristics of a receiver will determine his or her compliance with the messages (Beaumont, 1999). Substantial research has identified the effects of characteristics of the receiver on the persuasion process. These include gender, age, initial attitudes, prior knowledge, involvement and commitment, social status, and various other personality traits (Ajzen, 1992; Manfredo & Bright, 1991), as well as intelligence and self-esteem (Petty & Cacioppo, 1981).

More detailed studies, with regard to gender differences, found that women were more persuadable than men. This may be due to the different social roles that men and women have learned. Men have been socialised to be assertive and independent which would result in resistance to influence while women have been socialised to be co-operative and harmonious (Beaumont, 1999). In some studies of age differences, age is a factor in attitude change via persuasive communications and there have been produced inconsistent findings. Some studies have found that older adults are less likely to yield to influence than younger adults (Olson & Zanna, 1993). However, others found that when personal experiences were involved, attitude change occurred in people over 50 as much as in those aged 18 to

25. It is concluded that attitude change can occur at any time throughout a person's life (cited in Beaumont, 1999).

However, although the individual differences contribute to the effectiveness of persuasion, there is a consensus that receiver effects generally have less influence on persuasion impact than source, message and channel effects (Petty and Cacioppo, 1981).

Contextual Factors

With regards to contextual factors (or situational factors), a number of contextual factors can serve as intervening variables to influence the impact of persuasion. These include mood, distractions, forewarning, and affective reactions (Pearce, 1988; Ajzen, 1992; Beaumont, 1999).

In the review of the effects of those variables, first, it was assumed that audiences are more likely to be persuaded if they are in a pleasant setting or in a good mood (Pearce, 1988). Distractions such as external noise or internal preoccupation with other matters can have an adverse effect on persuasion (Ajzen, 1992). In processing the persuasive message, the message might activate affective reactions such as pleasure, joy, fear or worry. These affective reactions to the persuasive message could be the major influence on the individual's attitude toward the object (Beaumont, 1999).

4.6 Summary

This chapter reviewed the literature relevant to the concepts of attitude and behaviour change which are targeted as the management goals of interpretation for environmental protection. There are several important issues in applying those targeted concepts into this current research.

First, there is no consensus on the definitions and measurements of attitude and behaviour. Therefore, it is important to define and measure attitude and behaviour based on the same degree of general or specific level.

Secondly, it is suggested that the influence of unidimensional or multidimensional aspects of attitudes on predicting behaviour vary differently according to types of behaviour and situations. Therefore, the multiple measures of both attitude and behaviour are useful to understand and predict behavioural change by the influence of interpretation in a variety of tourism situations.

Thirdly, in addressing the relationships between attitude and behaviour, it has been assumed that an understanding of a person's attitudes will lead to a better understanding and accurate prediction of his or her behaviour. However, numerous theories of the behaviour change process and empirical studies of this have suggested that the role of other situational factors and internal psychological factors should be acknowledged in influencing different types of behaviour and situations.

Through the reviews of key attitude-related theories and persuasion theories, it is suggested that interpretation management must consider the improved process models of behavioural change by considering the core attitude related variables (value, knowledge, awareness, feelings, behavioural intentions) and other psychological variables (responsibility, norms, locus of control) as well as the individual background characteristics and interpretation experiences factors (message, source, channel, mediating processing, contextual (or situational) factors).

In responses to the complexity and difficulty of behavioural change through persuasion in tourism settings, three distinct models of behavioural change are suggested: process by persuasion (Roggenbuck, 1992) including the applied behavioural analysis; the central route to persuasion; and the peripheral route to persuasion. Three distinct models for persuasion can be applied to behavioural change according to types of behaviour (spontaneous vs voluntary behaviour) and the receiver's motivation and ability to process the interpretation programmes.

The next chapter will discuss the empirical studies of the effects of interpretation on attitude and behaviour change in terms of different aspects of environmental conservation issues and different tourism settings. The impacts of several main variables on attitude and behavioural change used in the interpretation field will be reviewed in more detail.

CHAPTER

5

Chapter 5 Interpretation In Action

5.1 Introduction

The fourth topic of the current research is reviewed in the literature of the empirical studies of the effects of interpretation on the development of attitude and behaviour in the context of environmental conservation issues and responsible behaviour in nature-based tourism and protected areas.

As discussed in Chapter 3, tourism experiences might enhance visitors' environmental concerns and promote conservation behaviour. However, in some areas, the increase in visitor numbers and behaviour by the visitors has led to a number of negative impacts on the environment such as habitat destruction, changes to the wildlife behaviour, and pollution within recreation settings (Roggenbuck, 1992; Ballantyne and Hughes, 2004). It has been recognised that interpretation can play an important role as a visitor management tool in protected areas by modifying visitor behaviour. Therefore, this chapter focuses on the review of empirical studies which have provided critical evidences supporting this premise. First, this chapter reviews whether and when interpretation actually influences visitors' attitudes and behaviour with respect to natural resource protection. Next, it addresses the important factors influencing the effectiveness of interpretation on attitudinal and behavioural change.

5.2 The Effectiveness of Persuasive Interpretation as a Visitor Management Tool: Study Results

Although there is widespread advocacy for education and interpretation as a solution to managing tourists' impacts on the natural environment, few empirical evaluation of the effectiveness of interpretive programmes in promoting tourist's environmentally sustainable attitudes and low-impact behaviours have been conducted in a variety of resource settings (Orams and Hill, 1998; Roggenbuck, 1992; Beaumont, 2001). Through the review of existing empirical studies, the three main issues discussed in this section as follows:

(1) Measurement objectives of interpretation

(2) The failure of interpretation and why?

(3) Understanding the influential factors on the effectiveness of interpretation

       (e.g. channel factors, message factors, source factors and receiver factors)

5.3 Measurement Objectives of Interpretation

The first issue focuses on the review of targeted measurement objectives employed in empirical studies with regard to evaluating the management role of interpretation in nature-based tourism settings. In the reviews of several studies, the management objectives of interpretation for environmental conservation have been evaluated in two main approaches: (1) changes in visitor knowledge, awareness, attitudes and behavioural intentions regarding the rules and management policies for environmental protection, and (2) changes in visitors' actual behaviours in the context of selection of the advocated route or place and site-specific appropriate behaviour.

5.3.1 Effects of Interpretation on Visitors' Knowledge, Attitudes, Behavioural Intentions

One line of research to determine the beneficial outcomes of interpretation as a visitor management tool has focused on the underlying behavioural variables such as knowledge or beliefs, attitudes, and behavioural intentions. This approach is based on the traditional perspective of simple assumptions of the knowledge-attitude-behaviour link, later attitude-related theories or the central route to persuasion. From this perspective, initial research has assumed that interpretation designed to increase knowledge or favourable attitudes regarding appropriate behaviour and/or management policies may be successful in modifying visitor behaviour in the long-term (Manning, 2003).

Therefore, earlier empirical efforts to determine the beneficial effects of interpretive programmes have tended to measure either one target variable or two target variables which were mainly knowledge or attitudes regarding site-specific conservation issues and/or management policies related to low-impact practices in site-specific perspective rather than general environmental conservation issues and long-term conservation behaviour. The integrative reviews of the findings of previous studies summarised by Beaumont (2001) have indicated that interpretation can be effective in increasing knowledge or in fostering at least short term attitude change after experiencing the interpretation even though inconsistent findings on the effectiveness of interpretation as a visitor management tool have been produced (see Fazio, 1979; McAvoy and Hamborg, 1984; Nielsen & Buchanan, 1986; Olsen *et al.,* 1984; Cable *et al.,* 1987; Howard *et al.,* 2001; Madin & Fenton, 2004). However, some studies showed mixed results providing increased knowledge with limited favourable attitude change (Lee & Balchin, 1995), whereas others which simply measured environmental attitudes have found no significant changes in attitudes (Eagles & Demare, 1995).

In response to the inconsistent findings on the effectiveness of interpretation, recent researchers have begun to examine three distinct measures of the attitude constructs regarding knowledge or beliefs, attitudes, and behavioural intention as antecedents of responsible behaviour in multiple ways as well as to explore the link between these key antecedent variables and actual behaviour. The review of the empirical studies of the effects of interpretation on three key measures and the link between them has been mixed. Some studies have found that interpretation has a significant impact on increasing knowledge and promoting favourable attitudes toward the environment or management policies, which in turn lead to visitors' willingness to engage in low-impact behaviour. Thus, it was assumed that the positive link of knowledge, beliefs, attitudes and intention may modify inappropriate on-site behaviour or promote long-term conservation behaviour (Roggenbuck and Passineau, 1986; Bright *et al.,* 1993; Moscardo and Woods, 1998; Howard, 2000). For example, Roggenbuck and Passineau (1986) evaluated the effectiveness of interpreter-guided field trips at the Indiana Dunes National Lakeshore on changing behaviour by increasing knowledge and building supportive attitudes. They found that anti-littering messages and role modelling by the interpreter influenced changes in children's actual littering behaviour through changing their attitudes toward protection and conservation of park resources, as well as changing their behavioural intentions not to litter and to recycle after the interpreter-guided field trip experiences.

On the other hand, recent researchers found only modest levels of effect on awareness and behaviour and an unclear link between knowledge, attitude, intentions and behaviour (Orams, 1997; Tubb, 2003; Espiner, 1999; Beaumont, 2001). For example, a study of visitors to Lamington National Park, Australia conducted by Beaumont (2001) investigated the impacts of interpretation and ecotourism experiences on overnight and day visitors' knowledge, attitude, intentions, and behaviour regarding general environmental protection and long-term conservation behaviour. The results showed that increased knowledge did not correspond to a significant change in pro-environmental attitudes and behaviour as a result of the park experiences. However, both post-visit and follow-up participants questioned within four months of the visit indicated that their conservation views regarding the need to protect the natural environment had been changed by their experiences. Surprisingly, it was found that only follow-up participants indicated that they had actually engaged in some long term conservation behaviour since their return.

5.3.2 Effects of Interpretation on Visitors' Actual Behaviours

The previous section reviewed empirical studies of the effects of interpretation in targeting knowledge, beliefs, attitudes and behavioural intentions based on the attitude-based theories perspective such as the central route to persuasion approach or the theory of reasoned action. However, it remains unclear whether changing attitudes or knowledge will lead to changes in a particular behaviour. According to Clark *et al.* (1972a), although visitors may profess a protective attitude toward the environment, they might exhibit an opposite behaviour (almost everyone is against littering, but almost everyone litters). It means that interpretation/education may stimulate positive attitudes, but does not automatically result in a reduction in inappropriate behaviour. Thus, another line of studies has examined the interpretation-behaviour link directly based on the applied behaviour analysis perspective, the peripheral route to persuasion, or the norm theory. Based on this perspective of the direct link between the interpretive messages and behaviour, the researchers have assumed that if visitors are informed of the persuasive message such as rewards or punishments, overt behavioural change will occur, at least in the short term. Some studies have been conducted to determine whether persuasive interpretation actually reduces inappropriate behaviours or visitor impacts on the environment in recreation settings (Clark *et al.*, 1972b; Oliver, Roggenbuck and Watson, 1985; Orams and Hill, 1998; Orams, 1997; Widner & Roggenbuck, 2000; Littlefair, 2003).

There are two main issues drawn from the review of the measurement of the effects of interpretation on actual visitor behaviour. First, much previous research in measuring visitor behaviour has focused on specific on-site inappropriate behaviour such as unintentional or uninformed behaviour (e.g. theft, off-trail hiking, tree damage, picnic table carving, wildlife feeding, visitor safety, and littering) (Widner & Roggenbuck, 2000) as well as the selections of appropriate routes or site (Roggenbuck, 1992) rather than on long-term conservation behaviour. In more recent examples, a study of visitors to Mon Repos Conservation Park, Australia was conducted by Howard (2000). In this study of interpretive programmes for turtle conservation, visitors who participated in the interpretive programmes reported that they had actually taken action to conserve turtles (e.g. volunteering at Mon Repos, releasing turtles in nets, and reporting sightings of turtles to the park agency) in the six months since their visit. However, only a few studies have examined long-term conservation behaviour (Beaumont, 2001). Of these, studies by Orams (1997) and Dresner & Gill (1994) found that interpretation had significant impacts on long-term conservation behaviour (e.g. buying ecologically friendly products, making a donation to an environmental organisation, recycling, using public transport, minimal impact practices) whilst others found there was no impact (Beaumont, 2001).

Another main issue drawn from the literature is that two different approaches to assessing actual behaviour have been measured: self-reported behaviour and observed behaviour. Both different measurements of self-reported or observed behaviour have its strengths and weaknesses. Self-reported behaviour related to low-impact behaviour has been measured in several studies (Orams, 1997; Howard, 2000; Beaumont, 2001), as discussed above, due to it being easier to measure tourists' behaviour in the short term and their being less influence from situational factors than in observed behaviour (Cable *et al.*, 1986; Littlefair, 2003).

With regard to the observed behavioural measure, some studies have employed the observation technique in measuring actual visitor behaviour (Orams and Hill, 1998; Chandool, 1997; Espiner, 1999; Widner and Roggenbuck, 2000; Littlefair, 2003). For example, the recent study of the effects of hazard warning signs on visitor behaviour at Fox and Franz Josef Glaciers, New Zealand conducted by Espiner (1999) showed that the observed appropriate visitor behaviour regarding the access restrictions to the terminal faces of Fox and Franz Josef Glaciers (e.g. 'not touching or getting closer to the ice face beyond the roped enclosure') was significantly increased with the introduction of hazard warning signs when compared with the original signs at two different glacier sites. However, there were found to be significant differences in the frequency of appropriate visitor behaviours between the observation periods. This study using observation technique of actual visitor behaviour indicated that the variation of the findings might be manipulated due to the effects of situational factors related to the weather, general conditions, timing of observations, and the presence of other visitors (namely, social facilitation) (Espiner, 1999).

5.4 The Failure of Interpretation and Why?

The failures of interpretation in reducing visitor impacts on the natural environment were found in some of the literature to be caused by the wide diversity of visitors looking for different recreation experiences and having different motives to perform the particular inappropriate behaviours (Lucas, 1981; Roggenbuck, 1992). For example, Lucas (1981, cited in Chandool, 1997) attempted to redistribute visitors to more lightly used trails at the Selway Bitterroot Wilderness by giving visitors an informational brochure about the current use of various trails in the forest. It was discovered that the brochure was ineffective because visitors either failed to receive the brochure or those who did get them received them too late in this route planning and decision process. In addition, it was found that visitors sometimes doubted the accuracy of the brochure's information about use. Thus, it is suggested that it is important for managers to understand where and how visitors receive information about low-impact behaviour.

In the review of the study of visitors to Tangalooma, Australia conducted by Orams (1997), it was indicated that visitors increased their knowledge about the dolphins and changed self-reported behaviours such as 'obtaining more information on dolphins', 'removing beach litter', 'involvement in environmental issues', and 'making a donation to an environmental organisation' as a result of their interpretive programme experiences. However, there were no significant differences in participants' attitudes to and behavioural intentions regarding protection of the dolphins and the issue of pollution between the experimental and control groups. One possible reason for the apparent failure of interpretation was 'social desirability' as participants in both control and experiment groups know the 'socially desirable' answer to a question about environmental attitudes. Chandool (1997) attempted to evaluate the impacts of interpretation on visitors' attitudes, norms, and behaviour regarding taking petrified wood from the Petrified Forest national park, U.S. based on the Theory of Reasoned Action. This study showed site-specific interpretation failed to shape visitors' theft of the petrified wood through influencing their attitudes and norms regarding theft behaviour. One of the major reasons for the failure in achieving the management goals of interpretation was assumed to be that the message content might not be effective to influence the visitor's wood theft behaviour. It was suggested that managers needed to deliver the salient belief-targeted message regarding the outcomes of wood theft rather than focusing on the history of the area, punishment of wood theft, and dangers along trails. The other major factors of the failure might include (1) the inappropriate application of the theory of reasoned actions to spontaneous types of wood theft; (2) measurement problems (behaviour measurement through observation, personal norm measure rather than use of social norm, measurement in different time).

To sum up, many studies of measurement objectives have evaluated specific management policies or low-impact behaviour in site-based interpretation, rather than general environmental issues or general environmentally responsible behaviour. There are also different conceptualisations and measurements of knowledge, attitude, and behaviour in different settings. It is seen that there is lack of research into the three main key antecedents of behavioural modification and their relationships with behavioural responses on the persuasive process of the types of behavioural changes in different situations.

5.5 Understanding the Influential Factors on the Effectiveness of Interpretation

Given the complexity of the attitude-behaviour change process and the conflicting results of the effects of interpretation on attitude-behaviour change, it was suggested that many contextual factors such as source, message, channel, and receiver factors influence the success of persuasive interpretation (Ajzen, 1992; Roggenbuck, 1992). In other words, the immediate benefits of interpretation are difficult to measure, and the change of visitor attitudes with subsequent behavioural responses may result not from a single variable such as interpretation but from other factors, such as social norms, past experiences, prior existing attitudes and source credibility (Ajzen, 1992; Roggenbuck, 1992; Bright *et al.*, 1993). Therefore, it is difficult to generalise the conclusions that can help design effective interpretation strategies in influencing attitude and behaviour change.

In the review of previous studies, much insight on how to create effective interpretive programmes has been discussed in more detail in empirical studies. Four major lines of research have attempted to understand the effective strategies of when and how interpretation influences different types of behaviour and/or attitudes in the context of several factors: (1) channel factors; (2) message factors; (3) receiver characteristics; (4) theoretical approaches.

5.5.1 The Effects of Different Channel Factors on Knowledge Gain, Attitude Change, and Behavioural Responses

Most studies have assessed the differing effectiveness of various media in achieving the educational and management goals of interpretation. However, the findings on the most effective method in managing the impacts of the visitor remain unclear. For example, Olson, Bowman, and Roth (1984) evaluated the effects of interpretation on the visitor's knowledge and attitudes regarding natural resource management policies and practices in four Ohio State nature preserves. In their study, particularly, they investigated the effects of different media such as brochures, on-site signs, off-site presentations and on-site guided hikes on various management policies (e.g. picking wildflowers, burning vegetation, camping, etc) through comparing differences between pre-test and post-test scores. Of the more than 1,000 visitors sampled, the findings of this study showed that post-test participants demonstrated significant gains in both knowledge and attitudes across the three different methods compared to both pre-test participants and the control group. The most effective method for knowledge and attitude change was brochures, followed by personal services while signs were the least effective.

The more recent study found significant effects of personal services on change in appropriate visitor behaviour at Lamington National Park, Australia (Littlefair, 2003). This study investigated the different effects of four interpretive treatments on different types of on-site inappropriate behaviours related to shortcutting of the trail, picking up litter, and noise, compared to the control groups. The four interpretive treatments included: generic environmental interpretation, role modelling of appropriate behaviour by the guide, verbal appeals from the guide, and the complete programme including all three methods. Although there were found to be slight differences in the types of behaviour across the four treatments, visitors' inappropriate behaviours were reduced most when visitor impacts were specifically addressed by role modelling by the guide and/or verbal appeals from the guide (Littlefair, 2003).

By contrast, several researchers have indicated that there were no significant differences between personal services and non-personal interpretive programmes if the goals of interpretation are to educate and inform visitors about natural resources and management policies rather than to entertain the visitor (Nielsen and Buchanan, 1986; Roggenbuck, 1992; Manning, 2003). For instance, Nielson and Buchanan (1986) compared the effects of the visitor centre and an interpreter guided tour on park visitors' knowledge about fire ecology in Grand Teton national park and their attitudes towards natural fire management policies. Both programmes were found to be effective in increasing knowledge and positive attitudes towards park management policies compared to a control group, but there were no differences in the effectiveness of the two different types of interpretive methods.

Other studies have emphasised that use of multiple media to convey the persuasive message is generally more effective than a single medium in improving knowledge, attitudes and behavioural modification (Roggenbuck, 1992; Manning, 2003). For example, Oliver, Roggenbuck and Watson (1985) indicated the effectiveness of three interpretive methods on reducing inappropriate behaviour regarding litter and tree damage. The three methods included a brochure, a brochure plus personal contact from a uniformed park ranger, and a brochure plus personal contact plus a request for camper assistance in reporting others' inappropriate behaviour to the park staff. The results of this study showed that participants exposed to different types of interpretive methods were found to be significantly more effective in reducing littering and tree damage behaviour than the control groups who had no treatments applied. In particular, the brochure plus the personal contact was significantly more effective than the brochure alone.

Another study of the effects of site-based interpretation at the Great Barrier Reef, Australia supported the view of the effects of multiple methods on targeted objectives (Madin and Fenton, 2004). They indicated that interpretation was effective in educating visitors about a variety of conservation issues in relation to the Great Barrier Reef environment. In particular, the results indicated that visitors with high levels of participation in interpretive activities increased their awareness and knowledge in relation to two main topics such as reef environment and human impacts compared to those with lower levels of participation in interpretive activities. Therefore, it was suggested that visitors were able to increase their knowledge related to the reef environment through their higher levels of involvement in interpretive activities on-site.

5.5.2 The Effects of Message Factors on the Success of Persuasion

Another area of research into influential persuasive factors has emphasised the important role of the message content and the cognitive or affective responses of the messages by the recipients of the persuasive effectiveness of interpretation. In response to this perspective, several studies have evaluated the effects of the interpretive messages in increasing visitors' knowledge and modifying their attitudes so that they were more supportive of the protection of the wilderness and a variety of relevant management policies (Olson et al., 1984; Cable et al., 1987; Bright et al., 1993; Manfredo and Bright, 1991; Ballantyne and Hughes, 2004). For instance, Cable, Knudson, Udd, and Stewart (1987) tested the effects of the interpretive messages on visitors' attitudes regarding the management role of the Canadian Forestry Service. The results indicated that the interpretive messages had a positive impact on favourable attitudes toward the Canadian Forestry Service.

Much insight into the different effects of several messages factors (e.g. the message content, the structure, style, order of presentation of the arguments, and emotional versus non-emotional appeals) has been identified to determine the success of interpretation (Ajzen, 1992; Petty et al., 1992; Knopf and Dustin, 1992). The study of the effects of interpretive messages at the Selway Bitterroot Wilderness conducted by Cole, Hammond and McCool (1997) found that hikers exposed to the messages regarding low-impact camping practices at a trailhead increased their knowledge about appropriate behaviour compared to those who were not exposed to the messages. It was also discovered that as the number of messages increased, the attention per message and retention decreased. They found that visitors exposed to eight messages did not acquire any more new low-impact knowledge than those exposed to two messages. Cole et al. (1997) concluded that messages should be clear and concise containing not more than two to four different minimal impact messages. Other techniques to increase visitor's attention to minimal impact behaviour messages might be required.

The effects of different types of belief-targeted messages designed on the basis of attitude-related theories or other theoretical approaches has been evaluated by several researchers. Bright, Manfredo, Fishbein, and Bath (1993) used the theory of reasoned action and the central route to persuasion, they noted the importance of clear message and the receiver's motivation and ability to process the messages. They examined the public's attitude and behavioural intentions toward the National Park Service's controlled burn policy. The results of this study indicated that the effects of belief-targeted messages regarding the outcomes of the controlled burn policy were different across positive and negative treatments groups which were divided by their prior attitudes toward the controlled burn policy. In more detail, the belief-targeted messages strengthened the visitor's beliefs, attitudes, and intentions for people who held prior positive attitudes toward supporting the controlled burn policy. However, the people who held prior negative attitudes were less likely to be persuaded by the new belief-targeted message about the outcomes of a controlled burn policy. For one of the reasons of different effects of the persuasive messages across two groups, it was assumed that an individual's perception of credibility of the source regarding the land management agency may also have mediating effects on response to the content of the message (Bright *et al.*, 1993). This might be that the mixed messages can weaken source credibility. Therefore, it was assumed that clear and consistent messages based on defined management objectives can help establish source credibility (Fazio, 1979, Douchette and Cole, 1993; Reid and Marion, 2003).

In addition, Vander Stoep and Garmann (1988) tested the impacts of different types of messages based on low-impact behaviour of youth groups at historical monuments. There were different types of messages designed to target three issues: an awareness of consequences of behaviour; awareness of consequences plus resource protection; and awareness of consequences of behaviour, resource protection, and an incentive (rewards for appropriate behaviour). The results of this study found that all message interventions had significant impacts on behavioural change. However, the recent study by Ballantyne and Hughes (2004) found different preferences of the persuasive messages regarding visitors' bird feeding behaviour at three warning sign interventions designed according to three main theories (e.g. the theory of planned behaviour by Ajzen, 1991; protection motivation theory by Rogers and Prentice-Dunn, 1997; and Constructivist theory by Hein, 1998). The results of this study showed that the persuasive messages based on the negative impacts of bird feeding on birds' health and survival (the Constructivist approach) were most likely to influence visitors' bird feeding behaviour rather than the other types of messages regarding the dangers of bird feeding to humans (Protection Motivation Theory) or the negative impacts of bird feeding on other visitor's picnic experience and the long-term dependency of birds on humans (Theory of Planned Behaviour). It was also suggested that the impacts of different types of the persuasive messages might vary across different ranges of visitors, as different visitors perceive and process messages in different ways because of their diverse interests, beliefs, experiences and attitudes toward the objects.

Another interesting element in recent research findings was the impact of emotional involvement such as fear, concern, joy or pleasure in the message content areas on the persuasive process of attitude and behavioural modification (Howard, 2000; Ballantyne and Packer, 2005). The 'fear or emotional tension arousal' message is one of the important elements in warning situations regarding visitor safety, hazard, and interactions with animals. For example, Beckmann (2002) provided the empirical evidence regarding river safety behaviour and indicated that the key safety messages at a 'swimming conditions sign (Take Care/Unsafe)' had less impact on changes in visitor's understanding of river safety behaviour and intention to swim in the river. The main reasons for the limited effects of safety messages were assumed to be either lack of availability of the information material or an inappropriate message slogan (e.g. 'Don't Croak in the River') and its associated picture of the safety behaviour (e.g. a frog clinging to a reed). As seen in the example, several studies have indicated that the influences of fear-based messages vary according to different segments of the visitor population (McCool and Braithwaite, 1992; Beckmann, 2002).

With regard to the emotion of joy or pleasure, Howard (2000) provided the empirical evidence that the interpretive experiences such as at a visitor centre and guided turtle watching tour at Mon Repos Conservation Park, Australia promoted visitor's self-reported behaviour through influencing increased knowledge regarding turtle conservation and arousal reactions to the trip experiences. The results showed that visitors' arousal reactions had a significant impact on behavioural intentions and self-reported behaviour for turtle conservation rather than increased knowledge in the last six months after the visit to Mon Repos. Therefore, it was concluded that affective experiences to the object (e.g. environmental settings, problems, or interpretive experiences) need to be considered as important in promoting long-term conservation behavioural modification as cognitive domains as suggested in other research (Orams, 1996/97; Howard, 2000; Ballantyne and Packer, 2005).

5.5.3 The Impacts of the Receiver Factors on the Effectiveness of Interpretation

As reviewed in the previous section, the recipients' cognitive or affective responses to the persuasive communication are also important in promoting attitude and behaviour change as message factors. Several studies have found that the beneficial outcomes of interpretation have been limited due to various characteristics of the receiver. Therefore, a better understanding of specific receiver characteristic is required to determine the success of interpretation on the targeted objectives. Several receiver factors have been identified in previous research: (1) socio-demographic; (2) social or normative groups; (3) the persuasive processing factors (e.g. the perceived relevancy of messages and timing of delivery) (Ajzen, 1992; McCool and Braithwaite, 1992). Among various receiver factors, most empirical studies explore the effects of differences of socio-demographic characteristics of the participants on knowledge, attitude, and behaviour (Cable *et al.*, 1986; Lee and Balchin, 1995). For example, Negra and Manning (1997) considered that identifying specific subgroups of visitors would allow the design of more focused interpretative strategies to address each group's needs and interests, while providing appropriate educational opportunities. They determined visitors' current levels of environmental awareness and behaviour, the ethical perspectives through which they perceived nature and their expectations of their visit. From their data they distinguished four visitor subgroups, each with a different perspective on spiritual, ecological, moral/ethical and economic values, and noted that different interpretive strategies could address these different perspectives.

Another line of research into the characteristics of the visitor has identified the impacts of the recipients' interests, existing attitudes, experience and level of prior knowledge on the cognitive process of the messages (Roggenbuck, 1992; Petty *et al.*, 1992; Beaumont, 2001). For example, Manfredo and Bright (1991) examined the persuasion process of how the information package influenced visitors' beliefs which in turn affected their behaviour related to the wilderness use at the Boundary Waters Canoe Area Wilderness (BWCAW), U.S. It was noted that the information package had only a moderate impact on changing beliefs and affecting behaviour. The results of this study indicated that visitors with less knowledge and less experience were more influenced by the information package than those with higher knowledge and prior experiences. In other words, visitors with higher experience levels were less likely to be persuaded by new information (Manfredo and Bright, 1991). Similarly, the important influences of prior knowledge and prior experiences on the limited effectiveness of persuasive interpretation have been identified in other studies (Lisowski and Disinger, 1991; Bright *et al.*, 1993; Beaumont, 2001). The study by Bright *et al.* (1993) also indicated the different effects of interpretation on changes in beliefs, attitudes, and behaviour between two treatment groups. They felt that a number of factors may have an effect on the success of the outcome of a communication strategy, including recipient characteristics such as the initial direction of people's attitude, the extent to which the attitudes were held and prior knowledge.

Furthermore, recent studies have identified that the receiver's responses to the interpretation experiences may also be influenced by the perceived relevancy of the information provided and the ability to process the message, as well as the format and timing of the message delivery (Espiner, 1999; Tubb, 2003; Ballantyne and Hughes, 2004; Porter and Howard, 2003). For instance, Porter and Howard (2003) found that although the brochures regarding dingo warnings were distributed to all visitors to Fraser Island prior to entry to the Island, some visitors did ignore the messages completely and did not read the brochure due to the lack of relevancy of the information provided to them. However, for visitors who had read the brochure on the island, it was found to have increased knowledge about appropriate behaviour in interacting with the dingo. Therefore, it was suggested that the timing of the message delivery and the perceived relevancy of the information appears to play an important role in the success of interpretation in influencing behaviour change.

5.5.4 Theoretically Grounded Messages, Delivery, and the Role of the Receiver

According to the review of empirical studies above, the effective interpretation strategies of different types of behavioural change (e.g. the short-term vs the long-term behaviour; the spontaneous vs voluntary behaviour; illegal vs inappropriate behaviour) have been utilised based on different theoretical perspectives in order to determine the way in which types of the message content and types of delivery methods of the message are most effective to the targeted receivers.

As reviewed in the Chapter 4, the three major persuasive models of the attitude-behaviour change require application to different types of behaviour and situations to target receivers (e.g. low motivation and low ability to process the message vs high motivation and high ability to process the message). However, as reviewed in the previous section, many empirical studies of interpretation in the context of natural resource areas have evaluated the management role of interpretation without utilising a particular theoretical framework. Some studies have attempted to test the effects of a single theory such as the theory of reasoned action or the central route to persuasion (e.g. Manfredo and Bright, 1991; Bright et al., 1993; Chandool, 1997) as well as norm theory (e.g. Cialdini, 1996) or applied behaviour analysis (e.g. Clark et al., 1972a,b).

The contradictory findings of the effects of different interpretation interventions designed on different theoretical base have been examined above. The research has emphasised the importance of multiple theoretical approaches to influence various types of visitor behaviour (see for the review, Widner and Roggenbuck, 2000). For example, a study of visitors in Petrified Forest National Park by Widner and Roggenbuck (2000) tested the effects of three treatments on reducing the theft of fossil wood. Utilising different theoretical approaches regarding theory of attitude-related theory, the applied behaviour analysis approach, and norm theories, the interventions included signs developed by three main theories basis, a signed pledge (or freely written and public commitments), and a uniformed volunteer (the applied behavioural analysis or normative social-influenced theory). It was found that all three interpretive methods significantly reduced theft of wood over control conditions. There were no significant differences between the effectiveness of each of the methods. All three interventions tested in this study have been designed based on multiple theories approaches incorporating the applied behavioural analysis, norm theories, and attitude-related behaviour theories. They concluded that the interventions developed by the multiple theories would be more effective in influencing visitors' theft behaviour or controlling other inappropriate visitor behaviour rather than the interventions using a single theoretical viewpoint.

5.6 Summary

The overall research for an evaluation of interpretation as a visitor management technique has focused on the core targeted outcomes either by influencing underlying behavioural variables such as knowledge, attitudes, behavioural intentions, or by directly modifying actual behaviour in the context of environmentally sensitive areas. According to the review of several studies, although mixed results of the effects of interpretation on target variables have been produced, the interpretation was generally effective in improving visitor knowledge, attitudes and behavioural modification, but not all versions of the various interpretive programmes were successful in all types of responsible behaviours and for all visitors (Roggenbuck, 1992). There are three main specific reasons for mixed findings. Firstly, the negative impacts of the visitor on the natural environment occur over time rather than one visit to the site. Thus, the immediate benefits of interpretation provision in reducing visitor impact on the environment are difficult to measure. Secondly, it is difficult to measure the concept of attitudes because of the unclear conceptualisation and various measurement techniques. Thirdly, the change of visitor behaviour may result not from the interpretation but from other factors, such as social norms, previous experiences so that it is difficult to identify the direct impact of various factors on changes in visitor behaviour (McDonough, 1986; Weiler, 1992, cited in Littlefair, 2003; Kuo, 2002).

From the review of theoretical constructs and empirical studies, the following suggestions and future research for effective interpretation on environmental sustainable attitudes and behaviour in protected areas has been identified (e.g. Roggenbuck, 1992; Doucette and Cole, 1993; Maning, 2003; Reid and Marion, 2003; Beckmann, 2002; Ballantyne and Packer, 2005).

(1) Management objectives

- Interpretation can influence visitors' behaviour through either modifying beliefs, attitudes, and intentions or changing actual behaviour according to different situations and management objectives in particular sites. However, most research has focused on one or two target variables such as knowledge, attitude, and actual behaviour. There is a lack of empirical studies in evaluating the effects of interpretation on visitor behavioural modification through measuring the three key objectives of beliefs, attitudes, and intentions in the long-term as well as investigating the link between those key objectives with responsible visitor behaviour.
- Most studies have focused on specific attitudes based on the site-specific issues and on-site specific behaviours (e.g. mainly uninformed or unintentional behaviours) targeted for management policies and the objectives of site-based interpretation at a certain site rather than long-term conservation behaviour in general perspective.
- Thus, there is a need to examine the effects of interpretation on the multiple measurements of attitudes and behaviour in terms of both site-specific and general perspectives.

(2) Channel Factors

- Most research has focused on the effects of different interpretive methods on attitude and behaviour change. Personal services such as personal contacts with the park rangers, the guided-walk tour, role modelling by the park staff, and use of volunteers can be effective information strategies. Non-personal services such as brochures, signs, and visitor centres are as effective as personal services in influencing visitors' attitude and behaviour regarding environmental conservation. It was found that the use of multiple media to deliver messages can be more effective than the use of a single medium (Manning, 2003).
- However, there is a need to examine the multiple effects of interpretation as well as the direct effects of each of method on targeted objectives.

(3) Message Factors

- Several researchers have concluded that messages should be clear, concise and consistent. Also, the source of the message being perceived as credible and the message's object being perceived as relevant, and the timing of the message delivery are also important. A combination of message contents based on different theoretical approaches is likely to be most effective. In particular, information on the impacts, cost, and consequences of problem behaviours, and the emotional appeals of the problems or a particular behaviour can be an effective information strategy.

- However, there has been little research into message effectiveness to determine the success of the persuasive interpretation on attitude and behaviour change. Much contemporary interpretation concentrates on the cognitive domain of learning which emphasises 'the transmission of large amounts of knowledge by the expert 'teacher' (Markwell, 1996:10).

- Therefore, there is needed to determine how cognitive or affective processes of the interpretation experiences influence visitors' attitude development and their subsequent behaviour for environmental conservation.

(4) Receiver Factors

- Understanding the target visitors' characteristics and their responses to cognitive and affective experiences of the persuasive interpretation is critical in influencing the success of interpretation on attitude and behaviour change. In particular, it was suggested that visitor's interest, existing attitudes, prior knowledge and past experiences have a mediating effects on their preferences and perceptions of the message content and ability to process the message.

- Therefore, management may need to use a range of approaches to target the diverse interests, beliefs, experiences and attitudes held by visitors to specific site areas.

- In summary, there is no consensus to generalise the best effective interpretation strategies in designing the message, delivery of the message, and target audience based on different theoretical approaches. Therefore, the conclusion drawn from the review of the literature is that the next question needs to focus on when and how interpretation influences changes, in which types of behaviour, in which target groups, and why interpretation fails to achieve the management goals of the development of attitude and behaviour and in what situation, rather than simply asking whether interpretation influences visitor's environmental attitude and behaviour.

CHAPTER

6

Chapter 6 Methodology I:
Research Process & Research Case Study Sites

6.1 Introduction

Previous chapters have explored the literature in areas relevant to sustainable tourism, interpretation, theories and models related to attitudinal and behavioural change and persuasive interpretation, and empirical research into attitude-behaviour change through interpretation. Chapter 6 and Chapter 7 discuss the methodology of this study through the structure of the overall research process (see Figure 6.1) in order to examine the research objectives.

Chapter 6 begins with an explanation of the structure of the overall research process. Next, based on a brief review of the limitations and problems of the literature related to research questions and objectives, the conceptual framework for this study is introduced and modified to explain the relationships of key elements affecting behavioural modification. Additionally, the selection procedure for the case study and a brief background of the selected sites are presented.

In the following Chapter 7, the actual methods in the main field study are addressed in more detail in order to develop the appropriate techniques based on the research objectives.

6.2 Research Process

The research process model adopted for this research provides a schematic description of the interactive relationship between a central research focus and the process, which begins with the development of an initial theory, and ends with a tentative empirical generalisation (Marshall and Rossman, 1995; Frankfort-Nachmias and Nachmias, 1996). The model consists of several major stages including problem, hypothesis, research design, measurement, data collection, data analysis, and generalisation (Frankfort-Nachmias and Nachimias, 1996). The structure of the overall research methodology for the current study is presented in Figure 6.1. In its first section, Chapter 6 includes the three main stages which contain the identification of the research problems and questions, the development of the conceptual frameworks, conceptualisation of the key elements of the research objective, and selection of research sites. Research questions and objectives are presented based on the review of problems and theories in relation to attitude and behaviour change, particularly, in the interpretation fields. The conceptual framework is proposed and modified in order to examine research questions and objectives. In developing the appropriate research strategy to explore how to achieve research questions and objectives, selecting the research sites best suited to all research object criteria was one of the most important procedures. Dorset Heritage Coast was selected as the sustainable case study site for this study. Within the Dorset Heritage Coast, the Lulworth and Charmouth Coasts were selected as the two specific case study sites to identify the site specific management issues and policies regarding responsible behaviour and conservation at each site. This information forms the basis of the questionnaire deal with Chapter 7.

In the next section the research design strategy is presented. This includes selection of the most effective methods for the research investigation, the nature of the research instruments, the sampling plan, the development of questionnaire design, the procedure of data collection and the techniques of data analysis. The development of the research design strategy is discussed in Chapter 7.

Figure 6.1 Research Process

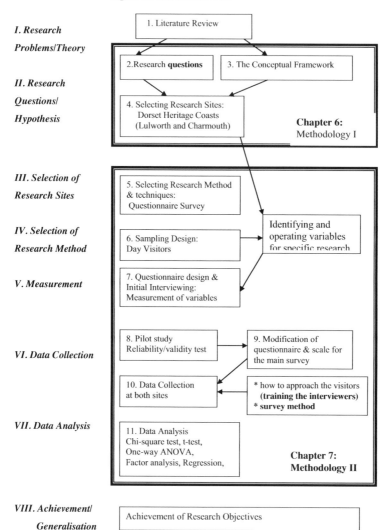

I. Research
Problems/Theory

1. Literature Review

II. Research
Questions/
Hypothesis

2.Research **questions**

3. The Conceptual Framework

4. Selecting Research Sites:
   Dorset Heritage Coasts
   (Lulworth and Charmouth)

Chapter 6:
Methodology I

III. Selection of
Research Sites

5. Selecting Research Method
& techniques:
Questionnaire Survey

IV. Selection of
Research Method

6. Sampling Design:
Day Visitors

Identifying and
operating variables
for specific research

V. Measurement

7. Questionnaire design &
Initial Interviewing:
Measurement of variables

VI. Data Collection

8. Pilot study
Reliability/validity test

9. Modification of
questionnaire & scale for
the main survey

10. Data Collection
at both sites

* how to approach the visitors
(training the interviewers)
* **survey method**

VII. Data Analysis

11. Data Analysis
Chi-square test, t-test,
One-way ANOVA,
Factor analysis, Regression,

Chapter 7:
Methodology II

VIII. Achievement/
Generalisation

Achievement of Research Objectives

6.3 Research Questions

The significant contribution of interpretation as a visitor management tool for environmental conservation has been well recognised in the context of sustainable tourism (Moscardo, 1999; Kuo, 2001; Beaumont, 2001; Tubb, 2003). Interpretation can manage negative impacts of tourism at heavily used sites under the most pressure through providing visitors with information about alternative sites, routes, or activities as an attempt to move visitors away from those sites (Moscardo, 1998/99). Interpretive programmes can also help to enhance visitors' understanding of the features of the site and to influence visitors to be more aware of the conservation issues. In turn, it can help to modify their previously inappropriate behaviour and to promote long-term conservation behaviour (Cooper *et al.*, 1998; Orams and Hill, 1998; Moscardo, 1998/99; Kuo, 2002; Sam & Weiler, 2002).

With regard to the widespread support for the significant role of interpretation as a visitor management tool in the achievement of the goals of sustainable tourism, recently, several efforts have been directed at determining the beneficial effectiveness of interpretation in promoting pro-environmental attitudes and behaviour in environmentally sensitive areas or at natural heritage sites (Moscardo, 1999; Orams, 1997; Tubb, 2003; Beaumont, 2001; Kuo, 2002). In particular, several researchers have showed the successful impacts of interpretation in modifying inappropriate visitor behaviours resulting from increased knowledge or attitudes change (Roggenbuck, 1992; Ham & Weiler, 2001; Kuo, 2002; Cable *et al.*, 1986). In this way, as mentioned in the review of the empirical research in Chapter 5, some of researchers have attempted to examine the relationships between attitudes and behaviour or between knowledge and behaviour or between knowledge and attitudes in order to construct an effective message to the target audience in maximising the effectiveness of interpretation.

However, the effectiveness of interpretation on pro-environmental attitude and environmental behaviour has been a topic of much debate. The previous literature review section has shown that it is very difficult to change tourists' attitudes and behaviour as the result of a single interpretive experience. The overall empirical research of an evaluation of the effects of interpretation on knowledge, attitudes and behaviour change are likely to suffer inconsistencies and inefficiencies in terms of different management issues and different tourism settings. One of the reasons for these inconsistencies may result from the complex processes of behavioural change and the influences of various situational factors. The various influential factors include the attributes of the interpretive programmes and the presenters, as well as those of the recipients, or indeed the ways in which knowledge, attitudes, and behaviour were conceptualised and measured (Orams, 1997; Cable *et al.*, 1986; Beaumont, 2001; Ballantyne and Packer, 2005). With regard to the unclear and complex relationship between attitudes and behaviour, depending on the types of behaviours or issues and the difficulties in measuring the effects of interpretation on attitude and behaviour change, the evaluation of how interpretation influences attitude-behaviour change presents a challenging research topic.

Given the research problems, the conceptualisation of attitude and behaviour based on site-specific perspectives and multiple measurement approaches were employed. It was also considered necessary to integrate the various factors associated with the target behaviour as part of a combination of different strategies (Ham and Krumpe, 1996; Ballentyne and Packer, 2005). In this way, the purpose of this study attempts to develop a more complete and integrated model for the evaluation of the impacts of visitor interpretation experiences on attitudes and behavioural modification process in site-specific settings. Thus, it is hoped that this research will make a significant contribution to understanding of 'when', 'why' and 'how' site-based interpretation may influence a certain type of behaviour towards local environmental conservation to the target visitors in a particular situation (Ballantyne and Hughes, 2004; Monroe, 2003).

The results of this assessment can provide helpful feedback for improvement and development of interpretation programmes in order to maximise their effectiveness in the process of the planning and designing site-based interpretive programmes.

6.3.1 Conceptual Research Questions

This research is both an exploratory and explanatory study, which aims to examine the management role of interpretation in promoting positive attitudes toward site-specific conservation issues and support for responsible environmental behaviour in order to achieve the environmental goal of sustainable tourism at natural heritage sites or protected areas. To achieve the purpose of this study, the structure is divided into two areas of investigation to answer the two main research questions as follows:

1.   Is interpretation effective in promoting visitors' positive attitude and intentions towards local environmental conservation issues and responsible environmental behaviour?

2.   How does interpretation influence visitors' behavioural intentions toward specific responsible behaviour along with the attributes of visitors and attitude components?

6.4 The Conceptual Framework

In order to explore the main research questions, a conceptual framework was developed to provide an overview of the key elements of the behavioural modification process by interpretation. An outline is provided in Figure 6.2 (see Page 143). The first section begins with selecting the key elements affecting environmental behavioural change based on a review of the psychology literature and the persuasion communication theories. The next part deals with how the research is processed based on the proposed conceptual framework and research questions for the current study. In particular, the relationships between selected variables and responsible environmental behaviour are explored and modified based on two stages of research objectives. Furthermore, more details about the specific objectives of the two research questions are introduced.

6.4.1 The Development of the Conceptual Framework

Due to the complex relationships among the various factors in the behavioural change process, there are many models and theories to identify various factors influencing environmental behaviour (see Chapter 4). In selecting the appropriate theoretical framework for the study, it was critical to choose and define the appropriate variables depending on research objectives and different settings. Previous researchers suggested that it is unlikely that a single strategy will effectively control all inappropriate behaviours in park settings and it is important to take a multi-strategy approach. Therefore, researchers should draw from as many theories as possible in developing the evaluation of interpretation intervention (Christensen & Dustin, 1989; Knopf & Dustin, 1992; Johnson and Vande Kamp, 1994; Widner and Roggenbuck, 2000).

However, there is a lack of a substantiated framework for the behavioural modification through persuasive interpretation in tourism and interpretation fields. It therefore needs careful work to produce effective strategies which incorporate a number of the variables influencing environmental behaviour change as have been identified by other researchers (Knapp and Volk, 1997).

As mentioned in Chapters 4 and 5, there are two major theories. The Theory of Reasoned Action proposed by Ajzen and Fishbein (1980) has been widely used as the basis of the theoretical framework by several researchers in the literature of attitude and behaviour change resulting from interpretation. This theory is useful to predict and explain behavioural intentions and why people have or have not engaged in various types of behaviour (Fishbein & Manfredo, 1992). Ham and Krumpe (1996) supported that the Theories of Reasoned Action and Planned Behaviour provide a useful and empirical guide not only to develop the influential messages of the target audience but also to evaluate the effectiveness of interpretation. However, Fishbein and Ajzen's model has its own limitations and cannot encompass all factors in influencing responsible environmental behaviour. Empirical research based on the Theory of Reasoned Action has produced mixed results depending on different management issues and a wide range of behaviours regarding environmental conservation issues in natural areas or environmentally sensitive areas.

The traditional persuasive communication model proposed by the Hovland group (1953) which incorporated context (e.g. source of message, message content, media channel, and receiver), target (e.g. beliefs, attitudes, and behaviour), and mediating variables served to organise thinking about the persuasion process in the 1950s and 1960s. However, limitations of the conceptual framework have been identified including the inconsistent findings in the empirical research of the effects of contextual factors, lack of attention of the dependent target variables and the content of persuasive messages, and the passive role of the receiver in the persuasion process (Ajzen, 1992). In response to the limitations of the Hovland group's persuasive communication model, recent research in persuasive communication theory has focused on the examination of the contents of persuasive messages and the active role of the receivers in the persuasion process on targeted dependent variables (beliefs, attitudes, and behaviour) (Ajzen, 1992).

With regard to this point, the main antecedent variables of responsible environmental behaviour, adopted from the review of the several models of persuasive interpretation (Cable et al., 1986; Orams, 1997; Ham and Krumpe, 1996; Ballantyne and Packer 2005), were selected for the framework of this study which integrated attitude-based theories (Cottrell, 2003b; Hines et al., 1986/87; Fishbein & Ajzen, 1980) and persuasion communication models (Petty & Cacioppo, 1981; Hovland group, 1953, cited in Ajzen, 1992) within tourism settings, instead of applying a single theory of attitude and behaviour change.

The four levels of variables related to environmentally responsible behaviour have been identified by previous researchers including individual background variables, interpretation variables, attitudinal variables, and situational variables. To date, attitudinal variables which are several strong indicators and determinants of environmentally responsible behaviour include awareness of the issues, environmental attitudes, and intention to act (Orams, 1996a; Hines et al., 1986/87; Cottrell, 2003b).

Other psychological factors in influencing responsible environmental behaviour have been identified such as locus of control, responsibility, social norm and environmental sensitivity (Hines et al., 1986/87; Newhouse, 1990; Hwang et al., 2000). Individual background factors also affect the environmental attitude-behaviour relationship including socio-demographic factors, previous experience, and environmental group memberships (Cable et al., 1986; Beaumont, 2001). Additionally, situational factors such as economic constraints, social pressures, and opportunities to choose different actions may interfere with attitudes and behaviour (Hines et al., 1986/87). With regard to persuasive interpretation factors, they include the source of a message, message content, media channel, receiver factors, other mediating process factors (i.e. reception, acceptance, and integration), and situational factors (i.e. distraction and forewarning) (Petty and Cacioppo, 1981; Ajzen1992; Cable et al., 1986; Roggenbuck, 1992).

In selecting the appropriate key elements affecting environmentally responsible behaviour through persuasive interpretation based on previous research, this study attempts to integrate the three key elements of visitor characteristics, attitudes as message content factors, and interpretation experiences as channel factors. There need to be considered in the behavioural change process at the planning and implementation stage of an effective interpretation programme within the particular tourism settings.

6.4.2 The Procedure for Selecting the Key Elements Affecting Behavioural Modification Through Interpretation

The conceptual framework of this study is proposed in Figure 6.2. It is assumed that the main object of this study can be achieved through effective interpretation influencing responsible behavioural change regarding local environmental conservation in the context of sustainable tourism. The three levels of selected key elements affecting the target behavioural outcomes of interpretation are clearly identified as the appropriate variables to be considered relevant to the study in this section. The three levels of key elements are connected by their relationships or inter-relationships with the behavioural objectives.

First, behavioural intention and attitude were selected as the main antecedent variables of environmentally responsible behaviour. Cable et al (1986) and Orams (1996a) indicated that if the objective of interpretation aims to influence visitors' behaviour, it is valuable to measure behavioural intentions and attitudes in order to understand the basis of the behaviour of participants.

Behavioural intention was selected as the behavioural modification objective to identify the long-term effects of interpretation (Kuo, 2002; Cable et al., 1986). Behavioural intention can be understood as the expressed willingness to act upon a certain action (Hines et al., 1986/87; Hungerford & Volk, 1990). Parcel (1984) indicated that behavioural intention can be used when it is not possible to measure revealed behaviour. Many other studies have also found that behavioural intention is strongly related to environmental behaviour, or at worst moderately related (Hines et al., 1986/87; Cottrell & Graefe, 1997). In tourism settings, the measurement of behavioural intention as behavioural modification would be more practical and efficient than measuring actual behaviour through observation (Cable et al., 1986). However, it is necessary to be aware of the gap between actual behaviour and behavioural intentions (Hwang et al., 2000).

Figure 6.2 The Conceptual Framework of Behavioural Change through Interpretation in the Context of Conservation and Sustainable Tourism

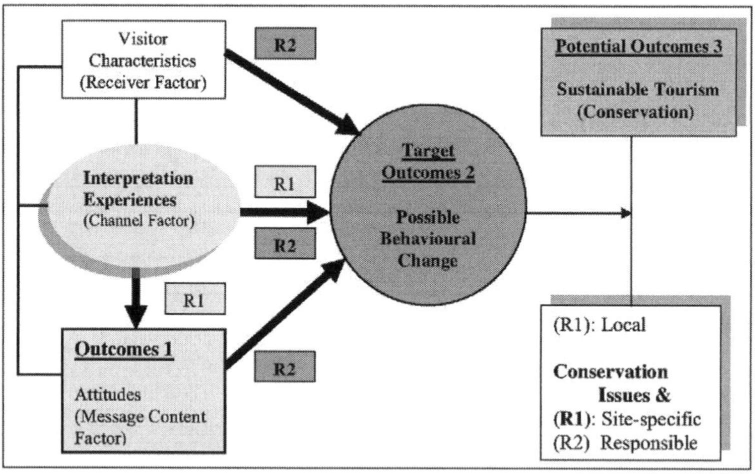

Note: (R1) indicates the specific objectives of the first research question;

(R2) indicates the specific objectives of the second research question

Attitude may serve in this study as a complex and inter-mediate factor, as either a strong determinant affecting behavioural intention or as the basis for a beneficial outcome of interpretation experiences. Attitude change could be influenced by the inter-relationships between interpretation experiences and

144

visitor characteristics, and in turn, attitudes will influence behavioural intentions and subsequently actual behaviour (Beaumont, 2001). As suggested by Ajzen (1992), it is essential to understand visitors' beliefs and other aspects of their attitudes which influence their behaviour in order to obtain the additional information about how to construct an effective message. As reviewed in the literature, when interpretation focuses on the knowledge component in changing behaviour, the failure of the effectiveness of interpretation has been found in many of empirical studies (Orams, 1996a). With regards to this point, several researchers have also emphasised that interpretation should focus on both cognitive and affective domains in influencing visitor behaviour in order to maximise the effectiveness of programmes in nature-based tourism (Iozzi, 1989; Orams, 1996a; Ballentyne and Packer, 2005). Therefore, this study included both cognitive and affective components of attitudes to determine the primary beliefs and feelings of the visitors affecting the target behaviour in order to either construct effective message content for the target audience or to examine the beneficial effects of interpretation on attitudes.

In addition to persuasion related factors, this study focuses on interpretation channel factors. Interpretation channel factors have been accepted as an important variable in the messages' effectiveness (Cable et al., 1986; Jacobson, 1988; Reid and Marion, 2003). The previous empirical research related to the different effects of various types of interpretive programmes has produced mixed results in changing visitor attitudes and behaviour (Chandool, 1997; Ajzen, 1992). One of the reasons for the inconsistent findings might be that visitors may use the different types of programmes to choose the type of nature-based activities or attractions which best suit to their interest and preferences (Madin and Fenton, 2004; Porter & Howard, 2003). Another reason for this may be that each individual perceives and responds differently to their experiences of the particular programmes (Ballantyne and Packer, 2005). With consideration of these problems, it is recommended to examine both the different effects of each interpretation method and the multiple effects of the various programmes depending on visitors' participation in the particular programmes on the desired target outcomes of interpretation (i.e. attitudes and behavioural intentions) (Madin and Fenton, 2004). The results of this evaluation help to tailor visitors' preferences and interest and to determine the strength and weakness of particular programmes in maximising delivery and design of effective interpretation to the target visitors.

Individual background characteristics are another key element to understand the process of responsible environmental behaviour (Cottrell & Graefe, 1997; Hines et al., 1986/87). In particular, it has been shown that one of the key difficulties of changing tourists' attitudes and behaviour through interpretation is due to a wide range of different demographic visitors (e.g. school children groups, adults, local residents, national and foreign tourists) and the non-captive audience within tourism settings (Orams, 1997; Ballantyne and Packer, 2005; Ham and Krumpe, 1996). Therefore, the desired behavioural outcomes as a result of an individual's interpretation experiences might be differently achieved depending on the visitor's background characteristics, their pre-visit experiences, their perception and responses to the interpretation experiences (Ajzen, 1992; Ballantyne and Packer, 2005). Therefore, the visitor-characteristics variable is necessary to determine which of the persuasive messages and method delivery methods are most effective in influencing the target visitor groups' behaviour for effective interpretation design (Christensen and Cole, 2000; Monroe, 2003).

Overall, the procedure of the selection of all three main key elements is presented and identified as the important factors which should be considered in the behavioural modification process through interpretation. They are the visitor background characteristics, interpretation channel, attitudes (i.e. message content), and behavioural intentions as the antecedent variables of behavioural modification in Figure 6.2.

6.4.3 The Modification of the Relationships of Selected Key Variables through the Two Stage Processes of the Research

The important role of selected key variables affecting behavioural modification was explained based on the review of previous theories and models. This part deals with how the research is processed through the two stages of investigation of the main research questions based on the proposed conceptual framework (See Figure 6.2). The relationships between selected sub-variables of the three key elements and desired target behavioural outcomes are addressed and modified based on the two-stage research process as part of site-specific or multiple measure approach.

Stage 1. The Effects of Interpretation on Attitudes and Behavioural Intentions (R1)

For the major objective of the first stage, it is assumed that the potential outcome of interpretation is to help ensure the successful contribution of interpretation as an effective visitor management tool to conservation and sustainable tourism through promoting the two beneficial outcomes of interpretation (i.e. attitudes and behavioural intentions) at the specific case study sites.

In order to examine the first research question, as recommended by Ham and Krumpe (1996), the first step is to identify local conservation issues and management policies regarding visitor impacts caused by the problem behaviours and responsible environmental behaviour within the particular sites. This process is reviewed in more detail in a later section of this chapter in relation to the background of the specific case study sites (see 6.6).

The next step is to determine which management policies regarding conservation issues and responsible environmental behaviour might or might not be achieved by site-based interpretation. In this stage, the researcher needs to decide the selection of the conservation topic associated with local management policies in either a single measure or a multiple measure approach. Based on the review of the literature, it is recommended to measure the range of site-specific conservation topics covered by site-based interpretation (Maddin and Fenton, 2004). For instance, although the beneficial outcomes of interpretation have been clearly recognised, the inconsistent findings of empirical studies have been produced in previous research. One of the reasons for this results from the fact that the effectiveness of interpretation depends largely on the type of visitor impact, the type of behaviour, the behaviour involved and motives for the behaviour (Roggenbuck, 1992). In this sense, the use of multiple approaches in the measurement of attitude and behavioural intentions is required in order to provide a more accurate predictive model of environmental behaviour (Rajecki, 1982) and to maximise the effectiveness of interpretation on various topics (Ham and Krumpe, 1996; Lee and Balchin, 1995). This approach will provide helpful guidance to identify the strengths and weaknesses of site-based interpretation as an effective management strategy upon a variety of management policies and practices.

With regard to this point, in the current study, various categories of responsible environmental behaviour were selected including uninformed, undesirable, responsibility-denial, and the long-term conservation behaviours (Roggenbuck, 1992; Han and Weiler, 2002). In addition, a multi-set of responsible behaviour was associated with a wide range of local management policies and conservation issues at a particular site. The main conservation issues regarding local management policies were selected based on the key site-based interpretation theme after reviewing the interpretation management plan and strategies at the research case sites described later.

Overall, the desired beneficial outcomes of interpretation in the first stage of investigation are assessed to determine the effects of interpretation on multidimensional attitudes and behavioural intentions in relation to various local conservation issues and a multi-set of responsible behaviours. They were assessed by compared differences between visitor groups depending on their experiences of the particular programmes on-site. Therefore, it is assumed that visitors who experience the interpretive

147

programmes will have higher levels of positive attitudes and behavioural intentions than those who have no experience the interpretive programmes on-site.

Stage 2. The Relative Contributions of The Three Key Elements to Specific Behavioural Intentions Toward Responsible Environmental Behaviour (R2)

Following the process of the first stage, the second stage aims to provide a better understanding of when, why, and how interpretation may influence or fail to influence a certain topic or a certain type of behaviour to the target visitors in the particular situations.

The specific objectives of the second stage are "what are the main influential factors to promote specific responsible behavioural intentions?" and "how are the most important factors associated with specific behavioural intentions?". It would be helpful to understand if these factors do indeed contribute to the specific behavioural intentions and if so, it is worth examining to what extent or in what direction.

For the major objective of the second stage, it is assumed that the effectiveness of interpretation on desired site-specific behavioural outcomes varies and are dependent upon a number of variables associated with attitude components (as the belief-targeted message content), message delivery, and visitor characteristics. In order to investigate the relative contributions of the three key elements influencing a multi-set of specific responsible behavioural intentions, the following section addresses the relationships among key elements and also explores the procedure for selecting the sub-variables of the three key elements. Based on this point, several assessments of the assumptions of the specific relationships between independent variables and dependent variables are presented as specific objectives of the second stage.

Stage 2.1 Behavioural Intentions: Dependent variable

For the second stage investigation, behavioural intentions towards specific responsible behaviour were selected as a dependent variable to measure possible behavioural modification in relation to local responsible environmental behaviour.

A multi-set of site-specific responsible behaviour were employed because the management goal of site-based interpretation is to modify a wide range of visitor behaviour including both uninformed or undesired behaviours which might cause negative impacts for the specific site. In particular, additional research monitoring other important factors contributing to the effectiveness of site-based interpretation on site-specific responsible behaviour is essential to a basis for practitioners to tailor effective interpretation techniques for both message content and message delivery to the needs, preferences, and perceptions of each target group.

For this stage, it is assumed that different types of specific responsible behavioural intentions are differently influenced by the relative contribution of the three key levels of elements such as belief or feeling components of specific attitudes, interpretation channel factors, and visitor characteristics variables.

Stage 2.2 Independent Variables

There are three independent variables, namely, attitude, the interpretation channel, and the visitor characteristic. The following section deals with the modified definition of each independent variable, the selection of sub-variables of the three independent factors, and the assumptions of the relationship between each key factor and behavioural dependent variables.

- **Attitude**

According to the review of the attitude construct, attitudes are multidimensional, consisting of three components – belief (the cognitive component), feelings/emotions (the affective component), and intention (conative component) (Cottrell, 2003b). While attitude has been defined in a variety of ways, most definitions may not be readily apparent. Recent research has emphasised the distinction between attitude, intention and behaviour (Fransson & Gärling, 1999; Kaiser et al., 1999). As behavioural intention is measured independently from attitude components (Hienes et al., 1986/87; Orams, 1996a), this study proposed the environmental attitudes that refer to the collection of both feeling and belief which a person holds toward environmentally related behaviours or issues.

Most previous studies show only a weak or non-existent link between attitude and behaviour (Baron and Byrne, 1987, cited in Adams, 2003; Uitto et al., 2004). That is, they indicate that positive general attitudes toward the environment do not necessarily lead to environmentally responsible behaviour (Baron and Byrne, 1987, cited in Adams, 2003). However, other researchers suggest that strong specific and narrowly defined attitudes toward a particular behaviour that has been acquired through direct experience have a stronger influence on that behaviour than general attitudes (Ajzen & Fishbein,

149

1980; Cottrell & Graefe, 1997; Hines et al., 1986/87; Newhouse, 1990; Hungerfore & Volk, 1990; Adams, 2003).

Bring this assumption provided by previous researchers into interpretation research, the effectiveness of interpretation in influencing visitors' behaviour can be substantially improved by addressing specific messages targeting primary beliefs and emotional feelings toward particular behaviour that are relevant and important to the target audience (Ballantyne and Hughes, 2004; Orams, 1996a; Monroe, 2003). Several types of beliefs and feelings have been identified by previous research into the effectiveness of belief-/feeling- targeted messages on desired behavioural change. They include awareness of the positive or negative consequences of the behaviour, the social acceptability of the behaviour, the ease with which the action can be taken, different levels of moral development (e.g. fear of punishment, consideration for justice, social norms, fairness and self-respect) (Monroe, 2003; Christensen and Dustin, 1989) and emphasise of emotional factors (Orams, 1996a; Ballantyne and Packer, 2005).

In particular, with regard to low impact behaviour at park settings, the inappropriate behaviour of visitors may be due to visitors simply not being aware of the potential negative environmental impacts of their activities (Tribe et al., 2000). Therefore, it is important to influence visitors' awareness of the positive or negative consequences of the particular behaviour. Manning (2003) also suggests that the type of belief targeted messages may be warranted when applied to issues such as visitor safety and protection of critical and sensitive resources. In particular, the visitor will always pay more attention when the basic human emotions of fear, anxiety and pity are aroused (McCool & Braithwaite, 1992; Heylin, 1993).

In selecting sub-variables of attitudinal components for the message content variable in this study, the measurement of attitudes was proposed in multidimensional approaches in terms of both belief and feeling components of attitudes ranged from general to specific perspectives. They include general attitudes toward local environmental conservation issues (e.g. 'importance of protection of critical and sensitive resources', 'concern or care for the resources') and specific attitudes toward the particular responsible behaviour (e.g. 'the positive or negative consequences of the particular behaviour', 'support for the particular behaviour' and 'the basic human emotions of fear, anxiety and pity').

Based on this discussion, this study attempts to identify the different impacts of primary types of beliefs and the emotional domain of specific attitudes depending upon the different types of specific

150

behaviour and in what direction, as has been recommended by previous researchers (Ham and Krumpe, 1996; Lee and Balchin, 1995). The hypothesis is that specific attitudes toward a particular behaviour will have more impact on specific behavioural intentions than will general attitudes.

- **Interpretation Channel**

The second independent variable identified here is the interpretation channel. The multiple assessment of the interpretation channel is essential to understand different strengths and weaknesses of the interpretive programmes on the specific behavioural outcomes (i.e. attitudes and behavioural intentions). Several sub-variables of multiple media measurement were selected such as the visitor centre, reading of the Code of Conduct brochure, and the levels of interpretation participation.

Previous research has shown inconstant findings on the effectiveness of different interpretation methods (Candoll, 1997; Ajzen, 1992). In general, recreation managers support the view that personal contact with the visitor has more impact on knowledge, attitudes, and behaviour than non-personal methods such as brochures, signs, visitor centres, and other interpretive media (Martin and Taylor, 1981; McAvoy and Hamborg, 1984; Roggenbuck, 1992; Reid and Marion, 2003). However, recent research suggests that well-designed trailhead signs or brochures are in some cases as effective as a visitor centre or a personal guide in influencing visitor behaviour (Roggenbuck and Berrier, 1982; Widner and Roggenbuck, 2000).

With respect to the inconsistency of the effects of the particular interpretation media on behavioural outcomes identified by previous research, this study focuses not only on determining how each selected channel influences the desired target outcomes, but also assesses what type of media is most effective on the beneficial behavioural outcomes.

First, the effects of a Visitor Centre were assessed. Previous researchers have emphasised the important role of the visitor centre in achieving the holistic goals of sustainability including economic, environmental, and cultural and social sustainability (Fallon and Kriwoken, 2003). According to the review of the literature (Fallon and Kriwoken, 2003; Knudson, Cable, & Beck, 1995), visitor centres serve many different functions, including marketing and access, enhancement and information, management, and substitution for the attractions themselves (Moscardo, 1998/99; Wylde, 1996; Pearce, 1991). The primary function of a centre is to provide tourists with information and orientation about the site, as well as toilet and restaurant services (Moscardo, 1993). In addition, a centre plays an important role as a management tool in promoting 'sense of place' and awareness of the local environmental

151

conservation issues. Thus, it can help reduce visitor pressure on resources and undesirable visitor behaviour as well as foster visitors' attitudes toward more environmentally sensitive tourist activities (Moscardo, 1999; Wylde, 1996; Pearce; 1991).

With regard to the multiple functions of a visitor centre as a visitor management tool, this study attempts to determine the main effects of a visitor centre on attitudes and behavioural intentions toward local conservation issues and appropriate behaviours by comparing the differences between visitor groups divided by their experiences of the visitor centre at a particular site. In addition, in examining visitors' involvement in, preferences for and responses to different interpretive methods, reading a Code of Conduct brochure and their levels of interpretation participation were considered.

In particular, reading a Code of Conduct brochure was considered important to determine visitors' levels of awareness of contents of a Conduct of Conduct brochure and to assess the effects of that particular brochure on attitudes and behaviour. In terms of the levels of interpretation participation, this variable is defined as the total number of interpretation programmes in which visitors participate on-site, including both non-personal programmes (i.e. signs, brochures, exhibition/display, interactive computer programme, films) and personal contacts (e.g. talking with staff, and guided walks) (Maddin and Fenton, 2004). With respect to the specific assumption in the relative contributions of different interpretation channels, it is suggested that if the goals of interpretation are to inform or educate rather than to entertain the visitors, the use of multiple interpretive methods is very important for successful interpretation in order to attract and to reach the needs of a range of targeted audiences (Manning, 2003; Jacobson, 1988; Littlefair, 2003).

Based on the above discussion, it is assumed that the multiple media approaches combining non-personal and personalised channels will have more impact on specific behavioural intentions than use of a single medium. It is assumed that the particular interpretive programmes will have different impacts on various types of attitudinal components and behavioural intentions towards local conservation issues and responsible behaviour in the context of the Visitor Centre, reading of the Code of Conduct, and levels of interpretation participation.

- **Visitor Characteristics**

As reviewed in the literature, visitor characteristics are critical in determining the effectiveness of interpretation on desired attitude and behaviour change. This study focuses on how the different visitor groups modify the types of specific behavioural intentions depending on their experiences of the particular interpretation programmes and/or their attitudes toward the types of specific behaviour.

Sub-variables of the visitor characteristics were selected in relation to socio-demographics and pre-existing environmental experiences. First, a wide range of socio-demographic variables have been linked to environmental action, such as age, gender, education, income and family type (Barr, 2003) as well as ethnicity, income ('income' repeated – see line above) and place of residence (Adams, 2003). In general, research has provided the evidence for higher levels of pro-environmental behaviour amongst younger, female, well-educated, wealthy individuals in nuclear families (Hines et al., 1986/87). However, in this study, gender, age, education and place of residence were selected as visitor demographic background variables.

In addition, several researchers have emphasised the significant role of pre-existing environmental attitudes and previous environmental experiences (or environmental involvement and pre-trip experiences) on pro-environmental attitudes and behaviour (Cable et al., 1986; Beaumont 2001). For this study, 'previous experiences of this site', 'previous experience of natural areas', and 'pre-existing environmental involvement' were selected. With regard to the review of persuasion models in the previous chapters of this study (See Chapter 4), an individual's characteristics which include the receiver's valuation of the importance of the information, prior attitudes, pre-visit experiences, environmental involvement, and other recalled items of information (or prior knowledge) can affect the process of information integration and the effectiveness of persuasive communication (Cable et al., 1986; Ajzen, 1992; Beaumont, 2001). It is noted that 'interpretation is generally more effective with visitors who are less experienced and who are less knowledgeable' (Manning, 2003: p.25).

With respect to the inconsistent relationships between visitor characteristics and behaviour, it can be assumed that different visitor characteristic variables are differently associated with different types of specific responsible behavioural intentions corresponding to the interaction of their experiences with the particular interpretation and specific attitudes.

6.4.4 Research Specific Objectives

The previous section examined the procedure of selecting the three key elements influencing the three main target outcomes of interpretation (e.g. attitude change, behavioural intentions change, and its potential contributions to sustainable tourism and conservation). Also, several key assumptions were also discussed concerning the relationships among selected key sub-variables and desired behavioural outcomes.

Table 6.1 The Variables Based on the Conceptual Framework of the Study

Categories of the Three key Elements and Outcomes of the Study **(The First Stage)**	Independent and Dependent Variables **(The Second Stage)**	Sub-variables of each key element
Visitors characteristics (Receiver Factor)	Receiver (Independent variable)	Social-demographics; Previous trip experiences; Environmental involvement
Interpretation Experiences (Channel Factor)	Interpretation channel (Independent variable)	The Visitor Centre; Reading of the Code; The levels of interpretation participation
Outcomes 1 of Interpretation: Attitudes Change	Attitudes (Message content) (Independent variable)	• Belief components: The importance of protection; Awareness of the consequences of types of behaviours; Support for management policy regarding types of behaviours • Feeling components: 'Danger', 'concern', 'worry' regarding the issues or types of behaviours
Outcomes 2 of Interpretation: Behavioural Intentions Change	Targeted Dependent Variable (the different types of Site-Specific responsible behavioural intentions)	Site-specific responsible behaviour; General responsible behaviour; Long term conservation behaviour
Potential outcomes 3 of Interpretation (Conservation and Sustainable tourism)	Assumption of Possible Behavioural Change	Local conservation issues; Management policies regarding site-specific responsible behaviour

Overall, Table 6.1 summarises the categories of selected three independent variables and sub-variables affecting behavioural modification to examine the target outcomes of interpretation through investigation of the two research questions in this study.

The following section presents the specific objectives of the two research questions. Before examining the main research questions, first, it was important to identify various local environmental conservation issues and practices in order to relate the effectiveness of site-specific interpretation to the context of the particular research case study sites. In this sense, it was critical to examine the validity and reliability of multidimensional measurement of attitudes and behavioural intentions in a site-specific context. It was also necessary to explore who visits the site, what visitors' attitudes and behavioural intentions toward local conservation issues and responsible behaviour are, and how visitors experience and respond to interpretive programmes on-site.

Next, the first research question can be investigated through both exploratory and descriptive research, examining the management role of interpretation in contributing to conservation and sustainable tourism in relation to local management policies and conservation practices.

i). The specific objectives of the first research question are:
• To examine the main effects of the Visitor Centre on attitudes and behavioural intentions toward local conservation issues and responsible behaviour, by comparing the differences between visitor groups divided by their experiences of the Visitor Centre
• To examine the different impacts or the multiple effects of the particular interpretation programmes on attitudes and behavioural intentions by comparing the differences between visitor groups depending on their participation in various types of interpretation methods in the context of the reading of the Code of Conduct brochure and the levels of interpretation participation

The second research question can be considered through explanatory research, identifying the impact of the main factors on the dependent variable regarding specific responsible behaviours.

ii). The specific objectives of the second research question are:
• To investigate the relative contributions of interpretation methods, attitudes, and visitor characteristics to different types of specific responsible behavioural intentions
• To examine the inter-relationships between the most influential factors and different types of specific responsible behavioural intentions
• To identify which of the primary belief or feeling components of attitudes are the most significant contributors to different types of specific responsible behavioural intentions

155

- To assess which of the interpretation channel factors are the most significant contributors to different types of specific responsible behavioural intentions

- To identify which characteristics of the visitors are the most significant contributors to different types of specific responsible behavioural intentions.

6.5 Selection of Research Case Sites

As explained in the research objectives and the conceptual framework are the first step in the research process. The next step is to select the research sites. The following section presents the selection procedures and the backgrounds of the two selected case study sites. This information helps to identify the major management issues and appropriate behaviours within the specific case study sites and to determine the target issues of responsible behaviour in measuring attitudes and behavioural intentions. This part deals with the selection procedure; a brief background of the Dorset Heritage Coast (the Jurassic Coast); the selection procedure for the two specific case study sites; and a brief background of the Lulworth Coast and Charmouth Coast.

6.5.1 Selection Procedure for Research Case Sites

This study is to examine the role of interpretation in achieving the environmental goals of sustainable tourism by managing visitor behaviours. In order to achieve the main objective, the research focuses on protected natural areas that are designed to conserve the natural environment and to manage tourism in a more sustainable way. England's finest countryside and landscapes are protected under numerous national designations by the Countryside Agency such as National Parks or Areas of Outstanding Natural Beauty or Heritage Coasts. These areas are protected by law to conserve and enhance their natural beauty not just for the present, but also for future generations (The Countryside Agency, 2005a).

Among national designations of protected natural areas, Heritage Coasts sites were selected as the case study sites. Heritage Coasts are stretches of undeveloped coastline which contain features of scenic natural beauty or special significance around England and Wales. There are several reasons why Heritage Coasts were chosen for the main study site. First, Heritage Coasts are easily accessible and have become popular destinations to attract a wide range of commercial day visitors including both tourists and local residents. These areas are managed not only to conserve unspoilt coastline of special scenic and environmental value from undesirable development, but also to improve the accessibility for visitors. Many of these coasts are part of larger National Parks or Areas of Outstanding Natural Beauty

(AONBs). Therefore, the majority of Heritage Coasts have a similar purpose to AONBs, but put with a greater emphasis on recreation management. Indeed, many areas of beautiful coastline and wider countryside are easily accessible by a network of public footpaths and national trails (The Countryside Agency, 2005b; Britain Express, 1996a).

This enables a direct comparison to be made between commercial day tourist visitors, local residents, and people who undertake guided or interpretive activities. As the number of visitors to heritage coastal areas has grown, many negative impacts on the environment caused several problems for wildlife and coastal areas, especially during the summer time. For example, in Norfolk, sensitive dune reserves are vulnerable to erosion and there are concerns over disturbance to internationally important shore nesting birds. Uncontrolled dogs cause the most serious problems in this area. Other problems such as traffic and parking congestion, in particular, during the summer time, affect locals and other tourists (Norfolk Coast Partnership, 1995).

In response to negative impacts, positive visitor management and interpretation techniques have been adopted in order to overcome the negative problems and to address environmental concerns, as well as to develop sustainable tourism through improved co-operation and joint action by all partners (Norfolk Coast Partnership, 1995).

With regards to the growing concern for a sustainable approach in managing negative problems caused by visitors through interpretation, there has been a lack of ongoing research regarding the effect of interpretation as a positive visitor management tool at the heritage coastal areas. As these reasons and the objectives of this research are the basis for the direction of choosing this study area, heritage coasts provide excellent study sites to examine the role of interpretation in promoting environmentally responsible behaviour.

A more detailed background of Heritage Coasts sites is presented in the following section. As reviewed, two research sites were selected in order to compare the two cases and to identify common features and differences rather than selecting just one case. In this study, Dorset heritage coastal areas were chosen, in particular the Lulworth Heritage Coast and Charmouth Heritage Coast.

6.5.1.1 Heritage Coast Scheme

The "heritage coast" classification scheme was initiated in 1972. Unlike National Parks and Areas of Outstanding Natural Beauty (AONBs), the Heritage Coast scheme is a non-statutory designation, and the designations can be given by the Countryside Agency with the agreement of local authorities and land owners. Much of the designated coastline is owned by the National Trust, through its Enterprise Neptune campaign (Britain Express, 1996a).

Heritage Coasts cover a total of 1027 km (35%) of the scenic English coastline. There are currently 32 designated Heritage Coasts in England(Britain Express, 1996a). Figure 6.3 shows the location of Heritage Coasts around England and the names of sites are presented in Table 6.2 (Source: Countryside Agency, 2005b). The first Heritage Coast to be defined was Beachy Head with its famous white cliffs in Sussex and the latest was the Durham Coast.

Figure 6.3 The Location of 32 sites of Heritage Coasts in England

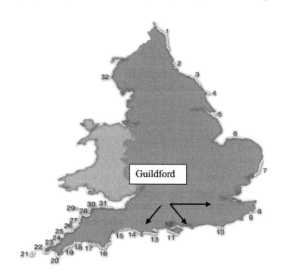

Table 6.2 The Names of 32 sites of Heritage Coasts in England

• North & Yorkshire	• South East
1. North Northumberland;	8. South Foreland; 9.Dover-Folkestone;
2. Durham; 3. North Yorkshire and Cleveland;	10. Sussex Downs;
4. Flamborough Headland;	11.Tennyson, Isle of Wight;
5. Spurn;	12.Hamstead, Isle of Wight
32. St. Bees Head	
• East Anglia	• South West
6. North Norfolk; 7. Suffolk	13. Purbeck; 14. West Dorset; 15. East Devon; 16. South Devon; 17.Rame Head; 18.Gribbin Head-Polperro; 19.Trevose Head; 20. The Lizard; 21. Isles of Scilly; 22. Penwith; 23. Godrevy-Portreath; 24. St.Agnes; 25. Trevose Head;26. Pentire Point-Widemouth; 27. Hartland; 28. Hartland (Devon); 29. Lundy; 30. North Devon; 31. Exmoor

(Source: Countryside Agency, 2005b)

As explained, the Heritage Coast scheme was used for the specific case study areas. In choosing of the representativeness of the research sites, the following criteria were used: First, the management plans or strategy for tourism should be adopted under the principles of sustainable tourism development in terms of conservation of natural sites as the primary goals of sustainable tourism. Secondly, an interpretation strategy plan should be implemented as a key visitor management strategy in managing the negative impacts of visitors. The main objectives of the interpretation plan should seek to promote responsible environmental behaviour for conservation of the site beyond enjoyment of visitors and understanding of the site. The existence of the site-specific Visitor Code of Conduct is critical to develop the basis for the measurement of behaviour statements and to examine the effects of interpretation in managing inappropriate visitor behaviour. Thirdly, the availability of a variety of interpretive programmes was also important, including the visitor centres, signs, brochures, and guided walks. On this basis, it is essential to survey people who undertake an experience both with and without interpretation for the comparison analysis in evaluating interpretative experiences. Moreover, the other criterion includes convenience of location and access in order to reduce time and cost constraints.

Finally, participation of local interpretive centre staff was also considered. In this initial stage, the researcher contacted the interpretive centre staff by e-mail or phone in order to request the agreement of conducting visitor research and to review management problems and themes and objectives of interpretation in each of the sites. More details will be discussed in Chapter 7.

A number of Heritage Coasts sites for the research were narrowed down to the two English regions among the eight regions of England and Wales in consideration of convenience of location (short distance from Guildford), time constraints, and cost-effectiveness in order to enhance the feasibility of the field research. Based on these conditions, it was first decided to select Heritage Coast sites within the South East and South West regions. As seen in Table 6.2, South East region includes five Heritage Coasts; Sussex, South Foreland, Dover Folekstone, two Heritage Coasts on Isle of Wight (Tennyson and Hamstead). More than two-thirds (638 km) of England's heritage coast (a total of 1,027 km) can be found in the South West including the Dorset and East Devon Jurassic Coast, South Devon, Isles of Scilly, Lundy, North Devon, and Exmoor regions.

Table 6.3 shows the estimation of each site satisfying each of the six criteria in terms of choosing the proposed sites within the South East region and the Dorset Coast. As seen in Table 6.3, the Dorset Heritage Coast was selected as the research site satisfying all six criteria.

Table 6.3 Estimation of the Proposed Site within The South East Region and Dorset

The Criterion	Sussex	Dover Foreland-Folkestone	Isle of Wight	Dorset
Management plans for sustainability	•	•	•	•
Interpretation strategy plan	•		•	•
The site-specific Visitor Code			•	•
Interpretation facilities (e.g. the visitor centre)	•	•	•	•
Convenience of location/access	• (by car or train)	• (by car or train)	(By boat)	• (by car or train, Coastlink bus)
Participation of local interpretive centre staff	No response	-	-	•

Note: The symbol '•' indicates a satisfied criterion among the seven criteria for each of the sites

6.5.1.2 Brief Background of the Dorset Heritage Coast (the Jurassic Coast)

The Dorset Heritage Coast, known the Jurassic Coast, provides a good of a case study site in terms of the importance of conservation value and the success of sustainable tourism management. Recently, the Jurassic Coast has received the Destination Award at the 2005 Tourism for Tomorrow Awards, which recognises and promotes the world's leading examples of best practice in responsible tourism development (Jurassic Coast Team, 2005).

The Dorset Coast is situated in the South West of England, UK (see Figure 6.4) and protected under several national conservation designations including World Heritage Site, Heritage Coast, AONB, Sites of Special Scientific Interest (SSSI) and others (e.g. SAC, SPA). First, the Dorset Coast is part of the Jurassic Coast, which was also classified as England's first Natural World Heritage Site in December 2001. It comprises 95 miles (155 km) of unspoilt cliffs and beaches, from Exmouth in East Devon to Old Harry Rocks in Purbeck. The Jurassic Coast World Heritage Site is both nationally and internationally important for nature conservation value in terms of special features of geology, geomorphology (the landforms), and fossils which represent an immense 185 million years of earth history, as well as scenic coastlines and beaches (Jurassic Coast Team, 2004a).

Further protection is also provided through established statutory planning policies, including 13 geological and biological Sites of Special Scientific Interest (SSSI) which are regulated by English Nature, the government conservation agency, as well as seven Special Areas for Conservation (SAC) and three Special Protection Areas (SPA) along the Jurassic Coast (Jurassic Coast Team, 2004a).

The two Dorset Heritage Coasts are situated within the Jurassic Coast along with Purbeck Coast in East Dorset and West Dorset Coast. Purbeck Coast extends from Arne, in the creeks and flats of Poole Harbour along a spectacular series of chalk and limestone cliffs and the beauty spots of Lulworth Cove and Durdle Door to Weymouth Bay. West Dorset Coast ranges from the Isle of Portland's limestone greys and the white, shingle curve of Chesil Beach, to picturesque villages at Lyme Bay, Charmouth and Golden Cap, the south coast's highest point (Britain Express, 1996b, c). Many parts of Dorset's coast and countryside also lie within the Dorset Area of Outstanding Natural Beauty (AONB) which recognises nationally important landscapes, conserving both the Jurassic World Heritage Site and the wider surrounding countryside areas (Jurassic Coast Team, 2004a; the Dorset AONB Partnership, 2004).

161

Figure 6.4 Location of The Dorset Heritage Coast and National Conservation Designations in the South West

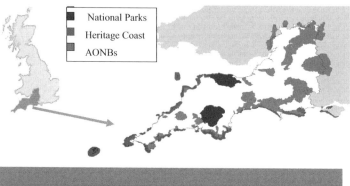

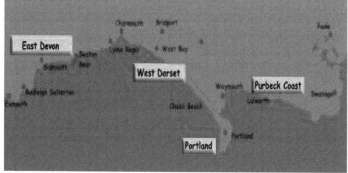

(Source: South West Observatory/Environment, 2006; www.great-britain.co.uk/world-heritage)

With respect to the significant importance and the attractiveness of nature conservation value, the Dorset Heritage Coasts are popular for valuable educational resources with their unique fossil exposures and other geological specimens along the coast and are highly accessible through gateway towns and the South West Coast Path. In addition, the coastal beaches also attract visitors for recreational purposes (the Dorset AONB Partnership, 2004; Jurassic Coast World Heritage Steering Group (JCWHSG), 2003; Jurassic Coast Team, 2004a).

Given the unique geological and coastal environment of the Dorset region, this area has long been a popular tourism destination attracting a large number of domestic visitors each year as well as overseas tourists (Dorset Tourism Data Project, 2002; Dorset Coast Forum, 1998). Over the last decade, tourism growth has been examined and has shown an increase in domestic tourist numbers to Dorset from 3.0 million in 1990 to 5.6 million in 2000, particularly concentrated during summer time (The Dorset For You Partnership, 2005).

Increasing numbers of visitors to the Dorset Coast brings pressures on the coastal environment and local communities. In order to minimise a conflict between tourism development, and conservation and sustainable use of coastal and geological resources, several management plans and strategies have been established and reflect a commitment to put the principles of sustainability into practice (The Dorset For You Partnership, 2005; The Dorset Coast Forum, 1999).

There are a range of management plans and county-wide strategies which have relevance for tourism or local management issues where different local agencies and partnerships co-operate. These include the Dorset Coast Strategy (the Dorset Coast Forum, 1999), the Dorset AONB Management Plan (the Dorset AONB Partnership, 2003), and the Jurassic Coast World Heritage Site Management Plan (JCWHSG, 2003a). For example, according to the Jurassic Coast World Heritage Site Management Plan and Framework for Action, "the overall aim is to manage the Site and this wider area, World Heritage Coast, in a cohesive way, and that recognises it as an 'attractor' for visitors (including local people), and leads to increased understanding, appreciation and support for conservation of the World Heritage Site, and to tangible benefits for the quality of life of local people and visitors." (Jurassic Coast World Heritage Site (JCWHS) Framework for Action, 2003a:p.3). As seen in this plan, the main policy of management at Dorset Coast focuses on conservation of the site as the primary goal through managing human activities. The policies and practical objectives of management plans and strategies have been developed in order to achieve the holistic goals of sustainability which guarantee the quality of nature, the visitor experience and the sustainable development of its region (the Jurassic Coast World Heritage Steering Group (JCWHSG), 2003a).

Based on the review of several management plans and strategies established by the partnerships of Dorset Council and other agencies within the Dorset Coast region, the Dorset Coast can be regarded as a case of sustainable tourism (Johnson, 2002). In terms of practices and strategies to achieve the sustainability, Dorset County Council emphasises that interpretation is a key component to the approach in order to contribute more widely to the environmental sustainability of coastal and geological environments (Johnson, 2002). The main directions and actions of interpretation projects for the Jurassic Coast are adhering to the policies and objectives of the Jurassic Coast World Heritage Site Management Plan and Framework for Action as well as to the recommendation of a scoping study on interpretation facilities undertaken by the Natural History Museum (2003) (JCWHSG, 2005). For instance, according to the Scoping Study on interpretation facilities, it is stated that "interpretation of the Jurassic Coast World Heritage Site should allow intellectual, emotional and physical engagement with the landscape, science and history of the coastline, for people who live close by and those who visit for study and recreation" (Natural History Museum, 2003: p.4). Based on a review of the main theme of interpretation, the main goal of interpretation of the Jurassic Coast highlights the behavioural objectives such as "what the visitor can do to help conservation of the site", "you can play part in conservation", and "please help us preserve the cliff by keeping to the path" (p.15).

In this sense, the Dorset Coast site is suitable as a research site to examine the management role of interpretation on behavioural modification towards conservation of the site in the context of sustainable tourism management.

6.5.1.3 Selecting the Two Case Sites

The following part discusses the procedure of selecting two specific case sites after examining the interpretation theme and visitor centres at major locations within the Dorset Coast region. According to the Scoping Study on interpretation facilities for the Jurassic Coast, the key concept of interpretation for the Jurassic Coast is a unique 'Walk through Time' which is the lead story to link up the total picture of past life and natural earth processes over 185 million years of geological and biological change (Natural History Museum, 2003).

Due to the extensive and diverse characteristics of the site, however, the Jurassic Coast Interpretation Plan and the Natural History Museum Scoping Study recommended that site-wide themes of interpretation focus on primarily geological coastal stories such as the rocks, fossils, the coastal landforms, and conservation and sustainability of the World Heritage Site. Additionally, site-specific themes also include marine life, wildlife, and location-specific social and cultural history stories depending on Gateway Towns and coastal sites (JCWHSG, 2005).

With regards to the main theme of Interpretation Strategy and the Scoping Study, a site-specific interpretation facilities project has been initiated through co-operation and collaboration by all local and national stakeholders along the Jurassic Coast Sites and Gateway Towns. In particular, Dorset

Coastlink has been developed by voluntary groups and local stakeholders in order to raise awareness of the relatively unknown and unexplored marine and geological environment along the Dorset Coast (Dorset Coast Forum, 1999; Dorset Coastlink & Bournemouth University 1997a). It is indicated that the Dorset Coastlink is the first marine awareness network of its kind in the UK (Dorset Coastlink & Bournemouth University 1997a).

Recently, Dorset Coastlink includes the network of the five main visitor centres such as Charmouth Heritage Coast Centre, Chesil and the Fleet Nature Reserve Centre, Lulworth Heritage Centre, Purbeck Marine Wildlife Reserve, Kimmeridge, and Durlston Marine Project (See Figure 6.4). Each Coastlink interprets their own particular features of the coast but emphasises the importance of the marine influence on their site. The site-specific theme and main attributes of each visitor centre focus on mainly marine life and geology (Dorset Coastlink & Bournemouth University, 1997a).

Figure 6.5 Locations of Coastlink Visitor Centres

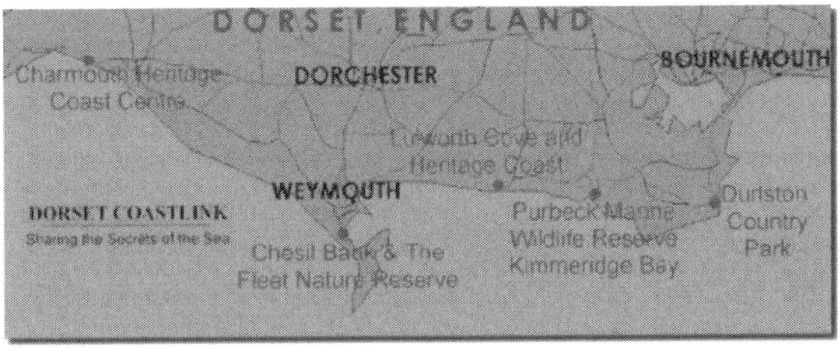

(Source: Dorset Coastlink & Bournemouth University 1997)

The specific case study sites were selected based on the primary theme presented in Dorset Coastlink visitor centres, the JCWHS interpretation action plan, and the Natural History Museum Scoping Study on interpretation facilities. In particular, as examined, the main themes of each centre based on Dorset Coastlink visitor centres are as follows:

- Charmouth Heritage Coast Centre: local geology and fossils
- Chesil Beach (The Fleet Nature Reserve): coastal lagoons
- Lulworth Cove Heritage Centre: evolution of coastal landforms

- Kimmeridge Bay (Purbeck marine Wildlife Reserve): marine habitats and ecology, rockpooling and the natural stone

- Durlston Country Park (Marine Research Area): seabirds and dolphins
    (Source: Dorset Coast Forum 1998; Dorset Coastlink & Bournemouth University 1997a)

Although the two case sites of Lulworth Coast, and Charmouth coast areas were selected based on the similar primary theme, there are also different site-specific features including tourism activities, management issues, and specific local attractions at each specific location. Therefore, by comparing the two cases as well as identifying common or contrary features, it is expected to be more helpful to identify the effective role of interpretation and the strengths and weakness of interpretive programmes at each site.

6.6 Brief Review of the Two Selected Case Sites

The following section presents the brief background of these two cases and compares the main attributes of each site.

6.6.1 Lulworth Heritage Coast

Location and Designation

The Lulworth Coast is situated within the Purbeck Heritage Coast in East Dorset, half-way between the resorts of Swanage and Weymouth and stretches along 5 miles of beaches between White Nothe in the west and Warbarrow Bay in the east (The Lulworth Estate, 2004a; Dorset Coastlink & Bournemouth University, 1997b).

With regards to the significant natural conservation value of Lulworth, it forms part of the 95 mile coastline of Dorset and East Devon World Heritage Site, the Jurassic Coast and Purbeck Heritage Coast. It also is protected under the numerous designations such as SSSI (Site of Special Scientific Interest), AONB (Areas of Outstanding Natural Beauty) which help to conserve its unique natural heritage (The Lulworth Estate, 2004a).

Geology and Tourism Attractions

The unique geology of Lulworth Coast contains several tourism attractions including Lulworth Cove, the Durdle Door, Fossil Forest, and wildlife as well as human activities and archeological heritage. In particular, the area between Lulworth Cove and Durdle Door is known as a 'honey spot' in the regions of the South West and is also internationally a well-known tourist destination for its stunning coastal scenery and geology, representing some of the finest examples of geology and geomorphology in Europe. Lulworth Cove coastline itself is a beautiful shell-shaped cove which was formed by coastal erosion through the interaction of weather and sea. The rocks at the Lulworth Coast represent Cretaceous time periods dating between 150 million years old and 65 million years old which lie within the continuous earth history of 185 million years at the Dorset and East Devon World Heritage Site (The Lulworth Estate, 2004b; Lulworth Cove Online, 2003).

One of the famous attractions near Lulworth Cove, the Fossil Forest can be found here. It is an example of fossilised rings of algae, 'tufa' that gathered around tree trunks nearly 150 million years ago. The huge tufa remains in the present although much of the wood has been eroded by the weather or taken in the past by fossil hunters. In particular, Fossil Forest is within the Army Range and can be accessed through the footpath at the eastern side of the beach near Cove. The footpath is open most weekends and in August (The Lulworth Estate, 2004c; Lulworth Cove online, 2003).

In addition, this geological diversity supports a wide variety of wildlife including a famous butterfly, the "Lulworth Skipper" which first was discovered near Durdle Door in 1832. Further around Lulworth, tourists could also experience its rich archaeological heritage including Lulworth Castle and the Lulworth Equestrian Centre (Lulworth Cove online, 2003).

Tourism Pressure and Management Issues

The spectacular landscapes and the unique geological features attract a large number of geologists and walkers with educational and recreational purposes, such as relaxing on the beaches, swimming or diving in the cove, as well as collecting fossils or rocks. There are also numerous guided boat trips leaving from the Lulworth cove showing the highlights of the spectacular coastal views. (The Lulworth Estate, 2002; Dorset Coastlink & Bournemouth University, 1997b).

The tourism growth at the Lulworth Coast has been increasing with approximately, over half a million visitors each year. Some 30% of visitors come during July and August with 10% visiting the site during the winter months, between November and February (The Lulworth Estate, 2002). However, the increasing tourism pressure brings considerable management problems, particularly, in relation to the erosion of paths and landscape and the domination of the car park in the area surrounding Lulworth

Cove. On the contrary, the economic benefits to a rural area are significant, offering substantial full time and seasonal employment and contributing to the local economy and social stability.

In order to minimise the negative impacts of the tourism pressure and to achieve the environmental, economic and social goals of sustainability, several management policies have been set up by the Lulworth Estate, which has owned much of Lulworth including Lulworth Castle and Lulworth Cove Heritage Centre since 1641 (Dorset Coastlink & Bournemouth University, 1997b; The Lulworth Estate, 2002).

In terms of visitor management policies, several activities and access for visitors are restricted at Lulworth, including limited beach access, climbing, fossil collecting, and there is a Visitor Code of Conduct. The limited beach access for visitors is managed depending on the area of Lulworth. Visitors can access all the beaches via the sea by boat or the Southwest Coast Path, which has been granted, managed and maintained by the Lulworth Estate for over 100 years. The beaches to the west of the coast, Middle Beach and Durdle Door are open to the public, providing car parking and refreshment facilities in the Dudle Door Holiday Park. However, the beaches to the east, Fossil Forest and Mupe Bay are only open at weekends, and throughout August when the army ranges are closed (The Lulworth Estate, 2002).

The Lulworth Estate also prohibits visitors from climbing the cliffs due to danger of unstable cliffs and frequent rock falls, the damage of the chalk cliffs, and the disturbance to wildlife. However, as professional and semi-professional climbers visit Lulworth to collect fossils or for scientific research, they tend to encourage visitors without experiences or equipment to climb dangerous and unstable cliff formations (The Lulworth Estate, 2002).

In particular, the Visitor Code for appropriate behaviour when collecting fossils or walking on the beach is published and distributed to visitors for their own safety and for conservation of the site through delivering various types of interpretation (Lulworth Estate, 2004). For example, it is recommended for visitors to collect fossils from beaches. However, hammering the cliff face or collecting fossils from the cliffs is banned by the Lulworth Estate. The Lulworth Estate encourages visitors to take a small hammer and hard hats when collecting fossils because of frequent falling rocks caused by weather and birds. (UK Fossils Network, 2005a; The Lulworth Estate, 2002).

Additionally, it is recommended to follow the Visitor Seashore Code to minimise the negative impact of visitors on the environment and to be responsible for their own safety and danger as follows:

- Respect marine wildlife
- Keep the shore tidy (e.g. "take your litter home")
- Watch the tides
- Beware of cliffs

(Source: Dorset Coastlink & Bournemouth University, 1997c)

Interpretation at the Lulworth Cove

Interpretation plays an important role for visitors to understand better the unique environment and management policies at Lulworth Coast. The various interpretation facilities include signs, brochures, guides, publications, the Internet website, and the Lulworth Cove Heritage Centre. As mentioned above, the Heritage Centre at Lulworth Cove is one of the Coastlink visitor centres at the Dorset Coast. It is open every day with free admission and provides tourism facilities such as the souvenir shops, toilets, restaurants and car park. The Centre provides various informative exhibitions and displays showing the geological features of Lulworth regarding its famous geology, the fossils, the coastal erosion process by the sea, and wildlife which are the site-wide themes of interpretation for the Jurassic Coast. In 2002 the Centre expanded the displays regarding the local social history from the stone, the bronze, and iron ages to the present day. Educational tours for school children, students and the public are also made available by the Centre staff (Lulworth Estate, 2004d).

6.6.2 Charmouth Heritage Coast

Location and Designations

The second case study was undertaken in the Charmouth Heritage Coast in West Dorset, on the South West Coast of England. The Charmouth Coast lies within West Dorset Heritage Coast, which stretches from Seaton in the west, along Chesil beach, to the Bill of Portland in the east. It is known as 'the Jurassic Coast' which represents the Jurassic period 190 million years ago and comprises 185 million years' of earth history and is internationally important for its unique and rich geological heritage and fossils (Britain Express, 1996c). With respect to such importance of the site, this area is protected through numerous designations including 'Heritage Coast', 'the Jurassic Coast World Heritage Site', 'AONB', 'Site of Special Scientific Interest' (See JCWHS management plan).

169

Tourism Attractions and Geology

Charmouth is one of the most famous and popular sites for fossil collecting in the UK. Its wealth of Jurassic fossil attracts a large numbers of commercial collectors and international tourists every year. Jurassic fossils such as dinosaur footprints, huge ammonites, and marine fossils have been discovered at the Charmouth Coast (UK Fossils Network, 2005). With regard to the history of the earliest pioneers of geology, the history of Mary Anning who was an early famous fossil collector has been well recognised around Lyme Regis and Charmouth (The Natural History Museum, 2003). In particular, the beach below the Balck Ven Landslide between Charmouth and Lyme Regis is the best place for fossil collecting. Other beach activities, bathing and rock-pooling are also available in this area (UK Fossil Network, 2005b).

Management Issues

Considering the growth of 'geotourism' and the importance of geological science and nature conservation value (Hose, 1995), the National Trust, which owns the Charmouth Coast, is responsible for managing visitor safety and the negative impact of tourism as well as conserving the site. Sustainable land use and management policies are similar to those of Lulworth Coast including cliff erosion and the fossil collecting activity. The unstable cliffs and landslips have been frequently collapsing by the sea in rough weather, especially, during winter time at this site and can be very dangerous for visitors. The natural cliff erosion and the frequent rock falls always uncover a huge number of fossils which could be washed away and destroyed by the sea at any time. Therefore, careful management policy is required in both promoting responsible fossil collecting by the public and conserving the natural cliff erosion to the minimum. For example, collecting fossils from the beach is allowed, but visitors are banned from climbing or hammering the cliff face to collect fossils (Jurassic Coast Team, 2004b; Dorset Coastlink and Bournemouth University, 1997d;Charmouth Heritage Centre, 2006).

For effective visitor management, the Visitors' Code and interpretation have been provided the public with the best advice in relation to responsible fossil collecting and appropriate behaviours for conservation of the site and visitor management. The Code of Conduct for fossil collecting and recording scheme for key scientifically important fossils have been initiated through a series of working group meetings led by the Charmouth Heritage Coast Centre and Dorset County Council's World Heritage Team since 1998 (UK Fossil Network, 2005b; Charmouth Heritage Coast Centre, 2005) **(See Appendix 1).**

The full Code for fossil collecting is of more relevance to the more experienced collectors and it encourages people to collect responsibly in order to protect the scientific interest and their own safety. It is recommended that visitors report the discovery of important fossils to museums or related organisations such as Charmouth Heritage Coast Centre in order to contribute to scientific research (Charmouth Heritage Coast Centre, 2005). It is noted that the policies regarding responsible fossil collecting and the Visitor Code can contribute to sustainable tourism management and benefit heritage conservation, as well as foster geological understanding (English Nature, 2000). In general, the Seashore Code is also provided for visitor safety and to minimize behaviours which impact on the marine environment, as mentioned above in the section on Lulworth Heritage Coast (6.6.1).

Interpretation at the Charmouth Coast
The management objectives of interpretation at this site aim to help the visitors to be aware of safe and responsible fossil collecting and to understand the unique geological features of the site. Further, it is assumed that interpretation can manage the visitors' inappropriate behaviours and encourage visitors' support for conservation of the site. In particular, various interpretive programmes such as signs, brochures, publications, guided walks, and the official website provide useful information about the Visitors' Code for fossil collecting and the Seashore Code.

In particular, the Charmouth Visitor Centre is essential to introduce the visitors to the local geological and coastal environment and to encourage safe and responsible fossil collecting. The Centre is an active member of Dorset Coastlink along with Lulworth Cove Heritage Centre (Dorset Coastlink & Bournemouth University, 1997a). It is a registered charity and is funded by various organisations including National Trust, English Nature, WWF (World Wildlife Fund), and West Dorset District Council, and by public donations (JCWH Steering Group, 2005). The Centre also relies on the help and involvement of the local community through 'Friends of Charmouth Heritage Coast Centre Organisation' and voluntary works (Charmouth Hertiage Coast Centre, 2005).

Since the Centre opened in 1985, the number of visitors has increased from approximately 55,000 in 1998 to more than 75,000 in 2005, including over 4,800 school children as part of education programmes (Charmouth Heritage Coast Centre, 2005). The visitor pressure to promote geotourism and responsible fossil collecting is considerable. The Centre was expanded and renovated in 2005 in order to manage visitors with more sustainable approaches.

171

The Centre provides a large variety of programmes and various events and activities throughout the year for both the public and schools including display/exhibition, films, and interactive computers. The main theme of interpretation within the Centre contains the global importance of fossil sites, the process of Black Van landslides, Mary Annying's home and birth place of earth science, wildlife, marine life, and sustainable tourism management activities. In particular, interactive computers enable visitors to take a virtual dive beneath the waters of Lyme Bay, or to identify the fossils they have found on the Charmouth beach. A number of ongoing research projects on local biodiversity, geology and coastal science are managed by the Centre and educational tours and guided walks for school children and the public are also made available by the Centre staff. The Centre provides tourism facilities including toilets, a cafe, Charmouth Fossil Shops and car parks (Charmouth Heritage Coast Centre, 2005).

6.6.3 Comparison of the Two Selected Case Sites

The procedure of selection and the background of the selected two case sites were investigated. Table 6.4 presents the summary of the comparative aspects of the Lulworth and the Charmouth Coasts. It shows that the case sites are appropriate for this study according to six selection criteria. It is noted that both case sites promote sustainability and the best practice of interpretation as the key management visitor strategy based on the policies and practices of Dorset Coast Strategy, Jurassic Coast World Heritage Site Management Plan and Action Strategies. The main conservation issues and management policies regarding the site-specific responsible environmental behaviour for protection of the site are also addressed at both sites. This information will be the basis of the research objective topics to develop the measurement and conceptualisation of attitudes and behavioural intentions in the multiple approaches in the methodology design process.

These two cases have some similarities in terms of management policies regarding climbing, fossil collecting, and the Visitor Code for appropriate behaviours. Both sites are managed to protect the natural cliff erosion, fossils, coastline and landscapes, wildlife and marine life, which are the main interpretation themes.

However, many different features are also found at both sites. In particular, the Lulworth Coast is owned by the private landowner, the Lulworth Estate. There is limited beach access in the end of East side and Fossil Forest when the Army Ranges are opened at the Lulworth Estate. In contrast, commercial fossil collecting activity is popular on the Charmouth beach. The beach can be accessed through both Lyme Regis and Charmouth. As the Charmouth Coast is owned by a voluntary stakeholder, the National Trust, public donations and community involvement are also encouraged in this area.

Table 6.4 The Comparative Aspects of Two Selected Case Sites

	Lulworth	Charmouth
1. Management plan	Dorset Coast Strategy; Jurassic Coast World Heritage Site Management Plan and Action strategies; Scoping study on Interpretation Facilities; Dorset AONB management plan	
2. Management Issues	Limited beach access in the end of East side and Fossil Forest due to Army Ranges Prohibited climbing and collecting fossils from the cliffs	Popular for the commercial fossil collecting activity on the beach Prohibited climbing and collecting fossils from the cliffs
3. Stakeholder	The private land owner, the Lulworth Estate	National Trust
4. Tourism and Visitor Numbers	One of the most popular tourist destination along the Dorset Coast. 600,000 visitors to the Lulworth site in 2003	One of the most popular destinations for commercial fossil collecting 66,000 educational and family group visitors to the Charmouth Heritage Coast Centre in 2003
5. Code of Conduct	Fossil collecting code, Seashore code	Fossil collecting code, Recording scheme for important fossils Seashore code
6. Site-wide or site-specific Interpretation Themes	Geology, coastal process, fossils, rocks, local social history	Geology, coastal process, fossils, marine life, wildlife, history of early geology science
7. Interpretation facilities	Lulworth Heritage Centre, Guided walks, educational tour, signs, brochures, the official web site, publications	Charmouth Heritage Coast Centre, guided walks, educational tour, signs, brochures, the official web site, publications
8. Participation of the Centre Staff for the research	Very helpful	Very helpful

(Source: the reviews of this section by the author)

6.7 Summary

This chapter examines several elements of designing the research methodology strategy based on the overall research process in Figure 6.1. First, the limitations and problems of the research drawn from the previous studies in relation to the evaluation of interpretation on attitudes and behaviour change are reviewed to develop the research questions and objectives. The conceptual framework of this current study is proposed and modified to provide the overview of complex relationships among key elements affecting behavioural modification through interpretation. The two stages of research objectives are addressed with specific objectives of the two main research questions.

The aims of this study are to determine if attitudes and behavioural intentions toward local environmental conservation are affected or changed by visitors' involvement in the interpretation experience and to explore the various factors or variables that may mediate such effects or changes. Based on research questions and objectives, the research sites were selected through the procedure of satisfying all criteria. According to several management plans and strategies established by the partnership between Dorset County Council and other stakeholders, it is concluded that the Dorset Coast represented a sustainable tourism destination, and interpretation of the Dorset Coast play a key visitor management tool as one of the best practices in sustainability at this site. It is also addressed that the key objective of interpretation of the Jurassic Coast aims to achieve conservation of the site through encouraging stewardship and responsible use of the landscape in a sustainable way (Natural History Museum, 2003). Finally, the Lulworth Coast and Charmouth Coast areas of the Dorest Heritage Coast, in the South West of England, UK were selected to allow an exploration of the connections between interpretation, conservation, and sustainable tourism.

By reviewing the structure of the research methodology, this chapter has established an outline of the general goals and the conceptual framework, and brief background of selected research objective sites.

The next chapter explains the details of the procedures of selecting appropriate research methods, the development of questionnaire measurement, the procedure for data collection, and then, suitable techniques of data analysis used in the main field study to examine the results and construct a conclusion that fulfils the research objectives.

CHAPTER

7

Chapter 7 Methodology II:
Methods and Techniques

7.1 Introduction

While the previous Chapter 6 provided the research questions drawn from a review of the research problems in the literature, the conceptual framework, and a brief background of the sample case sites, this chapter presents an overviews of how the research operates systematically to achieve the research objectives.

Selecting and designing the appropriate research methods and techniques is a crucial factor determining the potential of achieving the purpose and objectives of the study. Figure 7.1 shows the research process of methods and techniques used to undertake the study and to analyse the data collected. First, it begins by selecting the appropriate research methods and research design techniques through the reviews of the advantages and disadvantages of quantitative and qualitative methods. The following section of this chapter explores the process of development of questionnaires including types of survey methods, types of population, sample size, question form, question content, measurement of variables, pilot study, reliability and validity of the measurement. Next, the data collection techniques and response rates are described in detail. Finally, several data analysis techniques used in this study are discussed, followed by the limitations of methods and techniques at the end of this chapter.

Figure 7.1 The Process of the Research Method and Techniques

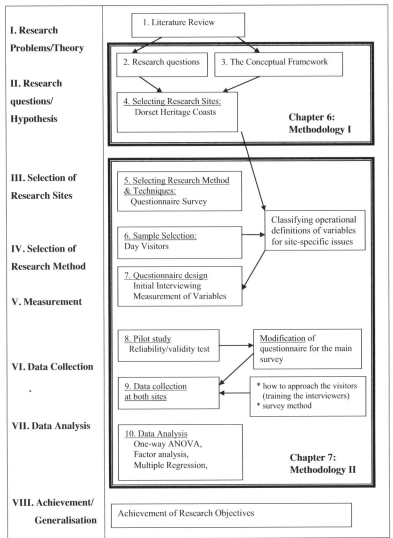

7.2 Selecting Research Methods and Techniques

It is critical to choose the appropriate method to fit the research objectives. After reviewing the advantages and limitations of each research method, this study employed quantitative methods to examine the relationship between numerous variables related to attitudes and behaviour and the effectiveness of interpretive programmes by a comparison between visitor groups according to their experiences of the particular programmes. For the purpose of a comparative study, independent pre- and post-visit surveys were used to compare the differences between groups. The pre- and post-visit samples were screened to ensure that the same people are not interviewed in both parts of the questionnaire and are selected at random using a self-administered questionnaire. More detailed information about this is discussed in the following section.

7.2.1 Types of Methods

Various methods have been suggested for determining the effect of interpretive programmes on visitor attitudes, beliefs, and behaviour (Ballantyne *et al*., 1998). These include questionnaire surveys (Masberg & Savige, 1986; Orams, 1997; Lee & Balchin, 1995; Howard, 2000; Beaumont, 2001; Tubb, 2003; Madin & Fenton 2004), focus groups, interviews (Stewart *et al*., 1998), and observation (Moscardo & Wood, 1998; Littlefair, 2003; Tubb, 2003).

Each of these data collection methods has both advantages and some inherent limitations. The following sections describe briefly both the strengths and weakness of each qualitative and quantitative research method.

7.2.1.1 Quantitative Research

Quantitative research is a good means of investigating a social or human problem, based on testing theories or hypotheses in order to demonstrate causality between variables, their relationship and the degree of them (Neuman, 2000; Brannen, 1992). Quantitative methods are ideal for gathering and recording simple information on the incidence of attitudes, meanings, and perceptions among the population as a whole while qualitative methods provide the means to explore them on an individual basis (Veal, 1997). That is, it allows a much larger sample size, representativeness of a wider population and range of questions to be addressed, but with a corresponding loss in the richness of the data (Ballantyne *et al*., 1998; Blaikie, 2000).

Most quantitative research is generally associated with a positivist approach, leading to laws or generalisations that describe the world and allow good predictions to be made. However, applying positivism is limited to when studying smaller groups in the shorter term and when people respond to specific situations as they see them and make value-led choices (Arksey and Knight, 1999).

As reviewed in looking at both the advantages and limitations, it is for these reasons that the quantitative method was chosen for the present study, to explore the characteristics, attitudes, and experiences of a certain wider population in the particular study setting as well as to establish the relationships between variables which can be used to speculate on explanations for certain findings. Many researchers most commonly used the questionnaire method to evaluate the effectiveness of interpretive programmes (Madin and Fenton, 2004; Tubb, 2003; Orams, 1997; Beaumont, 2001).

7.2.1.2 Qualitative Research (Interview or Observation)

Compared with the quantitative research reviewed in previous section above, qualitative methods provide "depth and detail" (Patton, 1980, cited from Heffernan, 1998). As qualitative methods which are associated with an interpretivist approach allow for broader exploration of participants' perspective, it provides a more complete understanding of individual characteristics, their experience, and behaviour in specific situations (Ballantyne *et al.*, 1998; Arksey and Knight, 1999).

However, this method involves significant cost in the time and effort involved in both data collection and data analysis. It also tends to be limited to small sample sizes and few research questions, which is considered by critics to be unrepresentative and consequently cannot allow generalisations to be made (Ballantyne *et al.*, 1998; Mason, 1996).

Qualitative research methods have been employed in evaluating interpretation. In particular, in-depth interviews, participant observation, and focus groups were mainly used to study visitor use of interpretation (Ballantyne *et al.*, 1998; Tubb, 2003; Stewart *et al.*, 1998).

7.2.1.3 Questionnaire Survey in This Research

Overall, as methodological approaches for the evaluation of the effects of interpretation were reviewed, questionnaire survey was selected as the main research method in this study. Concerning the limitations of the questionnaire method, the qualitative methods have also been included at the initial stage. This approach was complemented by qualitative data derived from the informal exploratory interview which provided a background for understanding site-specific issues and interpretation theme at each site (see section 7.3.1 in this chapter for more details). At the initial stage, the research involved contacting the various managers to elicit their involvement in the study and to gather basic information in the context of both the Lulworth and Charmouth coastal areas. More details were reviewed in the following sub-section in 7.3.

7.2.2 Choice of On-Site Visitor Survey

In order to achieve the first research question, the comparative study was applied by using an independent survey method before and after visitor participation at the Visitor Centre (pre-test/post-test survey). For the appropriate technique of data collection survey methods, self-administered questionnaires were employed in both pilot and main surveys.

7.2.2.1 Pre-Visit/Post-Visit Survey Design

The questionnaire survey has been designed from exit surveys and applied to both pre- and post- visit, along with a follow-up survey. Previously, questionnaire studies of interpretative programmes that are restricted to 'exit surveys' have been described as methodologically weak because 'exit surveys' are unlikely to assess prior attitudes accurately and are prone to 'faking good' (Lee & Balchin, 1995). Alternatively, the more acceptable survey technique is to compare the results of two samples, pre- and post-visit (Lee & Balchin, 1995). A comparison of pre- and post-visit samples will enable the assessment of visitor knowledge gain and/or awareness increase and can give emphasis to changes in attitudes or behaviour as a result of interpretation (Thom, 1980).

McArthur and Hall (1993) recommended that it can be used for an evaluation of interpretive programmes where it is not possible to survey the same visitors both pre- and post-visit. The same people could not be interviewed both before and after they had experienced the interpretive programmes, as they would then have been 'sensitised' by the pre-visit interview, which might threaten the internal validity and external validity (Lee and Moscardo, 2005). Previous researches using an independent pre-and post-visit survey have highlighted that the pre-visit and post-visit groups need to be matched in the distribution of socio-demographics, previous experiences, and psychographic variables. Therefore, the matched pre- and post-visit samples enable an assessment of the obvious effect of the messages and media on visitors' attitudes and behaviour change (Beaumont, 2001; Tubb, 2003). Many researchers used this method to evaluate the effectiveness of the interpretive programmes on visitors' attitudes and behaviour change (Olson *et al.*, 1984; Orams, 1997; Beaumont, 2001; Tubb, 2003; Madin & Fenton, 2004). Furthermore, some research used follow-up survey 2-4 months later to see whether visitors' actual behaviour changed in the long term, and also enabled a comparison to be made of the pre-visit and post-visit responses of the same group of individuals (Beaumont, 2001; Orams, 1997; Howard, 2000).

In this study, an independent survey pre- and post-visit to the Visitor Centre was originally planned. However, the initial pilot study revealed considerable difficulties in conducting the pre-/post-visit questionnaire in the field. As suggested by previous researchers (Orams, 1997; Lee and Balchin, 1995; Beaumont, 2001), the profiles of pre-visit and post-visit samples need to be similar in terms of matching several contaminating factors such as socio-demographics, previous experiences, and psychographic variables in order to compare directly the effects of interpretation on the main indicators. However, the results of the initial pilot survey implemented on August, 2004 at the Charmouth coastal area revealed that it was difficult to match the similar profiles of both groups in the field settings. Therefore, a conventional comparison of non-treatment (pre-visit) and treatment (post-visit) groups by the Visitor Centre experience would be inadequate. A safer approach was suggested that the increased variance can be controlled by making the groups sufficiently large to rely on randomisation in order to achieve equivalence (Lee and Balchin, 1995; Sekaran, 2000). One of the reasons might be that there still remain uncontrolled variables although the suspected confounding factors are matched across the groups (Oppenheim, 1996; Sekaran, 2000).

Therefore, a large random sample approach was adapted in the main survey in pre-visit and post-visit survey design. Any of the visitors to the site were asked to complete a pre-visit questionnaire (non-treatment of the visitor centre experience) if they had no experience to the Visitor Centre. On the other hand, they were asked to complete a post-visit questionnaire (treatment of the visitor centre experience) if they have participated in the Visitor Centre on-site. In this sense, large amounts of data from a wider sample at various stages of their trip experiences was potentially useful in additional investigation of the profile of visitors who had not been to the visitor centre and the impacts of various other interpretive programmes on visitors' attitudinal variables (Moscardo *et al.*, 1997). For further analysis, in determining the main effects of the visitor centre, all respondents from both pre-and post-questionnaires were divided into the three main sub-groups according to their previous experiences and participation in the visitor centre, and their intention to visit the centre on-site, instead of comparing the pre-visit and post-visit samples. The post-visit questionnaires were only analysed to examine visitors' experiences of the Visitor Centre on-site. For more detail, this is addressed in the Chapter 8.

7.2.2.2 Self-Administered Questionnaire

The self-administered questionnaire was chosen for this study as the appropriate technique for collecting data. This technique is considered to have several advantages. They are as follows: a high response rate; accurate sampling; less time consuming; a minimum of interviewer bias and socially desirable responses; quicker responses through a large number of response choices (de Vaus, 19991; Oppenheim, 1996). With regard to the time element, questionnaires could be left with the independent day visitors to complete at a convenient time during relaxing on the beach or sitting near the entrance of the visitor centre immediately after exiting the centre. The questionnaires designed with multiple choice questions could be useful for visitors to easily scan and quickly check the large number of questions to reduce their completion time. Anonymous, self-administered format questionnaires help to reduce the socially desirable responses which might be increased in face-to-face situations (de Vaus, 1991). However, it is acknowledged that the self-administered format may have excluded some potential respondents due to literacy or language difficulties and incomplete response (Beaumont, 2001; Veal, 1997).

7.3 Sample Selection

The specific sampling method adopted in the present study is explained in this section, first, sample and the sample size.

7.3.1 Sample

For the sample subjects, visitors are to be surveyed to assess their level of attitudes and behavioral intentions as a result of the visitor centre experience. The study population group focused on independent day visitors to both sites (e.g. the Lulworth Coast and Charmouth Coast). As reviewed in Chapter 6, the data indicated that the majority group of subjects was independent domestic tourists to the case study sites during the summer peak visitation season between May and September. Also, visitors to Dorset are mainly in the 35 to 64 age groups and noticeably fewer visitors aged between 16 and 24 (Dorset For You Partnership, 2005; Dorset Tourism Data Project, 1998; see Chapter 6).

Based on the objectives of the current study and the key characteristics in the Dorset tourism market, the sampling frame comprised English-speaking adults (over 18 years old) at fixed placements at each of two Dorset Coasts. At entrance points and near the visitor centres, interviewing was chosen for distributing pre-visit or post-visit questionnaires. Non-participants groups in the Visitor Centre were targeted mainly at beach areas for comparison with the participant groups in the Visitor Centre. This random sample was considered with English-speaking day visitor population to the each site (e.g. the Lulworth and Charmouth coast sites) during periods of peak season.

In selecting the sampling design, several researchers have emphasised that it is necessary to make trade-offs in sample design under certain circumstances with practical limitations such as time, resources, costs, and access to the field (Oppenheim, 1996; Frankfort-Nachmias and Nachmias, 1996). Sekaran (2000) indicates that a non-probability sampling method can be used when elements in the sampling design do not have a known or predetermined chance of being selected as a subject. The specific methods of a non-probability sampling include convenience sampling, judgment sampling and quota sampling (Sekaran, 2000). In this study, due to consideration of limitations of time and financial cost, a non-probability convenience sampling method was used. Convenience sampling method is most often used for exploratory research purposes although this method has disadvantages in terms of a lack of generalizability of the whole population (Sekaran, 2000).

7.3.2 Sample Size

The effect of sample size should be considered with the absolute size of the sample regardless of the size of the population (Veal, 1997). The main criteria need to be considered for determining sample size as follows:

- Sample sizes larger than 30 and less than 500 are appropriate for most research
- Where samples are to be broken into sub-samples, a minimum sample size of 30 for each category is necessary
- For simple experimental research with tight experimental controls (matched pairs, etc), successful research is possible with samples as small as 10 to 20 in size (cited from Sekaran, 2000, p.296).
- In multivariate research (e.g. multiple research and MANOVA), a sample size of 150-200 for each group should be estimated (Hair *et al.*, 1998).

- In factor analysis, the sample should have at least 300 cases, with 500 being very good, and 1,000 excellent (Tabachnick and Fidell, 1996).

With consideration to those criteria above and employing the multiple regression and factor analysis for data analysis methods in this research, the samples were targeted for a minimum of 300 to a maximum 500 participants, with at least 200 participants of each pre-visit or post-visit groups for the visitor survey. The final sample size in this study was targeted for 412 visitors at the Lulworth Coast and for 442 at the Charmouth Coast. This moderately sized sample was considered to be adequate for the conduct of multivariate analyses and divided into sub-samples by the experimental control variable (e.g. visitor groups according to their experience of the Visitor Centres).

7.4 Questionnaire Development

Once the techniques of data collection method and sampling are chosen, the questions can be constructed. However, this process had been dealt with several difficulties and problems in terms of not only assessing environmental attitudes and behaviour from site-specific perspectives and multiple measurement approaches of the indicator but also the shortcomings of the theoretical and methodological backgrounds. In this response, several research phases of questionnaire development for this study were conducted to determine the direction of the main survey in site-specific case study settings and to obtain the basic details of visitor profiles and their experiences as well as the important antecedents of responsible environmental behaviour in a particular situation. Table 7.1 shows the process of the research phases of questionnaire development with specific objectives at each phase.

The following sub sections deal with each of the research phases presented in Table 7.2. They include as follows: (1) the preliminary questionnaire development process; (2) the important consideration factors in designing questionnaires; (3) measurement of variables; (4) the pilot study process; (5) reliability and validity of the questionnaire.

Table 7.1 The Research Phases of Questionnaire Development

Time	Phase	Sample/process	Objectives
12/2003-03/2004	Co-operation in the selected sample sites	Sending e-mails to the managers at heritage coasts sites	Obtaining co-operation and involvement from the managers at each site
06/2004	Personal interview Development of Initial pilot survey questionnaire	Selecting the Charmouth Heritage Coast Centre; Observation of the Centre, and other interpretation facilities; Personal interview with the staff and guide in the Centre	Identifying the themes and the main environmental problems and the specific issues related to the Charmouth coast
08/2004	Preliminary pilot survey	Pre-/post-exposure questionnaires Targeting 200 random sampling (collected 92 for pre-visit and 115 for post-visit group)	Testing questionnaire wording, procedures etc. Investigating details of local environmental issues and responsible behaviour
03/2005 –	Questionnaire Design for the main study	Personal interview with the staff or visiting the Centre at the Lulworth Coast Questionnaire design Measurement of variables	Identifying the themes and issues related to the sample site Developing questions and statements of attitudes and behavioural intentions
05/2005 – 06/2005	The Second and Third Pilot surveys for both sites	Targeted 50 questionnaires at each site	Testing questionnaire wording, procedures etc. Developing attitude statements Testing reliability and validity of attitudes and behavioural intentions scaling
06/2005 – 07/2005	The main survey Phase 1:Lulworth Phase 2:Charmouth	Data collection the same way as the pilot survey	Targeting 200 random sampling for pre-exposure group Targeting 200 random sampling for post-exposure

7.4.1 The Preliminary Questionnaire Development Process

7.4.1.1 Co-operation and Involvement at the Specific Site

The initial stages of the study involved contacting the various staff in the visitor centre to elicit their involvement in the study. A letter was sent to the visitor centre managers at each of the heritage coast sites through e-mail, particularly, South East Heritage Coast and Dorset Coast areas, indicating the purpose of the research and asking for their participation in the survey. As reviewed in Chapter 6, site-specific case sites were selected including the Lulworth and Charmouth heritage coast through several criteria. Visitor Centre staff at the sample sites agreed to participate in the study and informal exploratory interviews were conducted with Meirel Whaites, the staff of the Charmouth Heritage Coast Centre in June, 2004, May, 2005 and Maddy Pfaff, a manager of the Lulworth Cove Heritage Centre, in May, 2005. Permission was obtained from both staff for the visitor survey to be conducted with day visitors within both sites on the Dorset Heritage Coast (see Appendix 2.).

7.4.1.2 Obtaining Details of the Site-Specific Issues

Obtaining details of the site-specific issues and responsible behaviour was desirable for a background to the survey and to identify management policies and conservation issues so as to develop a basis of statements and question items in the context of the attitudes and/or behavioural intention measurement.

- Printed Material and Interpretation Facilities

Publications, brochures, and other written information were obtained from the Charmouth Heritage Coast Centre and the Lulworth Cove Heritage Centre. In particular, the Visitor Code of Conduct brochure for fossil collecting was published and distributed by the Charmouth Heritage Centre. The Visitor Code were applied to develop various statements regarding site-specific responsible behaviour and general minimal impact behaviour at the case study sites. In addition, details of facilities, signs, and interpretive information available at both the visitor centres were also gathered during visits to the study sites for both informal interviews with the centre staff and the initial pilot survey.

- The Informal Exploratory Interview at the Initial Stage

The informal exploratory interview was conducted with the managers of both the visitor centres. Staff at both centres agreed to be involved in the informal exploratory interviews at this initial stage so as to gather information on the site-specific management issues and the problem behaviour caused by visitors as well as brief information related to the Centre and interpretation (See Appendix 2).

Through interviewing the managers, the main issues were similar with both sites and identified including cliff erosion, fossil collecting and coastal protection. As reviewed in Chapter 6.6, the management policies associated with each of these conservation issues include climbing, the erosion of the footpath, responsible behaviour for fossil collecting, and beach litter. Furthermore, they also advised the designs of questions regarding attitudes and behaviour toward three local environmental issues and management policies and reviewed and confirmed the final draft of questionnaires before conducting the main field visitor survey.

7.4.1.3 The Preliminary Study at the Charmouth Coast

The findings of the preliminary survey data identified several problems and suggestions in terms of the methodological approaches and techniques. This following modification from the pilot questionnaire helped to improve and make clear results for the main study.

The purposes of the initial pilot survey were (1) to obtain details of visitors profiles; (2) to improve the validity and reliability of the main indicators measured including knowledge, awareness, attitudes, and behavioural intentions related to local environmental issues; (3) to identify the primary belief and feeling components of the attitude measurement; (4) to find an easier way for the participants to answer; (5) to identify the main contributors of responsible environmental behaviour.

Pre-testing of the preliminary questionnaire was carried out with English-speaking adults (including students and researchers at the University of Surrey and local residents in Surrey County) to check wording, sequences of the questions, and length of the questionnaire prior to the final versions of the initial pilot questionnaires and is attached in Appendix 3. The first pilot survey was conducted on English day visitors at the Charmouth coastal area which was one of the case study sites in August 2004. In a total of 207 questionnaires obtained from a distribution of 260, 92 pre-visit questionnaires and 115 post-visit questionnaires were collected at this phase. As noted in previous section 7.2.2.1, pre- and post-visit questionnaires were developed to determine the effects of the Visitor Centre on behavioural objectives. Several modifications for the main survey questionnaires were suggested based on the information drawn from the findings of the initial survey.

Both pre-visit and post-visit questionnaires were designed to find out details of the visitors' knowledge, awareness, attitudes, and behavioural intentions according to their experience of the visitor centre. In addition, their experiences of the interpretive programmes, reason to visit, the experiences of the site and sociodemographics were also included. In particular, more questions for post-visit questionnaires were added to examine the participants' evaluations of the Visitor Centre experiences. The questionnaires include mainly closed questions. Some open-ended questions were employed as part of a qualitative method in order to provide an identification of the respondent's detailed and conceptual understanding of the local issues and the targeted problem behaviours at the Charmouth coastal areas.

In order to answer those aims of this stage, the outcomes and modifications of questionnaires were identified based on the information drawn from the results of the initial study as follows. The more detailed measurement of each indicator will be discussed in the following sub-section 7.3.3.

(1) Visitor Profile and Interpretation Experiences

Initially, this study was designed to categorise two groups: a pre-exposure group who had no experience to the Visitor Centre and a post-exposure group who had experience, to examine the effects of the centre on environmental knowledge, attitudes and responsible behavioural intentions. Comparing the profile of tourists who visit national parks or protected areas with visitors who visit the Charmouth coastal areas, tourists in this coastal area were generally day visitors and motivated by relaxation and tourist activities and were less motivated by learning. In general, it has been shown that 'ecotourists' who visit natural areas have a strong interest in learning, along with high levels of pro-environmental attitudes (Ballentyne *et al.*, 1998; Beaumont, 2001). In this sense, as the coastal areas were selected as the sample site in this study, it would be better to categorise the three subgroups of the sample by the visitor centre experience of the respondents. The first sub-group would be categorised as 'mindless' visitors who have no motivation to learn new things and want to relax and have fun with family on the beach. The second group would be categorised as 'pre-exposure' (pre-visit) visitors who intend to visit the visitor centre but have no experience of the centre. Finally, the third group would be categorised as a 'post-exposure' (post-visit) group who have experience of the centre. Therefore, the outcomes of this survey suggested a division into three groups including a combination of visitors' motivation perspective and their participation in the Visitor Centre. The additional questions regarding the visitors' intention to visit the Centre and perceptions of the role of the Visitor Centre were included in the main questionnaire.

(2) Reliability and Validity of Multiple Indicators

A problem with self-administered data collection on knowledge, attitudes and behavioural intentions is that it can be difficult to find whether or not the respondent's answer to items of each indicator is honestly true. In order to minimise this problem, several techniques were discussed. First, reliability tests of each of the scales were made. The results of the reliability test showed that an acceptable Cronbach's alpha ranged from .74 for the behavioural intentions measure to .90 for the knowledge measure. However, twelve items of attitude scale did not interrelate highly (Cronbach's alpha= .64) in the initial study. After dropping out two items, Cronbach's alpha of ten items of attitude scale was at .70. It was recommended that particular attention needed to be paid to development of attitude statements for the further stages. As suggested by Hair *et al.*, (1998), the lower limit for Cronbach's alpha was .7 for internal consistency reliability but it can be acceptable with at least to .6 in exploratory research. Therefore, three sub-scales were moderately acceptable in the initial study. In addition, the factor analysis was conducted to assess the construct validity and to examine the underlying sub-dimensions of each of three indicators (e.g. knowledge, attitudes, and behavioural intentions). The results of factor analysis of all scales were acceptable.

(3) Social Desirability Bias on Attitude Measurement

With regards to attitude statements, several items in the attitude scale needed to be modified to improve reliability for the main field survey. Attitude statements consisted of 12 questions focusing on the Charmouth coastal area to reflect the diversity of information provided within the Visitor Centre or by other site-based interpretive programmes. These attitude items were developed with a combination of existing measurement statements developed by Tubb (2003), Madin & Fenton (2004), Orams (1997) and the construct of attitudes reviewed in the literature. The four main constructs of the attitude measurement included as follows: i) the importance of environmental protection and responsible behaviour (Tubb, 2003; Lee and Balchin, 1995); ii) awareness of coastal pollution and visitor impact (Orams, 1997; Madin & Fenton, 2004); iii) awareness of the negative consequences of tourist activities (i.e. fossils collecting) (Tubb, 2003); iv) visitor support for management policy regarding fossil collecting (Aipanjiguly *et al.*, 2003). Most of these were cognitive/belief-type statements but emotional items were also included.

The highlighted results indicated that visitors who had experienced the Charmouth Heritage Coast Centre had changed significantly in only the part of their attitudes related to 'fossil collecting' issues when compared to the visitors who had no experience of the Centre. In contrast, there were no significant differences on overall attitudes related to general environmental issues between the sub-samples. Several assumptions can be considered to explain results found in this initial pilot survey including 'pre-environmental attitudes' (Beaumont, 2001), and 'social desirability' (Ryan, 1995).

First, it may be due to a 'ceiling effect' in that most people had reasonably strong environmental attitudes and high levels of environmentally responsible behaviours. In addition, the results of the strong pro-environmental attitude might be due to 'social desirability'. It would be difficult to determine whether a response to attitude statements reflects true attitudes or is simply given as the socially/politically correct answer because most respondents know the 'desirable' answer to a question about environmental attitudes (Ryan, 1995; Orams, 1997). The results of this study showed that most pre-exposure respondents considered 'fossil collecting' as an activity that harms the environment. In contrast, the post-exposure respondents who had experienced the visitor centre thought that fossil collecting activities were one of the main attractions in promoting tourism in the Charmouth coastal area.

Thus, in order to cover this point, wording for attitude statements related to the particular tourist activities such as 'fossil collecting' needed to be more clear and specific as this has ambiguous outcomes of this behaviour. Instead of focusing on the statements regarding general tourism impact, it was suggested that the site-specific issues and the positive or negative consequences of the particular activities (e.g. fossil collecting) needed to be re-designed to avoid social-desirability and to improve the reliability of attitudes measurement.

(4) Open-ended Questions

The open-ended type recall questions were employed to provide an indication of the visitors' overall conceptual understanding of the local environmental issues and to support alternatively the findings by comparison with the results of quantitative data. The main attention was paid to the special environmental issues (e.g. cliff erosion, safety, and inappropriate behaviour causing the negative impact on environment) related to the Charmouth coastal area in open-ended questions.

The recall questions indicated if visitors could understand how to change their behaviour in order to minimise their environmental impact. Additionally, the questions were also examined to see the respondents' overall understanding of connections between their behaviour and the tourism problems of the site. The example question is based from Tubb (2003) such as "what steps might you take to ensure that you are not having a negative impact on the natural environment?". For the post-visit questionnaires, more detailed responses regarding awareness and concerns about the specific issues related to the Charmouth coastal area were examined in the open-ended questions. These questions were combined to address concepts requiring the respondents to recall information. It allows us to see how acquired new knowledge becomes implanted in the structures of existing knowledge (Tubb, 2003). Alternatively, this information helped to re-design the additional items of attitudes scale regarding the site-specific policies and the consequences of the problem behaviour in the main survey questionnaires.

However, the response rate in answering the open-ended questions was low because the respondents tended to avoid spending a long time to write the answer. With some of the open-ended questions repeated and a lot of questions included, the length of time spent on the initial pilot questionnaire was considered to be too long (15 to 25 minutes), and it was necessary to revise the form and exclude some of the variables to narrow down the focus of the research.

(5) Selecting the Main Contributors to Responsible Environmental Behaviour

Due to a lack of adequate data or previous studies in this field, several variables were considered to identify the major contributors of responsible environmental behaviour as well as those of the visitors' experiences of the site. The outcomes of the important contributors to a multi-set of behavioural intentions were identified through the multiple regression and correlation analysis. Therefore, the priority was placed on the outcomes of this survey and mutually exclusive factors are removed.

Initially, in order to explore the visitors' experiences of the site and level of environmentally responsible behaviour, behavioural intention items were combined with both travel intentions and environmental behavioural intentions. It consisted of thirteen 5-point Likert-type questions. These behavioural intention statements included the main two sections, which are travel intention and environmental behavioural intention. A sample of questions included as follows:

- Travel intentions : "I will recommend this site to friends", "I will revisit this area"
- Environmental behavioural intentions: "I will follow the Code of Conduct", " I will remove litter", " I intend to make a donation to an environmental organisation".

A principal component factor analysis was undertaken to explore underlying factors that summarise the structure of this set of 13 behavioural intention items, and to reduce the number of variables into a smaller set of factors for later multivariate analyses. The results of factor analysis showed that the four factors were clearly categorised into one factor regarding travel intentions and the three factors regarding environmental behavioural intentions.

As seen in the outcomes of this phase, the important contributors of different set of behaviour were varied according to the types of behaviour. For example, the results of the preliminary survey revealed that satisfaction and motivation (e.g. learning about the site and fossils) were among the most influencing contributors to two items of travel behavioural intentions statements (e.g. recommendation and revisit to the site) rather than attitudes and knowledge. This finding supports the studies by Moscardo (1999) and Orams (1997) that satisfaction, as one of the basic goals of interpretation, can be one of the important factors in encouraging visitor experiences.

The results of this survey also showed that responsible environmental behaviours were significantly associated with attitudes and levels of interpretation participation. However, the knowledge variable was not related to the environmental behavioural intentions. One of the assumptions of these findings might be due to a lower level of knowledge of the visitors related to site-specific issues, such as fossils, geology, and local conservation issues.

Therefore, the knowledge variable as one of the antecedents of responsible behaviour was excluded for the main survey. The travelling intentions were also excluded due to the different contributors from those of environmental behavioural intentions. As a result, the priority was placed on attitudes and environmental behavioural intentions as the major variables. The conceptual framework for the relationships of the antecedent variables and responsible behaviour were modified based on the outcomes of the initial stage.

Overall, several modifications drawn from the outcomes of the initial survey were recommended in designing the questionnaires for the main survey. The priority of the main antecedent variables of responsible environmental behaviour was narrowed down to develop the focus of the conceptual framework for the research. The several limitations would be also considered including a small number of sample size for this initial study and different visitor samples between the initial survey and the main survey. Although a total of 207 respondents were enough to conduct the factor analysis and regression analysis in this stage, sample size might need to be increased to approximately 300 to 500 as discussed in the previous section. Despite this, as a preliminary study, the conclusions can be a good indicator for a major study. In addition, due to time and seasonality, different demographic visitors might be different from the sample respondents used in the initial pilot survey in terms of education, age, motivation, place of residence and their previous experiences. Therefore, the main survey was planned to be carried out during the peak summer seasonality to minimise the sample bias.

7.4.2 Questionnaire Design for the Main Study

As noted in the previous section, several techniques in the preliminary processes were employed to obtain the detailed information as much as possible from the initial stage including the informal interviews, printed materials, observations of the interpretation facilities at each site, and the initial pilot survey.

The final questionnaire for the main study (See Appendix 3) was designed to obtain answers to the research questions set out in Chapter 6 and to explore details of respondents' environmental attitudes and behavioural intentions, as well as demographic, trip experiences, and interpretation experiential variables that may influence the dependent variable. In developing the final questionnaires, a number of points were considered including length, question style, sampling approach, wording of the questions, layout, measurement of variables, the feedback of evaluation of the initial pilot and the second pilot survey, and reliability and validity of the questionnaire.

7.4.2.1 Design of the Questionnaire

(1) Length and Open-ended or Closed-ended Questions

In order to achieve a higher response rate and accurate response through self-administrated questionnaires for day visitors, some modification regarding the length of the questionnaires and closed-ended questions were recommended based on the outcomes of the initial pilot survey and several researchers (Veal, 1997; Oppenheim, 1996; Beaumont, 1999). In order to reduce the length of the questionnaire using both sides of the page, the main survey questionnaires were re-designed to comply with less than 30 questions and less than 15 minutes to answer, so that it can achieve a balance between the amount of information to be obtained from respondents and keeping the questionnaire an acceptable length as noted by Beaumont (1999).

The majority of questions for the main survey questionnaires were closed-ended questions. Consideration of several advantages in using the closed-ended approach were given regarding it being time-consuming for respondents to answer and for researchers to analyse and enable direct comparisons to be made among different sub-samples (Veal, 1997; Beaumont, 1999). In particular, questions about attitudes and behavioural intentions were developed in the closed-ended approach based on the detail information of the initial study.

As identified by the initial pilot survey, the problems of using open-ended questions were shown through the many unanswered responses regarding attitudes and behavioural intention questions due to a respondent's limited time or lack of motivation to answer the long length of the questionnaires as noted by Veal (1997) and Beaumont (1999). However, open-ended questions were useful to obtain more details about respondents' opinions and understanding related to local environmental issues and responsible behaviours for safety and hazard.

With consideration of the benefits of the open-ended approach, a few open-ended questions were employed where specific details were sought including an 'other (please specify)' category in multiple choice category questions such as motivation, activities, the place of residence, and lists of learning concepts as a result of the Visitor Centre experience.

(2) Sampling approach

Other ways of increasing a higher response rate and of motivating the respondents to answer the questions were considered in sampling approach. As recommended by de Vaus (1991) and Oppenheim (1996), a front cover introduction page for the main survey questionnaires started with asking the respondents' participation to an on-site survey. The respondents were then given detailed information about the purpose of the questionnaire as part of the PhD research and the duration of questionnaire (approximately 15 minutes). The brief explanation of the importance of honesty and confidentiality in answering the questions was given to the respondents. At the end of the instructions, the respondents were asked to return the completed questionnaires to the researchers or the Visitor Centre.

(3) Wording of Questions

As suggested by Veal (1997), the following main principles were used as the guidance when wording the questions for the questionnaire.

- use simple language
- avoid ambiguity
- avoid leading questions
- ask just one question at a time

Wording of questions was evaluated through the second pilot study and modified for the final questionnaires.

(4) Identifying the Questionnaires

Pre- and post-visit questionnaires were developed for different visitor groups depending on their experience of the Visitor Centre at each of the case study sites. As mentioned in the previous section, one half of the visitor group who had experienced the Visitor Centre on-site were asked to answer questions for post-visit questionnaires (participant group in the visitor centre) while the other half of the visitor group who had no experienced the Visitor Centre on-site were asked for pre-visit questionnaires (non-participant group in the visitor centre).

One type of questionnaire for different groups (pre-visit vs post-visit) was used instead of two different types. This was due to the large scope of the sample site across the beach and the Visitor Centre environments to aid easier distribution to respondents. Therefore, as seen in Table 7.3, both pre-visit and post-visit questionnaires consist of four main sections but the fourth section was only allowed for the post-visit group of respondents to answer the questions with regard to on-site the Visitor Centre experience. The identification of these groups was important and categorised with a filter question in the beginning and an indication in the end of the third section of the questionnaires to distinguish different groups. For example, the questionnaire started with a filter question that functions to distinguish pre-visit and post-visit groups according to the respondent's participation in the Visitor Centre on-site. A sub-question followed asking whether the respondent had an intention to visit the Visitor Centre on-site to identify the other sub-sample group of respondents as suggested by the outcomes of the initial pilot survey (see the section 7.4.1.3, visitor profile and interpretation experiences).

The following indications were placed at the end of the third section to invite post-visit groups proceeding to the next questions in the fourth section while pre-visit groups were instructed to end answering questions and return the questionnaire to the researcher or the Centre. Additionally, the identification box was placed at the top of the front page of the questionnaire to indicate pre-visit or post-visit questionnaire by the researcher when collecting data.

7.4.2.2 Structure of Questionnaire

The questionnaire was divided into four parts. Sections One and Three collected personal data from respondents' involvement in interpretive programmes and trip details (Section One), to demographic characteristics (Section Three) in order to build the visitor profile. As noted by Sekaran (2000), a nominal scale was mainly employed for obtaining personal data in Section One and Three. Section

195

Two explored the respondents' attitudes and behavioural intentions toward three local environmental issues and a multi-set of responsible behaviour associated with three main issues using an interval scale. Section Four focused on the respondents' experiences of the Visitor Centre on-site including both nominal and interval data. The structure of the questionnaires and grouping variables into the sub-sections were presented in Table 7.3.

As suggested by de Vaus (1991) and Oppenheim (1996), questions were arranged from easy to more difficult and from concrete to abstract questions. After starting with a filter question for identifying different groups, easy to answer factual questions were asked including trip details, use of interpretation and perception of the functions of the Visitor Centre.

In the next section, more complex and abstract questions were placed including respondents' environmental attitudes and behavioural intentions. In particular, the positive and negative statements, as well as different topics of the statements on environmental attitudes and behavioural intentions were mixed up to avoid response set bias and the possibility of one question influencing the responses to another.

The third section asked respondents' demographic characteristics such as age, gender, educational level, and place of residence, which people are often sensitive about answering. In the final section, the questionnaire for the post-visit group then moved to ask for the respondent's evaluation of the Visitor Centre and their experiences. A copy of the main survey questionnaire is attached in Appendix 3.

7.4.2.3 Measurement of Variables

This section examines the measurement of variables within each of four sections of the questionnaire.

Section One and Three: Measurement of Visitor Characteristics
(1) Measurement of Interpretation Experiences

The respondent's involvement in the particular interpretive programmes was measured using a nominal scale including participation in the Visitor Centre during previous times or on-site in order to identify the sub-groups of visitors according to the Visitor Centre experiences (i.e. pre-visit and post-visit groups) in the first section. The other variables of the interpretation experiences were also measured using nominal scale such as 'reading of Code of Conduct for fossil collecting' (yes/no/ don't know options), and 'level of use of interpretive programmes' (multiple-choice options).

Additionally, the respondents were asked to rate how they perceive the function of the Visitor Centre using a 5 point Likert scale ranging from 1 'strongly disagree' to 5 'strongly agree'. The categories of the multiple functions of the visitor centre which were developed based on the review of Fallon and Kriwoken (2003)'s study contained five concepts including i) 'to provide entertainment'; ii) ' to provide a useful source of tourist information about local facilities'; iii) 'to provide a good introduction to local attractions'; iv) 'to educate people'; v) 'to help people understand the local environment'. This was addressed in more detail in Section 6.4.2.2: Interpretation Channel Factor, in Chapter 6.

(2) Measurement of Trip Features

Trip characteristics of the visitors contained pre-existing environmental experiences and on-site trip experiences variables. First, for the previous environmental experiences variables, previous experiences of the site were measured with yes/no options. The respondents were also asked to indicate how often they visit natural areas on the ratio scale ranging from 'less than once per year' to 'more than 10 times per year'. 'Previous involvement into environmental activities' variable was modified from the multiple items developed by Beaumont (2001). The categories of environmental activities included 'none', 'volunteer work for environmental conservation', 'regular reader of environment, nature or wildlife magazines', 'membership of a conservation organisation' and 'other'.

Secondly, on-site trip experience variables contained 'motivation for visiting the site', 'travel party', satisfaction, and on-site experiences. The statements related to motivations were developed from the classification developed by Ballentynes et al. (1998) and then confirmed the categories of motivations for visiting the site through factor analysis in the initial pilot study of this research. The categorised statements for motivation consisted of i) 'learning about the protection of nature' or 'learning about fossils'; ii) 'enjoying the beauty of nature'; iii) 'having a relaxing time'; iv) 'having a good time with family/friends', and 'other'. In addition, the respondents who had experienced the Visitor Centre on-site were asked to indicate their opinion about their overall experiences of the site. The statements of on-site experiences were matched with the categorised statements of motivations. This variable was arranged in the final section for the post-visit group questionnaires. Furthermore, all the variables were measured using the nominal scale. However, overall satisfaction of the site was measured using the interval scale. For example, the respondents were asked to rate how satisfied they were in their experience of the site on a five-point Likert type scale ranged from 1 'strongly disagree' to 5 'strongly agree'.

Table 7.2 Structure of the Questionnaire and Measurement of Variables

Categories of the Four key Elements and Sections of the Questionnaire	Sub-variables	Measurement
• Section One **Interpretation Experiences**	• Use of the Visitor Centre; • Reading of the Code; • The levels of interpretation participation • The perceptions of the function of the visitor centre	Nominal Nominal Multiple choice Interval
• Section One **Visitors Trip Details**	• Previous trip experiences; • Previous environmental involvement; • motivation; • visiting group composition;	Nominal or ratio Multiple choice Nominal Nominal
• Section Two **Attitudes**	• Overall awareness of the threats to the environment • Beliefs components: The importance of protection; Awareness of the consequences of types of behaviours; Support for management policy regarding types of behaviours • Feelings components: 'concern' or 'worry' regarding the issues or types of behaviours	Interval
• Section Two **Behavioural Intentions**	• Site-specific responsible behaviour; • General responsible behaviour; • Environmental activism behaviour	Interval
• Section Three **Visitors Characteristics**	• Overall satisfaction of the site ; • Demographics (Section Three)	Interval Nominal
• Section Four **Visitor Centre Experiences** Sub-variables only included in Post-visit Questionnaires (Participation in the Visitor Centre)	• On-site experiences of the site; • Learning ; • Evaluation of the Visitor Centre experience; • Understanding and attitudes change by the Visitor Centre; • Satisfaction of the Centre	Nominal Nominal Interval Interval Interval

(3) Measurement of Demographic Characteristics

Demographic variables were measured using nominal scale. The classification of place of residence variable was modified from the initial pilot study because the majority of visitors were from the South of England. They were categorised such as 'Dorset region', 'the South West of England', 'the South East of England', 'Elsewhere in the UK' or 'overseas'.

Section Two: Measurement of Attitudes and Behavioural Intentions

(4) Statements on attitudes scale

As reviewed in Chapter 6, selecting various types of the salient belief and feeling components of attitudes was a difficult task because of approaching site-specific issues and the lack of methodological background and previous empirical research of this case study site

With respects to the attitude measure in the context of site-specific issues and multi-dimensional approaches, it is critical to examine the validity of scale in environmental attitudes, reliability (internal consistency), and multi-dimension of the attitudes (factor principal component analysis). Therefore, reliability and content validity were checked prior to the main study and then factor analysis was conducted in the data analysis process.

In classifying operational definitions of the attitude measure, the survey focused on three local environmental issues and responsible behaviour associated with each of three local environmental issues and management policies, in order to reflect the diversity of information provided within the Centre or by the interpretive programmes at case study sites. The main topics included cliff erosion, fossil collecting and beach litter.

Attitude measurement was developed with a combination of existing measurement statements as in the guidelines set by Tubb (2003), Brown (1999) and Madin & Fenton (2004), Lee and Balchin (1995) and the multidimensional concepts of the environmental attitudes constructs identified by previous researchers (Monroe, 2003; Ajzen & Fishbein, 1980; Orams, 1996; Ballantyne and Packer, 2005). As reviewed in the conceptual framework of this study in Chapter 6 and the modification from the preliminary study in the above Section 7.4.1.3, the multidimensional measurement of attitudes was comprised of each of the sub-dimensions as follows: (i) the importance of environmental protection towards each of three local environment issues and responsible behaviour (Tubb, 2003); (ii) awareness of the negative or positive consequences of each of types of behaviour (i.e. climbing, collecting fossils from the cliffs, picking up beach litter) (Tubb, 2003; Brown, 1999; Lee and Balchin, 1995; Fishbein & Ajzen, 1975); (iii) visitor support for the management policies regarding each type of behaviour (Aipanjiguly et al., 2002); (iv) feelings of concern about three local environmental issues or types of behaviour (Lee and Balchin, 1995).

It consisted of 31 statements on a 5 point Likert type scale raging form 1 'strongly disagree' to 5 'strongly agree'. Alternatively, the measurement of nine items for feelings of 'concern' or 'worry' components were used with unipolar items ranging from 1 'not at all seriously' to 5 'very seriously', instead of using bipolar semantic differential scale as suggested by Oppenhaim (1996) and Bagozzi et al., (2002). All attitude statements were presented in Table 7.3 following sub-dimensions of each of topics in Table 7.3.

In order to minimise the response set bias, some items were made in a negative manner (Oppenheim, 1996). Wording of each of the statements were modified based on guidelines suggested by Oppenheim (1996) and then reviewed by academic experts for content validity. Some minor changes to the items were made as a result of several pilot studies prior to the main study. An overall awareness question added in this study. about threats to the environment was measured on a five-point scale from 'not at all serious' to 'very serious'.

Table 7.3 Statements on Attitudes

Dimensions of attitudes	31 Statements (9 for Cliff Erosions; 13 for Fossil Collecting; 8 for Beach Litter; 1 for REB)
• Beliefs components (B): **B1- The importance of environmental protection**	It is important for visitors to behave in environmentally responsible way (REB 1)
	It is important to keep cliff erosion to a minimum (Cliff Erosion 1)
	It is important to protect fossils for future generations (Fossils Collecting 1)
	It is important to protect the quality of the coastal area (Beach Litter 1)
B2- Awareness of the consequences of types of behaviours (B2.1(e): Negative outcomes about environmental damage)	Climbing the cliffs will damage the environment (Cliff erosion 2)
	Walking off the footpaths will not damage the cliffs (Cliff erosion 3)
	Collecting fossils from the cliffs will damage the cliffs (Fossils Collecting 2)
	Beach litter does not contribute to water pollution (Beach Litter 2)
	Picking up litter will reduce the amount of water pollution (Beach litter 3)
(B2.1(s): Negative outcomes about personal safety)	It is safe to climb the cliffs (Cliff Erosion 4)
	It is dangerous to climb the cliffs (Cliff Erosion 5)
	It is safe to collect fossils from the cliffs (Fossils Collecting 3)
	It is dangerous to collect fossils from the cliffs (Fossils Collecting 4)
(B2.2: Positive outcomes about fossil collecting)	Fossil collecting helps in the progress of scientific research (Positive Fossils Collecting 5)
	Fossil collecting helps one to learn about fossils (Positive Fossils Collecting 6)
	Fossil collecting activities by visitors make a positive contribution to the economy of the local area (Positive Fossils Collecting 7)
B3- Visitor Support for management policies regarding types of behaviours	Visitors should be allowed to climb the cliffs (Cliff Erosion 6)
	Visitors should be allowed to collect the fossils from the cliffs (Fossil Collecting 8)
	Visitors should not be allowed to collect fossils from the cliffs (Fossil Collecting 9)
	Visitors need to report the discovery of special fossils to the Visitor Centre (FC 10)
	Visitors should help to remove beach litter, even if it did not belong to them (BL 4)
	Visitors do not need to help remove beach litter, even if it did not belong to them (BL 5)
• Feelings components (F): **F1(a) – 'concern' or 'worry' regarding the issues**	The cliffs are eroding rapidly (Cliff Erosion 7)
	Important fossils are damaged by visitors (Fossil Collecting 11)
	There is too much litter on the beach (Beach Litter 6)
	Pollution on the coast is being increased by beach litter (Beach Litter 7)
F1(b) - 'concern' or 'worry' regarding types of behaviours	People do not keep to the footpaths on the cliffs (Cliff Erosion 8)
	People climb the cliffs (Cliff Erosion 9)
	People collect the fossils from the cliffs (Fossil Collecting 12)
	People take special fossils home (Fossil Collecting 13)
	People dispose of litter on the beach (Beach Litter 8)

(5) Measurement of Behavioural Intentions

Behavioural intention was measured by the extent of visitors' willingness to participate in certain coastal conservation activities. Based on the review of the conceptual framework in Chapter 6 and the modification of the preliminary study of this research, multiple-act criteria for responsible environmental behaviour were employed and consisted of three sub-dimensional aspects of behavioural intentions toward responsible environmental behaviour as follows: (i) site-specific responsible behaviour (i.e. uninformed behaviour); (ii) general responsible behaviour (i.e. unintentional and responsible-denial behaviour); (iii) environmental activism behaviour.

Table 7.4 Statements on Behavioural Intentions

Dimensions of Behavioural Intentions	Statements
Specific Responsible Behaviour	I will keep to the footpaths on the cliffs I will not climb the cliffs I will not collect fossils from the cliffs I will inform the Visitor Centre, if I discover special fossils I will follow the Code of Conduct (e.g. the countryside code, the fossil collecting code, the safety code)
General Responsible Behaviour (Minimal Impact Behaviour)	I intend to behave in a way that will not harm plants and animals I do not intend to disturb any marine life I will pick up beach litter when I see it, even if did not belong to me
Environmental Activism Behaviour	I will tell people about the importance of the geological environment in this area I intend to become more involved in environmental issues I intend to make a donation to an environmental organisation I intend to become involved in volunteer work for environmental conservation activities I intend to become a member of an environmental organisation

For this study, site-specific responsible behaviour referred to uninformed behaviour which degrades the environment in unfamiliar park settings. General responsible behaviour referred to careless actions 'which the recreationist knows is wrong or inconsiderate, but which he or she does without thinking' (Roggenbuck, 1992: p.163). This might be both unintentional and responsibility-denial behaviour. In this sense, the statements for the site-specific responsible behaviour and general responsible behaviour were developed based on the Visitor Code of Conduct (i.e. the fossil collecting Code of Conduct and Seashore Code). In particular, the items of site-specific responsible behaviour focused on the management policies related to three local environmental issues at the case study areas.

For another sub-dimension of behavioural intention, environmental activism behaviour was selected among five types of behaviours (i.e. environmental activism, non-activist political behaviours, consumer behaviours, ecosystem behaviour, specific behaviour) set by Monroe (2003). The items of environmental activism were developed from the existing statements set by previous studies by Orams (1997) and Beaumont (2001). The behavioural intentions scale consisted of 13 statements using a 5 point Likert type scale ranging from 1 'strongly disagree' to 5 'strongly agree'. As mentioned earlier, all questions were guided and improved by the results of the interviews with the staff at the Charmouth Heritage Coast Visitor Centre and the pilot studies. (see Table 7.4)

Section Four: Measurement of Visitor Centre Experiences

(6) Measurement of the Visitor Centre Experiences for Post-Visit Questionnaires

In 'Section Four' for post-visit questionnaires, this section was designed to investigate the respondents' experiences of the Visitor Centre related to i) their evaluation of the centre experiences; ii) learning; iii) change in understanding and attitudes toward local environmental issues; and iv) satisfaction of the Centre experiences. First, the respondents were asked to indicate their immediate impression of interpretive programmes within the visitor centre. The six items developed by Howard (2000) were used including both cognitive experiences (i.e. educational) and affective experiences (i.e. enjoyable/exciting/ fulfilling/ stimulating/ inspiring) on a 5-point semantic differential scale.

Respondents were also asked to indicate the most enjoyable aspects of learning about the site during the experience of the Visitor Centre with several options. The aspects of learning were categorised based on the main theme of the Visitor Centre including 'geology of the coast', 'fossils', 'marine life', 'conservation', 'responsible environmental behaviour', 'history', 'other' and 'none of them'.

The five-point Likert-type scale ranging from 1 (not at all) to 5 (a great deal) was used in four questions to determine change in respondent's understanding of the site, and awareness of and attitudes toward environmental conservation issues as a result of the Visitor Centre experience. Respondents were also asked to indicate their overall satisfaction with the Visitor Centre experiences on a five-point scale ranging from 1 (not at all satisfied) to 5 (very satisfied).

7.5 Pilot Study

Based on several suggestions and modification from the results of the preliminary study on visitors to the Charmouth coastal area in August 2004, the questionnaire was re-designed and quite extensively altered in the second pilot study stage. Two pilot studies were carried out in May and June 2005 in order to develop the final version of the questionnaire prior to the actual main study. Due to lack of methodological background and focus on site-specific environmental issues, as suggested in the previous section, this second pilot stage mainly focused on developing the various components of the attitude constructs and rewording of the statements on attitude and behavioural intention measurement in order to reduce social desirability and to enhance reliability of scales. In this sense, the content validity was also examined in developing underlying structure of multi-dimensional aspects of the attitudes and behavioural intentions through factor analysis.

7.5.1 The Second Pilot Study at the Lulworth Coastal Areas

In the second pilot study on visitors to the Lulworth coastal area in May 2005, the forty-one English speaking day visitors at the Luworth coastal areas were interviewed using the pilot questionnaire to check the response rate, the selection of the interviewing areas, the time taken to complete the questionnaire by respondents, the clearness of the wording, the sequence of the questions, and the reliability of the statements of attitudes and behavioural intentions.

(1)   Response rate and selection of the interviewing areas

Most visitors were willing to stop to complete the questionnaire in the front of the restaurant areas near the visitor centre and the beach area when the majority of visitors had a rest. However, one third of the visitors were unwilling to stop to complete the questionnaire at the entrance to the Visitor Centre. As suggested as an alternative method, the interviewer distributed the questionnaires to visitors when they exited the centre and asked them to complete the questionnaire in the comfortable seating area and to return to the interviewers later.

(2) Length

The respondents indicated that they took 5 (mainly for pre-visit questionnaires) to 15 minutes (for post-visit questionnaires) to complete the pilot survey questionnaire.

(3) Open-ended questions or closed-ended questions

Open-ended questions were included to ask respondents if they had any suggestions about the Visitor Centre in the fourth section of the questionnaires. However, most respondents ignored this question and did not answer it. Therefore, this question was excluded from the main study questionnaires.

(4) Wording of Questions and Added Questions

Motivation items were added with an 'other' option as the respondents added their motivation for visiting the site on this section. Five items regarding on-site experiences of the site which were matched with the categories of motivation items included in the fourth section to examine the different experiences of which post-visit respondents had as a result of the site.

The filter question to identify the sub-groups based on visitor centre experiences was divided into two questions. First, the respondents were asked to indicate whether they visited the centre today with yes/no option. Next, if no, they were asked to indicate whether they plan to visit the centre today with yes/no option. A question on overall awareness of the threats to the environment was added prior to the attitude statements to compare the response of overall awareness between sub-groups as a result of their different experience. Most respondents indicated that the questions were easily understood.

(5) Structure of questionnaire

Questions on overall satisfaction and demographic information were arranged into the third section in order to move the appropriate flow of the questions after asking the visitors' experiences of the visitor centre into questions related to trip details.

(6) Attitude measurement

Wording of the statements on attitude measurement was altered in order to improve reliability of attitude scale and to develop the underlying multidimensional structure of the attitude constructs through factor analysis. This helps to minimise response set bias and reduce socially desirable responses. As reviewed in above Section 7.4.2.3, the main underlying components of the attitude constructs included as follows: i) importance of environmental protection; ii) awareness of the negative or positive consequences of types of behaviour; iii) visitor support for management policies related to types of behaviour; iv) feeling of 'concern' about environmental issues or types of behaviour.

The major modification of each of sub-dimensions of attitudinal components was made as follows:

- Statements related to 'importance of environmental protection' were reworded and simplified with three main environmental resources and the importance of responsible behaviour added.

- Several negative items of the statements were added into the underlying sub-dimensions related to the awareness of the negative consequences of three main types of responsible behaviour.

- Statements related to 'visitor support for management policies regarding types of responsible behaviour' were also added in terms of three main types of responsible behaviour (i.e. not climbing the cliffs, not collecting fossils from the cliffs, picking up beach litter) and some of the statements were reversed in a negative direction to minimise response set.

- The emotional components of the attitude constructs focused on 'negative feelings of concern and/or worry related to three main issues or types of behaviour'. Some statements related to positive feelings of 'fun', 'respect', 'appreciation', 'surprise' regarding the geological landscapes or fossils were eliminated due to the low inter-correlated items in the results of reliability test. The statements for feelings of 'concern' or 'worry' over three local environmental issues were separated from belief type statements due to the length of attitude statements to fit in the structure of questionnaires.

(7) Behavioural intention measurement

Minor wording changes to the statements on behavioural intention were made. One item related to 'I will tell people about the importance of the geological environment in this area' developed from the review of Orams (1997)'s study, was added. The final version of behavioural intention measurement consisted of thirteen statements.

7.5.2 The Third Pilot Study at Both Case Study Sites

The third pilot study was carried out with the final version of the questionnaires in May and June 2005 at both the Lulworth and Charmouth coastal areas. In total, forty-nine English-speaking day visitors at the Lulworth coastal areas and fifty visitors at the Charmouth coastal areas were interviewed after distributing 65 questionnaires at each site. Although some of the added questions were included in the final version of questionnaires, the respondents took 10 to 20 minutes on average to complete the questionnaires. The reliability test of the attitude and behavioural intention scales was moderately acceptable. The feedback from the third pilot study did not involve substantial changes to content or meaning. Minor modification was made in minor wording changes in the introduction of the front page of the questionnaire to ask the respondents for the honest response on each question.

7.6. Reliability and Validity of the Questionnaire

It is essential to test the survey instrument for reliability and validity in establishing the truthfulness and credibility of the findings of the research (Veal, 1997; Newman, 2000; Hair at al., 1998).

Reliability

Veal (1997:35) defines that reliability is 'the extent to which research findings would be the same if the research were to be repeated at a later stage or with a different sample of subjects'. In other words, reliability is considered with 'stability' and 'consistency of measurement' across time, place, and different samples, and across the various items in the instrument. First, 'stability' of measurement refers to the ability of a measure to maintain stability over time. Two tests of stability include test-retest and parallel-form reliability. In particular, test-retest reliability is obtained when the same measure is repeated to the same respondents at the two different times (Sekaran, 2000:205). On the other hand, 'consistency' is established by examining the correlation of the items and subsets of items in measuring the instrument. There are two assessments of consistency:

interitem consistency reliability (the Cronbach's coefficient alpha is used for interitem consistency reliability) and split-half reliability (Sekaran, 2000:206). Hair *et al.*, (1998:583) explained that 'the indicators of highly reliable constructs are highly intercorrelated, indicating that they all are measuring the same latent construct. As reliability decreases, the indicators become less consistent and thus are poorer indicators of the latent construct'.

In testing reliability, several techniques were suggested to increase the reliability of the measures (Newman, 2000). Firstly, it is important to develop unambiguous, clear theoretical definitions of each measure in the quantitative method. The next step is to use as precise a level of measurement as possible. This study used a 5-point Likert scale which was used in the previous studies of Tubb (2003) and Orams (1997). The third step is to use Cronbach's alpha in order to examine internal consistency reliability of multiple indicators. Cronbach's alpha is a reliability coefficient and indicates how well the items measuring a concept in a set are positively correlated to one another (Sekaran, 2000). Sekaran (2000) suggested that 'the closer Cronbach's alpha to 1, the higher the internal consistency reliability.' (p.308). As suggested by Hair *et al.* (1998) and Sekaran (2000), if Cronbach's alpha is over .8, it is considered to be good, those in the .7 range, acceptable, and at least to .6 in exploratory research. However, reliabilities less than .60 are considered to be poor. Finally, pre-tests and pilot studies can be used with duplication to confirm the reliability of measurement (Neuman, 2000).

For this study, multiple questions were used to measure attitudes, and a multi set of behavioural intentions variables. All the negatively worded items measuring the attitudes were reversed prior to reliability tests. The Cronbach's alpha coefficient was used to measure the internal consistency reliability for the main indicators (e.g. attitudes, and behavioural intentions) and several items in a set of attitudes and behavioural intentions were modified and eliminated to increase reliability through the pilot studies. In terms of the reliability coefficient for the multidimensional aspects of the attitude constructs, the value of Cronbach alpha coefficient ranged from .70 for the ten attitudes items in the preliminary study (the Charmouth Coast) and .715 on 25 items in the second pilot study (the Lulworth coast), to .888 (for the Lulworth Coast) and .875 (for the Charmouth Coast) on 31 items in the final main study.

For the behavioural intention measure, Cronbach's alpha ranged from .74 for the thirteen behavioural intentions items in the preliminary study (the Charmouth Coast), .834 on 12 items in the second pilot study (the Lulworth Coast) to .847 (for the Lulworth Coast) and .814 (for the Charmouth Coast) on the thirteen items in the final main study. Therefore, all the instrument scales for both the pilot and main questionnaires were considered to have an acceptable and good reliability.

Validity

With regard to 'validity', it is defined as the extent to which 'the information collected by the researcher truly reflects the phenomenon being studied' (Veal, 1997:35). In other words, measurement validity refers to how well the conceptual and operational definitions of the indicators fit with each other (Neuman, 2000). There are three methods of measuring validity: content validity, criterion-related validity, and construct validity (Neuman, 2000; Sekaran, 2000).

First, content validity is known as 'face validity' and 'sampling validity' which adequately represent the content population of the property being measured (Sekaran, 2000). That is, it ensures that 'the measures of the variables include an adequate and representative set of items that tap the concept' (Sekaran, 2000:207). Content validity is subjectively to assess the correspondence between the individual items and the concept consisting of a set of items through ratings by expert judges and pre-tests (Hair *et al.*, 1998). For this study, content validity of the instrument (i.e. attitudes and behavioural intentions) was provided using various methods including the concepts from the review of the literature, the preliminary study, two pilot studies, and the panel of judgments by academics experts and supervisors.

Secondly, 'criterion-related validity' ensures that the measure differentiates individuals in a manner that helps to predict a criterion variable (Sekaran, 2000). Two different validities are included as follows: predictive and concurrent validity. Predictive validity refers to the ability of the measuring instrument to differentiate among individuals in a manner as to help predict a future criterion. Concurrent validity is established when the measure discriminates individuals who are known to be different in a manner as to help to predict a current criterion variable (Sekaran, 2000). It refers to the extent to which one measures of a variable can predict a criterion variable currently (Tull and Hawkins, 1990). That is, 'an indicator must be associated with pre-existing indicator that is judged to be valid (i.e., face validity)' (Neuman, 2000: 168). Due to the complex of and interrelationships between interpretation experiences and the main indicators of attitudes and behavioural intentions, the test for concurrent and predictive validity is considered to be inappropriate for this study.

Finally, construct validity refers to 'how well the results obtained from the use of the measure fit the theories around which the test is designed.' (Sekaran, 2000:208). Construct validity consists of convergent and discriminate validity. Convergent validity applies when two instruments measuring the same concept correlate highly. With regards to discriminate validity, the empirical results of two variables are predicted to be uncorrelated (Sekaran, 2000). That is, it is expected that the two variables measuring the different concepts based on theory have independent constructs. For this study, as suggested by Sekaran (2000), factor analysis was used to test construct validity and to establish the multidimensional constructs of attitude and behavioural intention.

7.7 Data Collection Procedures

7.7.1 Questionnaire Administration

The main survey was administered at both the Lulworth and Charmouth coastal areas in June and July 2005. Prior to conducting the survey, the research assistants were trained in the way of approaching the sample to interview every visitor with the introductory comments emphasising the purpose of the survey and the confidentiality of the research in order to increase the response rates. The research assistants helped to guide the respondents to complete the sections of the questionnaires for pre-visit or post-visit questionnaires and where to return the completed questionnaires. The five research assistants were situated in the main five areas of the site, such as car park, beach areas, restaurants, and the entrance of the Visitor Centre for interviewing the visitors. The research assistants asked every visitor to grant permission to participate in the survey. If they rejected, the interviewers moved to the next visitor to ask them to participate in the survey. The interviewers also asked whether or not they were interviewed by other assistants on-site and previous time to ensure the independent random pre- and post-visit samples. That is, the pre-and post-visit samples were screened to ensure that they had not already participated in the survey on-site.

7.7.2 Responses Rates

(1) Lulworth Coast

At the Lulworth coastal area, 575 survey questionnaires were distributed. The number of valid questionnaires returned was 216 for pre-visit questionnaires (Visitor groups with non-participation in the Visitor Centre) and 205 for post-visit questionnaires (Visitor groups with participation in the Visitor Centre). Most questionnaires were collected during interviewing the sample at that visit.

Table 7.5 Response Rates at the Lulworth and Charmouth Coasts

	Lulworth		Charmouth	
	Number of questionnaires distributed	Number of valid questionnaires returned	Number of questionnaires distributed	Number of valid questionnaires returned
Total	575	421	610	453
Pre-visit	280	216	284	211
Post-visit	295	205	326	242
Response rates		73.2%		74.3%

(2)   Charmouth Coast

In total, 610 questionnaires were distributed and a total of 453 valid questionnaires were obtained at the Charmouth coastal area on the spot. Of those, 211 were pre-visit respondents who had not visited the Visitor Centre at the time of interview to complete pre-visit questionnaires survey and 242 were post-visit respondents who had visited the Centre to complete post-visit questionnaires.

Overall, the valid response rates of the samples were respectively high with 73.2% at the Lulworth Coast and 74.3% at the Charmouth Coast. Some questionnaires were returned either by mail by the respondents or the Visitor Centre staff after the survey, as the interviewers indicated the address of the researcher in the introduction section of the front page of the questionnaire. Prior to the analysis of the data, if the questionnaires were not responded to in an honest manner or a majority of questions were not completed, those questionnaires were eliminated.

7.8 Data Analysis

The Statistical Package for the Social Sciences Version 12.0 for Windows was used to analyse the data obtained from the survey. As seen in Table 7.6, various main data analysis procedures were applied to explore the research objectives which were the focus of the study according to the types of scales and methods.

Table 7.6 Data Analysis Methods

Objectives	Analysis	Methods	Measurement of Variables	
			Independent variables	Dependent variables
Frequency distribution	Descriptive statistics (Univariate methods)	Percentages Mean, S.D	Nominal Interval	-----
Test of differences	Inferential Statistics (Bivariate methods)	Chi-square test t-test ANOVA test	Nominal Two groups Three groups	Nominal Interval Interval
Underlying structure	Factor analysis (Multivariate methods)	Exploratory Factor analysis	Interval	
Test of association or prediction	Regression Analysis (Multivariate methods)	Multiple regression	Interval Dichotomous (Dummy variables)	Interval

(Source: Adopted from Hammond, 1995; Black, 1999)

7.8.1 Descriptive Statistics

A descriptive statistics procedure was applied to explore a profile of the sample, allowing for a picture of the distribution of data for each variable and getting a feel for the data. First, the frequency test was used to describe the nature of the responses, for example, demographic details, visitor use of interpretive programmes, and trip details. Next, the mean, the standard deviation, and the variance in the data were made of the interval scaled variables such as the perceptions of the functions of the Visitor Centre, overall awareness, satisfaction, attitudes and behavioural intentions using a five-point Likert scale.

7.8.2 Inferential Statistics

Inferential statistics were conducted to compare the differences between the variables in order to determine the effects of the independent variables (mainly, the Visitor Centre, as well as demographic variables) on visitors' attitudes and behavioural intentions. These techniques include Chi-square test, t-test, and ANOVA test.

7.8.2.1 Chi-Square test

As seen in Table 7.6, the Chi-square test can be used to examine the relationships between the independent variables measured on the nominal or categorical data (Puri, 1996). For this study, a chi-square test was conducted to examine if significant differences existed between the independent variables, such as demographic variables of the respondents and sub-groups of the Visitor Centre experiences.

7.8.2.2 t-test

Both the t-test and the one-way ANOVA test are applied to compare the mean difference between different groups of a single independent variable with the dependent variable measured on the interval or ratio data (Black, 1999). However, the t-test is used to compare the different impact of two groups on the dependent variable (Black, 1999). Several assumptions must be considered including independent samples, the homogeneity of variances, normal distribution, and the large sample size (over 30 samples). In this study, a t-test was employed to identify the mean differences between the independent variables with two groups (i.e. gender, reading of Code of Conduct) and the dependent variables (i.e. attitudes, or behavioural intentions). To interpret the results of a t-test, the significant differences between two groups can be considered when the p-value is less than 0.05.

7.8.2.3. ANOVA test

The ANOVA test is applied to compare the mean scores between two or more different groups of the independent variables to the dependent variables. With regards to the advantages of the ANOVA test, it allows researchers to handle data that has designs involving more than two conditions and to investigate the effect of more than one independent variable on the dependent variable. Therefore, it provides whether or not the mean score significantly varies across different conditions (Pallant, 2005).

There are different types of the ANOVA test according to use of the number of the independent variables and the dependent variables. First, One-way ANOVA is the typical method used to determine if the mean differences between the sub-groups of the sample. The number of independent and dependent variables should be one single variable for one-way ANOVA. Next, two-way ANOVA (i.e. a two dimensional design A × B) or factorial ANOVA (i.e. a three dimensional design A × B × C) is applied to where there are two or more than three of the independent variables and a single dependent variable. It allows the researcher to measure the interaction of independent variables and their effects on a single dependent variable (Iversen and Norpoth, 1987; Black, 1999). Multivariate analysis of variance (MANOVA) is often used when there are number of independent variables and multiple dependent variables, instead of repetitive computations of ANOVA (Hammond, 1995).

Prior to proceeding with this analysis, several assumptions for the data in the ANOVA test must be met in terms of independent random sample data collection, normal distribution of scores, the homogeneity of variance across groups (if not, the transformation of the data can be applied for the heterogeneity of variance), and an interval or ratio data of the dependent variable (Iversen and Norpoth, 1987; Black, 1999).

To interpret the results of an ANOVA test, the F statistic value and the p-value need to be examined. The F-ratio refers to the between-groups mean square divided by the error mean square (or within groups) (Howitt and Cramer, 1997). The p-value presents the probability of getting the F-ratio by chance alone. If the p-value is less than 0.05, the F-ratio is considered as significant (Brace *et al.*, 2000). It means that significant differences between groups exist.

Further, multiple comparisons could be computed to identify where the differences exist through the post hoc test (Black, 1999). There are various types of post hoc tests including Duncan,

Newman-Keuls, Tukey A, Tukey B, Scheffe, and Dunnett's. Among them, a Scheffe test is the most conservative in the sense that it seems to be strict finding of significant differences between groups (Bryman and Cramer, 1999). However, the Tukey HSD post-hoc test allows the researcher to perform every possible comparison and is more lenient than the Scheffe test (Coakes and Steed, 1997). Therefore, both the Scheffe and the Tukey post-hoc test were applied to find out which pairs had showed differences.

For this study, a one-way ANOVA test was employed to compare the mean differences between three sub-groups of the Visitor Centre experiences with the dependent variables (i.e. attitudes and behavioural intentions). Further, a post hoc test (Scheffe and Tukey test) was conducted as well. In addition, after examining the multiple regression analysis, a factorial ANOVA test (two-way or three-way ANOVA) was employed to examine the interaction of the independent variables and their effects on the dependent variables (i.e. specific types of behavioural intentions).

7.8.3 Factor Analysis

Factor analysis was conducted to explore and discover the multidimensional aspects or the main construct of the attitudes and behavioural intentions measured in this study. As indicated by Hair, Anderson, Tatham and Black, (1998), the factor analysis is useful to explore whether rational underlying structure exists in the multivariable data and to reduce many items of each variable into a smaller set of factors.

According to the purpose of the research, the researchers can approach two different types of factor analysis – exploratory and confirmatory factor analysis. Exploratory factor analysis is applied to explore the inter-relationship among a set of variables. The purpose of exploratory factor analysis is to summarise and describe the data by grouping correlated variables. It is performed in the early stages of research, providing a tool for the initial identification of the latent variables and for generating hypothesis about underlying processes (Hutcheson and Sofroniou, 1999; Tabachnick and Fidell, 1996). On the other hand, confirmatory factor analysis is to confirm specific hypotheses or theories concerning the structure underlying a set of variables. This can be applied for modelling data using already identified latent variables (Hutcheson and Sofroniou, 1999). For the purpose of the current study, exploratory factor analysis was conducted in the data analysis process.

Prior to proceeding to the factor analysis, it is essential to monitor a number of assumptions and considerations suggested by Coakes and Steed (1997) and Hair *et al.*, (1998) as follows: (i) Sample size (a minimum of five subjects per variable is required); (ii) Normality; (iii) Linearity; (iv) Homogeneity of sample; (5) Conceptual linkages.

In terms of confirming the appropriateness of the factor analysis, it is important to examine the Bartlett test of sphericity and the Kaiser-Meyer-Olkin measure of sampling adequacy. The Bartlett test of sphericity is a statistical test to examine the statistical probability on the correlation matrix (Hair *et al.*, 1998). It means that the correlation matrix has significant correlations among at least some of the variables. It is addressed that its test should be considered appropriate when there are significant differences ($p < 0.5$) (Pallant, 2005; Hair *et al.*, 1998). Next, the Kaiser-Meyer-Olkin (KMO) measure of sampling adequacy is applied to assess the degree of inter-correlations among the variables. The KMO statistics ranges from 0 to 1, reaching 1 when each variable is perfectly predicted without error by the other variables. According to the guidelines of the measure of sampling adequacy, 0.8 or above is considered good but below 0.5 is unacceptable (Hair *et al.*, 1998; Hutcheson and Sofroniou, 1999).

After monitoring the satisfied assumptions, several steps in factor analysis include such as (1) extracting a set of factors from the data set, (2) determining the number of factors, (3) rotating the factors to increase interpretability, and finally, (4) interpreting the results (Tabachnick and Fidell,

1996). First, in terms of the factor extraction technique (1), there are several methods which can be used to extract the underlying factors from a data matrix. Principal component analysis is the most commonly used approach as a first step in factor analysis in order to select the factors which explain as much of the variance in the sample as possible (Hutcheson and Sofroniou, 1999). Therefore, principal component analysis was employed for the present study.

Next step is to determine the number of factors (3) which best represent the underlying relationship among the variables. Three main techniques can be used: (i) latent root criterion, (ii) percentage of variance, and (iii) scree test (Hair *et al*, 1998). Hair *et al.*, (1998) recommended that the researchers need to use different criterion in determining how many factors to extract in order to arrive at the best presentation of the data.

Latent root criterion (i) is known as the eigenvalue rule and is one of the most commonly used techniques in order to determine the number of factors to extract. The easiest method is to select and retain any factors with an eigenvalue of 1.0 or greater than 1.0 (Pallant, 2005; Hutcheson and Sofroniou, 1999). However, criticism of latent root criterion is made due to the retention of too many (or too few) factors in some situations. Therefore, when the number of variables is between 20 and 50, an eigenvalue rule of 1.0 as a cut-off point is most reliable (Hair *et al.*, 1998). With regard to the percentage of variance criterion (ii), approximately 60% of the total variance (sometimes even less) is generally accepted in social science (Hair *et al.*, 1998). Thirdly, the scree test (iii) is a technique to examine the plot to find a point at which the shape of the curve changes direction and begins to straighten out. All the factors above the curve when it first begins to become a horizontal line should be extracted as the cut-off points (Pallant, 2005).

Once the number of factors has been identified, the following stage is to select a rotational method (3) for the adequate interpretation of the factor matrix. There are two different approaches including unrotation and rotation methods. Unrotated factor solution is a more complicated method to interpret and report the underlying solution. Compared to this, the rotation approaches present the pattern of loadings in a way that is easier to interpret without changing the underlying solution while (Hair *et al.*, 1998; Tabachnick and Fidel, 1996). In selecting two sub-types of rotation approaches (i.e. Varimax (i.e. uncorrelated) or Oblique (i.e. correlated)), Varimax (Orthogonal) rotational solutions were used in the present study. They are easier to interpret and report and seemed to give a clearer separation of the factors (Hair *et al.*, 1998). It reflects the assumption that the underlying constructs are not correlated (Tabachnick and Fidel, 1996).

Furthermore, the guideline for identifying significance of factor loadings was determined based on the sample size suggested by Hair *et al.*, (1998). The sample size of this present study is over 400. Therefore, the communalities of each variable were employed exceed 0.30 as an acceptable factor loading and as cut off value for this study in order to offer sufficient explanation within one factor. Finally, the validity and reliability of the results of the factor analysis were assessed by the split samples method and the value of Cronbach's alpha coeffient.

7.8.4 Multiple Regression Analysis

Multiple regression analysis was used to investigate the relative contributions of the independent variables to the dependent variable (i.e. each of different types of specific behavioural intentions) in this study. Pallant (2005:140) emphasises the usefulness of multiple regression analysis which allows a more sophisticated exploration of the interrelationship among a set of variables' although it is based on correlation. This analysis is a multivariate statistical technique used to examine the value of a single dependent variable by using multiple independent variables (Hair *et al.*, 1998).

In this analysis process, there are several main consideration criteria to be monitored for the validation of a regression analysis. First, it is important to identify different types of specific objectives of the regression analysis, including the selection of the dependent and independent variables. Two types of objectives of multiple regression analysis include prediction and explanation according to the research problems (Hair et al., 1998). With the purpose of explanation, multiple regression is to assess the degree and direction (positive or negative) of the relationships between dependent and independent variables in terms of three perspectives: i) the importance of the independent variables; ii) the types of relationships found; iii) the interrelationships among the independent variables (Hair et al., 1998). For this study, the specific objective of multiple regression analysis focused on the explanatory contributions of the independent variables (i.e. interpretation experiential variables, demographics, specific attitudes) to the dependent measure (i.e. each of types of specific behavioural intentions) in the context of three perspectives.

Prior to proceeding to the analysis, non-metric independent variables needed to be replaced as dummy variables. Several assumptions should be also considered as follows: i) linearity of the phenomenon measured; ii) constant variance of the error terms; iii) independence of the error terms; iv) normality of the error term distribution. Three assumptions can be assessed through an analysis of residuals and partial regression plots as well as normal probability plot (Hair et al., 1998).

Having met the assumptions of regression and the adequate sample size, the next step is to assess three basic tasks: (1) selecting a method for specifying the regression model to be estimated; (2) assessing the statistical significance of the overall model in predicting the dependent variable; (3) determining the degree of multicollinearity and is impact on the results (Hair et al., 1998). With regard to selecting appropriate methods to find the best regression model (1), there are a number of different types of multiple regression analysis such as standard multiple regression, moderated regression analysis (MRA), stepwise multiple regression and etc (Pallant, 2005). For the purpose of this study, stepwise multiple regression, which is the most commonly used sequential approach to variable selection, was employed. This approach has the key advantage which allows 'the researcher to investigate the contribution of each independent variable to the regression model' (Hair et al., 1998:178). As indicated by Hair et al., (1998), in the analysis process by stepwise approach, the independent variable with the greatest contribution is selected and added first in terms of its predictive power for this study.

For the statistical significance of the overall model (2), the F ratio, R square (R^2), the adjusted coefficient of determination (adjusted R^2), the beta (β), and the standard error of the coefficients, value should be examined in explaining the dependent variable. The F-ratio provides a measure of the statistical significance of the model. The F-ratio is considered to be significant when the p-value is less than 0.05. The R square (R^2) value is the square of a measure correlation between the observed value and the predicted value. It provides the proportion of the variance in the criterion variable which is accounted for by the model. Therefore, a larger F-ratio and the R^2 value indicate that the regression model has more explained by variance (Brace *et al.*, 2000). Compared to the unadjusted R^2 value, the adjusted R^2 value refers to the decreasing ratio of estimated coefficients according to the different numbers of independent variables or different sample size and compensates for overfitting of the data (Hair *et al.*, 1998: p.182). The beta (β) value reflects a measure of how strongly each independent variable is associated with the dependent variable. It can be used as a guide to compare and determine which independent variable has the most influence on the dependent variable, when collinearity is minimal (Hair *et al.*, 1998).

However, caution for the level of significance of the estimated regression coefficients in the model must be considered (Hair *et al.*, 1998; Brace *et al.*, 2000). When using a sample of the population for estimating the regression model, the researcher needs to examine the standard error of the coefficients in order to ensure the representativeness of the general population from the results. Hair et al., (1998) suggested that caution for this matter should be made in terms of the sample size. It means that 'as the size of the sample increases, the samples become more representative of the population, and the variation in the estimated coefficients for these large samples will become smaller'. However, it is also addressed that larger samples do not guarantee that the coefficients will not equal zero (Hair *et al.*, 1998: p.182).

The final key issue in linear regression is to assess the degree of multicollinearity and its impact on the results. It indicates a situation where an independent variable is related (r =.8 and above) to one or more of the other independent variables in the regression model (Pallant, 2005). The impact of multicollinearity can distort the results substantially and should be assessed through i) calculating the tolerance and VIF values and ii) using the condition indices and decomposing the regression coefficient variance. A high tolerance value (close to 1.0) and a low VIF value (close to 1.0) indicate low levels of collinearity (Hair *et al.*, 1998). In this study, the tolerance and VIF values were used as a guide to ensure the impact of multicollinearity is minimal in the model.

7.9 Limitations of the Study

Several potential sources of error and limitations might affect the quality of research outcome during the various stages of the research process because of the nature of the explanatory study and the methodological techniques employed.

The Disadvantages of Quantitative Research

First, this research employed only quantitative research methodology. Alternatively, in order to overcome and minimise the lack of depth of response, the researcher combined the qualitative and quantitative approaches in the preliminary study. In this stage, the informal interviews with the Visitor Centre staffs and open-ended questions in the pilot study questionnaires were employed to identify the depth and detail of the issues in terms of the primary local environmental issues, pre-existing level of knowledge and awareness, the primary beliefs, and the types of targeted site-specific responsible behaviour.

Survey Design Error

An independent pre-visit and post-visit test design was chosen and modified using the random sampling approach in this research. One of the advantages of use of this design was considered in reducing the internal validity of the research. However, some errors appeared to be unavoidable in certain areas, in particular sampling biases. For example, one of difficulties of this research was found in controlling the characteristics of the visitor groups. In approaching the independent pre-visit samples who might be assumed to have no experience of the site or the interpretive programmes by the researcher in the initial stage, the majority of visitors who had just arrived at the car park or the entrance of the site were unwilling to participate in the survey. Therefore, this research extended the sample size groups of the population to the site across the beach users and the non-participants or participants in the Visitor Centre. In this sense, in determining the direct effects of the Visitor Centre on the dependent variables by comparing the differences between sub-groups of the sample, the respondent's previous experiences of the site and awareness of the research issues acquired from participating in the other types of interpretive methods (i.e. signs, brochure, or guided walks) might manipulate the direct effects of the Visitor Centre on attitudes and behavioural intentions. It is ensured that it is impossible to control all manipulating variables because of the nature of the field research, compared to the experimental or science research.

Sampling Error

A study sample was drawn from the population of visitors to each of the case study sites – the Lulworth Coast and Charmouth Coast. The specific criteria of the sample focused on English speaking day visitors during summer seasons and selected only two sample sites among five coastlink Visitor Centre along the Jurassic Coast areas. Therefore, caution is indicated in generalising the findings beyond the case sample sites in this research due to the restricted sample and different site-specific issues.

Measurement Error

One of the major problems of measurement error was on the development of the instruments of multidimensional aspects of attitudes and a multi set of responsible behaviour. Due to lack of methodological background and empirical research at the case study sites, the construct validity of attitudes and measurement equivalence might be a criterion problem. Caution must be taken regarding the validity, reliability, and sensitivity of the scale measures. For this study, the construct of attitudes and behavioural intentions was based on specific information regarding local environmental issues and site-specific responsible behaviour, instead of measuring the general attitudes towards the natural environment based on well known scale - New Environmental Paradigm (NEP) by Dunlap and Van Liere (1978) or using measurement verified based on the Theory of Reasoned Action by Fishbein and Ajzen (1975/80). In addition, self-rating methods regarding attitude and behavioural intention measure might lead to social desirability response bias.

In order to overcome the difficulties and ensure the validity of the attitude or behavioural intention measurement, this research has conducted the repetitive pilot studies prior to the main study using multiple approaches (i.e. informal interviews, the judgment panel of social psychology academics, open-ended questions).

Nevertheless, in order to provide the beneficial evidence of interpretation that can contribute to pro-environmental attitudes and behavioural intentions in the natural settings, several efforts were made as follows: a sufficiently large number of samples, two sample case study sites (the Lulworth and Charmouth coastal areas) which have similar environmental issues for the comparisons of the results of the research, and several pilot studies prior to the main field study. This helped to minimise the impact of limitations or errors at each of the research process stages.

7.10 Summary

This chapter focuses on selecting appropriate research methods and techniques through several research process stages (i.e. research design, the appropriate data collection methods, development of questionnaires design, data administration and data analysis) as seen in Figure 7.1.

First, the independent pre- and post-visit sample design and self-administered questionnaires for on-site survey were selected. An operational procedure including random sampling, questionnaire development processes and measurement of variables are discussed. Moreover, the questionnaires for the main survey were tested and evaluated by the repetitive pilot studies. Reliability and validity of the attitude and behavioural intention scales were thoroughly considered and found to be acceptable. The outcomes of the processes are reflected in the corrections and amendments to the final questionnaire. Finally, data administration, response rates and several data analysis techniques, and limitations of the methods and techniques are discussed.

CHAPTER

8

Chapter 8 Case Study 1:
Lulworth Coastal Area

8.1 Introduction

This chapter presents the results of the survey of visitors to the Lulworth coastal area. As seen in Figure 8.1, the results are presented in four stages. For each stage, it provides the main objectives as well as the analytical tools. The first stage provides a general picture of the characteristics of the respondents and their interpretation experiences, as well as their overall attitudes and behavioural intentions toward local conservation issues and responsible behaviour (Stage 1). Stage 2 explores the effectiveness of the Lulworth Heritage Visitor Centre by comparisons of the mean score of the attitude and behavioural intention measures among the three subgroups dependent on their experiences of the Visitor Centre (Stage 2). Thirdly, all multidimensional scales of attitudes and behavioural intention statements are categorised into the factors underlying the factor analysis (Stage 3). Finally, the important determinants of each intention toward the three main specific behaviours were investigated by multiple stepwise regression analysis (Stage 4). Additionally, this stage 4 also investigated the indirect or direct effects of the important determinants on each of the specific behavioural intention and specific attitude.

After examining the findings from the Lulworth Coastal Area in Chapter 8, Chapter 9 follows the same structure based on the findings from the Charmouth Coastal Area.

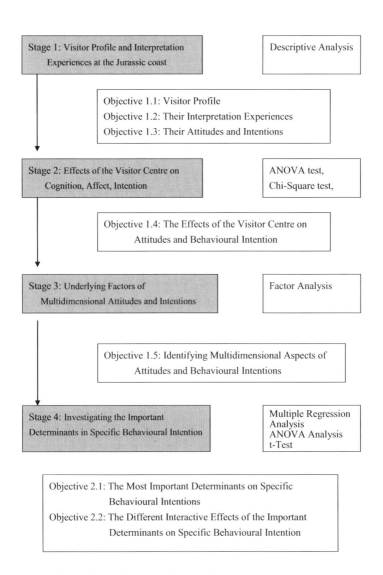

Figure 8.1 The Structure of the Results from the Lulworth Coastal Area

Stage 1: Visitor Profile and Interpretation Experience at the Lulworth Coastal Area

8.2 Visitor Profile

8.2.1 Demographic Profile of Visitors

A total of 421 participants took part in the survey at the Lulworth coastal area.

Of these, at this time of the interview, 216 had not yet been to the Visitor Centre at that visit, while 205 had visited the Centre. A more detail analysis of the respondents' experiences of the Visitor Centre is provided in Stage 2.

Table 8.1 Profile of the Total Survey Sample

		Total (N=421)	%
1. Gender	Male	**215**	**51.1**
	Female	**206**	**48.9**
2. Age	18-25	62	14.8%
	26-35	123	29.3%
	36-45	111	26.4%
	46-55	71	16.9%
	56-65	42	10.0%
	Over 66	11	2.6%
3.Education	None	27	6.4%
	High school qualification	60	14.3%
	College or professional Diploma	148	35.2%
	University degree	186	44.2%
4. Residence	Dorset region	82	19.5%
	South West of England	61	14.5%
	South East of England	196	46.7%
	Other Counties of England and Wales	74	17.6%
	Overseas	7	1.7%
5.Previous visits to this site	First-time visitors	143	34%
	Repeat visitors	278	66%

Overall, as seen in Table 8.1, the total number of males (51.1%) was slightly more than females (48.9%). The majority age group of participants was between 26 and 35 years old (29.3 % of all respondents). Some 44.2% of all participants stated they had university degrees. Visitors from Dorset accounted for 19.5 % of respondents and 61.2 % were from the South West and South East of England. Some 17.6% of respondents were from other counties of England and Wales. There were 1.7% of overseas respondents who were mainly from Germany, New Zealand and Canada. About 66% of respondents revisited the Lulworth coastal area.

8.2.2 Travel Features

Most respondents (39.3%) were travelling with their partner, followed by family including children (23.1%).

Table 8.2 Group Party

Group party	Total (n=421) %
Alone	2.6%
Friends	20.0%
Spouse/partner	39.3%
Friends and family	14.0%
Family including children	23.1%
An organised tour group	1.7%
With guide	0.2%

8.2.3 Environmental Involvement

As shown in Table 8.3, using multiple response analysis, 63 % of all respondent (N=421) indicated that they have not been involved in any organisations or other activities related to the environment. Some indicated that they were members of environment organisations (18.7%), and regular readers of environmental magazines (11.3%) as well as were involved in environmental activities such as volunteer work (2.4%).

231

8.2.4 Previous Environmental Experiences to Natural Areas

This study also examined respondents' experiences of natural areas during previous trips. Some 37.1 % of respondents (N=421) had visited natural areas more than 10 times during previous years. The results also showed that the majority of participants had previous experiences of natural areas at least from 3 to 4 times per year (23%) and from 5 to 10 times per year (24.7%).

Table 8.3 Pre-Environmental Experiences and Environmental Involvement

	Total (n=421) %
1.Environmental Involvement	
No	63.0%
Yes	<u>37%</u>
Volunteer work	2.4%
Regular reader of magazines related to environment, nature or wildlife	11.3%
Member of Environment organizations	18.7%
Other (e.g. work, teaching or degrees)	4.6%
2. Previous Visits to Natural Areas	
Less than once per year	1.9%
1 to 2	13.3%
3 to 4	23.0%
5 to 10	24.7%
More than 10 times per year	37.1%

8.2.5 Motivation

As presented in Table 8.4, the most important motives for this trip were "to have a good time with family/friends" (35.9%), which was followed by "to enjoy the beauty of nature" (34.7%), "to have a relaxing time" (17.1%), "to learn about the need to protect this area" (5.7%) and "to learn about fossils" (2.2%). It was found that some respondents were interested in "taking photos" (4.1%) and "doing physical exercise/sports activities" (0.3%) (e.g. walking or diving).

Table 8.4 Motivation

	Total (n=421)
To have a good time with family/friends	35.9%
To enjoy the beauty of nature	34.7%
To have a relaxing time	17.1%
To learn about the need to protect this area	5.7%
To learn about fossils	2.2%
Other	4.4%

8.3 Interpretation Experiences

8.3.1 Levels of Participation in Interpretive Programmes

'The level of participation in interpretive programmes' variable was defined in terms of the total number of interpretive programmes which respondents had used at the site. Most respondents (53%) were likely to use one or two interpretive programmes while 38.2% of respondents did not use any programmes on-site.

Table 8.5 Levels of Interpretive Programmes Participation

The total number of interpretive programmes	Total (n=421)
None (n=161)	38.2%
1	29.7%
2	23.3%
3	6.2%
4	1.9%
5	0.7%

8.3.2 Use of Different Types of Interpretive Programmes

In terms of using different types of interpretive programmes, the most commonly used media by respondents during their visits were exhibition/displays (44.2%) within the Visitor Centre, signboard (32.5%), and brochure (10.5%) while personal interpretive programmes were the least commonly used.

Table 8.6 Use of Types of Interpretive Programmes

	Total (n=260)
Signboard	32.5%
Brochure	10.5%
Publications	3.4%
Exhibition/displays	44.2%
Films	3.6%
Computer interactions	0.9%
Talked to the staff	1.8%
Guided walks	2.2%
Others (e.g. Maps)	0.9%

8.3.3 Reading of Code of Conduct

This study also examined whether the respondents had read the Code of Conduct for fossil collecting. Almost of 96.4% of all respondents (n=421) had not read the Code of Conduct leaflets.

8.3.4 The Perception of the Role of the Visitor Centre

All respondents (n=421) were asked to indicate on a 5-point scale whether they agreed or disagreed with the five statement items, about the role of a visitor centre.

Table 8.7 The Role of the Visitor Centre

	Mean	SD
Visitor centres are good places to educate people	4.208	1.0222
Visitor centres are designed to help people understand the local environment	4.086	1.0656
Visitor centres provide a useful source of tourist information	3.978	1.0542
Visitor centres provide a good introduction to local attractions	3.902	0.9868
Visitor centres provide entertainment	3.165	0.9607

Note: Used a 5-scale from 1 (strongly disagree) to 5 (strongly agree)

As indicated in Table 8.7, most respondents agreed that "Visitor Centres are good places to educate people" (mean=4.21, SD=1.02), followed by "Visitor Centres are designed to help people understand the local environment" (mean=4.09, SD=1.06) whereas the respondents agreed the least with the statement that "Visitor Centres provide entertainment" (mean=3.17, SD=0.96).

8.3.5 Experiences of and Plans to Visit the Lulworth Heritage Visitor Centre

Table 8.8 provides information about experiences of and plans to visit the Visitor Centre during previous visits and/or this time.

Table 8.8 Experiences and Plans to Visit the Visitor Centre

	Q1: Have you visited the Centre today?		
1.1 On-site experiences to the Centre (N=421)	No, I didn't visit today		Yes, I did visit today
	N= 216		N= 205
1.2 Plan to visit the Centre (N=214)	No, I plan to visit	Yes, I plan to visit	
	N= 156	N= 58	
Missing numbers (N=2)	(72.9%)	(27.1%)	
	Q2: Have you visited the Centre before?		
2.1 Previous experiences to the Centre (N=417)	No, I didn't before		Yes, I did before
Missing numbers (N=4)	N=256 (61.4%)		**N=161 (38.6%)**
2.2 The number of previous visits to the Centre (N=150)		Rarely	N=53 (35.3%)
		1 to 2 times	N=32 (21.3%)
Missing numbers (N=11)		3 to 10 times	N=51 (34.0%)
		More than 10 times	N=14 (9.3%)

First, respondents were asked to indicate whether or not they had visited the Centre during this visit to the site. Among all respondents (n=421), one half of respondents (participant groups in the visitor centre; n=205) indicated that they had visited the Centre whereas another half of respondents (n=216) had not visited the centre during this time to visit the site. Additionally, only respondents who had no experienced the centre during this time (non-participant groups in the visitor centre; n=216) were asked to indicate whether or not they have a plan to visit the Centre during this time to visit the site. Among all pre-visit respondents (n=216), only 27.1% of them indicated that they (n=58) had a plan to visit the Lulworth Heritage Visitor Centre.

Next, all respondents (N=421) were asked to indicate their previous experiences of the Visitor Centre. A total of 38.6 % of them indicated that they (n=161) had visited the Lulworth Heritage Visitor Centre during previous times. In terms of the numbers of visits to the Visitor Centre during previous times (n=161), almost 55.3% of previous visitors (n=161) had visited the Centre between one and ten times while 9.3% of previous experiences respondents (n=161) had visited the Centre more than ten times.

8.4 Evaluation of the Visitor Centre Experience

In order to evaluate the effect of interpretive programmes, in particular, this study focused on the effectiveness of the Visitor Centre on-site. The additional information about the evaluation of their experiences of the Centre by post-visit respondents (participants in the visitor centre on-site; n=205) are presented in this section.

8.4.1 Evaluation of the Visitor Centre Experiences for Post-Visit Respondents On-site (N=205)

As seen in Table 8.8, of all respondents (n=421), post-visit respondents (n=205) indicated that they had visited the Visitor Centre on-site. The additional questions regarding the effectiveness of the Visitor Centre experiences were asked to post-visit respondents (n=205) who indicated that they had visited the Centre on-site. Among post-visit groups (n=205), 78.5% of respondents indicated that they had already experienced the Centre in previous visits to the site. In particular, the post-visit sample (n=205) was asked about their experience, using a number of scales (e.g. educational/ not educational, enjoyable/not enjoyable) where 5 is positive to 1 is negative. Table 8.9 shows that the experience of visiting Lulworth Heritage Visitor Centre was described as educational (mean=4.08, SD=0.807), and enjoyable (mean=3.99, SD=0.855).

Table 8.9 Key Experiences to Interpretive Programmes

	Total (n=205)	
	Mean	SD
Educational /Not Educational	4.08	0.807
Enjoyable /Not Enjoyable	3.99	0.855
Fulfilling/ Disappointing	3.74	0.886
Stimulating/ Boring	3.72	0.877
Inspiring/Uninspiring	3.69	0.899
Exciting/Dull	3.57	0.851

8.4.2 Learning for Post-Visit Respondents On-Site (N=205)

Post-visit respondents were also asked to report what they had learned in the Visitor Centre. The results of their learning are summarised in Table 8.10. A total of 49.5% of respondents (n=205) indicated that they learned about the geology of the coast, followed by responsible environmental behaviour (13.8%) while 9.7% of visitors indicated that they did not learn anything.

Table 8.10 Learning

	Post-visit (n=205)
Geology of the coast	49.5%
Responsible environmental behaviour	13.8%
None of them	9.7%
Fossils	8.2%
Conservation	8.2%
History	8.2%
Marine life	2.6%

8.4.3 The Effectiveness of the Visitor Centre for Post-Visit Groups (n=205)

The study examined whether the Lulworth Heritage Visitor Centre helped increase respondents' satisfaction, understanding, awareness, and attitudes toward conservation of the site. As indicated in Table 6.11, generally, respondents (n=205) were satisfied with their visits to the Lulworth Heritage Visitor Centre, and the mean level of their overall satisfaction was '3.85' (SD=0.96) on a 5–point scale, ranging from 1 (not satisfied at all) to 5 (satisfied very much).

Table 8.11 The Effects of the Visitor Centre for Post-Visit Groups (n=205)

	Post-visit (n=205)	
	Mean	SD
Satisfaction	3.85	0.964
Awareness change	3.34	1.047
Understanding change	3.12	1.139
Attitude change	3.04	1.151

Note: Using a 5 point-scale (1=strongly disagree to 5= strongly agree)

Visitors were also asked whether or not their understanding and awareness of the environmental issues of the site were changed after visiting the Visitor Centre. The analysis in visitors' awareness (mean=3.34) was higher than the analysis in understanding (mean=3.12) or attitude (mean=3.04) on a 5-point scale, ranging from 1 (not at all changed) to 5 (a great deal changed).

8.5 Key Experiences after Visiting the Lulworth Coastal Area for Post-Visit Groups (Participant Groups at the Visitor Centre; n=205)

Respondents were asked to indicate the most important elements of their experience of visiting the Lulworth Coastal Area. Almost 55.1% of post-visit respondents (N=205) indicated that they enjoyed the beauty of nature while only 11.8% of respondents indicated they learned about the need to protect this area or about fossils.

Table 8.12 Key experiences after visiting the Lulworth Coastal Area

	Post-visit (N=205) %
I enjoyed the beauty of nature	55.1%
I simply had a good time	17.9%
I had a relaxing time	15.3%
I learned about the need to protect this area	8.7%
I learned about the fossils	3.1%

8.6 Satisfaction

All participants (n=421) were asked to indicate their satisfaction. Most respondents (N=421) were very satisfied with the experiences of the Lulworth coastal area (mean=4.25, SD=0.910).

Table 8.13 Overall Satisfaction

	The total samples (n=421)
Not at all satisfied	1.0
Dissatisfied	3.8
Neutral	14.8
Satisfied	30.0
Very satisfied	50.5

Note: Using 5-point scale (1 =not at all satisfied, 5= very satisfied)

8.7 Awareness of the Seriousness of the Threats to the Environment

Respondents were also asked to indicate how serious the threats to the environment are at the Lulworth coastal area, using a 5-point scale, ranging from 1(not at all) to 5 (very much). The overall mean level of all respondents' (n=421) awareness was 3.42 (SD=1.07).

8.8 Attitude: Beliefs and Feelings of Concern

The study tested respondents' attitudes towards specific conservation issues and responsible behaviour with two components of the specific attitudes including 22 items of belief and 9 items of feelings of concern. Belief components of specific attitudes were measured on the level of agreement/ disagreement using a 5-point Likert-type scale. Seven items of the 22 statements were explained negatively to reduce the response bias while 15 items were positive. All seven negative items were reverse coded prior to further analysis. In addition, feeling components of the specific attitudes were measured on level of concern for the environmental issues and problem behaviours using a 5-point Likert type scale (1=not all seriously to 5=very seriously).

Table 8.14 Attitude Statements (Beliefs and Feelings of Concern)

I think that…… & I am concerned that ……..	Mean	SD
1. I think that it is important to protect the quality of the coastal area	4.73	0.650
2. I think that beach litter does **NOT** contribute to water pollution *(= does contribute to water pollution)	4.71	0.810
3. I think that it is important for visitors to behave in an environmentally responsible way	4.68	0.724
4. I think that picking up litter will reduce the amount of water pollution	4.60	0.798
5. I think that it is important to protect fossils for future generations	4.53	0.826
6. I think that it is important to keep cliff erosion to a minimum	4.51	0.917
7.I think that it is **safe** to climb the cliffs (* dangerous to climb)	4.37	0.975
8. I think that it is dangerous to climb the cliffs	4.35	1.004
9. I think that visitors do **NOT** need to help remove beach litter, even if it did not belong to them * (=do need to help)	4.34	0.949
10. I am concerned that pollution on the coast is being increased by beach litter	4.34	0.909
11. I am concerned that people dispose of litter on the beach	4.33	0.938
12. I think that visitors should help to remove beach litter, even if it did not belong to them	4.30	0.988
13. I think that it is **safe** to collect fossils from the cliffs (*= dangerous to collect)	4.13	1.037
14. I think that collecting fossils from the cliffs will damage the cliffs	4.10	1.027
15. I think that visitors need to report the discovery of special fossils to the Lulworth Heritage Visitor Centre	4.08	1.021
16. I think that it is dangerous to collect fossils from the cliffs	4.08	0.982
17. I think that climbing cliffs will damage the environment	4.02	1.094
18. I am concerned that there is too much litter on the beach	4.00	1.012
19. I think that visitors **should be allowed to climb** the cliffs *(=should not be allowed to climb)	3.99	1.165
20. I think that visitors should not be allowed to collect fossils from the cliffs	3.95	1.076
21. I think that walking off the footpaths **will NOT damage** the cliffs *(=will damage)	3.93	1.193
22. I think that fossil collecting helps the progress of scientific research	3.75	1.089
23. I am concerned that important fossils are damaged by visitors	3.72	0.991
24. I think that visitors **should be allowed to collect** the fossils _from the cliffs_ *(=should not be allowed to collect)	3.71	1.145
25. I am concerned that the cliffs are eroding rapidly	3.69	0.974
26. I am concerned that people take special fossils home	3.65	1.058
27. I think that fossil collecting helps one to learn about fossils	3.59	1.082
28. I am concerned that people collect the fossils from the cliffs	3.56	1.032
29. I am concerned that people climb the cliffs	3.47	1.057
30. I am concerned that people do not keep to the footpaths on the cliffs	3.44	1.108
31. I think that fossil collecting activities by visitors make a positive contribution to the economy of the local area	2.87	1.203

Note: * negative items reverse coded prior to further analysis; Using a 5-point Likert type scale

The main concepts of the attitude statements included the specific environmental issues of the site such as cliff erosion, fossil collecting, and coastal pollution. All 31 attitude statements were computed and summed up for overall attitude measure. Overall, the total mean score of all 31 attitude statements was generally high (mean=4.05, SD=0.478) with the reliability (Cronbach's Alpha=.888). As indicated in Table 8.14, most respondents showed a strongly positive environmental attitude towards the importance of environmental protection regarding the quality of coastal areas, responsible behaviour, fossils, and cliff erosion. In particular, most respondents agreed strongly with 'it is important to protect the quality of the coastal area (mean=4.73)', and 'beach litter contribute to water pollution (mean=4.71)'. Yet, they generally disagreed with the economic benefits of fossil collecting activities (mean=2.87).

With regards to two key specific conservation issues in this site, 'cliff erosion' and 'fossils', most visitors agreed positively with belief statements regarding 'cliff erosion' and 'fossil collecting'. For example, visitors indicated that they agreed with the belief statements, 'it is important to keep cliff erosion to a minimum' (mean=4.51), 'it is dangerous to climb the cliffs' (mean=4.35), and 'climbing the cliffs will damage the cliffs' (mean=4.02). In addition, most respondents also strongly agreed with belief statements regarding negative impacts of 'fossil collecting' (i.e. 'it is safe (=dangerous) to collect fossils from the cliffs' (mean= 4.13); 'collecting fossils from the cliffs will damage the cliffs' (mean=4.10) rather than other statements regarding positive impacts of 'fossil collecting' i.e. 'fossil collecting helps in the progress of scientific research' (mean=3.75); 'fossil collecting helps one to learn about fossils' (mean=3.59).

With regard to 'visitors' support for management policies regarding specific responsible behaviour for conservation of the site, most participants agreed positively with the belief statements regarding three conservation topics (i.e. 'visitors do NOT need (*= do need) to help remove beach litter, even if it did not belong to them' (mean=4.34); 'visitors need to report the discovery of special fossils to the Lulworth Heritage Visitor Centre' (mean=4.08). However, they agreed less with two types of belief statements regarding the 'climbing' (i.e. 'visitors should (*=should NOT) be allowed to climb the cliffs' (mean=3.99) and 'fossil collecting' policies (i.e. 'visitors should not be allowed to collect fossils from the cliffs' (mean=3.95) (* negative statements for this: mean=3.71).

In terms of feelings of concern components of specific attitudes, most of the respondents have high levels of concern about coastal pollution (mean=4.34, S.D.=0.91) while they have moderate levels of concern about people 'collecting the fossils from the cliffs' (mean=3.56), 'walking off the footpaths' (mean=3.43, S.D.=1.11), and 'climbing the cliffs' (mean=3.47, S.D.=1.06).

8.9 Behavioural Intentions

This question was used to examine the degree of commitment respondents had to changing their behaviour toward conservation. The thirteen statements of behavioural intention were measured on a 5-point Likert scale (1=strongly disagree to 5=strongly agree). The thirteen statements for behavioural intentions include the three types of behavior, 'specific responsible behaviour at particular site', 'general environmental behaviour', and 'environmental activism'. The overall behavioural intention scale was created as the sum of the items divided by 13 to compute an overall score. The overall mean score of intentions toward environmentally responsible behaviour was generally high with 3.68 (SD=0.63) with the reliability coefficient of 0.847.

Intentions to change behaviour toward the environment were strongest in relation to 'behaving in a way that will not harm plants and animals' (mean=4.64, SD=0.66), 'following the Code of Conduct'(mean=4.51, SD=0.81) and 'not disturbing the marine life' (mean=4.46, SD=0.87)'. The respondents' intentions toward the environmental activism were less favourable on four statements including 'involvement with environmental issues (mean= 3.14)' 'donation (mean= 2.71)', 'membership of environmental organisations (mean=2.24)' and 'volunteer work (mean=2.16)'.

Table 8.15 Behavioural Intentions

I intend to....	Mean	SD
I intend to behave in a way that will not harm plants and animals	4.64	0.655
I will follow the Code of Conduct	4.51	0.807
I do not intend to disturb any marine life	4.46	0.871
I will keep to the footpaths on the cliffs	4.39	1.002
I will inform the Lulworth Heritage Visitor Centre, if I discover special fossils	4.25	1.007
I will not climb the cliffs	4.20	1.094
I will not collect fossils from the cliff	4.15	1.088
I will pick up beach litter when I see it, even if it did not belong to me	3.59	1.193
I will tell people about the importance of the geological environment in this area	3.48	1.247
I intend to become more involved in environmental issues	3.14	1.057
I intend to make a donation to an environmental organisation	2.71	1.535
I intend to become a member of an environmental organisation	2.24	1.204
I intend to become involved in volunteer work for environmental conservation activities	2.16	1.082

With regard to specific behavioural intention, most visitors have higher levels of willingness with 'informing the Centre about the discovery of special fossils' (mean=4.25), 'not climbing the cliffs' (mean=4.20), 'not collecting the fossils from the cliffs' (mean=4.15) while they have lower levels of willingness with 'removing beach litter' (mean=3.59).

Summary of Stage 1: The Visitor Profile and Interpretation Experience at the Lulworth Coastal Area

This study has provided an insight into the visitor profile, their experience of this site and various interpretive programmes, as well as attitudes and behavioural intentions towards the environmental issues and responsible behaviour.

Research Objective 1.1: Who is Visiting the Lulworth Coastal Area?

First, the data indicates that well-educated adults, couples and families including children groups, younger and middle aged adults (between 25 to 45 years old), domestic and repeated visitors were the major demographic groups. Almost 37% of visitors were involved in environmental organisations or activities and most respondents were likely to visit natural areas more than three times per year. The pre-existing attitude variables showed that respondents who visited the Lulworth coastal areas were already interested in and concerned for the natural environment. The most important motives for respondents were having a good time with family/friends and enjoying nature.

Research Objective 1.2: What Did They Experience during Their Visit to the Lulworth Coastal Area?

Experiences of The Sample Site

Most respondents were also very satisfied with their visit to the Lulworth Coastal Area. This study also found that the important experiences after visiting the Lulworth Coastal Area by post-visit respondents (n=205) were 'enjoying the beauty of nature', followed by 'having a good time' while 'learning experience' was generally the least important experiences. This was corresponded with their important motives for visiting this site.

Experiences of Various Interpretive Programmes

The results show that the most important information sources used were 'exhibition/display' and 'signboard' while almost 38% of respondents did not use any information during their visit to this site. Additionally, only 3.6% of all visitors (n=421) read the Code of Conduct brochure on fossil collecting which presented important information related to responsible environmental behaviour to help protect this part of the Jurassic coastal area.

In order to evaluate the effects of interpretive programmes, in particular, this study focused on the effects of the Lulworth Heritage Visitor Centre. With regard to the role of the Visitor Centre, most respondents agreed with the educational role of the Visitor Centre. After the experience of visiting Lulworth Heritage Visitor Centre, the results indicated that their experience of the Visitor Centre was educational and enjoyable. Post-visit respondents (n=205) showed that they learned mostly about 'geology of the coast' and 'responsible environmental behaviour'. Respondents who had visited the Centre indicated that they had a moderate level of satisfaction of the Centre experiences as well as a moderate level of awareness, understanding and attitude change toward environmental conservation.

Research Objective 1.3: Attitude and Behavioural Intentions toward Conservation Issues and Responsible Behaviour

In terms of respondents' attitudes and intentions toward conservation issues and responsible behaviour, most visitors had strongly positive environmental attitudes on the 'coastal protection' and beach litter issue rather than the two other site-specific issues (protection of cliff erosion and fossils). Overall, visitors were likely to be aware of the local environmental issues and problems, and they were concerned about the negative impacts of problem behaviour on the environment. In turn, they were likely to behave in a responsible environmental way in order to protect the Lulworth coastal area. However, the results present that a majority of visitors had a lower level of behavioural intentions to engage in environmental activism and removing beach litter behaviour.

Stage 2: The Effects of the Visitor Centre on Attitudes and Intentions by Comparison among the Three Sub-Groups

The main aim of this study was to explore the effects of interpretation experiences provided at the Visitor Center on visitors' attitudes and behavioural intentions. For this purpose, first, three subgroups were categorised depending on their experience of the Visitor Centre: **(1) Group A:** 'those who had not visited the Centre at all and had no intention of doing so', **(2) Group B:** 'those who had a plan to visit the Centre but had not visited before', and **(3) 'Group C:** 'those who had visited the Centre before and/or on this occasion'. Next step examined any significant differences that existed among those three sub-groups in visitors' demographic and other experience factors. Furthermore, after comparing the visitor profile among the three sub-groups, the effects of the Visitor Centre on attitudes and intentions were investigated. A series of Chi-Square and ANOVA tests were conducted to determine if there were any significant differences in the responses of the three sub-samples.

8.10 Formation of Three Sub-groups

To examine the effect of the Visitor Centre on visitors' attitudes and behavioural intentions, the study examined the different levels of visitors' experience of the Lulworth Heritage Visitor Centre for both pre-visit and post-visit respondents.

There were three main questions (1) visitors' experience of the Centre this time on this visit' (2) visitors' past experience of the Centre, and (3) visitors' intention to visit the Centre this occasion. Through those three main questions, the total sample was divided into four sub-groups (1) those who had not visited the Centre before and had no intention of doing so, (2) those who planned to visit the Centre on this occasion but had no previous experience of the Centre, (3) those who had not visited the Centre yet on this occasion but had previous experience of the Centre, (4) those who visited the Centre this occasion.

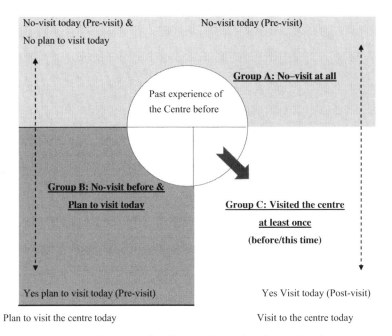

Figure 8.2 Diagram of the Three Sub-Groups of the Visitor Centre Experience

A series of ANOVA tests showed that there were significant differences between the four sub-groups. However, the post hoc test (Tukey method) indicated that there were no significant differences between (3) those who had not visited today but had previous experience of the Centre and (4) those who visited the Centre this time. Hence these two groups were combined, and three main sub groups were formed, as shown in Figure 8.2. These three sub-groups were used to determine the effects of the Visitor Centre on visitors' attitudes and behavioural intention in further analysis.

8.11 Description of the Overall Sample among the Three Sub-Groups

Overall, the individual characteristics of the three sub-groups had similar profiles. A series of chi-square tests indicated that there were no significant differences in most of the individual characteristic profiles among the three samples.

Table 8.16 Comparison of Visitor Profile by the Three Sub-Groups

	Group A: No-visit (n=122)	Group B: Plan to visit (n=44)	Group C: Visited at least once (n=255)	Chi-Square	Sig.
1. Age					
18-25	22.8%	9.1%	11.6%		
26-35	35.0%	54.5%	22.3%		
36-45	20.3%	20.5%	30.3%	38.169	.000
46-55	13.0%	13.6%	19.5%		
56-65	8.1%	2.3%	12.4%		
Over 66	0.8%	0%	4.0%		
2.Education					
None	7.3%	6.8%	6.0%		
High school qualification	11.4%	6.8%	17.1%	12.895	.045
College or professional diploma	26.8%	36.4%	38.9%		
University degree	54.5%	50.0%	38.1%		
3. Previous Experiences of Natural Areas					
Less than once to 2 times per year	23.8%	22.7%	9.8%	15.827	.003
3 to 4 times per year	20.5%	27.3%	23.5%		
More than 5 times per year	55.7%	50.0%	66.7%		
4. Motivation					
To have a good time with family/friends	46.7%	40.9%	29.4%		
To learn about the need to protect this area	**0.8%**	**2.3%**	**8.8%**		
To have a relaxing time	16.7%	25.0%	16.0%	24.75	.016
To enjoy the beauty of nature	31.7%	27.3%	37.4%		
To learn about fossils	**2.5%**	**0%**	**2.5%**		
Other (talking photos and doing sports)	1.7%	4.5%	5.5%		

However, significant differences were found in relation to age, education, previous experiences of natural areas, and motivation (See Table 8.16). Most (67.7%) of the third group who had visited the

248

Centre at least once were older adults (over 35 years old). Also, the third group (11.3%) were more interested in "learning about fossils or protection of the site" than the other two groups.

Table 8.17 shows that there were significant differences among three sub-groups in terms of the perception of the role of Visitor Centres, levels of interpretation and reading of the Code of Conduct. With regard to the perception of the role of Visitor Centres, the results of ANOVA test indicated that the 'plan to visit' group (B) had higher mean scores (mean=4.25) in one item, "visitor centres are designed to help people understand the local environment" than the 'no-visit' group (A) (mean=3.88) and the 'visited the Centre at least once' group (C) (mean=4.16). (See Table 8.17)

Table 8.17 Comparison of Interpretation Experiences by the Three Sub- Groups

	Group A: No-visit (n=122)	Group B: Plan to visit (n=44)	Group C: Visited at least once (n=255)		
• *ANOVA test*	*Mean(S.D)*	*Mean(S.D)*	*Mean(S.D)*	*F*	*Sig.*
1. Role of visitor centres Visitor centres are designed to help people understand the local environment	3.88 (1.088)	4.25 (0.918)	4.16 (1.076)	3.469	.032
Chi-Square test	*% (n)*	*% (n)*	*% (n)*	*Chi-Square*	*Sig.*
2. Level of Interpretation Participation None (n=161) Low level (1-2) (n=223) High level (3-5) (n=37)	75.4%(92) 23.8%(29) 0.8%(1)	47.7%(21) 52.3%(23) 0%(0)	18.8%(48) 67.1%(171) 14.1%(36)	120.369	.000
3. Read of Code of Conduct brochure Yes No	0 100%	0 100%	5.9%(15) 94.1%(240)	10.065	.007

A Chi-Square test was used to determine whether significant differences among the three subgroups existed in terms of levels of interpretation and reading of the Code of Conduct. The results of Chi-Square tests showed that there were significant differences between the three sub-groups (p=.000) in levels of interpretation participation. Most Group C respondents who had experienced the Visitor Centre before and this time were likely to use a number of different types of interpretive components while other Group A and Group B respondents were likely to use only one or two interpretive programmes which are mainly 'signboard' and 'brochures'. As seen in Table 8.17, Group C samples had reading the Code of Conduct brochure (5.9%) more than the other two groups (0%).

8.12 Comparison of Satisfaction by the Three Sub-Groups

No significant differences were found related to satisfaction between three subgroups

8.13 Comparison of Awareness of the Seriousness of Threats to the Environment among the Three Subgroups

The results of ANOVA test showed that there were significant differences (F=3.240, p=0.040) among the three samples. The 'visited the Centre at least once' group C (mean=3.53, SD=1.029) had a higher level of mean score than the 'no-visit' group A (mean=3.24, SD=1.135) and the 'plan to visit' group B (mean=3.30, SD=1.059) in their awareness of the seriousness of threats to the environment.

8.14 Comparison of Attitudes (Beliefs and Feelings of Concern) among the Three Subgroups

Differences of attitudes among the three groups toward specific environmental issues and problem behaviours were examined. As seen in Table 8.18, significant differences among the three sub-samples were found in beliefs about the specific issues regarding 'cliff erosion' and 'climbing', 'importance of protection' and 'negative impacts of fossil collecting', and 'support for picking up beach litter'. Overall, the Visitor Centre experiences appeared to have influenced significantly and positively visitors' level of beliefs and concerns toward 'cliff erosions' and 'climbing the cliffs',

250

followed by 'beliefs and concern of negative impacts of fossil collecting'. However, no significant differences were found on beliefs and concern toward 'negative impacts of beach litter' as well as beliefs about 'positive outcomes of fossil collecting' (e.g. 'helping science research' and 'economic value of the fossil collecting').

As expected, the 'visited the Centre at least once' group C had a higher score of these conservation issues than the other two groups (Group B and Group C). With regard to comparisons among the three sub groups, most of three different groups agreed positively with most specific issues about cliff erosion and fossil. It means that most visitors were already aware of specific environmental issues and negative impacts of problem behaviours even though Group A respondents who had not used any information also had moderate levels of attitudes.

More detailed, post-hoc tests showed that significant differences between Group B and Group C were found in beliefs about 'it is dangerous to climb the cliffs', 'it is safe (=dangerous) to collect fossils from the cliffs', and concern about 'people not keeping the footpaths on the cliffs'. This means that visitors were more aware of personal safety with relation to the consequences of 'climbing the cliffs' as a result of the Visitor Centre experience. In comparisons between Group A and Group C, Group A respondents had a lower level of attitudes toward specific issues regarding the 'cliff erosion' and 'fossils' issues, and were significantly different from Group C, who had experienced the Visitor Centre on these specific issues. Finally, in comparisons between Group A and Group B, no significant differences were found between the two groups.

Table 8.18 Comparison of Attitude by the Three Sub-Groups

	Group A: No-visit (n=122)		Group B: Plan to visit (n=44)		Group C: Visited at least once (n=255)		F	Sig.
	Mean	SD	Mean	SD	Mean	SD		
I think that it is *important* for visitors to behave in an environmentally responsible way	4.54	0.873	4.66	0.568	4.75	0.659	3.332	0.037
I think that it is *important* to protect the quality of the coastal area	4.57	0.792	4.66	0.645	4.81	0.555	6.481	0.002
I think that it *is important* to keep cliff erosion to a minimum	4.26	1.119	4.48	0.628	4.64	0.825	7.056	0.001
I think that it is *important* to protect fossils for future generations	4.31	1.035	4.50	0.629	4.64	0.718	6.863	0.001
I think that it is safe to climb the cliffs	4.22	1.080	4.09	1.117	4.48	0.878	4.999	0.007
I think that it is dangerous to climb the cliffs	4.24	1.037	4.07	1.108	4.45	0.958	3.834	0.022
I think that visitors should help to remove beach litter	4.12	1.065	4.11	1.146	4.42	0.905	4.562	0.011
I think that visitors do not need to help remove beach litter, even if it did not belong to them	4.16	1.039	4.27	1.042	4.43	0.875	3.431	0.033
I think that it is safe to collect fossils from the cliffs	3.87	1.164	3.89	1.125	4.30	0.921	8.738	0.000
I think that it is dangerous to collect fossils from the cliffs	3.82	1.099	3.89	0.868	4.24	0.910	8.819	0.000
I think that climbing cliffs will damage the environment	3.78	1.203	3.82	1.063	4.16	1.022	6.087	0.002
I think that visitors should be allowed to climb the cliffs	3.74	1.232	3.75	1.241	4.15	1.092	6.453	0.002
I think that visitors should not be allowed to collect fossils from the cliffs	3.69	1.165	3.84	1.010	4.10	1.018	6.537	0.002
I think that visitors should be allowed to collect the fossils from the cliffs	3.48	1.173	3.59	1.187	3.84	1.108	4.420	0.013
I am concerned that the cliffs are eroding rapidly	3.52	1.046	3.61	0.868	3.78	0.947	3.023	0.047
I am concerned that people take special fossils home	3.46	1.069	3.55	1.109	3.76	1.033	3.547	0.030
I am concerned that people collect the fossils from the cliffs	3.32	1.070	3.41	1.041	3.71	0.990	6.486	0.002
I am concerned that people do not keep to the footpaths on the cliffs	2.99	1.032	3.18	0.995	3.69	1.087	19.454	0.000
I am concerned that people climb the cliffs	3.24	1.068	3.30	0.904	3.61	1.055	5.983	0.003

Note: (a) Belief statements (I think that ....) using a 5-point scale (1=strongly disagree to 5=strongly agree);
(b) Feelings of concern statements (I am concerned that...) using a 5-point scale (1=not seriously concerned at all to 5=very seriously concerned)

8.15 Comparison of Behavioural Intentions by the Three Sub-Groups

As seen in Table 8.19, the question was used to examine the degree of commitment respondents had to changing their behaviour. In comparison, the results show that there were significant differences between the three groups in the specific environmental behaviour regarding 'not climbing on the cliffs', 'not collecting fossils', 'keeping to the footpaths', 'informing about the discovery of special fossils to the Lulworth Heritage Visitor Centre ', and 'involving in environmental issues'. The 'visited the Centre at least once' group C had a higher level of mean score in most of the six items than the 'no-visit' group A and the 'plan to visit' group B.

However, there were no significant differences among the three groups on environmental activism behaviour and other general environmental behaviour. Most visitors had a high level of positive intention toward 'not disturbing marine life' while they had a lower level of negative intentions toward 'removing beach litter', 'donation', and 'volunteer work'.

Table 8.19 Comparison of Behavioural Intention by the Three Sub-Groups

Dependent Variable	Group A: No-visit (n=122)		Group B: Plan to visit (n=44)		Group C: Visited before/this time (n=255)		F	Sig.
	Mean	SD	Mean	SD	Mean	SD		
I will keep to the footpaths on the cliffs	4.19	1.152	4.16	1.256	4.52	.846	5.966	.003
I will inform the Lulworth Heritage Visitor Centre, if I discover special fossils	4.01	1.072	4.00	1.121	4.40	.925	8.047	.000
I intend to behave in a way that will not harm plants and animals	4.49	.834	4.61	.618	4.72	.544	5.358	.005
I will not climb the cliffs	3.82	1.227	4.16	.963	4.38	1.001	11.577	.000
I will not collect fossils from the cliff	3.76	1.220	4.23	.912	4.33	1.001	11.914	.000
I intend to become more involved in environmental issues	2.85	1.104	3.11	.993	3.27	1.021	6.769	.001

Comparing different groups on behavioural intentions, the post-hoc tests show that significant differences between Group B and Group C were found in one type of intentions (e.g. 'I will inform the Lulworth Heritage Visitor Centre, if I discover special fossils'). Significant differences were also found between Group A and Group C on specific behavioural intentions related to 'keeping the footpaths on the cliffs', 'not climbing', 'reporting the discovery of the special fossils', and 'not collecting'. Interestingly, in the comparison between Group A and Group B, significant differences were found in behavioural intention toward 'not collecting the fossils' between Group A (mean=3.76) and Group B (mean=4.23).

Summary of Stage 2:

Research Objective 1.4: The Effect of the Visitor Centre on Attitudes and Behavioural Intentions

This study is to evaluate the effects of the Visitor Centre on respondents' beliefs, feelings and behavioral intentions toward conservation and responsible behaviour through comparison of the mean scores of the three subgroups. First, each group of visitor profile was examined between the three subgroups. Significant differences were found in relation to age, education, motivation, and participation pattern in the interpretive programmes. The 'visited the Centre at least once' respondents were more likely to be the older (between 36 to 55 years old), motivated by 'enjoying nature' and 'learning about the protection of the nature and fossils than pre-visit groups'. In terms of interpretation experience, respondents who visited the Centre at least once were more likely to participate in the different types of interpretive programmes.

Table 8.20 Comparison of Overall Three Attitudinal Indicators Among Three Samples

	Group A: No-visit (n=122)		Group B: Plan to visit (n=44)		Group C: Visited at least once (n=255)		F	Sig.
	Mean	SD	Mean	SD	Mean	SD		
Overall Attitude	3.88	.504	3.94	.545	4.15	.426	14.972	.000
Overall Intention	3.48	.632	3.62	.609	3.79	.616	10.155	.000

Overall, the effects of the Visitor Centre on attitudes and behavioural intention between the three subgroups were evaluated to determine if significant differences existed between the three subgroups.. Significant differences were found on most beliefs and feeling components of attitudes, and behavioural intentions toward fossils and cliffs for conservation issues at this site. Table 8.20 shows that the 'visited the Centre at least once' respondents (Group C) had a higher mean score for attitudes and behavioural intentions than the 'no-visit' group (Group A) and the 'plan to visit' group (Group B). More details, the results of post-hoc test indicated that significant differences between Group B and Group C were found in two items of attitudes toward 'danger of climbing' and 'danger of collecting' and in one item of behavioural intention toward 'reporting the discovery of special fossils to the Centre'. This indicates that the Visitor Centre experience appeared to affect visitors' awareness of danger regarding 'cliff erosion' and 'responsible fossil collecting'.

Interestingly, in comparison of behavioural intention between Group A and Group B, Group B respondents had higher levels of behavioural intentions regarding 'not collecting fossils from the cliffs' than Group A respondents. This indicates that Group B visitors who plan to visit the Centre had significantly higher levels of awareness of 'responsible fossil collecting' issues although both groups had not participated in the Visitor Centre. Overall, the direct effects of the Visitor Centre vary depending on types of specific responsible behaviour associated with each of conservation issues across different groups of visitors. That is, the Visitor Centre influenced visitors' attitudes and behavioural intentions regarding site-specific geological protection issues and responsible behaviour associated with these issues (e.g. 'not climbing' and 'not collecting the fossils'). There were no significant differences among three groups on attitudes and intentions regarding the 'coastal protection' and 'beach litter' issues. This means that the other potential factors might influence differently according to the types of behaviour with correlating with the Visitor Centre experience. Therefore, in Stage 4, this study examines the interactive effects of various factors on specific behavioural intention.

Stage 3: Factor Analysis

Introduction

For Stage 3, this section presents the results of an exploratory factor analysis using principal component analysis with a varimax rotation on all multivariable scale, attitudes and behavioural intentions. The factor analysis was performed to explore whether a rational underlying structure existed in the multivariable data and to reduce many items of each measure into a smaller set of factors. The structure of a set of factors represents the underlying psychological dimensions of a concept on the theoretical basis. The multidimensional aspects of environmental attitudes and a multi-set of responsible behaviour were reflected corresponding with three site-specific conservation topics and theoretically defined specific concepts (beliefs or feeling of concern components on the attitude scale; general or specific responsible behaviour on the intention scale). The communalities of the variables were examined to assess whether they meets acceptable levels of explanation. Variables with communalities less than .40 were excluded. Also, only factors with eigenvalues over 1 were retained as a cut-off point. The internal homogeneity of the subscales was examined by calculating Cronbach's alpha coefficients.

8.16 Factor Analysis of Attitudes

A principal component factor analysis with a Varimax (orthogonal) rotation was used to explore underlying dimensions that summarised the structure of the set of 31 attitudes (beliefs/feelings) item scale to assist in data reduction. The reliability test was high (0.888) with Cronbach alpha for the 31 items scale for beliefs/feelings of concern measure. The Bartlett's test of sphericity was significant (Chi-square=9198.558, p=.000), and the Kaiser-Meyer-Olkin measure of sampling adequacy was 0.878. This means that these variables were normally distributed and the correlation matrix indicated the possibility that grouping of attitude items could exist.

Table 8.21 shows that the eight factor structure was utilised and explained 62.72% of the total variance. Factor loadings of .40 or higher for the variables on each factor provided support its use as a latent construct. The internal consistency was high for six of the eight accepted factors, with Cronbach's alpha ranging from 0.78 to 0.87. Two factors (Factor 7 and Factor 8) had Cronbach's alpha of <.0.60.

The eight factors were interpreted as follows: the first factor, termed "negative impacts of fossil collecting" explained 11.8% with an eigenvalue of 3.665. The second factor, "negative impacts of climbing the cliffs" explained 10.4%. The third factor was labelled "concern of cliffs and fossils" with 9.97% of the variance and reflected respondent's feelings of concern of cliff erosion and damage of the fossils. Moreover, the fourth factor was termed "awareness of pollution and importance of coastal protection" with 8.86% of the variance. The fifth factor, "concern of coastal pollution" explained 8.34%.

Furthermore, "visitor support for beach cleaning" was labelled as the sixth factor with 7.27%. This factor represented two negative or positive beliefs in support of beach cleaning. The seventh factor, "positive impacts of collecting the fossils" focused on visitors' views of the benefits of fossil collecting (e.g. learning, contribution to scientific research or economy of the local area) explaining 5.71%. The eighth factor, "importance of protection for fossils and cliff erosion" explained 5.39%. This factor reflected the 'importance of protection for fossils and cliff erosion' and 'visitors' support for reporting the discovery of special fossils to the Centre'.

Table 8.21 Factor Analysis of Attitudes (Beliefs and Feelings of Concern Components)

	Factor 1	Factor 2	Factor 3	Factor 4	Factor 5	Factor 6	Factor 7	Factor 8	(A)	(B)
F1.Negative Impacts of Fossil Collecting									3.665	11.822
Visitor should (NOT) be allow to collect fossils *	.750									
It is dangerous to collect	.701									
Visitor should not be allowed to collect fossils	.639									
Collecting will damage the environment	.631									
It is safe to collect (= Dangerous to collect) *	.624									
F2. Negative Impacts of Climbing the Cliffs									3.222	10.394
It is dangerous to climb the cliffs		.852								
It is safe to climb the cliffs (=Dangerous to climb) *		.841								
Visitors should (NOT) be allowed to climb the cliffs		.751								
Climbing the cliffs will damage the environment		.615								
Walking off the footpaths will not damage the cliffs		.562								
F3. Concern for Cliff Erosion and Fossils									3.092	9.974
I am concerned that people climb the cliffs			.813							
I am concerned that people do not keep to the footpaths on the cliffs			.741							
I am concerned that the cliffs are eroding rapidly			.737							
I am concerned that people collect the fossils from the cliffs			.543							
I am concerned that important fossils are damaged by visitors			.514							
I am concerned that people take special fossils home			.467							
F4. Awareness of Pollution and Importance of Coastal Protection/Responsible Behaviour									2.754	8.885
Beach litter does contribute to water pollution *				.799						
Picking up litter will reduce the amount of pollution *				.752						
It is important for visitors to behave in environmental responsible way				.679						
It is important to protect the quality of the coastal area				.667						
Chronbach's alpha	.839	.837	.873	.782	.864	.883	.580	.522		

Note: * negative items reverse coded prior to factor analysis; (A)= *Eigenvalue*; (B)= *% of Variance*; *Mean(S.D.)*

Continued Table 8.21

	Factor 1	Factor 2	Factor 3	Factor 4	Factor 5	Factor 6	Factor 7	Factor 8	(A)	(B)
F5. Concern for Pollution by Beach Litter										
I am concerned that people dispose of litter on the beach					.877					
I am concerned that pollution on the coast is being increasing by beach litter					.871					
I am concerned that there is too much litter on the beach					.788				2.586	8.341
F7. Positive Outcomes of Fossil Collecting										
Fossil collecting helps one to learn about fossils							.742			
Fossil collecting by visitors make a positive contribution to the economy of the local area							.691			
Fossil collecting helps in the progress of science research							.688		1.769	5.705
F8. Importance of Protection of Fossils and Cliffs										
It is important to protect the fossils								.702		
It is important to protect the cliff erosion								.617		
Visitors should report the discovery of special fossils to the Lulworth Heritage Visitor Centre								.550	1.672	5.393
Chronbach's alpha	.839	.837	.873	.782	.864	.883	.580	.522		

Note: * negative items reverse coded prior to factor analysis; (A)= *Eigenvalue*; (B)= *% of Variance; Mean(S.D.)*

8.17 Factor Analysis of Behavioural Intention

Again, a principal component factor analysis with a varimax rotation was undertaken to explore underlying factors that summarised the structure of this set of 13 behavioural intention items, and to reduce the number of variables into a smaller set of factors. A total of 421 participants were asked to indicate their behavioural intention on a 5-point scale. The Bartlett's test of sphericity (Chi-Square test= 2052.763, p=.000) and the Kaiser-Meyer-Olkin measure of sampling adequacy test (=0.837) were measured. This result showed that these behavioural intention variables were normally distributed and the correlation matrix indicated the possibility that grouping of these variables could exist. Table 8.22 presents the two factors resulted from a factor analysis accounted for 59.7 % of the total variance. The reliability coefficient of 0.847 for the overall scale and the factor loadings of .40 or higher for the items on each factor provided support for its use as a latent construct.

Table 8.22 Factor Results of Behavioural Intentions (N=421)

	Factor 1	Factor 2
Factor 1: Environmental Activism	.837	
I intend to become involved in volunteer work for environmental conservation activities		
I intend to become a member of an environmental organisation	.807	
I intend to become more involved in environmental issues	.800	
I intend to make a donation to an environmental organisation	.690	
I will tell people about the importance of the geological environment in this area	.559	
I will pick up beach litter when I see it, even if it did not belong to me	.508	
Factor 2: Specific Responsible Environmental Behaviour		
		.769
I will not climb the cliffs		
I will not collect fossils from the cliffs		.717
I will keep to the footpaths on the cliffs		.713
I will follow the Code of Conduct		.702
I will inform the Lulworth Heritage Visitor Centre, if I discover special fossils		.682
I do not intend to disturb any marine life		.660
I intend to behave in a way that will not harm plants and animals		.645
Eigenvalue	3.716	3.261
% of variance	28.584	25.088
Chronbach's alpha	.820	.802
Mean (SD)	2.89(0.86)	4.37(0.67)

260

Summary of Stage 3:

The first factor, termed "Environmental Activism intentions" explained 28.6% of the total variance. It comprised the six variables which are 'telling the geological importance', 'removing beach litter', 'involvement in organisations', 'donation', 'other environmental issues', and 'volunteer work'. The second factor was labeled "specific responsible environmental behavioural intentions" which is related to the environmental problems and issues at the Lulworth coastal area. It explained 25.1 % of the total variance and combined seven measures which are 'not to climb the cliff', 'not to collect the fossils from the cliffs', 'inform the special fossils to the Centre' and another four items'.

Research Objective 1.5: Multi-dimensions of Attitudes and Behavioural Intentions

The Stage 3 demonstrates whether a rational underlying structure existed in the multivariate scale of attitudes and behavioural intentions. The results of factor analysis show that the different aspects of attitudes and behavioural intentions were clearly categorised to the three main topics regarding conservation issues and responsible behaviour in this study. At the Lulworth coastal area, eight factors were identified among the 31 attitude items and two factors were also identified among 13 behavioural intention statements.

Table 8.23 demonstrates that the three main topics regarding local conservation issues and responsible behaviour are related to each of specific attitudes toward each of the topics, 'cliff erosion (climbing cliffs)', 'fossil protection (fossil collecting)', and 'coastal protection (beach litter)'. Then specific factors for attitudes toward specific behaviour are also related to each of two types of responsible behavioural intentions.

Table 8.23 The Relationships between Three Main Conservation Topics and

Underlying Factors of Attitudes and Intentions

Three Main Topics Related to Local Conservation Issues	Factors on Attitudes	Factors on Behavioural Intentions
Cliff Erosion (Cliff Climbing)	Factor 2: Negative impacts of climbing the cliffs	Factor 2: Specific Responsible Environmental Behaviour
	Factor 5: Concern about cliff erosion	
		• 'Keep to the footpaths'
	Factor 8: Importance of protection for fossils and the cliffs	• 'Not climb the cliffs'
Fossil Protection (Fossil Collecting)	Factor 1: Negative impacts of fossil collecting	Factor 2: Specific Responsible Environmental Behaviour
	Factor 7: Positive outcomes of fossil collecting	• 'Report the discovery of special fossils to the Visitor Centre'
	Factor 3: Concern about fossils and Cliff erosion	• 'Not collect the fossils'
Coastal Protection (Removing Beach Litter)	Factor 4: Awareness of pollution and importance of protection & responsible behaviour	Factor 1: Environmental Activism
	Factor 3: Concern about pollution by beach litter	• 'Removing beach litter'
	Factor 6: Visitors' support for Beach cleaning	

Stage 4: Investigating the Relative Contribution of Important Factors on Specific Behavioural Intentions

Introduction

The previous section examined the effects of the Visitor Centre experiences on visitors' behavioural intentions and their attitudes. However, the results showed that the use of the Visitor Centre variable might be not the sole factor in determining visitor behaviour. According to Newhouse (1990), in order to understand how to encourage environmentally responsible behaviour, one must identify at least some of the factors that influence such behaviour.

With regards to this point, in the stage 4, the secondary objective of the current research is to investigate the relative contribution of selected three key elements (interpretation experiences, individual characteristics and attitudinal components) on specific responsible behavioural intentions. As a following step, this stage examines both the indirect or direct impacts of the most important variables on specific behavioural intention, and additionally, on attitudes.

- **Selection of Independent Variables and Dependent Variables**

In the process of identifying the important determinants for responsible environmental behaviour, the selection of dependent variables and independent variables must be examined before multiple regression analysis. The Figure 8.3 shows the relationships between various variables and specific behavioural intentions based on the conceptual framework for this study (see Chapter 6).

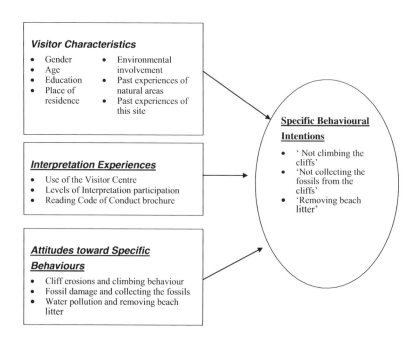

Figure 8.3 The Relationships Between Various Determinants and Behavioural Intention

First, this study focuses on behavioural intention, in particular, specific responsible behaviour as dependent variables. As mentioned in the previous Chapter 6, the main responsible behaviours for this study were chosen with regard to the local environmental issues and management policies at the Jurassic coastal area. Therefore, the three main specific responsible behavioural intentions were selected as dependent variables including 'not climbing the cliffs', 'not collecting the fossils from the cliffs'', and 'removing beach litter'. Additionally, the results indicated that interpretation was effective on only specific responsible behaviour but not on general environmental behaviour in the previous stage. The results of regression analysis help to understand to what extent interpretation contributes to each type of specific behavioural intention.

For independent variables, there are the three main independent variables as follow: interpretation experiences, individual characteristics, and attitudes. Individual characteristics contains as follow: gender, age, education, place of residence, previous environmental involvement, past experiences of natural areas, and past experiences of this site. Interpretation experiences variables include use of the Visitor Centre, level of interpretation participation, and reading the Code of Conduct brochure.

In terms of the attitude components, it includes only specific attitudes toward a certain type of specific issues and behaviour associated with each specific issue. This supports the assumption that specific attitudes might have stronger influence on specific behaviour than general attitudes (Cottrell, 2003a,b; Azjen and Fishbein, 1977/80). For example, specific attitudes toward cliff erosions and climbing the cliffs were selected to determine its relative power on behavioural intentions toward 'not climbing the cliffs'. More detailed information were also discussed in the previous Chapter 6.

- **The Three Steps for Data Analysis**

For this stage 4, three main steps were employed containing multiple regression analysis, two-way ANOVA analysis, and one-way ANOVA/ t-test analysis.

i) Regression Analysis 1: What Influences Specific Behaviour?

Multiple regression analysis helps to determine the important influential factors including specific attitudes and individual factors to each of the three specific behavioural intentions. First, this study examined the relative power of specific attitudes toward climbing the cliffs and individual factors on behavioural intention toward 'not climbing the cliffs'. Following this, specific behavioural intentions toward 'not collecting fossils from the cliffs' and 'removing beach litter' were analysed in the same way.

In each of the three regression models, all individual demographic and interpretation experience variables were transformed and coded as dummy variables (1,0) before beginning the regression analysis. The main independent variables were added to multiple regression analysis using stepwise estimation method. The scatter plots and the Pearson correlation coefficients r showed that there was a linear relationship between the independent variables and the dependent variable. It was also ensured that the independent variables were not highly correlated with each other to reduce the multicollinearity (Tolerance is over 0.5 or near 1; Durbin-Watson is over 0.75). Some of the independent variables were excluded, when its tolerance was less than 0.5 during the multiple regression analysis. In particular, as some of the attitude statements were explained negatively to reduce the response bias, these items were highly correlated with each other (e.g. 'it is dangerous to climb the cliffs' (= 'it is safe to climb the cliffs'); 'visitor should not be allowed to collect fossils from the cliffs (='visitor should be allowed to collect fossils from the cliffs').

ii) Two-way (a×b) or Three way (a×b×c) ANOVA Analysis 2: Interrelationships of the Most Important Determinants on Behavioural Intentions

After the multiple stepwise regression analysis, two-way or three-way ANOVA analysis was conducted to examine the interrelationships between only the most important individual determinants and each of the specific behavioural intentions.

iii) One-way ANOVA Analysis and t-test 3: The Direct Effects of The Most Important Determinants on Behavioural Intentions and Attitudes

When no interaction between individual factors and behavioural intentions could be assumed in the second Two-way or Three-way ANOVA analysis, it is possible to examine the direct effects of each of the important individual determinants on each of the behavioural intentions. For additional investigation, the direct effects of the most influential individual determinants on attitudes were also examined. Finally, this study investigated the comparison of the effects of different types of interpretation on behavioural intentions and attitudes.

8.18 Specific Behavioural Intention toward 'Not Climbing the Cliffs'

8.18.1 The Important Determinants on Specific Behavioural Intention

Figure 8.4 shows that there were several factors to influence behavioural intention toward 'not climbing the cliffs'. These six independent variables explained 34% of the variability of the dependent variable (F=36.715, p=0.000). Variables with lower Tolerance (less than 0.5) were excluded before the analysis (e.g. 'it is dangerous to climb the cliffs'). Tolerances of each variable were over 0.7 and Durbin-Watson was 1.948. This means that there was no multicollinearity between various variables.

As expected, the specific attitudes were the stronger than other individual variables. In more detail, the specific attitudes toward 'I am concerned about people climbing the cliffs (β= 0.292, t=6.494, p=.000)', 'I think that visitors should not be allowed to climb the cliffs (β= 0.171, t=3.350, p=.001)', 'I think that it is safe (=dangerous) to climb the cliffs (β=0.149, t=3.079, p=.002)' were the strong determinants in influencing specific behavioural intention toward 'not climbing the cliffs'. Other specific attitudes statements were not significantly associated with specific intention in this model (e.g. 'it is important to protect the cliff erosion', 'climbing the cliffs will damage the environment').

In terms of individual factors, age (β=0.151, t=3.679, p=.000) and gender (β=0.138, t=3.395, p= .001) also contributed to the regression model. For interpretation experience variables, levels of interpretation participation (β=0.094, t=2.299, p=.022) were moderately related to behavioural intentions toward 'not climbing the cliffs'. 'Use of the Visitor Centre' and 'reading the Code of Conduct brochure' variables had no relationships with intention.

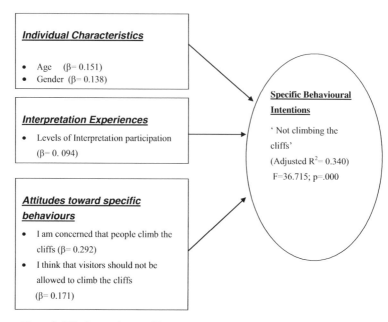

Individual Characteristics

- Age   (β= 0.151)
- Gender (β= 0.138)

Interpretation Experiences

- Levels of Interpretation participation
  (β= 0. 094)

Attitudes toward specific behaviours

- I am concerned that people climb the cliffs (β= 0.292)
- I think that visitors should not be allowed to climb the cliffs
  (β= 0.171)

Specific Behavioural Intentions

' Not climbing the cliffs'
(Adjusted R² = 0.340)
F=36.715; p=.000

Figure 8.4 The Determinants of Specific Intention toward 'Not Climbing the Cliffs'

The findings imply that as visitors' concern for the problem behaviour and understanding of consequences of the specific behaviour increase, there is a simultaneous increase in their willingness to take responsible action regarding 'not climbing the cliffs', and in turn, it might lead to their actual specific behaviour. In terms of the role of interpretation, the Visitor Centre experiences and reading the Code of Conduct brochure might not strongly influence visitors' behavioural intention toward 'not climbing the cliffs'. However, even though there was no strong impact by a single type of interpretation experience, when visitors use more, different types of interpretation, their willingness in 'not climbing the cliffs' increases.

Other demographic variables were also moderately and positively related to behavioural intentions. This indicated that different individual groups have different attitudes and behavioural intention. The next section showed that the indirect effects of the three different individual factors on behavioural intentions were compared by age, gender, and level of interpretation participation. The third section examines the direct effects of visitor sub groups on attitudes and behavioural intentions.

8.18.2 Interrelationships of the Important Determinants on Behavioural Intentions

The three factors way of ANOVA analysis was conducted to examine the interactive effects of the main individual characteristic variables on behavioural intention toward 'not climbing the cliffs'. Table 8.24 shows that visitors who are female, older and used a number of interpretive programmes, have higher levels of behavioural intention toward 'not climbing the cliffs' than those who are male, younger, and have no use of interpretation during their visit.

Table 8.24 Interactive Effects of the Important Determinants on Behavioural Intention toward 'Not Climbing the Cliffs'

Level of Interpretation Participation	Gender	Age			
		18 to 35		36 to over 65	
		Mean	Std. Error	Mean	Std. Error
None	**Male**	**3.370**	0.150	4.237	0.165
	Female	3.892	0.167	4.375	0.161
Lower level (1-2 media)	Male	3.644	0.151	4.231	0.126
	Female	4.478	0.150	4.712	0.125
Higher level (3-5 media)	Male	4.333	0.415	4.786	0.271
	Female	4.000	0.454	**4.833**	0.293

Dependent Variable: Behavioural Intention toward 'not climbing the cliffs'

Additionally, no association between age, gender, and levels of interpretation participation by three –way ANOVA analysis was found (F=0.173, p= 0.678). It means that the effects of each individual factor can be examined.

269

8.18.3 The Direct Effects of Gender, Age, and Level of Interpretation Participation on Attitudes and Behavioural Intention toward 'Not Climbing the Cliffs'.

The direct effects of the main influential factors on attitudes and behavioural intentions toward 'not climbing the cliffs' were different between sub samples involving gender, age, and levels of interpretation participation variables.

(1) Gender

First, the direct effects of gender on both attitudes and behavioural intention were examined. Significant differences were found between females and males. Female groups had higher mean scores in feelings and behavioural intention toward 'not climbing the cliffs' than male ones. Females also held a higher level of beliefs about the negative impacts of climbing the cliffs (e.g. danger of climbing the cliffs, and environmental damage by climbing the cliffs) than males. This suggests that females were more aware of personal safety and negative environmental impacts of climbing the cliffs than male, and in turn, increased their willingness not to climb the cliffs.

(2) Age

The two distinct groups were divided into a younger group (between 18 to 35 years) and an older group (between 36 to 65 years). The older group had a higher mean score in 'It is dangerous to climb the cliffs', 'I am concerned that people climb the cliff', 'I think that visitors should not be allowed to climb the cliffs' than younger groups.

(3) Level of Interpretation Participation

Groups were divided into the three distinct groups which ranged from non-user, to lower level of use of interpretation, to higher level of use of interpretation groups. Lower-level groups used at least one or two types of interpretive programmes. Higher-level groups used from three to five types of interpretive programmes.

The results of the ANOVA test indicated that visitors who used a higher number of different types of interpretation programmes had a higher mean score on the behavioural intention, 'I will not climb the cliffs'. There were also significant differences among the three different levels of interpretation participation on beliefs statements regarding 'I think it is dangerous to climb the cliffs', ' visitors should not be allowed to climb the cliffs', 'it is important to protect the cliff erosion' and 'I am concerned that the cliffs are eroded rapidly'. However, no significant differences were found in the belief statement regarding 'climbing the cliffs will damage the environment'. This indicates that levels of interpretation participation were significantly effective in behavioural intentions toward 'not climbing the cliffs' through increasing visitors' concern toward 'cliff erosion' and climbing behaviour and their awareness about negative impacts of climbing the cliffs.

8.19 Intention Toward 'Not Collecting Fossils from the Cliffs''

8.19.1 The Important Determinants on Specific Behavioural Intention

The second regression model explained 36.8% of the variation in the dependent variable, specific behavioural intention toward 'not collecting the fossils from the cliffs'. The model as a whole was also significant, indicating that there was a strong linear association between behavioural intention toward 'not collecting the fossils' and the independent variables (F=41.390, p=0.000). Tolerance score was over 0.7 in all independent variables and Durbin-Watson was over 1.943. It indicated that no multicollinearity was found between the independent variables.

Overall, specific attitudes toward 'not collecting fossils from the cliffs' and level of interpretation participation (β=0.167; t=4.160, p=0.000) influenced significantly and positively the behavioural intention toward 'not collecting fossils from the cliffs'. However, interestingly, behavioural intention was also influenced in reverse by the belief toward positive outcomes of fossil collecting with learning experiences (β= -0.115, t=-2.857, p=0.004) and education variable (β= - 0.086; t= - 2.153, p=0.032).

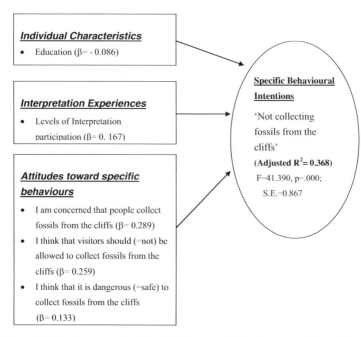

Individual Characteristics

- Education (β= - 0.086)

Interpretation Experiences

- Levels of Interpretation participation (β= 0. 167)

Attitudes toward specific behaviours

- I am concerned that people collect fossils from the cliffs (β= 0.289)
- I think that visitors should (=not) be allowed to collect fossils from the cliffs (β= 0.259)
- I think that it is dangerous (=safe) to collect fossils from the cliffs (β= 0.133)

Specific Behavioural Intentions

'Not collecting fossils from the cliffs'
(Adjusted R^2= 0.368)
F=41.390, p=.000;
S.E.=0.867

Figure 8.5 The Determinants of Specific Behavioural Intentions toward 'Not Collecting

Fossils from the Cliffs''

Once again, specific attitudes were more significant than level of interpretation participation and education. In terms of specific attitudes toward 'fossil collecting', the types of specific attitudes were included in this regression model as follows:

- The importance of protection of fossils
- Visitors' support for fossil collecting management policy
- Beliefs of positive or negative outcomes of fossil collecting
- Feelings of concern toward the damage of the important fossils and collecting the fossils.

Significant positive effect of specific attitudes on behavioural intention were found in the three main types of attitudes 'I am concerned that people collect fossils from the cliffs (β=0.289; t=6.256, p=0.000)', 'I think that visitors should not be allowed to collect fossils from the cliffs (β=0.259, t=5.523, p=0.000)' , and 'I think that it is dangerous to collect fossils from the cliffs'(β=0.133; t=3.198, p=0.001) . By contrast, specific behavioural intention was negatively influenced by the beliefs regarding 'I think that collecting fossils helps one to learn about the fossils (β= - 0.115, t= - 2.857, p=0.004)'. Some of items with lower levels of Tolerance (less than 0.5) were excluded during regression analysis to reduce multicollinearity (e.g. 'it is safe (=dangerous) to collect fossils from the cliffs', 'visitor should (=not) be allowed to collect fossils from the cliffs', 'I am concerned about the important fossils being damaged by visitors').

Other beliefs related to negative environmental impacts of fossil collecting (e.g. 'I think that collecting fossils will damage the environment') and importance of protection of the fossils, positive outcomes of fossil collecting (e.g. scientific research and local economic contribution), and concerns about people taking fossils home were not related to behavioural intention. It implies that behavioural intention toward 'not collecting fossils from the cliffs' had a stronger association with specific attitudes (feelings of concern, safety, and support for that behaviour) toward the specific behaviour of 'not collecting the fossils'.

In terms of interpretation experiences variables, once again, the effects of levels of interpretation participation on behavioural intention (β= 0.167, t= 4.160, p=0.000) were stronger than the effects of a single type of interpretation including use of the Visitor Centre, and reading the Code of Conduct brochure in this model. For the individual characteristic variables, age and gender were not related to behavioural intention in this model. Previous experiences and environmental involvement variables did not influence behavioural intention.

8.19.2 Interrelationships of the Important Determinants on Behavioural Intentions toward 'Not Collecting Fossils from the Cliffs'

The two factors way of ANOVA analysis was performed to examine the interactive effects of the main individual characteristics variables on behavioural intention toward 'not collecting fossils from the cliffs'. As seen in Table 8.26, significant differences were found between lower level of education groups (between no education qualification and college qualification) and higher levels of education groups (university qualification). In particular, visitors who have higher levels of education (University degree) were significantly influenced by the level of interpretation participation. That is, when visitors with higher levels of education and without any interpretation experiences, held negative attitudes toward 'not collecting fossils from the cliffs' (mean=3.793), compared to those visitors with lower levels of education and no interpretation experiences (mean =3.986). However, when those higher educated people have experienced the different types of interpretation programmes, they learned the new appropriate behaviour at site, and in turn, changed positively their intention toward 'not collect fossils from the cliffs' (mean =4.800), when compared to visitors with lower levels of education and higher levels of interpretation participation (mean=4.593). The results indicated that the levels of interpretation participation played the important role in changing visitors' behavioural intention not to collect fossils from the cliffs between the two groups.

Table 8.25 Interrelationships between the Important Determinants and Behavioural Intention toward 'Not Collecting Fossils from the Cliffs'

Level of Interpretation Participation	Education			
	Lower level (none to college)		Higher level (University)	
	Mean	Std. Error	Mean	Std. Error
None	*3.986*	0.123	*3.793*	0.114
Lower level (1-2 media)	4.396	0.092	4.079	0.112
Higher level (3-5 media)	4.593	0.204	4.800	0.335

Dependent variable: Behavioural Intention toward 'not collecting fossils from the cliffs''

The results of two-way ANOVA analysis indicated that there was no association between education and levels of interpretation participation (F=0.825, p=0.439). Next analysis was performed to examine whether any differences on attitudes and behavioural intentions exist between the different groups.

8.19.3. The Direct Effects of Level of Interpretation Participation and Education on Attitudes and Behavioural Intention toward 'Not Collecting Fossils from the Cliffs'

The direct effects of the main influential factors on attitudes and behavioural intentions toward 'not collecting fossils from the cliffs' were examined between sub samples involving levels of interpretation participation and education variables in this section.

(1) Education (Visitor Number)

Significant differences were found on attitudes toward positive outcomes of fossil collecting and behavioural intention between the two levels of education groups, 'lower level (between none and college degree, n=234)' vs 'higher level (university degree; n=186)'. Interestingly, visitors who have higher levels of education with university degree held positive beliefs regarding 'I think that fossil collecting helps one to learn about fossils (mean=3.73)' than those who have lower levels of education (mean=3.47). However, visitors with a higher level of education agreed less with 'it is dangerous to collect the fossils from the cliffs (mean=3.94)' than visitors with a lower level of education (mean=4.19). Similarly, visitors with higher levels of education held less willingness not to collect the fossils from the cliffs (mean=3.98) than those with lower levels of education (mean=4.29). The results showed that visitors who have university degrees are interested in learning about the fossils and think 'it is not really dangerous to collect the fossils'. In turn, their positive attitudes toward collecting fossils influenced positively behavioural intention toward collecting fossils at this site.

(2) Levels of Interpretation Participation

Again, levels of interpretation participation variable were divided into the three main groups including 'none (n=161)', 'lower level (n=223)' and 'higher level (n=37)'. Significant differences were found among the three groups. For example, visitors who have experienced more a various types of interpretation, agreed strongly with beliefs 'it is dangerous to collect the fossils from the cliffs (mean=4.55)' and 'visitors should not be allowed to collect the fossils from the cliffs (mean=4.73)' than the two other groups. Higher levels of interpretation participation groups also agreed strongly with behavioural intention (mean=5.00), compared to 'non user groups '(mean=4.00)' and 'lower level groups (mean=4.44)'.

Table 8.26 The Direct effects of Levels of Interpretation Participation on

Attitudes and Intention (n=421)

Levels of Interpretation Participation	None (n=161)	Lower Level (1-2) (n=223)	Higher Level (3-5) (n=37)
	Mean (S.D)	Mean (S.D)	Mean (S.D)
Attitudes 'I think that it is dangerous to collect fossils from the cliffs'	3.97 (1.022)	4.31 (.847)	4.55 (.820)
'I think that visitors should not be allowed to collect fossils from the cliffs'	3.88 (1.097)	4.05 (1.027)	4.32 (1.018)
Behavioural Intention 'I will not collect fossils from the cliffs'	4.00 (1.165)	4.44 (.829)	5.00 (0.000)

As higher levels of interpretation users' awareness of the danger of collecting the fossils from the cliffs and favourable attitudes toward management policy related to 'not collecting the fossils' increase, they changed their behavioural intention toward 'not collecting the fossils from the cliffs' in a desirable direction. Lower level users also held favourable attitudes and intentions related to 'fossil collecting'. By contrast, visitors who had not experienced any other interpretation during their visits, held moderate levels of attitudes and intentions.

8.20 Behavioural Intention toward 'Removing Beach Litter'

8.20.1 The Important Determinants on Specific Behavioural Intention

The third multiple regression model indicated that the overall explanatory power of the variables on behavioural intention toward 'removing beach litter' was weak (adjusted R square =0.249), compared to the other two regression models for 'not climbing the cliffs' and 'not collecting the fossils from the cliffs'. The model as a whole was also significant, indicating that there was a strong linear association between behavioural intention toward 'beach litter' and the independent variables (F=23.118, p=0.000; S.E.=.940). Two statements (e.g. feeling of concern about 'water pollution being increasing by beach litter' and 'visitor do not need (=need to) to help removing beach litter) was excluded because Tolerance of two items was less than 0.5. Other items' Tolerance scores were over 0.8 in all independent variables and Durbin-Watson was over 1.824. It indicated that no multicollinearity was found between the independent variables.

The important influential determinants for behavioural intention toward 'removing beach litter' included 'specific attitudes for 'beach litter', age (β=0.144, t= 3.348, p=0.001), gender (β=0.108, t=2.473, p=0.014), and environmental involvement (β=0.101, t=2.340, p=0.020). Interestingly, interpretation experiences variables did not significantly influence behavioural intention in this model.

As expected, specific attitudes were the strongest factor to behavioural intention. For example, behavioural intention was significantly influenced by specific beliefs regarding 'visitors should help remove beach litter (β=0.408, t=8.819, p=0.000)' 'picking up beach litter will reduce the amount of water pollution (β=0.112, t=2.436, p=0.015)', and feelings of concern related to 'I am concerned that people dispose the beach litter (β=0.135, t=2.960, p=0.003)'. Other beliefs related to the importance of protection of the coast and feelings of concern about too much beach litter, water pollution by beach litter were not related to behavioural intention.

277

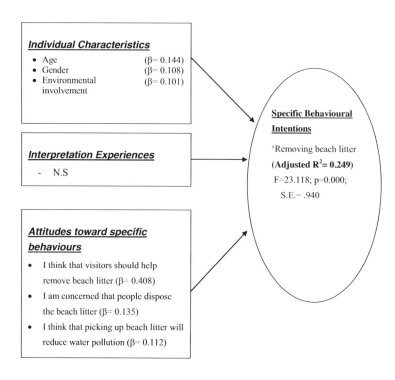

Figure 8.6. The Determinants of Behavioural Intention toward 'Removing Beach Litter'

With regard to the individual factors, different factors were found in this model, compared to the previous two models for 'not climbing the cliffs' and 'not collecting fossils from the cliffs'. In the two other regression models, there were no impacts of pre-existing environmental experience variables (e.g. visitors' previous experiences of the natural areas and Lulworth coastal area, and their previous involvement in environmental activities) on behavioural intention for 'not climbing the cliffs' and 'not collecting the fossils' while the interpretation variable significantly influenced those two specific responsible behaviours related to the particular local environment. By contrast, behavioural intentions toward 'removing beach litter' were significantly influenced by environmental involvement but not by interpretation variables. This suggests that it is very difficult to change human behaviour, in particular, responsible-denial or conservation behaviour as a result of short-term interpretation experiences. Even though picking-up beach litter is one of the most well-known responsible environmental behaviours in protected natural areas, 'removing beach litter' behaviour requires visitors to sacrifice time and convenience. Therefore, visitors who already have involvement in environmental organisations or activities hold stronger pro-environmental attitudes and behaviour as a 'conservation ethic' than those who simply have experienced natural areas and this site (in this study, those are negatively associated with responsible behavioural intention regarding 'removing beach litter').

The following section showed the interactive effects of environmental involvement, age, and gender on behavioural intention. Then, this study examined the direct effects of each of those factors on attitudes and behavioural intentions toward 'removing beach litter'.

8.20.2 Interrelationships of the Important Determinants on Behavioural Intentions toward 'Removing Beach Litter'

The three factors way of ANOVA analysis was performed to examine the interactive effects of the main individual characteristics variables on behavioural intention toward 'removing beach litter'. As seen in Table 8.27, significant differences were found between age, gender, and environmental involvement. In particular, visitors who were female, older, and had involvement in environmental organisations or activities, held higher level of behavioural intention toward 'removing beach litter (mean=4.042)' than those who were male, younger, and had no involvement in environmental organisations or activities (mean=2.960). However, the results of three-way ANOVA analysis indicated that there was no association between education and levels of interpretation participation (F=0.194, p=0.660). Next analysis was performed to examine whether any differences on attitudes and behavioural intentions exist between the different groups.

Table 8.27 Interactive effects of the Important Determinants On Behavioural Intention

toward 'Removing Beach Litter'

Age	Gender	Environmental Involvement			
		No		Yes	
		Mean	Std. Error	Mean	Std. Error
18 to 35	Male	**2.960**	0.133	3.364	0.246
	Female	3.524	0.145	3.977	0.176
36 to over 65	Male	3.597	0.131	3.775	0.182
	Female	3.907	0.133	4.042	0.235

Dependent Variable: Behavioural Intention toward 'removing beach litter'

8.20.3 The Direct Effects of Gender, Age, and Environmental Involvement on Attitudes and Behavioural Intention toward 'Removing Beach Litter'

The results of the t-Test showed that there were no interactions between the three determinants. Therefore, the direct effects of each of the visitor factors on attitudes and behavioural intention were examined as follows.

(1) Gender

Again, females held higher mean score of attitudes and behavioural intention toward 'removing beach litter' than males. Significant differences were found between females and males on most types of attitudes statements as follows:

Table 8.28 Comparison of effects of Gender on Attitudes toward 'Removing Beach Litter'

Specific Attitudes	Male(n=215)		Female (n=206)	
	Mean	S.D.	Mean	S.D.
'I think that beach litter contribute to water pollution'	4.61	.920	4.82	.664
'I think that visitors should help to remove beach litter'	4.18	1.081	4.42	.867
'I am concerned that people dispose litter on the beach'	4.20	.998	4.47	4.20
'I am concerned that pollution on the coast is being increasing by beach litter'	4.19	1.017	4.50	4.19

280

Similarly, females held higher mean scores on behavioural intention toward 'removing beach litter' (mean=3.82) than males (mean=3.38).

(2) Age

There were significant differences between two distinct age groups which were a younger group (n=185, between 18 to 35 years old), and an older group (n=235; between 36 to over 65 years old). Generally, the older group were more aware of the negative impacts of beach litter and were more concerned about 'beach litter' than the younger group. Significant differences were found on the four main attitude statements related to the importance of coastal protection, 'I think that picking up beach litter will reduce the amount of water pollution', 'I am concerned that there is too much litter on the beach', and 'I am concerned that people dispose of the beach litter'. Accordingly, the older group's behavioural intention toward 'removing beach litter' (mean= 3.34) was higher than the younger group's (mean=3.80).

(3) Environmental Involvement

Overall, visitors who have been involved in environmental organisations or activities had higher mean scores for feelings of concern and intention toward 'removing beach litter' (mean=3.82) than those who had no involvement in environmental organisations or activities on attitudes and behavioural intention (mean=3.50). Significant differences were found on attitudes as follows:

- I am concerned that people dispose litter on the beach
- I am concerned that pollution on the coast is being increased by beach litter
- I am concerned that there is too much litter on the beach

Overall, the results of the direct effects of each factor on attitude and behavioural intention were consistent with the results of the interactive effects of each factor on behavioural intention. However, even though most visitors have higher scores for favourable attitudes and awareness about negative impacts of beach litter, they have moderate scores for behavioural intention. This showed that the link between attitudes and behavioural intention was weak.

Summary of Stage 4

The Stage 4 for the secondary objective for this research investigated the relative contribution of interpretation experiences on specific behaviours with correlating determinants including individual background variables and specific attitudes. In particular, this stage examined both the indirect and direct impacts of the important variables on behavioural intentions, additionally, on attitudes as well. As mentioned in the introduction section for Stage 4, the results helped to answer the two sub-objectives: first, identifying the important factors to influence responsible environmental behavioural intentions; Second, examining different effects of the most influential determinants on behavioural intentions.

Research objective 2.1: To identify the important determinants in influencing specific responsible behavioural intentions?

Overall, the important determinants influencing the three types of specific behavioural intentions were identified as follows: specific attitude, gender, age, levels of interpretation participation, environmental involvement, and education. The results for this study indicated that specific attitudes toward each specific behavioural intention were the most influential determinants toward the three types of specific behaviour.

This research has provided the essential evidence that interpretation has a significant positive contribution to specific responsible behaviours. The results indicated that interpretation influenced directly the two types of specific behavioural intention toward 'not climbing the cliffs' and 'not collecting the fossils from the cliffs'. The mediate effects of interpretation on specific behavioural intention were examined in two different perspectives. First, interpretation influenced indirectly specific behavioural intention through specific attitudes toward a certain type of behaviour. This means that interpretation influenced visitors' attitudes toward specific behaviour, and in turn, increased visitors' attitude, this influenced specific behavioural intention in a desired direction. Secondly, in terms of the relative contribution of interpretation on specific behaviour with correlating factors such as gender, age, and education, interpretation significantly influenced all ranges of visitor sub-groups. Therefore, this study supports the idea that interpretation plays a key role in a significant positive contribution to specific responsible behaviour through influencing specific attitudes toward specific behaviour across a wide range of the visitor groups.

In terms of the type of interpretation experiences, this study indicates that levels of interpretation participation had a stronger positive impact on specific behavioural intention rather than 'use of the Visitor Centre', and 'reading the Code of Conduct brochure'. This finding from the regression analysis is consistent with the results of the effects of the Visitor Centre on behavioural intentions in Stage 2. The direct effects of the Visitor Centre were not significantly effective on behavioural intentions while significant effects were found on specific attitudes. It indicates that the Visitor Centre experience might influence indirectly visitors' behavioural intention through their specific attitudes. Although the reading the Code of Conduct brochure variable was not significantly associated with specific behavioural intentions, like the Visitor Centre experience variable, this brochure had limited positive effects on some types of attitudes and behavioural intentions regarding three conservation topics. Overall, the results suggested that the more visitors use a varied range of interpretation, the higher their level of behavioural intention when compared with those who used only a single type of interpretive programme.

Research Objective 2.2 : To explore any the inter-relationships of the different influential determinants on behavioural intentions?

Significant different effects of the important determinants on the different specific behaviours were found. It indicated that it is very difficult to change human behaviour related to conservation because other potential factors are related to types of long-term conservation behaviour (e.g. 'removing beach litter', 'recycling', 'involvement in volunteer work'). The reasons might be explained in several ways. For this study, apart from the impact of specific attitude on intention, the other potential factors were identified in influencing behavioural intention toward removing beach litter. For example, environmental involvement variables were significantly related to behavioural intention toward removing behavioural intention.

Interestingly, visitors' interest and education levels can also be one of the other potential factors in influencing specific behavioural intentions. For example, this study area is a popular destination for a type of special interest tourism, namely 'geotourism' related to the unique geological environment. Visitor characteristics at the Lulworth coastal area might be different from general ecotourists visiting natural areas or commercial visitors to coastal areas. For example, visitors who have university degrees were more interested in collecting the fossils as a learning experience and have moderate levels of willingness not to collect the fossils from the cliffs when compared with those who have lower levels of education. They held higher levels of willingness not to collect the fossils from the cliffs. However, interpretation experiences influenced their level of awareness of the negative impacts of fossil collecting during their visit to the site, and then, in turn, groups with higher levels of education showed an increased willingness not to collect the fossils from the cliffs as a result of interpretation. Overall, this showed that the effects of interpretation on behaviour can be limited dependent on visitors' pre-existing environmental involvement and their particular interest in or activities at the site.

284

CHAPTER

9

Chapter 9 Case Study 2:
The Charmouth Coastal Area

9.1 Introduction

This chapter presents the results of the survey for the visitors to the Charmouth coastal area. As

seen in Figure 9.1, the results are presented in four stages. For each stage, it provides the main

objectives as well as the analytical tools. This chapter follows the same of structure as in Chapter 8

for the results of the Lulworth coastal area. The first stage provides a general picture of the

characteristics of the respondents and their interpretation experiences, as well as their overall

attitudes and behavioural intentions toward local conservation issues and responsible behaviour

(Stage 1). Stage 2 explores the effectiveness of the Charmouth Heritage Visitor Centre by

comparisons of the mean score of attitudes and behavioural intentions among the three subgroups

dependent on their experiences of the Visitor Centre (Stage 2). Thirdly, all multidimensional scales

of attitudes and behavioural intention statements are categorised into the factors underlined by

factor analysis (Stage 3). Finally, the important determinants of each intention toward the three

main specific behaviours were investigated by multiple stepwise regression analysis (Stage 4).

Additionally, stage 4 also investigated the indirect or direct effects of the important determinants on

each of the specific behavioural intentions and specific attitudes.

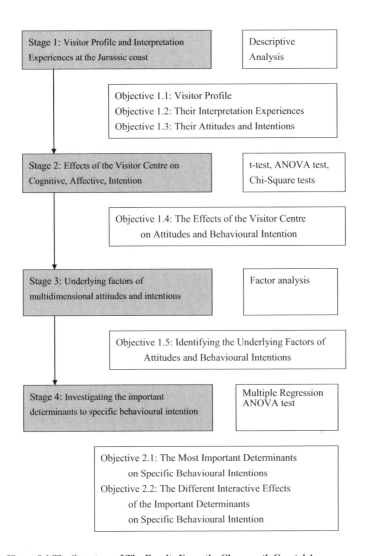

Figure 9.1 The Structure of The Results From the Charmouth Coastal Area

Stage 1: Visitor Profile and Interpretation Experiences at the Charmouth Coastal Area

9.2 Profile of Visitors to the Charmouth Coastal Area

Respondents were collected from 453 visitors to the Charmouth Coastal Area. Of those, 211 had not

visited the Visitor Centre at the time of interview and 242 had visited the Centre.

9.2.1 Demographic Profile of Visitors

Table 9.1 Profile of the Total Survey Sample

		Total (n=453)	%
1. Gender	Male	219	48.3
	Female	234	51.7
2. Age	18-25	30	6.6
	26-35	67	14.8
	36-45	135	29.8
	46-55	114	25.2
	56-65	75	16.6
	Over 66	32	7.1
3.Education	None	44	9.7
	High school qualification	74	16.3
	College and Professional Diploma	190	41.9
	University degree	145	32.0
4. Residence	Dorset Region	66	14.6
	South West of England	156	34.4
	South East of England	112	24.7
	Other Counties of England and Wales	114	25.2
	Overseas	5	1.1
5.Previous visits of this site	First-time visitors	164	36.2
	Repeat visitors	289	63.8

Table 9.1 presents the characteristics of the sample from the Charmouth coastal area. Overall, the

sample was composed of a predominantly middle-aged group of between 36 and 55 years (55% of

all respondents) and relatively well-educated adults with 73.9% having a college diploma or

university degree. A slight majority was female. The respondents were mostly from the South West of England (34.4%) while 14.6% were from Dorset region. Only 1.1% were from overseas, mainly Belgium, Spain, and the Netherlands. About 63.8% of respondents were revisiting to the Charmouth coastal area.

9.2.2 Travel Features

Overall 45.6% of respondents were travelling with family including children, followed by spouse/partner (29.8%).

Table 9.2 Group Party

Group party	Total (n=453) %
Alone	4.9%
Friends	8.9%
Spouse/partner	29.8%
Friends and Family	10.4%
Family including children	45.6%
With guided tour	0.4%
An organised tour group	0%

9.2.3 Environmental Involvement

As presented in Table 9.3, using multiple response analysis, 41.7 % of all respondents indicated that they have had been involved in organisations or other activities related to the environment. Some 22.8 % were members of environmental organisations. Some indicated that they were regular readers of environmental magazines (12.7%) as well as were involved in environmental activities such as volunteer work (3.4%).

9.2.4 Previous Environmental Experiences of Natural Areas

This study also examined respondents' previous experiences in natural areas during their previous trips. Some 45 % of respondents (n=453) had visited natural areas more than 10 times on previous trips.

Table 9.3 Pre-Environmental Experiences and Environmental Involvement

	Total (n=453) %
1.Environmental Involvement	
No	58.3%
Yes	41.7%
Volunteer work	(3.4%)
Regular reader of magazines related to environment, nature or wildlife	(12.7%)
Member of Environment organisations	(22.8%)
Other (e.g. Work, orteaching or recycling)	(2.8%)
2. Previous Environmental Experiences to the Natural Area	
Less than once per year	4.0%
1 to 2	12.6%
3 to 4	18.3%
5 to 10	20.1%
More than 10 times per year	45.0%

9.2.5 Motivation

Table 9.4 demonstrates that the most important motives for respondents was "having fun with family/friends (36.8%)", followed by "enjoying the beauty of nature (23.3%), "to have a relaxing time (19.5 %)", "to learn about fossils (15.3 %) and "to learn about the need to protect this area (1.3%). It was found that some respondents were interested in "doing physical exercise/leisure activities" (3.8%) (e.g. walking/running or taking photos).

Table 9.4 Motivation

	Total (n=453)
To have a good time with family/friends	36.8%
To enjoy the beauty of nature	23.3%
To have a relaxing time	19.5%
To learn about fossils	15.3%
Other	3.8%
To learn about the need to protect this area	1.3%

9.3 Interpretation Experiences

9.3.1 Levels of Participation in Interpretive Programmes

Most of the respondents (72.2 %) indicated they had used a number of various interpretive programmes while 27.8 % of respondents did not use any programmes during their visits.

Table 9.5 Levels of in Participation Interpretive Programmes

	Total (n=453)
None	27.8% (n=126)
Lower (1-3)	57.2%
Higher (4-7)	15.0%

9.3.2 Use of Different Types of Interpretive Programmes

The most commonly used media by all respondents were exhibition/displays programmes (28.7%) within the Visitor Centre, signboards (23.8%), and brochures (11.1%). Some 7.3% respondents indicated that they participated in guided walks.

Table 9.6 Types of Use of Interpretive Programmes

	Total (n=453)
Signboard	23.8%
Brochure	11.1%
Publications	8.5%
Exhibition/displays	28.7%
Films	12.0%
Computer interactions	6.6%
Talked to the staff	1.9%
Guided walks	7.3%
Others	0%

9.3.3 Reading the Code of Conduct

In terms of reading the Code of Conduct, just over 23% of all respondents (n=453) had read the Code of Conduct leaflets on fossil collecting whereas 77% of the sample had not read the Code of Conduct leaflets

9.3.4 The Perception of the Role of the Visitor Centre

All participants (n=453) were asked to indicate their perception of the role of the Visitor Centre. As indicated in Table 9.7, "visitor centres are good places to educate people" (mean=4.51, SD=0.872) and "visitor centres are designed to help people understand the local environment" (mean=4.48, SD=0.883) were found to be the two main perceptions about the role of the Visitor Centre. Respondents indicated that they agreed the least with the statement about the entertainment role of the Visitor Centre (mean=3.56, SD=0.979).

Table 9.7 The Role of the Visitor Centre

	Mean	SD
Visitor centres are good places to educate people	4.51	.872
Visitor centres are designed to help people understand the local environment	4.48	.883
Visitor centres provide a good introduction to local attractions	4.07	.905
Visitor centres provide a useful source of tourist information	4.03	.993
Visitor centres provide entertainment	3.56	.979

Note: Used a 5-scale from 1 (strongly disagree) to 5 (strongly agree); Cronbach's Alpha=0.772

9.3.5 Experiences of and Plans to Visit the Charmouth Heritage Coast Visitor Centre

Table 9.8 provides information about experiences of and plans to visit the Visitor Centre during previous visits and/or this time. First, respondents were asked to indicate whether or not they had visited the Centre during this visit to the site. Among all respondents (n=453), one half of respondents (participant groups in the visitor centre; n=242) indicated that they had visited the Centre whereas another half of respondents (n=211) had not visited the centre during this time to visit the site. Additionally, only respondents who had no experienced the centre during this time (non-participant groups in the visitor centre; n=211) were asked to indicate whether or not they have a plan to visit the Centre during this time to visit the site. Among all pre-visit respondents (n=211), some 39.9% of them indicated that they (n=83) had a plan to visit the Charmouth Heritage Visitor Centre.

Table 9.8 Experiences of and Plans to Visit the Charmouth Heritage Visitor Centre

	Q1: Have you visited the Centre today?			
1.1 On-site experiences of the Centre (N=453)	No, I didn't visit today (N= 211)		Yes, I did visit today (N= 242)	
1.2 Plan to visit the Centre (N=211) Missing numbers (N=3)	No, I plan to visit N= 125 (60.1%)	Yes, I plan to visit N= 83 (39.9%)		
	Q2: Have you visited the Centre before?			
2.1 Previous experiences of the Centre (N=453)	No, I didn't before N=296 (65.3%)		Yes, I did before **N=157 (34.7%)**	
2.2 The number of previous visits to the Centre (N=157) Missing numbers (N=5)			Rarely	N=30 (41.4%)
			1 to 2 times	N=69 (33.1%)
			3 to 10 times	N=33 (15.9%)
			More than 10 times	N=20 (9.6%)

Next, all respondents (N=453) were asked to indicate their previous experiences of the Visitor Centre. A total of 34.7 % of them indicated that they (n=157) had visited the Charmouth Heritage Visitor Centre during previous times. In terms of the numbers of visits to the Visitor Centre during previous times (n=157), almost 59 % of previous visitors (n=157) had visited the Centre between one and ten times while 9.6% of previous experiences respondents (n=157) had visited the Centre more than ten times.

9.4 Evaluation of the Visitor Centre Experiences

In order to evaluate the effect of interpretive programmes, in particular, this study focused on the effectiveness of the Visitor Centre on-site. The additional information about the evaluation of their experiences of the Centre by post-visit respondents (participants in the visitor centre on-site; n=242) are presented in this section.

9.4.1 Evaluation of the Visitor Centre Experiences for Post-Visit Respondents On-site (N=242)

Only post-visit respondents (n=242) were also asked to indicate the key experiences during their visit to the Charmouth Heritage Coast Visitor Centre. As seen in Table 9.9, the experience of visiting the Centre was described as educational (mean=4.38, SD=0.743), and enjoyable (mean=4.25, SD=0,778).

Table 9.9 Key Experiences to Interpretive Programmes

	Total (n=242)	
	Mean	SD
Educational /Not Educational	4.38	0.743
Enjoyable /Not Enjoyable	4.25	0.778
Inspiring/Uninspiring	3.99	0.841
Stimulating/ Boring	3.94	1.015
Fulfilling/ Disappointing	3.80	1.038
Exciting/Dull	3.64	1.012

Note: Used a 5-scale from 1 (strongly disagree) to 5 (strongly agree); Cronbach's Alpha=0.891

9.4.2 Learning

As summarised in Table 9.10, almost 41.3 % of respondents (n=242) indicated that they learned about fossils, followed by, geology of the coast (32.2%), while 2.9% of visitors indicated that they did not learn anything during their visits to the Centre.

Table 9.10 Learning

	Post-visit %(n=242)
Fossils	41.3%
Geology of the coast	32.2%
Conservation	8.7%
Responsible environmental behaviour	7.4%
Marine life	5.4%
None of them	2.9%
History	2.1%

.

9.4.3 The Effectiveness of the Visitor Centre

Table 9.11 shows the effects of the Visitor Centre on visitors' satisfaction, awareness, understanding and attitude change. Post-visit respondents (n=242) were very satisfied with their visit to the Centre with a mean of 4.18 (SD=0.825) on a 5-point scale. Visitors were also asked whether or not their understanding and awareness of the environmental issues of the site were changed after visiting the Visitor Centre. Visitors' awareness of change was higher (mean=3.56) than their understanding of change (mean=3.35). The mean level of their overall attitude change toward conservation at the site was '3.25' (SD=1.165) on a 5-point scale, ranging from 1 (not at all changed) to 5 (a great deal changed).

Table 9.11 The Effects of the Visitor Centre for Post-visit Groups only

	Post-visit (n=242)	
	Mean	SD
Satisfaction of visit to the centre	4.18	0.825
Understanding change of this site	3.35	1.143
Awareness change of environmental conservation	3.56	1.093
Attitude change toward conservation of this area	3.25	1.165

9.5 Key Experiences at the Charmouth Coastal Area

Respondents were also asked to indicate the most important experience after visiting the Charmouth coastal area. Some 33.3 % of post-visit respondents indicated they learned about fossils, followed by 'enjoying the beauty of nature' (25.8%) while only 16.3% indicated they simply had a good time on-site.

Table 9.12 Key Experiences after Visiting the Charmouth Coastal Area

	Post-visit (N=242)%
I learned about the fossils	33.3%
I enjoyed the beauty of nature	25.8%
I learned about the need to protect this area	16.3%
I simply had a good time	16.3%
I had a relaxing time	8.3%

9.6 Satisfaction of the Experiences at the Charmouth Coastal Area

Most of the respondents (N=453) were very satisfied with their experiences at the Charmouth coastal area with a mean of 4.54 on a 5-point scale.

Table 9.13 Overall Satisfaction

	Total samples %(n=453)
1. Not at all satisfied	0.2%
2. Dissatisfied	0.9%
3. Neutral	9.3%
4. Satisfied	25.6%
5. Very satisfied	64.0%

Note: Using 5-point scale (1 =not at all satisfied, 5= very satisfied)

9.7 Awareness of the Seriousness of the Threats to the Environment

Respondents were also asked to indicate how serious the threats to the environment are at the Charmouth coastal area, using a 5-point scale, ranging from 1 (not at all) to 5 (very much). The overall mean level of all respondents' (n=453) awareness was '3.78 (SD=0.99).

9.8 Attitudes: Beliefs and Feelings of Concern

The study investigated respondents' attitudes toward specific conservation issues and responsible behaviour. Two components of attitudes included the 22 items of belief and the 9 items of feelings of concern. As mentioned in the case of the results of the Lulworth coast area (see Chapter 9), the attitude statements were measured using a 5-point Likert-type scale. Each of the 31 statements were computed and summed to create an overall attitude measure. Overall, the total mean score of all 31 attitude statements was significantly high (mean=4.25, S.D.=0.422) with the reliability (Cronbach's Alpha=0.875).

296

Table 9.14 Attitude Statements (Beliefs and Feelings of Concern)

I think that…… & I am concerned that ……..	Mean	SD
1. *I think that beach litter does **NOT** contribute to water pollution *(= does contribute to water pollution)*	4.85	.637
2. I think that it is important for visitors to behave in environmentally responsible ways	4.84	.532
3. I think that it is important to protect the quality of the coastal area	4.77	.608
4. I think that picking up litter will reduce the amount of water pollution	4.73	.665
5. I think that it is dangerous to climb the cliffs	4.70	.702
6. *I think that it is **safe** to climb the cliffs (* dangerous to climb)*	4.69	.696
7. I think that it is important to keep cliff erosion to a minimum	4.63	.833
8. I think that visitors need to report the discovery of special fossils to the *Charmouth Heritage Visitor Centre*	4.61	.778
9. I think that it is important to protect fossils for future generations	4.55	.857
10. *I think that visitors **should be allowed to climb** the cliffs *(=should not be allowed to climb)*	4.42	1.027
11. I am concerned that pollution on the coast is being increasing by beach litter	4.42	.847
12. *I think that visitors do **NOT** need to help remove beach litter, even if it did not belong to them * (=do need to help)*	4.39	.962
13. I am concerned that people dispose of litter on the beach	4.39	.862
14. I think that visitors should help remove beach litter, even if it did not belong to them	4.36	.930
15. I think that climbing cliffs will damage the environment	4.35	.998
16. I think that collecting fossils from the cliffs will damage the cliffs	4.31	.899
17. I think that it is dangerous to collect fossils from the cliffs	4.31	.883
18. *I think that it is **safe** to collect fossils from the cliffs (*= dangerous to collect)*	4.28	.940
19. *I think that walking off the footpaths will **NOT** damage the cliffs *(=will damage)*	4.14	1.122
20. I am concerned that the cliffs are eroding rapidly	4.13	.906
21. I think that visitors should not be allowed to collect fossils from the cliffs	4.02	1.116
22. I think that fossil collecting helps one to learn about fossils	3.99	.925
23. I am concerned that people climb the cliffs	3.97	.968
24. I am concerned that important fossils are damaged by visitors	3.87	1.015
25. I am concerned that there is too much litter on the beach	3.86	1.019
26. I think that fossil collecting helps in the progress of scientific research	3.85	1.023
27. I am concerned that people take special fossils home	3.82	1.063
28. *I think that visitors **should be allowed to collect** the fossils from the cliffs *(=should not be allowed to collect)*	3.81	1.116
29. I am concerned that people collect the fossils from the cliffs	3.80	1.006
30. I am concerned that people do not keep to the footpaths on the cliffs	3.62	1.016
31. I think that fossil collecting activities by visitors make a positive contribution to the economy of the local area	3.38	1.141

Note: * negative items reverse coded prior to further analysis; Using a 5-point Likert type scale

As indicated in Table 9.14, most of the respondents showed a strongly positive environmental attitude toward the importance of environmental protection issues (i.e. the quality of coastal areas, responsible behaviours, fossils, and cliff erosion). In particular, most respondents agreed strongly with the coastal protection and 'beach litter' issue (e.g. 'beach litter contributes to water pollution' (mean=4.85) and 'it is important to protect the quality of the coastal area' (mean=4.77) than two other topics.

In terms of the belief statements regarding negative impacts of problem behaviour (e.g. climbing the cliffs and collecting fossils from the cliffs), most respondents agreed positively about the importance of protection of 'cliff erosion' (mean=4.63) and 'fossils' (mean=4.55) and they were more aware of the negative impacts of inappropriate behaviour on the geological environment. However, they agreed less with the three types of statements for the positive outcomes of fossil collecting activities which include 'fossil collecting helps one to learn about fossils' (mean=3.99), 'fossil collecting helps in the progress of scientific research' (mean=3.85), and 'fossil collecting activities by visitors make a positive contribution to the economy of the local area' (mean=3.38).

With regard to 'visitor support for management policies regarding specific responsible behaviour for conservation of the site, most participants agreed positively with the belief statements regarding three conservation topics (i.e. 'visitors should (*=should NOT) be allowed to climb the cliffs' (mean=4.42); 'visitors need to report the discovery of special fossils to the Lulworth Heritage Visitor Centre' (mean=4.61); 'visitors do NOT need (*= do need) to help remove beach litter, even if it did not belong to them' (mean=4.39; * positive statement for this: mean=4.36). However, they less agreed with a belief statement regarding 'fossil collecting' policy (i.e. 'visitors should not be allowed to collect fossils from the cliffs' (mean=4.01; * negative statements for this: mean=3.81).

In terms of feelings of concern toward the three environmental issues, most of the respondents had high levels of concern about coastal pollution (mean=4.42) and people 'disposing of litter on the beach (mean=4.39) than two other topics (e.g. 'cliff erosion' and 'fossils'). However, respondents had lower levels of concern about specific problem actions regarding 'walking off the footpaths' (mean=3.62), 'collecting fossils from the cliffs' (mean=3.80), and 'climbing the cliffs' (mean=3.97).

9.9 Behavioural Intentions

In terms of respondents' intentions toward general and specific responsible environmental behaviour, the overall mean score of intentions was high with 3.95 (SD=0.543). As expected, respondents agreed strongly with intentions to engage in general responsible environmental behaviour: 'I intend to behave in a way that will not harm plants and animals' (mean=4.85, SD=0.464), and 'I do not intend to disturb the environment' (mean=4.68, SD=0.666). The respondents' intentions towards the environmental activism in both groups were less positive on four statements including 'I intend to become more involved in environmental issues' (mean=3.53)' 'I intend to make a donation to an environmental organization' (mean= 3.10)', 'I intend to become a member of an environmental organization (mean=2.64)' and 'I intend to become involved in volunteer work for environmental conservation activities' (mean=2.32).

With regard to respondents' commitment to follow the specific responsible behaviour for conservation of the site, most respondents agreed positively on five behavioural intentions including 'I will follow the Code of Conduct' (mean=4.62), 'I will keep to the footpaths on the cliffs' (mean=4.64), 'I will not climbing the cliffs'(mean=4.54), 'I will inform the Lulworth Heritage Visitor Centre if I discover special fossils' (mean= 4.62) and 'I will not collect the fossils from the cliffs' (mean=4.35). However, 'I will tell people about the importance of the geological environment in this area' (mean=3.70), 'I will pick up beach litter when I see it, even if it did not belong to me' (mean=3.85) were less positive among the total sample.

Table 9.15 Behavioural Intentions

I intend to….	Mean	SD
I intend to behave in a way that will not harm plants and animals	4.85	.464
I do not intend to disturb any marine life	4.68	.666
I will keep to the footpaths on the cliffs	4.64	.768
I will follow the Code of Conduct	4.62	.724
I will inform the Charmouth Heritage Visitor Centre, if I discover special fossils	4.62	.769
I will not climb the cliffs	4.54	.837
I will not collect fossils from the cliff	4.35	.935
I will pick up beach litter when I see it, even if it did not belong to me	3.85	1.124
I will tell people about the importance of the geological environment in this area	3.70	1.073
I intend to become more involved in environmental issues	3.53	2.546
I intend to make a donation to an environmental organisation	3.10	1.245
I intend to become a member of an environmental organisation	2.64	1.404
I intend to become involved in volunteer work for environmental conservation activities	2.32	1.213

Note: Used a 5-scale from 1 (strongly disagree) to 5 (strongly agree); Cronbach's Alpha=0.814.

Summary of Stage 1: The Visitor Profile and Interpretation Experiences, Attitudes, and Behavioural Intentions at Charmouth Coastal Area

This study provides an insight into the visitor profile, their experiences of this site and various interpretive programmes, as well as attitudes and behavioural intentions towards conservation issues and responsible behaviour.

Research Objective 1.1: The Profile of Visitors to the Charmouth Coastal Area

Firstly, the data indicates that well-educated adults, couples and families including children groups, middle aged groups (between 35 to 45 years old), and domestic and repeated visitors were the major demographic profiles. Almost 41.7% of visitors were involved in environmental organisations or activities and most of respondents were likely to visit natural areas more than three times per year. This indicated that the pre-existing attitude variables showed that respondents who visited the Charmouth coastal areas were already interested in and concerned about the natural environment.

The most important motives in visiting the Charmouth coastal area for respondents were 'having a good time with family/friends' and 'enjoying nature'.

Research Objective 1.2: What Did They Experience During Their Visit to the Charmouth Coastal Area?

Experiences of The Sample Site and Various Interpretive Programmes

Most visitors were very satisfied with their visit to this site. In particular, post-visit groups (n=242) indicated that the key experiences after visiting the Charmouth coastal area by post-visit respondents (n=242) were 'learning about the fossils' and 'having a good time on-site' although their motivations to visit the site were 'having a good time with family' and 'enjoying nature'.

In terms of the interpretation experiences, the most important information sources used were 'exhibition/display' and 'signboard' while almost 27.8% of respondents did not use any information during their visits to this site. Additionally, some 23% of visitors (n=453) had read the Code of Conduct on fossil collecting which presented the important information related to responsible environmental behaviour for collection of fossils in order to help protect this part of the Jurassic coastal area. With regard to the Visitor Centre experiences, the results show that a majority group of visitors have experienced the Charmouth Heritage Visitor Centre previously, on-site experience being the most common use of the interpretive components in this area. With regard to the role of the Visitor Centre, most respondents agreed with the educational role of the Visitor Centre. After experiences of visiting the Charmouth Hertiage Visitor Centre, the results indicate that their experience of the Visitor Centre was described as educational and enjoyable. Also, they indicate that they learned mostly about 'fossils' and 'geology of the coast'. Moreover, respondents who had visited the Centre demonstrated that they had a high level of satisfaction of the Centre experiences while a moderate level of awareness, understanding and attitude change toward environmental conservation were held by participants in the Centre.

Research Objective 1.3: Attitudes and Behavioural Intentions toward Conservation Issues and Responsible Behaviour

Like the findings of the Lulworth coastal area, most visitors had strongly positive environmental attitudes on the 'coastal protection' and beach litter issue rather than the two other site-specific issues (protection of cliff erosion and fossils). Overall, visitors were likely to be aware of the local environmental issues and problems, and they were concerned about the negative impacts of problem behaviour on the environment. In turn, they were likely to behave in a responsible environmental way in order to protect the Charmouth coastal area. However, the results present that a majority of visitors had a lower level of intentions to engage in environmental activism and removing beach litter behaviour.

Stage 2: The Effects of the Visitor Centre on Attitudes and Intentions by Comparisons among the Three Subgroups

Introduction

The primary aim of this study was to assess the effects of interpretation experiences on visitors' attitudes and behavioural intentions. This study focused on the evaluation of the effectiveness of the Visitor Centre in this section. As mentioned in the results of the Lulworth Costal area, three subgroups were also revealed according to their experience of the Visitor Cetnre. Group A (n=89) consists of 'those who had not visited the Centre and had no intention of doing so', Group B (n=57) includes 'those who had a plan to visit without previous experience of the Centre', Group C (n=307) contains 'those who visited the Centre before and on this occasion'. In this Stage 2, first, this study examined whether or not any significant differences existed among the three sub-groups in terms of visitors' demographic and other experience variables through Chi-square tests or ANOVA tests. Next, after comparing the visitor profile among the three subgroups, the effects of the Visitor Centre on attitudes and intentions were investigated. In particular, a series of ANOVA tests were conducted to determine if there were any significant differences in the responses of the three sub-samples.

9.10 Description of the Overall Sample Comparing the Three Sub-Groups

Overall, a series of chi-square tests indicated that significant differences among the three sub-samples were found in age and motivation variables (See Table 9.16). However, there were significant differences in relation to gender, education, residence, group composition, past experiences of the site, environmental involvement, and previous experiences of natural areas.

Most of Group B and Group C were older middle-aged adults (over 36 years old) while most of Group A, who had not experienced the Visitor Centre at all, were younger adults. With regard to motivation, as expected, Group C who had experienced the Visitor Centre were more interested in 'learning about fossils' or 'protection of the site' while the other two groups (Group A and Group B) were more interested in 'having a good time with family/friends' and 'having a relaxing time'.

Table 9.16 Comparison of Visitor Profile by The Three Sub-Groups

	Group A (n=89)	Group B (n=57)	Group C (n=307)	Chi-Square	Sig.
1. Age					
18-25	10.1%	3.5%	6.2%	21.783	0.016
26-35	27.0%	10.5%	12.1%		
36-45	27.0%	29.8%	30.6%		
46-55	23.6%	24.6%	25.7%		
56-65	9.0%	24.6%	17.3%		
Over 66	3.4%	7.0%	8.1%		
2.Motivation					
To have a good time with family/friends	47.2%	42.1%	32.8%	33.232	0.001
To have a relaxing time	20.2%	31.6%	17.0%		
To enjoy the beauty of nature	22.5%	22.8%	23.6%		
To learn about fossils	5.6%	3.5%	20.3%		
To learn about the need to protect this area	0%	0%	2.0%		
Other (talking photos and doing sports)	**4.5%**	**0%**	**4.2%**		

Note: **Group A:** Not visited the Centre this time;

   Group B: Plan to visit the Centre; **Group C:** Visited the Centre before/this time

9.11 Comparison of Interpretation Experiences among the Three Sub-Groups

Table 9.17 shows that significant differences were found in the perception of the role of the Visitor Centres, levels of interpretation participation, and in whether they had read the Code of Conduct brochure. In terms of the perception of the role of the Visitor Centres, the results of the ANOVA test indicated that Group A, who had no experience of the Charmouth Heritage Visitor Centre, strongly agreed that visitor centres provide tourists information (mean=4.39) than Group B (mean=4.16) and Group C (mean=3.91).

Table 9.17 Comparison of Interpretation Experiences among the Three Sub-Groups

Chi-Square test	Group A (n=89) %(n)	Group B (n=57) %(n)	Group C (n=307) %(n)	Chi-Square	Sig.
Levels of Interpretive Participation (n=449)					
• No participation (0) • (n=126)	56.2% (50)	57.9% (33)	14.0% (43)	223.508	.000
• Lower levels (1-2) (n=191)	42.7% (39)	42.1% (24)	63.8% (196)		
• Higher levels (3-5) • (n=132)	1.1% (1)	0% (0)	22.1% (68)		
Reading Code of Conduct brochure (n=452)					
Yes (n=104)	11.2%(10)	5.3%(3)	29.7%(91)	43.811	.000
No & I don't know (n=348)	88.8%(79)	94.7%(54)	70.3%(215)		
• • **ANOVA test**					

The Role of the Visitor Centre (n=452)	Group A (n=89) Mean(SD)	Group B (n=57) Mean(SD)	Group C (n=307) Mean (SD)	F	Sig.
Visitor centres provide a useful source of tourist information about local facilities	4.39(0.79)	4.16(0.82)	3.91(1.05)	5.342	.000

Note: missing values are not included

Chi-Square tests were used to determine whether significant differences among the three subgroups existed in terms of levels of interpretation and reading of the Code of Conduct. The results of Chi-Square tests showed that there were significant differences between the three subgroups (p=.000) in levels of interpretation participation. As seen in Table 9.17, most Group C respondents who had experienced the Visitor Centre before and this time were likely to use a number of different types of interpretive components while other Group A and Group B respondents were likely to use only one or two interpretive programmes which are mainly 'signboard' and 'brochures'. With regard to reading the Code of Conduct brochure, Group C samples had reading the Code of Conduct brochure more than the other groups.

9.12 Comparison of Satisfaction by the Three Sub-Groups

No significant differences were found on related to satisfaction among the three subgroups.

9.13 Comparison of Awareness of Threats to the environment by the Three Sub-Groups

No significant differences were found on awareness of threats to the environment at Charmouth coastal area among the three subgroups.

9.14 Comparison of Attitudes (Beliefs and Feelings of Concern Components) among the Three Subgroups

In relation to the effects of the Visitor Centre on attitudes toward specific environmental conservation issues and responsible behavior, there were significant differences among the three subgroups in belief components of attitudes about the specific issues in terms of 'cliff erosion' and 'negative impacts of climbing', 'positive impacts of fossil collecting', 'visitor support for informing the discovery of special fossils to the Centre' and 'visitor support for picking up beach litter'. As expected, respondents demonstrated greater levels of these issues resulting from the experiences of the Charmouth Heritage Visitor Centre. However, there were no significant differences among the three subgroups in beliefs regarding 'negative outcomes of fossil collecting' and all types of beliefs and concern statements regarding the 'beach litter' issue.

Additionally, with regard to comparisons of levels of attitudes toward specific issues and behaviours among the three groups, post-hoc test (using Tukey and Scheffe methods) were performed whether significant differences exist among the subgroups. In particular, between Group B respondents who have a plan to visit without any previous experiences of the Centre and Group C respondents who had already experienced the Visitor Centre during previous visits and this one, significant differences were found relating to 'it is dangerous to climb the cliffs', 'climbing the cliffs will damage the environment', 'it is important to protect fossils for future generations'. In comparisons of mean differences between Group A and Group C, there were significant differences between these groups in relation to the consequences of problem behaviour associated with the cliff erosion and fossil issues. More detail, group A respondents agreed less with the five statements rather than Group C respondents in terms of the negative impact of problem behaviour associated with the cliff erosion issue (e.g. 'walking off the footpaths will damage the cliffs', 'visitor should not be allowed to climb the cliffs', concern about walking off the footpaths to the cliffs and climbing the cliffs').

With regard to the 'fossil collecting' issues, significant differences between Group A and Group C were found relating to 'it is important to protect fossils for future generations', 'visitors need to report the discovery of special fossils to the Centre', and two types of positive outcomes of 'fossil collecting' (e.g. helping in the progress of scientific research', 'a positive contribution to the local economy' and concern about fossil collecting and damage of important fossils.

With regards to the comparison of mean differences between Group A and Group B, Group B respondents who have a plan to visit during this visit to the site, had significantly higher levels of attitudes in three types of statements regarding 'visitors need to report the discovery of special fossils to the Centre', 'I am concerned that people do not keep the footpaths on the cliffs', and 'visitors should help to remove beach litter, even if it did not belong to them'. The Post-Hoc test results indicated that the Visitor Centre significantly influenced visitors' attitudes toward the negative impacts of 'climbing the cliffs' and the positive outcomes of 'fossil collecting'.

Table 9.18 Comparison of Attitudes of the Three Sub-groups

	Group A (n=89)		Group B (n=57)		Group C (n=307)		F	Sig.
	Mean	SD	Mean	SD	Mean	SD		
I think that it is dangerous to climb the cliffs	4.61	0.820	4.49	0.966	4.77	0.589	4.967	0.022
I think that it is safe (=dangerous) to climb the cliffs	4.55	0.798	4.60	0.704	4.75	0.657	3.322	0.007
I think that visitors need to report the discovery of special fossils to the Charmouth Heritage Visitor Centre	4.35	1.001	4.68	0.659	4.67	0.709	6.380	0.002
I think that it is important to protect fossils for future generations	4.33	1.042	4.30	1.101	4.66	0.716	8.185	0.001
I think that visitors should (=not) be allowed to climb the cliffs	4.19	1.195	4.28	1.065	4.51	0.954	3.959	0.001
I think that climbing cliffs will damage the environment	4.21	1.050	4.02	1.261	4.45	0.911	5.524	0.002
I think that visitors should help to remove beach litter, even if it did not belong to them	4.12	1.126	4.61	0.726	4.38	0.887	5.205	0.033
I think that walking off the footpaths will damage the environment	3.85	1.257	3.91	1.353	4.26	1.008	5.997	0.002
I am concerned that people climb the cliffs	3.66	0.941	4.00	0.982	4.05	0.959	5.727	0.000
I am concerned that important fossils are damaged by visitors	3.57	0.999	3.67	1.006	3.99	1.002	7.297	0.000
I think that fossil collecting helps in the progress of scientific research	3.57	1.075	3.63	1.011	3.96	0.991	6.627	0.013
I am concerned that people take special fossils home	3.56	1.055	3.65	0.973	3.93	1.067	5.047	0.000
I am concerned that people collect the fossils from the cliffs	3.57	0.999	3.61	1.031	3.91	0.991	5.012	0.002
I am concerned that people do not keep to the footpaths on the cliffs	3.29	1.079	3.88	1.019	3.66	0.978	6.926	0.037
I think that fossil collecting activities by visitors make a positive contribution to the economy of the local area	3.06	1.190	3.37	1.291	3.47	1.082	4.665	0.011

Note: (a) Belief statements (I think that ….) using a 5-point scale (1=strongly disagree to 5=strongly agree);

(b) Feelings of concern statements (I am concerned that…) using a 5-point scale (1=not seriously concerned at all to 5=very seriously concerned)

9.15 Comparison of Behavioural Intentions among the Three Sub-Groups

As seen in Table 9.19, the question was used to examine the degree of commitment respondents had to changing their behaviour. In comparisons between the three subgroups, the results provided that there were significant differences between the three groups in the specific environmental behaviour regarding 'not climbing on the cliffs', 'not collecting fossils', 'keeping to the footpath' and 'informing the Lulworth Heritage Visitor Centre about special fossils'. The 'visited the Centre at least once' group had a higher levels of mean score in most of the five items than the Group A who had not experienced the Centre and had no intention of doing so and the Group B who had a plan to visit the Centre without having previous experiences of the Centre before.

Table 9.19 Comparison of Behavioural Intentions of the Three Sub-Groups

Dependent Variable	Group A (n=89)		Group B (n=57)		Group C (n=307)		F	Sig.
	Mean	SD	Mean	Mean	SD	Mean		
I will keep to the footpaths on the cliffs	4.43	0.952	4.70	0.626	4.68	0.724	4.159	0.016
I will inform the Charmouth Heritage Visitor Centre, if I discover special fossils	4.27	1.063	4.68	0.540	4.70	0.672	11.784	0.000
I will tell people about the importance of the geological environment in this area	3.39	1.104	3.65	0.954	3.80	1.070	5.252	0.006
I will not climb the cliffs	4.22	0.997	4.65	0.694	4.63	0.791	7.984	0.000
I will not collect fossils from the cliffs	4.02	1.055	4.42	0.823	4.43	0.899	6.929	0.001
I intend to make a donation to an environmental organisation	2.67	1.295	3.26	1.275	3.20	1.199	6.785	0.001
I intend to become involved in volunteer work for environmental conservation activities	1.90	0.978	2.16	1.146	2.48	1.256	8.791	0.000
I intend to become a member of an environmental organisation	2.18	1.257	2.42	1.388	2.81	1.416	7.900	0.000

Again, this study performed Post-Hoc test by Tukey and Scheffe methods. Group A respondents were significantly different from Group B and Group C respondents on all 8 types of intention statements as seen in Table 9.19. Interestingly, Group B respondents agreed strongly on four types of specific behavioural intentions statements related to the climbing and collecting behaviours rather than Group A. For example, 'I will not climb the cliffs', 'I will not collect the fossils from the cliffs', 'I will inform the discovery of special fossils to the Centre' and 'I intend to make a donation to an environmental organisation'. Significant differences were found between Group A and Group C on all 8 types of behavioural intentions. However, there were no significant differences between Group B respondents and Group C respondents on all 8 types of behavioral intentions.

Summary of Stage 2:

Research Objective 1.4: The Effect of the Visitor Centre on Attitudes and Behavioural Intention

This study is to evaluate the effects of the visitor centre on respondents' beliefs, feelings and behavioural intentions toward specific local conservation issues and responsible behaviour through comparison of the mean scores of the three groups dependent on their experiences of the Visitor Centre. First, each group of visitor profiles were examined among three subgroups. Significant differences were found in relation to age, motivation, and participation pattern of the interpretive programmes.

Group C respondents who had visited at least once before this time were more likely to be older (between 36 to 55 years old), and have higher level of motivation for 'learning about the protection of the nature and fossils, compared to the other two groups. In terms of interpretation experience, respondents in Group C participated in the different types of interpretive programmes and had experience of the visitor centre previously. 'Plan to visit without experiences of the Centre' groups (Group B) used at least one or two types of interpretive programmes (e.g. brochure or signboard) before their experiences of the Visitor Centre, compared to Group A respondents who had no experienced the Centre before and had no interests to use any other information.

Overall, the effects of Visitor Centre on attitudes and behavioural intention among the three sub-groups, were evaluated to determine if significant differences existed among the subgroups. Significant differences were found on the part of the belief, or feeling components of attitudes and behavioural intentions in relation to the cliff erosion and fossil issues at this site. However, the Visitor Centre had no significant effect on attitudes and behavioural intentions related to the 'beach litter' issues. Table 9.20 shows that the Group C respondents had higher mean scores of overall attitudes (mean=4.31) and behavioural intentions (mean=4.01) than the other two groups. These results are similar to the findings of the Lulworth Coastal area.

Table 9.20 Comparison of Overall Attitudes and Behavioural Intentions among the Three Groups by Visitor Centre Experiences

	Group A (n=89)		Group B (n=57)		Group C (n=307)		F	Sig.
	Mean	SD	Mean	SD	Mean	SD		
Overall attitudes	4.08	0.436	4.24	0.390	4.31	0.410	10.883	0.000
Overall Intentions	3.68	0.543	3.95	0.521	4.02	0.525	13.941	0.000

Additionally, with regard to comparisons of Group B and Group C on attitudes and behavioural intentions by post-hoc test in ANOVA analysis, significant differences were found only in attitudes toward 'negative impacts of climbing the cliffs' between the two groups. However, there were no significant differences in all types of behavioural intentions between Group B and Group C. Interestingly, Group A respondents were significantly different from both Group B and Group C on specific attitudes and behavioural intentions regarding 'fossil collecting' and 'climbing the cliffs'.

Overall, the findings of the effects of the Visitor Centre at this site are similar with those of the Lulworth coastal area. The direct effects of the Visitor Centre vary depending on types of specific responsible behaviour associated with each of conservation issues and different groups of visitors. As the Visitor Centre influenced visitors' attitudes and behavioural intentions toward specific issues regarding 'climbing' and 'collecting fossils', the other potential factors might influence those behaviours with correlating with the Visitor Centre experience. Therefore, in Stage 4, this study examines the interactive effects of various factors on specific behavioural intention.

Stage 3: Factor Analysis

Introduction

For Stage 3, this section presents the results of an exploratory factor analysis on all multivariable scale: attitudes and behavioural intentions. The communalities of the variables were examined to assess whether they meets acceptable levels of explanation. Variables with communalities less than .50 were excluded. Also, only factors with eigenvalues over 1 were retained as a cut-off point. The internal homogeneity of the subscales was examined by calculating Cronbach's alpha coefficients.

9.16 Factor Analysis of Attitudes

A principal component factor analysis with a Varimax (orthogonal) rotation was used to explore underlying factors that summarised the structure of the set of 31 attitudes (beliefs/feelings) item scale to assist in data reduction. The reliability test was high (0.875) with 'Cronbach's alpha' for the 31 items scale for belief/feeling of concern measure.

In the process of factor analysis, the communality of one belief item, 'walking off the footpaths will damage the cliffs' was excluded in further analysis because factor loadings of this item was below 0.40. After removing this item, a principal component factor analysis was applied to the 30 items of attitude measure. Communalities of all 30 items of attitude were higher than 0.40. Also, the factor loadings of .40 or higher for all items on each factor provided support for its use as a latent construct.

The Bartlett's test of sphericity was significant (Chi-square=6268.639, p=.000), and the Kaiser-Meyer-Olkin measure of sampling adequacy was 0.837. This result supported that these variables were normally distributed and the correlation matrix indicated the possibility that grouping of attitudes items could exist.

The results of the analysis are presented in Table 9.19. Factor analysis of the 30 attitude statement items identified nine meaningful factors accounting for 69.47% of the total variance. The internal consistency was high for six of the nine accepted factors, with Cronbach's alpha ranging from 0.76 to 0.89. Three factors (Factor 6, Factor 7 and Factor 9) had Cronbach's alpha of < 0.60.

The remaining nine factors were interpreted as follow: the first factor, termed "negative impacts of fossil collecting" explained 12.3% with an eigenvalue of 3.690. The second factor, "negative impacts of climbing the cliffs" contained items related to visitors' understanding of ways in which climbing the cliffs may impact on the cliffs environment and visitors' support for the 'not climbing the cliffs' policy. This explained 8.58%. The third factor was labelled "concern for pollution by beach litter" with 7.79% of the variance and reflected the respondent's feelings of concern for coastal pollution by beach litter and disposing of litter on the beach. The fourth factor, "concern for fossils" (7.78% of the variance) indicated visitors' feelings of concern about damaging the important fossils, collecting fossils from the cliffs, and taking the fossils home. The fifth factor was termed "concern about cliff erosion" including 'climbing the cliffs', 'walking off the footpaths' and 'rapid cliff erosion'. This explained 7.09%.

For the sixth factor, namely, the term applied to the sixth dimension was difficult because there was a mix of several topics which were 'negative impacts of beach litter', 'importance of coastal protection', and 'importance of responsible behaviour'. This sixth factor (namely, "awareness of pollution and importance of protection and responsible behaviour") explained 6.92% of the variance. The seventh factor, "importance of protection for fossils and cliff erosion" explained 6.80%. This factor included two statements regarding the importance of protection for fossils and cliff erosion, and the additional statement which might be less relevant to those, were added such as 'visitors' support for reporting the discovery of special fossils to the Centre'. The eighth factor, was labelled "visitors' support for beach cleaning" with 6.19%. This factor represented two negative or positive beliefs in support of beach cleaning. Finally, the ninth factor, termed 'positive outcomes of fossil collecting' focused on visitors' views of the benefits of fossil collecting (e.g. learning, contribution to scientific research or economy of the local area) explaining 6.01% of the variance.

Table 9.21 Factor Analysis of Attitudes (Beliefs and Feeling of Concern Components)

	Factor 1	Factor 2	Factor 3	Factor 4	Factor 5	Factor 6	Factor 7	Factor 8	Factor 9	(A)	(B)	(C)
F1. Negative Impacts of Fossil Collecting										3.690	12.300	.879
I think that visitors should not be allowed to collect fossils	.810											
I think that it is dangerous to collect the fossils from the cliffs	.799											
I think that collecting fossils from the cliffs will damage the environment	.781											
I think that it is safe (=dangerous) to collect fossils from the cliffs*	.740											
I think that visitors should (NOT) be allowed to collect fossils from the cliffs*	.709											
F2. Negative Impacts of Climbing the Cliffs										2.576	8.588	.777
I think that it is dangerous to climb the cliffs		.869										
I think that it is safe(=dangerous) to climb the cliffs*		.839										
I think that climbing the cliffs will damage the environment		.665										
I think that visitors should (NOT) be allowed to climb the cliffs *		.602										
F3. Concern about Pollution										2.336	7.785	.822
I am concerned that people dispose of litter on the beach			.886									
I am concerned that pollution on the coast is increasing by beach litter			.865									
I am concerned that there is too much litter on the beach			.766									
F4. Concern about Fossils										2.335	7.784	.884
I am concerned that important fossils are damaged by visitors				.898								
I am concerned that people take special fossils home				.896								
I am concerned that people collect the fossils from the cliffs				.641								
F5. Concern about Cliff Erosion										2.127	7.088	.765
I am concerned that the cliffs are eroding rapidly					.773							
I am concerned that people climb the cliffs					.762							
I am concerned that people do not keep to the footpaths on the cliffs					.651							

Note: * negative items reverse coded prior to further analysis; *(A)= Eigenvalue; (B)= % of Variance; (C)=Cronbach's Alpha*

Continued Table 9.21

	Factor 1	Factor 2	Factor 3	Factor 4	Factor 5	Factor 6	Factor 7	Factor 8	Factor 9	(A)	(B)	(C)
F6. Awareness of Pollution and Importance of Coastal Protection/Responsible Behaviour												
I think that beach litter does not contribute to water pollution (=does contribute to)*						.833				2.076	6.920	.685
I think that picking up litter will reduce the amount of pollution						.678						
I think that it is important for visitors to behave in a environmentally responsible way						.552						
I think that it is important to protect the quality of the coastal area						.550						
F7. Importance of Protection of Fossils and the Cliffs												
I think that it is important to protect fossils for future generation							.807			2.041	6.803	.644
I think that it is important to keep cliff erosion to a minimum							.694					
I think that visitors need to report the discovery of special fossils to the Charmouth Heritage Visitor Centre							.586					
F8. Visitors' Support for Beach Cleaning												
I think that visitors do not need to help remove beach litter (=need to help)*								.908		1.856	6.186	.889
I think that visitors should help to remove beach litter, even if it did not belong to them								.902				
F9. Positive Outcomes of Fossil Collecting												
I think that fossil collecting activities by visitors make a positive contribution to the economy of the local area									.758	1.804	6.013	.638
I think that fossil collecting helps one to learn about fossils0									.758			
I think that fossil collecting helps in the progress of scientific research									.750			
Mean (S.D)	4.14 (0.82)	4.54 (0.67)	4.22 (0.78)	3.83 (0.93)	3.91 (0.79)	4.80 (0.44)	4.60 (0.63)	4.38 (0.89)	3.74 (0.79)			

Note: * negative items reverse coded prior to further analysis; *(A)= Eigenvalue; (B)=% of Variance; (C)=Cronbach's Alpha*

9.17 Factor Analysis of Behavioural Intention

Again, a principal component factor analysis with a varimax rotation was undertaken to explore underlying factors that summarised the structure of this set of 13 behavioural intention items, and to reduce the number of variables into a smaller set of factors. A total of 453 participants were asked to indicate their behavioural intention on a 5-point scale. The reliability test of 13 intention statements was 0.814. Communalities of all 13 items were higher than 0.40. The Bartlett's test of sphericity (Chi-Square test= 1986.368, p=.000) and the Kaiser-Meyer-Olkin measure of sampling adequacy test (=0.817) were measured. This result showed that these behavioural intention variables were normally distributed and the correlation matrix indicated the possibility that grouping of these variables could exist. Table 9.20 presents the three factors resulting from a factor analysis accounting for 61.41% of the total variance.

The first factor, termed "environmental activism intentions" explained 24.39 % of the total variance. It comprised the six variables concerning geological importance, removing beach litter, involvement in organisations, donation, other environmental issues, and volunteer work. The second factor was labeled "special environmental behavioural intentions" which is related to the environmental problems and issues in the Lulworth coastal area. It explained 18.9% of the total variance and combined four measures which are used to follow the code, to keep the footpaths, not to climb the cliff, and not to collect the fossils from the cliffs. The third factor, "general environmental behavioural intentions" explaining 18.11% of the total variance, combined three variables regarding general concern for the environment (e.g. reporting special fossils to the Charmouth Heritage Centre, not disturbing any marine life, not harming plants and animals).

316

Table 9.22 Factor Results of Behavioural Intentions (N=453)

	Factor 1	Factor 2	Factor 3
F1: Environmental Activism			
I intend to become involved in volunteer work for environmental conservation activities	.805		
I intend to become a member of an environmental organisation	.796		
I intend to make a donation to an environmental organisation	.787		
I intend to become more involved in environmental issues	.707		
I will tell people about the importance of the geological environment in this area	.632		
I will pick up beach litter when I see it, even if it did not belong to me	.455		
F2: Specific Environmental Behaviour			
I will not climb the cliffs		.844	
I will not collect fossils from the cliffs		.816	
I will keep to the footpaths on the cliffs		.580	
I will follow the Code of Conduct		.580	
F3: General Environmental Behaviour			
I intend to behave in a way that will not harm plants and animals			.823
I do not intend to disturb any marine life			.763
I will inform the Charmouth Heritage Visitor Centre, if I discover special fossils			.627
Eigenvalue	2.927	2.268	2.173
% of variance	24.394	18.901	18.109
Cronbach's alpha	.664	.771	.649
Mean factor score (SD)	3.19 (0.93)	4.54 (0.63)	4.71 (0.49)

Summary of Stage 3:

Research Objective 1.5: Multi-dimensions of Attitudes and Behavioural Intentions

In Stage 3, this study examines whether a rational underlying structure existed in the multivariate scale, attitudes and behavioural intentions. This analysis showes that the different aspects of attitudes and behavioural intentions were clearly categorised in the three main local conservation issues and responsible behaviour in this study. At Charmouth coastal area, nine factors were identified among the 30 attitude items and three factors were also identified among 13 behavioural intentions.

Table 9.23 demonstrates that the three main local conservation issues and responsible behaviour are related to each of specific attitudes in terms of each of topics, 'cliff erosion', 'fossils', and 'beach litter'. Then specific factors for attitudes toward specific behaviour are also related to each of three types of responsible behavioural intentions.

Table 9.23 The Relationships between Three Main Conservation Topics and Underlying Factors of Attitudes and Intentions

Three Main topics related to local conservation	Factors on attitudes	Factors on behavioural intentions
Cliff erosions	Factor2: Negative impacts of climbing the cliffs	Factor 2: Specific Behaviour
	Factor 5: Concern about cliff erosion	• 'Keep to the footpaths' • 'Not climb the cliffs'
	Factor 7: Importance of protection for fossils and the cliffs	
Fossil Protection (Fossil Collecting)	Factor:1 Negative impacts of fossil collecting	Factor 2: Specific behaviour & Factor 3: General behaviour
	Factor 9: Positive outcomes of fossil collecting	• 'Not collect the fossils' • 'Inform about the discovery of special fossils to the Visitor Centre'
	Factor 4: Concern for fossils	
Coastal Protection (Beach litter)	Factor 6:Awareness of pollution and importance of protection & responsible behaviour	Factor 1: Environmental activism
	Factor 3: Concern for pollution by beach litter	• 'Removing beach litter'
	Factor 8: Visitors' support for beach cleaning	

Stage 4: Investigating the Relative Contribution of Important Factors on Specific Behavioural Intentions

Introduction

In Stage 4, the secondary aim of this research is presented in order to investigate the relative contribution of interpretation experiences, individual characteristics and attitudinal components on specific behavioural intentions. Once again, Figure 9.2 shows the relationships between various variables and specific behavioural intentions.

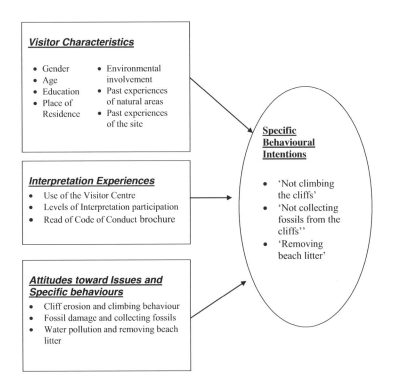

Figure 9.2 The Relationships Between Various Factors and Behavioural Intention

The structure of data analysis process in this Stage 4 is the same with the results of Stage 4 at Lulworth Coastal areas. Firstly, multiple regression analysis was performed in each of the three types of specific behavioural intentions. Before beginning the regression analysis, all individual demographic and interpretation experience variables were transformed and coded as dummy variables (1,0) before beginning the regression analysis. This analysis helps to determine the important influential factors including specific attitudes and individual factors to each of the three specific behavioural intentions. For all three types of regression models, the scatter plots and the Pearson correlation coefficients r showed that there was a linear relationship between the independent variables and the dependent variable. It was also ensured that the independent variables were not highly correlated with each other to reduce the multicollinearity (Durbin-Watson is over 0.75; Tolerance is over 0.5 or near 1).

Secondly, after identifying the important determinants on specific behavioural intentions through multiple stepwise regression analysis, two-way or three-way ANOVA analysis was conducted to examine the interrelationships between only the important individual determinants and each of the specific behavioural intentions. Finally, when no interaction between individual factors and behavioural intentions could be assumed in the second two-way ANOVA analysis, it is possible to examine the direct effects of each of the important influential variables on each of behavioural intentions. Additionally, the direct effects of the influential individual factors on attitudes were also examined.

9.18 Specific Behavioural Intention toward 'Not Climbing the Cliffs'

9.18.1 The Important Determinants on Specific Behavioural Intention toward 'Not Climbing the Cliffs'

Figure 9.3 showed that there were several factors to influence behavioural intention toward 'not climbing the cliffs'. These five independent variables explained 33.5% of the variability of the dependent variable (F=44.552, p=0.000) including specific attitudes, gender, and level of interpretation participation. As expected, the specific attitudes were stronger than other individual variables. Tolerance of each variable was over 0.6 and Durbin-Watson was 1.943. However, Tolerance score of one belief item was less than 0.5 because this item was highly correlated to the other ('I think that it is safe (=*dangerous) to climb the cliffs'). In further regression analysis, this item was excluded. This means that there was no multicollinearity between various independent variables.

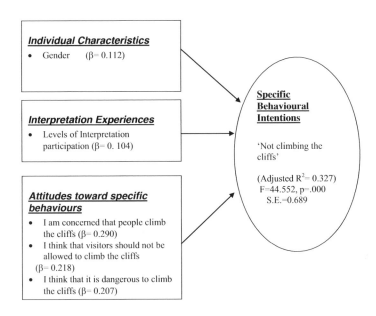

Figure 9.3 The Determinants of Specific Intention toward 'Not Climbing the Cliffs'

As with the results of the types of specific attitudes at Charmouth Coastal area, the specific attitudes toward 'I am concerned about the climbing the cliffs (β= 0.290, t=6.930, p=0.000)', 'I think that it is dangerous to climb the cliffs (β=0.207, t=4.639, p=0.000)' 'I think that visitors should not be allowed to climb the cliffs (β= 0.218, t=4.744, p=0.000)' were the strong factors to behavioural intention toward 'not climbing the cliffs'. Other specific attitude statements were not included in this model (e.g. 'it is important to protect the cliff erosion', 'climbing the cliffs will damage the environment').

In terms of individual factors, only gender (β=0.112, t=2.4846, p=0.005) contributed to the regression model. For interpretation experiences variables, levels of interpretation participation (β=0.104, t=2.378, p=0.018) were also moderately related to behavioural intentions toward 'not climbing the cliffs'. The 'use of the Visitor Centre' and 'reading the Code of Conduct brochure' variables had no the relationships with this intention.

321

The findings imply that as visitors' concern for the problem behaviour and understanding of consequences of the specific behaviour increase, there is a simultaneous increase in their willingness to take responsible action regarding 'not climbing the cliffs', and in turn, it might lead to their actual specific behaviour. In terms of the role of interpretation, Visitor Centre experiences and reading the Code of Conduct brochure might not strongly influence visitors' behavioural intention toward 'not climbing the cliffs'. However, even though there was no strong impact by a single type of interpretation experiences, when visitors use more different types of interpretation including the Visitor Centre experiences and brochure, their willingness regarding 'not climbing the cliffs' increases. Therefore, a single type of interpretation experience variable also influenced indirectly the behavioural intention.

For the demographic variables, gender was also moderately and positively related to behavioural intention. This indicated that different individual groups have different attitudes and behavioural intentions. The next section showed that the indirect effects of the two different individual factors on behavioural intentions were compared by gender and level of interpretation participation. The third section examined the direct effects of visitor sub groups on attitudes and behavioural intentions.

9.18.2 Interrelationships of the Important Determinants on Specific Behavioural Intention toward 'Not Climbing the Cliffs'

The three factors way of ANOVA analysis was conducted to examine the interactive effects of the main individual characteristic variables on behavioural intention toward 'not climbing the cliffs'. Table 9.24 showed that visitors who were female and used a number of interpretive programmes, have higher levels of behavioural intention toward 'not climbing the cliffs' (mean=4.87) than those who were male and have not used interpretation (mean=4.30) during their visit.

Table 9.24 Interactive effects of the Important Factors on Behavioural Intention Regarding 'Not Climbing the Cliffs'

Level of Interpretation Participation	Gender			
	Male		Female	
	Mean	Std. Error	Mean	Std. Error
None	4.30	0.944	4.48	0.759
Lower level (1-2 media)	4.30	1.035	4.69	0.751
Higher level (3-5 media)	4.56	0.810	4.87	0.424

Dependent Variable: Behavioural Intention toward 'not climbing the cliffs'

Additionally, no association between age and gender and levels of interpretation participation by three –way ANOVA analysis was found (F=0.577, p= 0.562). It means that the effects of each individual factor can be examined.

9.18.3 The Direct Effects of Gender and Level of Interpretation Participation on Attitudes and Behavioural Intention toward 'Not Climbing the Cliffs'.

The direct effects of the main influential factors on attitudes and behavioural intentions toward 'not climbing the cliffs' were different between sub samples involving gender and levels of interpretation participation variables.

(1) Gender

First, the direct effects of gender on both attitudes and behavioural intention were examined. As seen in Table 7.24, significant differences were found in the three types of attitudes and behavioural intention between female and male. Female groups had higher mean score in feelings and behavioural intentions toward 'not climbing the cliffs' than male. Even though there were no significant differences in other types of attitudes, females held higher level of beliefs about the negative impacts of climbing the cliffs (e.g. danger of climbing the cliffs, and environmental damage of climbing the cliffs) than males. This means that the awareness of personal safety and negative environmental impacts of climbing the cliffs affects emotionally the concerns about climbing the cliffs for females and in turn, increased their willingness not to climb the cliffs.

Table 9.25 The Direct Effects of Gender on Attitude and Behavioural Intention

	Male (n=219)		Female (n=234)	
Specific Attitudes	Mean	S.D.	Mean	S.D.
I think that it is important to protect the cliff erosion	4.51	.930	4.75	.712
I am concerned that the cliffs are eroding rapidly	**3.98**	.960	**4.28**	.827
I am concerned that people climb the cliffs	**3.82**	1.024	**4.11**	.891
I will not climb the cliffs	4.38	.948	4.68	.690

(2) Level of Interpretation Participation

With regard to the level of interpretation participation in groups, the results of the ANOVA test indicated that visitors who used a higher number of different types of interpretation programmes had higher mean scores on attitudes and behavioural intentions toward 'not climbing the cliffs'. Although there were no significant differences on all types of beliefs and feelings of concern regarding the importance of 'protection of the cliff erosion' and the negative impacts of 'climbing the cliffs' and personal safety, behavioural intention among the three groups was significantly effected by the level of interpretation participation. Compared with the direct effects of other interpretation variables, there were no significant differences in behavioural intention brought about by the use of the Visitor Centre, and reading of Code of Conduct brochure. Both types of interpretation experience variables were effective in influencing visitors' attitudes toward the negative impacts of climbing the cliffs and danger of climbing the cliffs. It indicated that levels of interpretation participation influenced visitors' behavioural intentions through increasing their awareness and concerns about the negative outcomes of climbing the cliffs by a single type of interpretive programme.

9.19 Specific Behavioural Intention Toward 'Not Collecting Fossils from the Cliffs'

9.19.1 The Important Determinants on Specific Behavioural Intention toward 'Not Collecting Fossils from the Cliffs'

The second regression model explained 40.3 % of the variation in the dependent variable, specific behavioural intention toward 'not collecting fossils from the cliffs'. The model as a whole was also significant indicating that there was a strong linear association between behavioural intention toward 'not collecting fossils' and the independent variables (F=61.483, p=0.000). Tolerance score was over 0.5 in all independent variables and Durbin-Watson was over 1.999. It indicated that no multicollinearity was found between the independent variables. However, Tolerance score of one belief item was less than 0.5 because this item was highly correlated to the other ('I think that it is safe (=*dangerous) to collect fossils from the cliffs', I think that visitors should be (=Not) allowed to collect fossils from the cliffs', 'I am concerned that important fossils are damaged by visitors'). In further regression analysis, this item was excluded. This means that there was no multicollinearity between various independent variables.

Overall, specific attitudes toward 'not collecting fossils from the cliffs' and gender (β=0.130; t=3.514, p=0.000) influenced significantly and positively behavioural intention toward 'not collecting fossils from the cliffs'. In terms of the interpretation experiences variables, the use of the Visitor Centre (β=0.080; t=2.149, p=0.032) variable was moderately related to behavioural intention in this model. However, no impacts of 'level of interpretation participation' and 'reading code of conduct brochure' were found.

Once again, specific attitudes were more significant than gender and the use of Visitor Centre variables. In terms of specific attitudes toward 'fossil collecting', a significant positive effects of specific attitudes on behavioural intention were found in the three main types of attitudes related to

'I think that it is dangerous to collect the fossil from the cliffs from the cliffs (β=0.306, t=6.876, p=0.000)', 'I think that visitors should not be allowed to collect the fossils from the cliffs (β=0.263, t=5.899, p=0.000)', and 'I am concerned that people collect fossils from the cliffs(β=0.164; t=3.759, p=0.000)'.

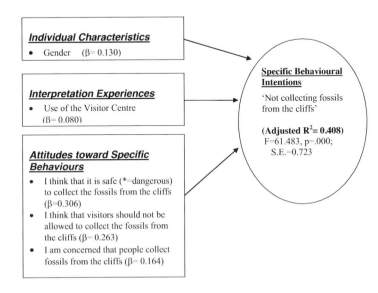

Figure 9.4 The Determinants of Specific Behavioural Intentions toward 'Not Collecting Fossils from the Cliffs'

Other beliefs and concerns of feelings related to negative environmental impacts of fossil collecting (e.g. ''I think that visitors should (*=Not) be allowed to collect fossils from the cliffs', 'I think that it is dangerous to collect the fossils from the cliffs', 'I am concerned that important fossils are damaged by visitors', 'I am concerned that people take fossils home') were highly correlated to each other and Tolerance score of these items was less than 0.5. In further regression analysis, they were excluded because of multicollinearity. Positive outcomes of fossil collecting for scientific research, learning about fossils, and its contribution to local economy were not related to behavioural intention. It implies that behavioural intention toward 'not collecting fossils from the cliffs' had a stronger association with specific attitudes (feelings of concern and support) toward specific behaviour of 'not collecting fossils'.

For the individual characteristic variables, age, education, and place of residence were not related to behavioural intention in this model. Previous experiences and environmental involvement variables also did not influence behavioural intention.

9.19.2 Interrelationships of Gender and the Use of the Visitor Centre on Behavioural Intentions toward 'Not Collecting Fossils from the Cliffs'

The two factors way of ANOVA analysis was performed to examine the interactive effects of gender and use of the Visitor Centre on behavioural intention toward 'not collecting fossils from the cliffs'. As seen in Table 9.25, visitors who were female with experience of the Visitor Centre from previous visits in addition to the surveyed visit held higher level of attitudes toward 'not collecting fossils from the cliffs' (mean=4.65), compared to visitors who were male and without experience of the Visitor Centre (mean =4.00). The results indicated that the use of the Visitor Centre played an important role in changing visitors' behavioural intention not to collect the fossils from the cliffs between the two groups of females and males.

Table 9.26 Interrelationships between the Important Determinants and Behavioural Intention toward 'not Collecting Fossils from the Cliffs'

Gender	The Use of the Visitor Centre			
	No, not visited before/this time		Yes, Visited before/this time	
	Mean	Std. Error	Mean	Std. Error
Male	4.00	1.113	4.21	1.000
Female	4.32	0.859	4.65	0.721

Dependent variable: Behavioural Intention toward 'not collecting fossils from the cliffs'

The results of two-way ANOVA analysis indicated that there was no association between education and levels of interpretation participation ($F=0.437$, $p=0.509$). The next analysis was performed to examine whether any differences in attitudes and behavioural intentions exist between the different groups existed.

9.19.3 The Direct Effects of Gender and Use of the Visitor Centre on Attitudes and Behavioural Intention toward 'Not Collecting Fossils from the Cliffs'

The direct effects of the main influential factors on attitudes and behavioural intentions toward 'not collecting fossils from the cliffs' were examined between sub samples involving gender and use of the Visitor Centre variables in this section.

(1) Gender

Significant differences were found in behavioural intentions toward 'not collecting fossils' between male and female groups. As expected, female groups held higher levels of behavioural intentions and attitudes toward the negative outcomes of collecting fossils than male groups. Significant differences were found in most types of attitude statements related to the importance of protection, negative outcomes of fossil collecting, visitors' support for the policy, and concerns about fossil collecting. Interestingly, male groups held slightly higher moderate levels on beliefs related to positive outcomes of fossil collecting regarding helping scientific research and the local economy than female groups.

Table 9.27 The Direct Effects of Gender on Attitudes and Behavioural Intention toward 'Not Collecting Fossils'

Specific Attitudes	Male (n=219)		Female (n=234)		t	Sig.
	Mean	S.D.	Mean	S.D.		
The Importance of Protection It is important to protect the fossils for future generations	4.42	.961	4.67	.730	*-3.088*	*.002*
Negative Outcomes Collecting fossils will damage the environment	4.19	.956	4.43	.827	*-2.915*	*.004*
It is dangerous to collect the fossils from the cliffs	4.19	.924	4.41	.831	*-2.702*	*.007*
Support for policy Visitors should not be allowed to collect the fossils from the cliffs	3.86	1.211	4.16	1.000	*-2.834*	*.005*
Feelings of Concern I am concerned that people collect the fossils from the cliffs	3.66	1.029	3.94	.967	*-2.918*	*.004*
I am concerned that the important fossils are damaged by people	3.65	1.058	4.07	.931	*-4.539*	*.000*
I am concerned that people take the important fossils	3.55	1.117	4.07	.944	*-5.363*	*.000*
Behavioural Intention I will not collect the fossils from the cliffs	4.15	1.036	4.53	.787	*-4.454*	*.000*

(2) Use of the Visitor Centre

This study showed the use of Visitor Centre was moderately related to behavioural intention toward 'not collecting fossils from the cliffs'. No significant effects of a total number of interpretation participation and reading the Code of Conduct were found on behavioural intention. As reviewed in the previous section, Stage 2, there were significant positive effects of the Visitor Centre on behavioural intention toward 'not collecting fossils from the cliffs' among the three different groups. Additionally, the Visitor Centre influenced significantly visitors' attitudes related to negative and positive outcomes of fossil collecting among the three groups. Compared to the direct effects of the level of interpretation participation and reading the Code of Conduct brochure, the results were similar to the effects of the Visitor Centre on specific attitudes. The findings indicated that even though there were no direct effects of each of the interpretation variables on behavioural intention, interpretation indirectly influenced behavioural intention through increasing visitors' attitudes through all types of interpretation experiences. Interestingly, a total number of interpretive participation was not significantly effective on attitudes and behavioural intention, compared to the other, singe types of interpretation experience. In conclusion, at Charmouth coastal area, a single type of interpretation experience, by itself, was significantly effective on visitors' specific attitudes.

9.20 Specific Behavioural Intention toward 'Removing Beach Litter'

9.20.1 The Important Determinants on Specific Behavioural Intention toward 'Removing Beach Litter'

The third multiple regression model indicated that the overall explanatory power of the variables on behavioural intention toward 'removing beach litter' was weak (adjusted R square =0.215), compared to other two regression models for 'not climbing the cliffs' and 'not collecting fossils from the cliffs'. The model as a whole also significantly indicated that there was a linear association between behavioural intention toward 'beach litter' and the independent variables (F=29.436, p=0.000; S.E.=0.991). Tolerance score was over 0.9 in all independent variables and Durbin-Watson was over 2.097. It indicated that no multicollinearity was found between the independent variables. However, Tolerance score of one belief item was less than 0.5 because this item was highly correlated to the other ('I think that visitors should help to remove beach litter', 'I am concerned that pollution on the coast is being increasing by beach litter'). In further regression analysis, this item was excluded. This means that there was no multicollinearity between various independent variables.

The important influential factors for behavioural intention toward 'removing beach litter' included 'specific attitudes for beach litter', gender (β=0.123, t=2.780, p=0.006), environmental involvement (β=0.081, t=2.104, p=0.043), and reading the Code of Conduct brochure(β=0.096, t=2.196, p=0.029). As expected, specific attitudes were the strongest factor in behavioural intention. For example, behavioural intention was significantly influenced by specific beliefs regarding 'visitors should help remove beach litter (β=0.392, t=8.876, p=0.000) ' and feelings of concern related to 'I am concerned that people dispose of beach litter (β=0.108, t=2.434, p=0.015)'. Other beliefs related to importance of protection of coast and feelings of concern about water pollution by beach litter were not related to behavioural intention.

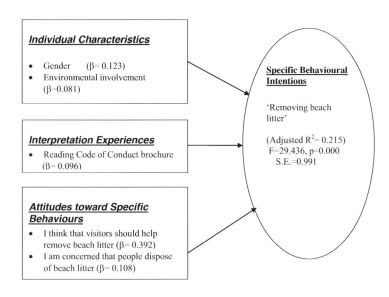

Figure 9.5 The Determinants of Behavioural Intention toward 'Removing Beach Litter'

With regard to the individual factors, different factors were found in this model, compared to the previous two models for 'not climbing the cliffs' and 'not collecting fossils from the cliffs'. In the two other regression models, there were no impacts of pre-existing environmental sensitivity variables (e.g. visitors' previous experiences of the natural areas and Charmouth coastal area, and environmental involvement) on behavioural intention for 'not climbing the cliffs' and 'not collecting fossils' while the interpretation variable significantly influenced those two specific responsible behaviours related to the particular local environment.

By contrast, behavioural intentions toward 'removing beach litter' were moderately and positively influenced by environmental involvement. Again, this suggests that it is very difficult to change human behaviour, in particular, conservation behaviour as a result of short-term interpretation experiences. Even though picking-up beach litter is one of the most well-known responsible environmental behaviours in natural protected areas, the 'removing beach litter' behaviour requires visitors to sacrifice time and inconvenience themselves. Therefore, visitors who already have involvement in environmental organisations or activities hold stronger pro-environmental attitudes and behaviour as a 'conservation ethic' than those who have simply experienced natural areas and this site.

The following section showed the interactive effects of environmental involvement, age, and gender on behavioural intention. Then, this study examined the direct effects of each of those factors on attitudes and behavioural intentions toward 'removing beach litter'.

9.20.2 Interrelationships between the Important Determinants on Specific Behavioural Intentions toward 'Removing Beach Litter'

The three factors - way of ANOVA analysis was performed to examine the interactive effects of gender, environmental involvement, and reading the Code of Conduct brochure on behavioural intention toward 'removing beach litter'. As seen in Table 9.28., significant differences were found among the three important variables. In particular, visitors who were female, had been involved in environmental organisations or activities and had read the Code of Conduct brochure held a great higher levels of behavioural intention toward 'removing beach litter (mean=4.24)' than those who were male, had not been involved in environmental organisations or activities, and had not read the brochure (mean=3.45).

Table 9.28 Interactive effects of the Important Determinants on Behavioural Intention toward 'Removing Beach Litter'

Gender	Environmental Involvement	Reading Code of Conduct Brochure					
		No (n=348)			Yes (n=104)		
		Mean	S.D	N	Mean	S.D	N
Male	No (n=264)	_3.45_	1.238	110	4.00	1.168	23
(n=219)	Yes (n=189)	3.74	0.991	62	4.13	1.058	23
Female	No (n=264)	3.92	1.071	105	4.12	1.013	25
(n=234)	Yes (n=189)	4.00	1.069	71	_4.24_	1.032	33

Dependent Variable: Behavioural Intention toward 'removing beach litter'

9.20.3 The Direct Effects of Gender, Environmental Involvement, and Reading Code of Conduct brochure on Attitudes and Behavioural Intention toward 'Removing Beach Litter'

The results of the ANOVA test showed that there were no interactions among three factors. Therefore, the direct effects of each of the visitor factors on attitudes and behavioural intention were examined as follows:

330

(1) Gender

Again, females held higher a mean score of attitudes and behavioural intention toward 'removing beach litter' than males. Significant differences were found between females and males on most types of attitudes statements related to negative impacts of beach litter and concerns about beach litter.

(2) Environmental Involvement

Overall, visitors who had been involved in environmental organisations or activities had higher mean score of intention (mean=4.05) toward 'removing beach litter' than those who had not been involved in environmental organisations or activities on behavioural intention (mean=3.75). Significant differences were also found on attitudes related to concern of water pollution by beach litter and visitors' support for removing beach litter as follows:

- I am concerned that people dispose litter on the beach
- I am concerned that pollution on the coast is being increasing by beach litter
- I think that visitors should help to remove beach litter

(3) Reading the Code of Conduct brochure

The direct effects of reading the Code of Conduct brochure were examined between two groups dependent on their having read the brochure. As expected, visitors who had read the brochure held higher levels of behavioural intention (mean=4.13) than those who had not read the brochure (mean=3.76). Interestingly, no significant differences were found on attitudes.

Summary of Stage 4

Stage 4 for the secondary aim of this research investigates the relative contribution of interpretation experiences on specific behaviours with correlating variables including individual background variables and specific attitudes. The results of Stage 4 are similar with the results of Stage 4 at the Lulworth coastal area.

Research objective 2.1: To identify the important determinants in influencing specific responsible behavioural intentions?

Overall, the important determinants in influencing the three types of specific behavioural intentions were identified as follows: specific attitude, gender, levels of interpretation participation, the use of the Visitor Centre, reading the special brochure, and environmental involvement. As predicted, the results for this study indicate that specific attitudes toward each of specific behavioural intentions were the most influential determinants on three types of specific behaviour.

This research provides the essential evidence that interpretation has a significant positive contribution to specific responsible behaviours at the Charmouth coastal area. The findings indicate that interpretation influenced directly and indirectly the two types of specific behavioural intention toward 'not climbing the cliffs' and 'not collecting fossils from the cliffs'. The mediate effects of interpretation on specific behavioural intentions were examined in two different perspectives. First, interpretation influenced indirectly specific behavioural intention through specific attitudes toward certain behaviour. That is, interpretation influenced visitors' attitudes toward specific behaviour, and in turn, improved visitors' attitudes influenced specific behavioural intention in a desired direction. Secondly, in terms of the relative contribution of interpretation on specific behaviour with correlating factors such as gender, and environmental involvement, interpretation had a significant impact on specific behavioural intentions across all ranges of visitor sub groups. It means that visitors who were females, and have been involved in environmental organisations or activities increased their behavioural intention as a result of interpretation experiences.

In terms of the type of interpretation experiences, this study indicates that the three types of interpretation experience variables were moderately related to each of the specific responsible behaviours. In particular, more visitors (n=104) used the Code of Conduct brochure which specialised in fossil collecting activities, and this might be enough to change visitors' attitudes and in turn, their behaviour in an appropriate way. The 'reading the Code of Conduct brochure' variable was also effective on behavioural intentions toward 'removing beach litter'. Overall, the results shows that when visitors were exposed to messages related to the consequences of specific

332

behaviour through either a single type or various types of interpretation, their attitudes and intention were influenced by that primary belief-targeted information.

Research Objective 2.2: To explore any different effects of the different variables on behavioural intentions?

There were significant differences by different variables on the different specific behaviour. As with the results of Stage 4 at the Lulworth coastal area, environmental involvement variables were moderately related to behavioural intention toward 'removing beach litter'.

Overall, the effects of interpretation on environmental behaviour can be limited depending on visitors' pre-existing environmental involvement and their particular interest or activities at the site. All types of behaviour are relatively associated with three key elements although there are different contributors of each type of site-specific behaviour. Therefore, it is important to understand visitors' beliefs and attitudes toward specific behaviour as well as their characteristics and participation in different types of interpretation.

CHAPTER

10

Chapter 10 Discussion

10. 1 Introduction

This chapter explores the highlighted findings of this study from Chapter 8 and Chapter 9 and discusses them with the findings from the literature review. It also presents answers to the core objectives of the research. The main purpose of this study was to examine the role of interpretation as a visitor management tool in promoting the antecedents of environmentally responsible behaviour in order to achieve the ecological goals of sustainable tourism at natural heritage sites. In order to change human behaviour through effective interpretation techniques, previous research has suggested that it is necessary to understand visitor characteristics, attitudes, and behavioural intentions which are considered as the antecedents of behaviour and as three key elements for effective interpretation design. To achieve this objective, this research attempted to evaluate the effects of interpretation on attitudes and behavioural intentions from a number of perspectives, including the assessment of the local environmental conservation issues (Discussion 1), the multiple effects of the different types of interpretive programmes (Discussion 2) and the relative impacts of interpretation along with the attributes of the visitor (Discussion 3 and Discussion 4).

Table 10.1 sets out the main items explained in this study related to attitudes and responsible behaviour as well as the main environmental issues. The three main topics regarding local environmental issues at the Jurassic Coast were 'cliff erosion', 'fossil protection (fossil collecting)' and 'coastal protection'. In addition, general environmental behaviour and environmental activism were explained. The three topics were related to each responsible behaviour and attitude which needs to be influenced by the current interpretation at this site. The multi-dimensional aspects of attitudes and behavioural intentions were clearly categorised to the three main topics by the results of factor analysis in this study (See Chapter 8 and 9 Stage 3). With regard to the suggestion of Madin and Fenton (2004), through measuring the range of the three main topics, this study identified the strengths and weaknesses of interpretive programmes.

Table 10.1 The Relationships between Attitudes and Responsible Behaviours

Topics of Conservation Issues	Categories of Responsible Behaviour	Various Elements of Attitudes toward responsible behaviour and conservation issues
1. Cliff Erosion (Cliff climbing)	• Not climbing the cliffs • Keeping to the footpaths	• Importance of protection of cliff erosion • Negative impacts of climbing the cliffs & walking off the trail • Safety aspects of climbing the cliffs • Support for the three types of appropriate behaviour • Feelings of Concern about the three types of issues and associated with behaviour
2. Fossil Protection (Fossil collecting)	• Not collecting the fossils from the cliffs • Reporting to the Centre about the discovery of important fossils	• Importance of protection of fossils • Negative or positive impacts of fossil collecting • Safety of fossil collecting
3. Coastal Protection (Beach litter)	• Removing beach litter	• Importance of protection of coastal areas • Negative impacts of beach litter
4. General Environmental Behaviour	• Not disturbing marine life • Not harming animals or plants • Following Code of Conduct • Telling the importance of geological environment to friends	• Importance of responsible behaviour
5. Environmental Activism	• Donation & Volunteer work • Involvement in environmental activities • Membership of environmental organisations	

The proposed conceptual framework is shown in the diagram below (Figure 10.1) to provide an overview of the key elements of the behavioural change process by interpretation in this study. The key elements affecting behavioural change have been identified based on a review of the social psychological literature and the persuasion communication theories and was modified for the current study.

336

With regard to the interpretation factors, Madin and Fenton (2004) suggested that researchers should seek to assess not only the effects of numbers of activities undertaken by visitors, but also the individual effects of the particular activities themselves upon the various topic areas for various interpretive programmes to be successful. For this study, the multiple effects of the different types of interpretation were examined including the effects of the Visitor Centre, reading the Code of Conduct brochure, and the levels of interpretation participation.

**Figure 10.1 The Structure of The Research for Discussion
based on the Conceptual Framework**

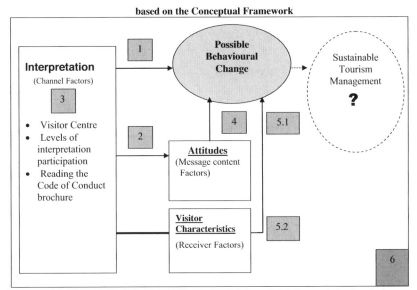

In terms of the individual attributes variables, several factors that influence behavioural change were considered including pre-existing environmental involvement and previous environmental experiences, socio-demographic factors, and psychological variables, particularly, attitudes and behavioural intentions.

The highlighted findings of this study are explained in the ordered numbers on the link of key elements in the above diagram as discussed in this chapter. There are three main sections. The first section focuses on the effects of interpretation on behavioural intentions (10.2.1) and then attitudes in terms of different aspects of environmental conservation issues (10.2.2).

The second section discusses the relative contributions of interpretation factors associated with the important individual attribute factors on specific behavioural intentions. In this second section, the influences of different types of interpretive programmes on behavioural intentions and attitudes are discussed briefly (10.3.1).

In addition, the relationships between attitudes and behavioural intentions are examined (10.3.2). Furthermore, visitor characteristics are addressed as other important factors in specific responsible behaviour (10.3.3) as well as the inter-relationships of interpretation and visitor characteristics (10.3.4). Finally, the third section addresses an overall view of the important role of interpretation in achieving the goals of sustainable tourism development at the end of this chapter (10.4).

Discussion 1: Is interpretation effective in promoting environmental attitudes and responsible environmental behavioural intentions?

The first section focuses on the first research question about "how effective the interpretive programmes are in promoting pro-environmental attitudes and behavioural intentions in relation to various aspects of local environmental conservation issues and responsible environmental behaviour at the Jurassic Coast. The results of this study showed that interpretation was successful in the two main conservation issues regarding 'cliff erosion' and 'fossil collecting', but there were no effects on the 'coastal protection' issue. The highlighted findings confirm that interpretation plays an important role as a visitor management tool in managing visitors' inappropriate behaviour which might influence negative impacts on the Jurassic Coast environment. This first section discusses the strengths or the weaknesses of interpretation on the types of responsible behavioural intentions and the types of attitudes in the context of three main environmental conservation issues and associated with responsible environmental behaviour. This section highlights the two main findings as follows:

- The types of responsible behavioural intentions
- The types of attitudes

10.2 The Role of Interpretation as a Visitor Management Tool

10.2.1 The Effects of Interpretation on Responsible Environmental Behavioural Intentions 　1　 (in Figure 10.1)

With regards to the types of responsible environmental behaviour, there were three main categories of responsible behaviour (i.e. general responsible behaviour, specific responsible behaviour, and environmental activism behaviour) which were identified as the three dimensions of responsible behaviour by the results of factor analysis. This study demonstrated that the majority of visitors to the Jurassic Coast had high levels of positive behavioural intentions regarding general and specific responsible behaviour but had low levels of positive intentions toward environmental activism behaviour (i.e. donation, volunteer work, and membership in environmental organisations).

Even though most visitors had high levels of pro-environmental behavioural intentions toward general or specific responsible behaviour (the overall mean score was over 4), the results of this study indicated that interpretation had at least some influence on the types of specific behavioural intentions regarding 'keeping to the footpaths', 'not climbing the cliffs', 'not collecting fossils from the cliffs' and 'informing the Centre about special fossil finds' at both sites (See Chapter 8 and Chapter 9). However, there were no significant impacts of interpretation on intentions regarding general environmental behaviour (e.g. 'not disturbing any marine life', 'not harming plants and animals', 'removing beach litter') and environmental activism behaviour. The results of the multiple regression analysis also supported this view that the level of interpretation participation influenced moderately only the specific behaviour (e.g. 'not climbing the cliffs' and 'not collecting fossils from the cliffs' but no effects on 'removing beach litter' behaviour). Comparison of behavioural intentions between the Lulworth and the Charmouth coastal areas, the results showed similar findings. Based on the findings of this study, it showed that the effects of interpretation varied and were dependent on the types of behaviour.

Several key findings are discussed as follows:
- **The Strengths of Interpretation**
(1)   Interpretation can modify specific inappropriate behaviour on-site
- **The Weaknesses of Interpretation**
(2)   The failure of interpretation in promoting 'removing beach litter'
(3)   The failure of interpretation in promoting long-term conservation behaviour

(1) Interpretation can modify specific inappropriate behaviour on-site

The key finding echoed the evidence of previous literature, which indicated that interpretation can be effective as a visitor management tool in modifying inappropriate visitor behaviour which may cause damage to natural and cultural resources through their experiences of interpretation on-site (Oram, 1996a,b; Moscardo & Wood, 1998; Ham & Weiler, 2002; Kuo, 2002).

Several researchers have showed the successful impacts of interpretation on specific behaviour (Moscardo & Wood, 1998; Widner & Roggenbuck, 2000). For example, Widner and Roggenbuck (2000) investigated the effects of interpretation on the theft of petrified wood in the Petrified Forest

National Park, USA. The results showed that interpretation was significantly effective in reducing visitors' wood theft behaviour.

(2) The failure of interpretation in promoting 'removing beach litter'

Despite the successful effects of interpretation on site-specific appropriate behaviour in this area, this study found that no significant effects of interpretation were found on 'removing beach litter' behaviour and other general responsible behaviour. In terms of behavioural intentions toward 'removing beach litter', this is inconsistent with the previous findings of other researchers that interpretation had a positive impact in reducing littering behaviour and even cleaning up littered areas (Clark *et al.*, 1972a,b; Oliver *et al.*, 1985; Roggenbuck & Passineau, 1986; Littlefair 2003).

As reviewed in the literature, the effects of interpretation on behavioural intention/behavioural change have produced mixed results (Beaumont, 2001). It is indicated that environmental interpretation alone did nothing to increase 'removing beach litter' behaviour, indicating that general education or interpretation about the environment does not automatically lead to a reduction in impacts and turn into a conservation ethic through a single short-term experience (Gudgion and Thomas, 1991; Orams 1997; Beaumont, 2001). Therefore, it is important to identify when interpretation can influence which types of behaviour in a particular situation. This finding was important in realising that interpretation could fail if planners do not have a good idea about visitors' conceptual understanding of topics which are to be presented (Loomis, 1996). That is, other authors have previously stated that simply providing environmental interpretation alone is not likely to result in behaviour change, and therefore, that interpretation needs to specifically refer to a behaviour or issue (Hungerford & Volk 1990; Iozzi 1989; Moscardo 1999; Orams 1997; Wearing & Neil 1999; Tubb 2003; Monroe, 2003).

One of the possible reasons for this might be that the presentation and the messages from the interpretive programmes in this area focused on the geological environment and fossils. Therefore, the reason for the ineffectiveness of interpretation on removing beach litter behaviour may be that the interpretive message did not deal with problems of beach litter and then were not strong enough to cause any change in this particular behaviour. The managers need to focus on specific messages in order to encourage visitors to take responsibility in removing beach litter in the interpretive planning in future at this area as well as the need to identify the barriers to this behaviour as perceived by the target audience. This point was also made by Monroe (2003).

(3) The failure of interpretation in promoting long-term conservation behaviour

Finally, the results of this study found that the effects of interpretation on long -term conservation behaviour globally were still in question. This finding is inconsistent with the conclusion that interpretation can promote long-term conservation behaviour globally (Ham and Weiler, 2002). Most visitors to the sample study sites showed unwillingness to follow environmental activism behaviour such as 'donation', 'volunteer work', and 'membership of environmental organisation'. Several reasons might be considered (i.e. visitor characteristics and ineffectiveness of interpretation).

However, interestingly, this study showed significant effectiveness on the part of the Visitor Centre on behavioural intention toward 'donation' at the Charmouth coastal area. The possible reason for this might be that the Chartmouth coast is owned by the National Trust, while the Lulworth coast is owned by a private owner, the Weld Estate (Lulworth Estate). In particular, public donations and membership of the Friends of the Charmouth Heritage Coast Centre were encouraged at the Charmouth coastal area (Charmouth Heritage Coast Centre, 2005). This shows that interpretation might enhance long-term conservation behaviour in the future, although there were slight differences between the Lulworth and Charmouth coast sites.

Reviews of the literature, Orams (1997) also found that interpretation was not significantly effective on influencing behavioural intentions toward the general environmental behaviour or environmental activism during a visit. However, he concluded that education programmes did influence tourists' intentions because significant increases in actual behaviour change were revealed through the results of the follow-up interview. Consistent with this, Beaumont (2001) also supported this view that ecotourism experiences enhanced visitors' long-term environmentally friendly behaviour after their return home through the results of the follow-up survey. This research agrees with the view of previous research (Beaumont, 2001; Orams, 1997) that interpretation may play an additional role in promoting long-term conservation behaviour but is still questionable. To examine the effects of interpretation on long-term conservation behaviour, follow-up surveys and further study could be conducted.

10.2.2 The Effects of Interpretation on Environmental Attitudes

2 (in Figure 10.1)

This study examined the multidimensional aspects of attitudes comprising cognitive (i.e. belief) and affective (i.e. feeling or concern) dimensions which were clearly categorised to the three main topics as shown in the previous section (Table 10.1) (see Chapter 8 and 9 Stage 3). In terms of different aspects of attitudes toward the three main topics, this study also found that the effects of interpretation varied depending on specific types of beliefs and feelings of concern toward a certain issue or certain problem behaviour.

In particular, the main findings showed that interpretation at the Jurassic Coast has a positive effect on attitudes towards at least the two specific topics of conservation issues regarding 'cliff erosion' and 'fossil collecting', but has no effect on general attitudes toward the 'coastal protection' issue and the importance of protection of natural resources. These highlighted findings help to easily identify the strengths or weaknesses of interpretation on the different types of beliefs and feelings of concern toward a certain topic at this site in a particular situation.

The four main findings are discussed as follows:
- **The Strengths of Interpretation on Specific Attitudes**
(1)   Interpretation can promote specific attitudes toward specific responsible behaviour .
(2)   Interpretation can change some aspects of attitudes of visitors in the opposite direction
- **The Weaknesses of Interpretation on General Attitudes**
(3)   Interpretation needs to strengthen 'feelings of concern' toward conservation.
(4)   The failure of interpretation to affect general attitudes regarding environmental protection and the 'coastal protection' issue.

(1)   Interpretation can promote specific attitudes toward specific responsible behaviour
First, the results of this study supported the view that interpretation can aid management policies toward specific conservation issues at each site. For example, 'cliff erosion' is one of the main environmental conservation issues at the Jurassic Coast as the cliff is rapidly eroded both by the natural impact of the sea, particularly during rough winter weather, and by visitors climbing the cliffs for the coastline views or for collecting fossils from the cliffs. Therefore, management polices prohibit those specific inappropriate behaviour for the protection of the cliff erosion and for visitor safety management (see Chapter 6: Case Study Sites). This research found that interpretation increased visitors' awareness and feelings of concern for the negative impacts of the problem behaviour (i.e. 'climbing the cliffs' and 'collecting fossils from the cliffs') and also enhanced their support for management policies toward regulation of the specific problem behaviour (i.e. 'visitors should not be allowed to collect fossils from the cliffs', 'visitors should not be allowed to climb the cliffs', 'visitors should help to remove beach litter').

This result corresponds with the evidence that interpretation can be effective as a visitor management tool in modifying visitors' attitudes so they are more supportive of wilderness and related land management polices (Manning, 2003; Tubb, 2003). This is also similar to the findings of Cable *et al.*, (1986) that visitors who were exposed to interpretive messages about fire ecology and the effects of controlled-burn policies were more aware of the ecological effects of fire and were more supportive toward fire management policies than visitors who were not exposed to the messages during their visits to the Yellowstone National park in Montana, USA.

(2) Interpretation can change some aspects of attitudes of visitors in the opposite direction
Secondly, this result indicated the idea that interpretation can change the different types of beliefs toward a certain behaviour in different directions (Lee and Balchin, 1995). Somewhat surprisingly, this study demonstrated that the different direction (positive or negative attitudes) between the Lulworth and the Charmouth coastal areas was found in relation to attitudes about specific behaviour, in this case, 'fossil collecting'.

With regard to the results of the Lulworth coastal area, visitors who had experienced all types of interpretive programmes were more aware of the negative impacts of fossil collecting and they disagreed with the beliefs about the positive outcomes of fossil collecting activities. However, beliefs regarding the positive outcomes of fossil collecting activities were significantly different as a result of interpretation experiences (i.e. the Visitor Centre and the levels of interpretation participation) at the Charmouth coastal area. That is, visitors who had experienced a number of interpretive programmes including the Visitor Centre showed moderate agreement with the view that some aspects of fossil collecting were positive (i.e. two statements including 'helping in scientific research' and 'economic contribution to the local area').

The several reasons for this finding can be considered including different management policies at different sites, visitors' interest and availability of tourism activities (Beckmann, 2002; Madin and Fenton 2004). For this study of the Jurassic Coast 'geo-tourism', is popular as the main natural attractions are related to geology and fossils as well as the beauty of the coastline or beach (Hose, 1995). In particular, at the Charmouth Coastal Area, fossil collecting is one of the main tourism activities and it is allowed for visitors to collect fossils from the beach, but not from the cliffs (Charmouth Heritage Coast Centre, 2005). Especially, the visitor Code of Conduct brochure for fossil collecting is published as the main management policy in this area to introduce responsible behaviour regarding safety, how to collect fossils, and where to collect fossils. By contrast, even though the 'fossil forest' is popular as the main attraction at the Lulworth coastal area, fossil collecting activities are not allowed from the cliffs because of a lack of fossils at this site. Visitors' access to the east of the Lulworth coast is also prohibited at a certain particular time when the army ranges are closed (see Chapter 6.6.1). Therefore, this finding may show that different management policy and visitor interests regarding available activities and environmental issues at each site were the important factors to influence a change in specific attitudes toward fossil collecting behaviour in different directions.

(3) Interpretation needs to strengthen 'feeling of concern' toward conservation

Another interesting finding of this research was that the effects of interpretation on visitors' attitudes were more effective in strengthening beliefs rather than affective components (i.e. feelings of concern) at both sites. That is, most visitors were more aware of and supportive for site-specific responsible behaviour (i.e. climbing the cliffs) as a result of the interpretation experiences.

However, these who have participated in various interpretive programmes still held a moderate level of environmental concern toward conservation issues and problem behaviour. In addition, the results of post-hoc test also demonstrated that no significant effects of the Visitor Centre between Group B and Group C were found on affective components (feelings of concern) about certain types of issues or problem behaviour although the results were slightly different at both sites. The possible reasons for this might be the fact that interpretation focuses on cognitive rather than affective components (Iozzi, 1989).

As reviewed in the literature, both cognitive and affective components for message content must be emphasised together in order to modify appropriate visitor behaviour (Orams 1996a,b). Therefore, this finding identifies one of the weaknesses of interpretation at this site and suggests that there is a need to strengthen an affective domain of attitudes.

(4) The failure of interpretation to affect general attitudes regarding environmental protection and the 'beach litter' issue

Interpretation had some influence to a limited extent in changing specific attitudes related to the consequences of the problem behaviour and support for the policies regarding 'not climbing the cliffs' and 'not collecting fossil'. However, there were no effects on general attitudes toward the importance of protection of the resources or attitudes toward 'removing beach litter'. The key finding of this study is consistent with those of Tubb (2003), that interpretation within the High Moorland Visitor Centre at Dartmoor National Park, UK was effective only in changing attitudes related to the feeding of wildlife, but that no effects on general attitudes toward the natural environment were seen.

Several factors for the ineffectiveness of interpretation on general attitudes might be considered. One of the possible reasons for this might be due to a 'ceiling effect' or 'social desirability' by significant life experiences (Chawla, 1999). Firstly, with respect to respondents' attitudes in this study, it demonstrated that all reported attitudes were strongly in favour of the specific behaviour and the three main conservation issues, particularly, 'water pollution by beach litter'. This agreed with the arguments of previous researchers and identified that both visitors to nature-based activities and the wider public have demonstrated that reported attitudes are generally environmentally favourable (Orams 1997; Beaumont 2001; Adams, 2003). A number of studies have found that the pre-existing attitudes of individuals participating in outdoor education, interpretive programmes and wilderness experiences were already strongly pro-environmental in their attitudes and did not change significantly following participation in the programme due to a 'ceiling effect' (Asfeldt, 1992; Beckmann, 1991; Beaumont, 2001)

Another possible explanation for why interpretation did not appear to change general environmental attitude was 'social desirability'. This finding is consistent with Orams' (1997) study. The study by Orams (1997) assessed whether people changed their behavioural intentions after a visit to Tangalooma, Australia. He found that a high percentage of visitors reported telling friends about dolphins and picking up litter from the beach. There were no significant differences between the control and experiment groups. Both groups had extremely positive intentions to behave in environmentally responsible way. He explained that the reason for the findings might be the influence of 'social desirability'. As most visitors are aware of environmentally responsible behaviour, visitors may have simply responded in a manner that is consistent with well-known and socially accepted views about environmental issues and positions, and not on the basis of how they really feel (Ryan, 1995; Orams, 1997; Ewert and Baker, 2001).

In addition to the 'ceiling effect' by previous environmental experiences or 'social desirability', this study demonstrated that other personality factors might be involved in influencing visitors' attitudes and behavioural intentions toward the 'coastal protection' issue as well as diminishing the effectiveness of interpretation. This finding reflects the weakness of interpretation at this site in promoting both attitudes and behavioural intentions toward this particular issue or this behaviour. However, there was no clear conclusion as to why interpretation was less effective in this topic.

For instance, there were significant differences in visitors' support for the clean-up beach litter policy as a result of the interpretation experiences. That is, visitors who used more amounts of interpretation methods or read the Code of Conduct agreed strongly with the attitude statement 'visitors should help to remove beach litter'. This finding is consistent with those of Asfeldt (1992) who found even where existing attitudes were high, participation could influence concern for the environment, particularly by strengthening existing concern. As people use more of the interpretive programmes and activities, their attitudes toward the specific behaviour increased.

However, it was difficult to determine whether a change in visitors' support for the clean-up beach litter policy was due to the effects of interpretation or the relative effects of other personality factors such as previous environmental experience or other psychological factors. The additional finding showed clearly the assumption that most visitors had only the moderate levels of behavioural intentions toward 'removing beach litter' even though people had strongly favourable attitudes of the 'coastal protection' issue rather than the other two site-specific issues.

This reinforces the need for interpretive designers to investigate existing levels of attitudes or other individual attributes in the target audiences before completing interpretive tools depending on specific management policy. More detailed information about identifying other personality factors is discussed in Section 10.3.

Overall, this study identified the different results of interpretation upon multidimensional attitudes and behavioural intentions regarding the three main topics. The successful effects of interpretation were found on specific attitudes and behavioural intentions toward local environmental issues regarding 'cliff erosion' and 'fossil collecting' in this area. However, the weaknesses of interpretation were also found in general attitudes toward environmental protection or the 'coastal protection' issue as well as behavioural intentions regarding general responsible behaviour, 'removing beach litter' and environmental activism.

The highlighted findings of this study confirmed that the majority of interpretation efforts succeeded in altering visitor about appropriate behaviour even though some efforts did not achieve their stated goals for various reasons. The additional findings also highlighted that different types of interpretation can influence the different types of beliefs related to ambiguous outcomes of the particular behaviour (i.e. 'collecting fossils from the cliffs') in different directions. The results of this study clearly support the idea of Lee and Balchin (1995:295) that 'attitudes should not be treated in a simplistic way and they are a complex mix of beliefs and emotions'. In order to promote responsible behaviour, it is important to examine what types of interpretive methods can be effective as well as which types of belief-targeted messages are more effective to the target audience and in what direction (Ham and Krumpe, 1996; Ballantyne and Hughes, 2004; Lee and Balchin, 1995). The next section focuses on identifying those main factors for the successful implications of effective interpretation techniques.

10.3 The Important Determinants Influencing Specific Responsible Behavioural Intentions

As reviewed in the previous section, this study provided the beneficial outcomes of interpretation on attitudes and behavioural intentions. The effectiveness of interpretation varied widely depending on the types of conservation topic and the types of behaviour. This indicated that it was not clear to support fully the contribution of interpretation in influencing environmental attitudes and behavioural intention in the various perspectives. The critical points considered in the previous section suggest that other factors might be involved in influencing the behavioural change process. Thus, it is important not only to acknowledge that interpretation is not the sole influence on the types of behavioural intentions but also to understand how other various individual factors associated with interpretation factors interact relatively with behavioural intentions.

In response to this, more detailed information is discussed in this second section regarding the additional research questions such as "how does interpretation influence specific responsible behavioural intentions along with the attributes of the visitors and attitude components?, "what are the main factors influencing different types of specific responsible behavioural intentions?". Those findings also provide the answers for the alternative research questions about "to what extent does interpretation contribute to influence behavioural change" and "why is interpretation not effective in influencing certain types of behavioural intentions". Answers to these questions will contribute to a better understanding of the process of why and how people behave differently in particular situations. They will also provide important implications for the practitioners in tailoring effective interpretation techniques of message content and message delivery to the needs, preferences, perceptions of each target group in order to manage visitors' appropriate behaviours.

For this study, several main factors selected from both the antecedents of environmental behaviour and persuasive interpretation factors were employed including interpretation channel factors as well as socio-demographics, previous environmental experiences, and attitudes of the visitors.

Those main factors are discussed including first, the multiple effects of the different types of interpretive programmes (10.3.1), the relative impacts of attitudes (10.3.2) and the visitor characteristics (10.3.3) as well as the inter-relationships of interpretation and the important factors (10.3.4).

Discussion 2: How do the different types of interpretation Influence Behavioural Intentions and Attitudes?

According to a review of the literature, to help ensure the success of park educational programmes or interpretive programmes, a clear communication channel between visitors and site managing agencies plays a key role in a message's effectiveness for the effective quality of interpretation. In response to this, this section focuses on determining what type of media is most effective on the beneficial outcomes in a particular situation (Jacobson, 1988; Nielsen and Buchanan, 1986). As mentioned in the first section (Discussion 10.2.1 and 10.2.2), all of the various interpretation methods appeared to be effective in promoting visitors' specific attitudes and behavioural intentions regarding 'cliff erosion' and 'fossil collecting' issues and the associated appropriate behaviours with the two main issues. Yet the direct impact of a single medium on the dependent variables was quite unclear. This is the limitation of the current study in explaining these problems. Although several factors were identified in the persuasive communication literature, this study focused on only the channel factors, including the Visitor Centre, reading the Code of Conduct brochure, and a total amount of participation in interpretative programmes. Therefore, it should consider that other persuasion context factors might mediate the direct effects of types of interpretation on dependent variables.

10.3.1 Which Aspects of Interpretation Channel Factors are the Most Effective?

3 (in Figure 10.1)

The highlighted findings of this study help understanding the additional effects of different interpretation methods and provide an answer as to which aspects of interpretation methods were more effective in a particular situation.

Several main findings are worthy of discussion, as follows:

(1) The levels of interpretation participation were one of the most important factors in influencing specific responsible behavioural intentions

(2) The different effects of the Visitor Centre to affect attitudes and behavioural intentions

(3) Other persuasive interpretation factors? Visitors' emotional experiences

(4) The effects of the Code of Conduct brochure in educating special interest groups about responsible 'fossil collecting' behaviour

(1) The levels of interpretation participation were one of the most important factors in influencing specific responsible behavioural intentions

In terms of the effectiveness of types of interpretive programmes, the key results of this study identified that levels of interpretation participation had influence moderately the specific responsible behavioural intentions at both sites, although there were slight differences between the Charmouth and the Lulworth coastal areas through the results of regression analysis (See Table 10.2).

Table 10.2 Comparison of the Relative Contribution of the Levels of Interpretation Participation on Specific Responsible Behavioural Intentions

Behavioural Intentions	Lulworth	Charmouth
• Not climbing the cliffs	• Levels of Interpretation participation (β=0.094)	• Levels of interpretation participation (β=0.104)
• Not collecting fossils from the cliffs	• Level of interpretation participation (β=0.167)	• Use of the Visitor Centre (β=0.080)
• Removing beach litter	• Environmental involvement (β=0.101)	• Reading the Code of Conduct brochure (β=0.096) • Environmental involvement (β=0.081)

(Note: Modified from the results of Multiple Regression Analysis (See Chapter 8 and 9 Stage 4)

This corresponds with the findings of previous research and identified that the use of multiple media was very important for successful effectiveness of interpretation as opposed to the use of a single type of media (Doucette and Cole 1993; Roggenbuck and Berrier, 1982; Littlefair, 2003; Manning, 2003). For instance, the findings of Littlefair (2003) showed that interpretation was most effective in reducing 'the shortcutting from the trails' behaviour when both verbal appeals from guided walk and role modelling were incorporated in the interpretative programmes. That is, visitors who participated in greater numbers of activities felt that they had improved levels of both behavioural intentions and specific responsible behaviour. This suggests that the use of multiple media can be more effective when delivering persuasive messages to reach a different range of a targeted audience than the use of a single medium (Manning, 2003). Previous research has suggested several outcomes of the multiple media approaches. One of the beneficial outcomes of multiple methods approaches is to attract the interest and to serve the needs of a heterogeneous audience (Jacobson, 1988). In addition, repetition of messages through different types of media also has a greater effect in maximising effectiveness of message (Thorn, 1995; Hockett, 2000).

In addition to the importance of the use of multiple media in order to modify visitors' behaviour, in terms of the assessment of the effectiveness of a single medium, the current study also suggests that it is necessary to understand the different effects of particular interpretive programmes themselves on dependent variables in a particular situation. More detailed information about this includes the effects of the Visitor Centre and the Code of Conduct brochure for fossil collecting activities.

(2) The different effects of the visitor centre to affect attitudes and behavioural intentions
In terms of the effect of the Visitor Centre on dependent variables (i.e. attitudes and behavioural intentions), the findings of this study indicated that the Visitor Centre, by itself, did not have a significant impact on recipients' levels of behavioural intentions, but had some influence on specific attitudes regarding the two main topics at the Jurassic Coast. This does not necessarily reflect a failure of the Visitor Centres in influencing visitors' behavioural intentions.

In light of largely inconsistent findings of previous empirical research and the current study of the effectiveness of the types of interpretive programmes, this current study agrees with the view of Ajzen (1992) that it is very difficult to determine whether differences in persuasion stem from variations in the communication channel or from associated contextual differences because the other associated context factors (i.e. receiver, message, source of message, and other channel factors) may confound the observed effect.

Several factors for the contradictory effectiveness of the Visitor Centre on attitudes and behavioural intentions might be considered, such as the mediating effects of visitors' use pattern of other media, their emotional response to interpretation, their interest and preferences for media, the amount of time visitors spent in each interpretive programme, effective design techniques, message content, other mediating process variables (e.g. attention, comprehension, and acceptance) and so on (Azjen, 1992; Chandool, 1997; Cable *et al.*, 1986; Reid and Marion, 2003).

For this study, one of the several possible reasons for ineffectiveness of the Visitor Centre on behavioural intentions may be due to the mediating effects by other media factors. One of the limitations of this study was that it was difficult to distinguish between the control groups who have not been exposed to any other interpretation and the experimental groups who have been exposed only to the Visitor Centre in tourism settings. That is, as visitors were already exposed to other interpretive programmes before visiting the Centre, other media which visitors have used might influence their awareness of appropriate behaviour. In turn, there was not a significantly greater impact of the Visitor Centre on behavioural intentions (See Table 10.3).

For example, three participant groups were categorised and labelled Group A, Group B, and Group C according to their experiences of and intention to visit the Visitor Centre during the previous visits and/or this time (See Chapter 8). According to the comparison of mean score on behavioural intentions by three groups, both Group B and Group C respondents held the higher levels of pro-environmental behavioural intention toward 'not climbing the cliffs', 'not collecting fossils' and 'removing beach litter' than a control group (Group A). Yet there were no statistically significant differences between the two treatment groups (Group B and Group C) at both sites through the results of post-hoc ANOVA analysis. As seen in Table 10.3, with regards to comparison of the use pattern of other media by the three groups, the results of the Lulworth coastal area (See Chapter 8) demonstrated that 52.3% of Group B respondents and 67.1% of Group C respondents had used at least one or two media (mainly, sign or brochure) while some 23.8 % of Group A had used during their visits to the Lulworth coastal area. Therefore, increased awareness of the visitors resulting from the use of other interpretive media might diminish the direct effects of the Visitor Centre on behavioural intentions between Group B and Group C respondents.

Table 10.3 Comparisons of the Level of Interpretation Participation among the Three Groups by the Visitor Centre Experiences

Level of Interpretation Participation	Three Groups by the Visitor Centre Experiences					
	Group A		Group B		Group C	
	L	C	L	C	L	C
None	75.4%	55.7%	47.7%	59.3%	18.8%	13.4%
Lower level of participation (1-2)	23.8%	44.3%	52.3%	40.7%	67.1%	64.3%
Higher level of participation (3-7)	0.8%	0%	0%	0%	14.1%	22.3%

Note: L=The Lulworth coastal area. C= The Charmouth coastal area;
Group A: No-visited the Centre this time; Group B: Plan to visit to the Centre;
Group C: Visited the Centre before and/or this time.

This additional finding indicates that the relative effects of the Visitor Centre associated with other types of media might reflect the weakness of the Visitor Centre in influencing behavioural intentions. Alternatively, the finding of this study might suggest that all other media equally, signs and booklets, may be almost as effective as the Visitor Centre. Previous research has showed that there were significantly different effects of different types of interpretive programmes depending on the targeted outcomes (knowledge, attitudes, and behavioural intention (Chandool, 1997; Ajzen, 1992). Ajzen (1992) suggested that the receiver acquires more information about physical and behavioural characteristics of the source from face-to-face or video messages than from information presented orally or in writing.

Inconsistent with this, this finding reflects the conclusion of Nielsen & Buchanan (1986) that there was no significant difference in the effectiveness of the two different types of interpretive techniques (e.g. Visitor Centre and Interpreter) when the goals of interpretation are to inform or educate rather than to entertain the visitors. Much of the previous empirical research has also indicated that well-designed trailhead signs or brochures were as effective as the Visitor Centre or a uniformed person in reducing inappropriate behaviour (Widner and Roggenbuck, 2000; McAvoy & Hamborg, 1984).

Therefore, the Visitor Centre should not be considered as the only approach in attempts to generate environmentally responsible behaviour. It may need to be used in co-ordination with other types of media based on the targeted objectives of the interpretation.

(3) Visitors' emotional experiences

However, the results of this current study demonstrated that the Visitor Centre had a significant impact on specific attitudes regarding the two main topics which were mainly presented within the interpretive programmes at the Centre, but on the effect on general attitudes toward environmental protection and beach litter was limited. For example, most respondents who had visited the Centre during their visits to the site this time indicated that their understanding, awareness and attitudes toward conservation issues of the site had been only moderately changed by the Visitor Centre experience (See Chapter 8.3 and Chapter 9.3). However, most visitors also indicated that they learned most about fossils or geological aspects of coastal areas as a result of the Visitor Centre experiences. This was consistent with the findings from comparison of mean scores among the three groups according to their Visitor Centre experiences. For instance, the Visitor Centre had a significant impact on visitors' specific attitudes toward 'cliff erosion' issues at both the Lulworth and Charmouth coastal areas. In addition, some influence of the Visitor Centre was found on specific attitudes toward 'positive outcomes of fossil collecting activities' at the Charmouth coastal area.

As far as the successful outcomes of the Visitor Centre in promoting specific attitudes regarding the two main topics are concerned, the possible reason for this finding might be that the other factors related to visitors' emotional experiences through the effective design techniques (i.e. message, pictures, exhibition, computer interaction, films, and personal contact) might influence visitors' emotional moods regarding satisfaction, enjoyment and feelings of 'worry' or 'concern' about local environmental issues. These emotional experiences through participating in interpretation might subsequently influence the main outcomes such as learning, attitudes and behaviour (Moscardo, 1999; Howard, 2000; Schänzel, 1998).

For example, more visitors who had visited the Centre indicated that they perceived the Visitor Centre's educational role, in contrast with visitors who had not visited. When they experienced the Visitor Centre, they felt the interpretive programmes were quite educational and enjoyable during their visit to the Centres at both sites. This perception and their experience of the Visitor Centre might influence both their satisfaction and positive emotional mood which, in turn, influence pro-environmental attitudes and behaviour regarding the two main issues of 'cliff erosion' and 'fossil collecting'.

This finding agrees with the view of Hull (1991) that feelings of having fun can still have emotional mood benefits, particularly as the positive effects of storing images and associated states in memory are well recognised. Howard (2000) also found that the affective domains of arousal were more important than knowledge in reporting behaviour change.

This research supports the significant impacts of emotional experiences of interpretation programmes in conjunction with cognitive experiences on visitors' learning, their awareness, appreciation and pro-environmental behaviour (Schänzel, 1998; Howard, 2000, Moscardo, 1999). However, this study did not examine the link between emotional responses to interpretation and dependent variables (e.g. attitudes and behavioural intentions). This study suggests that emotional responses to interpretive programmes can be considered as one of the important factors affecting behaviour change in future research. Further research is also needed on the complex relationship between the affective and cognitive processes on attitudes and behaviour change.

(4) The effects of the Code of Conduct brochure in educating visitors about responsible 'fossil collecting' behaviour

Additionally, this study attempted to examine the effects of reading the Code of Conduct brochure, particularly targeting on fossil collecting activities. The specific Visitor Code brochure for fossil collecting is designed to modify inappropriate behaviour and minimise the impacts of the visitors on cliff erosion, damage to important fossils, and disturbance of marine life at the site (See the Code of Conduct brochure for fossil collecting).

The highlighted finding showed that the specific Visitor Code brochure was also significantly effective in promoting both behavioural intentions and specific attitudes towards 'cliff erosion' and 'fossil collecting' issues and the responsible behaviour associated with those two main topics. In particular, visitors who had read the Code brochure indicated higher levels of intentions to engage in specific responsible behaviour, and even environmental activism behaviour, than those who had not read the brochure, particularly at the Charmouth coastal area.

This finding is consistent with the study of Howard *et al.* (2001) and Porter & Howard (2003) who examined the successful effects of visitors' readiness regarding the Be Dingo-Smart brochures on both their knowledge and appropriate behaviour at Fraser Island, Australia. They also showed most visitors did not read the brochure even though they received the message related to dingo warnings as part of the permit issuing system at Fraser Island. The reasons for lack of access of messages by visitors might be timing of the message delivery and the availability of information regarding visitors' interest in the certain activities (that is, the perceived relevance of the information provided) at each site (Beckmann, 2002; Madin & Fenton, 2004).

This study agrees with the viewpoint of Howard *et al.* (2001) who indicated that different visitor groups tend to see different communication media. Interestingly, it is notable that there were significant differences in terms of visitor use patterns of different media and their interest in available activities at both the Lulworth and Charmouth coastal areas. For example, with regard to visitor use patterns of media, the Visitor Centres was highly used by most visitors during previous visits and during the surveyed visit (i.e. 60.6% at the Lulworth and 67.8% at the the Charmouth coastal area), followed by signs and brochures at both sites. However, only a few visitors indicated they had read the Visitor Code of Conduct brochure related to 'fossil collecting' activities at both sites. Some 23% of visitors to the Charmouth coastal area had read the brochure while only 3.6% of visitors at the Lulworth coastal area had read the brochure (See Table 10.4).

Table 10.4 Comparisons of Visitors' Use Pattern of Types of Media

	Reading the Code of Conduct Brochure		Use of the Visitor Centre	
	Yes, I read	No, I didn't	Yes, at least once	No, never
Lulworth (n=420)	15 (3.6%)	405(96.4%)	255 (60.7%)	165 (39.3%)
Charmouth (n=452)	104 (23%)	348 (77%)	306 (67.7%)	146 (32.3%)

This finding indicates that visitors appeared to use the Visitor Code brochure for fossil collecting at the Charmouth coastal area more than at the Lulworth coastal area. It explains that visitors who were interested in fossil collecting activities appeared to use the particular media related to that information when that activity and its associated information were available for them. This finding is consistent with Howard *et al.*'s (2001) who explained that while birdwatchers wandering through the bush read the brown wooden route signs, visitors undertaking short walks read the interpretive panels (p.101). By contrast, most respondents who had visited the Lulworth coastal area had not read the particular brochure regarding fossil collecting activities due to availability of different activities or attractions at this site.

The results of this study and the review of the literature suggest that it is important to consider visitors' preferences and interests with regard to different types of media, according to the timing of media delivery and available activities at a particular setting. Madin and Fenton (2004) indicated that as regards the different effects of interpretive programmes on the different types of topics, this might be because visitors may use the different types of information to choose the type of nature-based activities or attractions which best suit their interests. Therefore, this finding confirms that the multiple use of methods to communicate persuasive messages is essential in shaping the effectiveness of the message. It is also critical to choose the appropriate media format wisely according to the particular advantages of each media as well as visitors' interests and preferences towards types of media in the particular settings.

Discussion 3: How Do Attitudes of the Visitors Influence Specific Responsible Behavioural Intentions?

Although previous findings help to show which types of programmes produce the greatest changes on specific behavioural intentions, there is still much unexplained variation in the outcomes. Other characteristics and attitudes of the visitors were considered to examine their relative contributions to specific behavioural intentions along with the impacts of interpretation channel factors.

This section focused first on the relationships between attitudes and specific responsible behavioural intentions (see 10.3.2), followed by the link between other individual attributes and specific responsible behavioural intentions (see 10.3.3 and 10.3.4).

355

10.3.2 Which the Primary Belief or Feeling Components of Attitudes Are the Most Significant Contributors? [4] (in Figure 10.1)

The results of this study indicated that a positive and significant link between attitudes and behavioural intention were found in three types of specific responsible behaviour (e.g. 'not climbing the cliffs', 'not collecting fossils from the cliffs', 'removing beach litter'). This supports the notion that environmental attitudes are one of the important factors in influencing environmentally responsible behaviour (Newhouse, 1990; Hines *et al.*, 1986/87; Hwang et al, 2000; Monroe, 2003). In particular, as reviewed in the literature, understanding visitors' beliefs and other elements of attitudes helps to answer the additional information about how to construct a persuasive message in order to maximise the effectiveness of the message itself (Ajzen, 1992; Knopf and Dustin, 1992).

This study emphasises the three main findings in the relationship between attitudes and behavioural intentions:

(1)   The relationships between attitudes and specific responsible behavioural intentions
(2)   Identifying the primary beliefs or emotional components of attitudes for target messages
(3)   Other factors?

(1) The relationships between attitudes and specific responsible behavioural intentions
This research highlighted the importance of understanding visitors' beliefs in order to influence a targeted behaviour. Despite the positive relationships between attitudes and behavioural intention, the findings of this study showed that there were inconsistent relationships between types of beliefs or emotion of attitudes and behavioural intentions. It is important to identify which types of beliefs have the greatest influence on specific behavioural intentions in a particular situation.

For instance, interestingly, no significant association was found between general attitudes towards conservation issues and the associated specific responsible behavioural intentions regarding each issue in this study. On the contrary, visitors' concern about and support for each specific behaviour (i.e. 'not climbing the cliffs', 'not collecting the fossils', and 'removing beach litter') were moderately related to each specific responsible behavioural intention at both sites (See Table 10.5). Yet, only a certain type of belief toward a given behaviour was related to specific behavioural intentions.

Table 10.5 The Link Between Attitudes and Behavioural Intentions

toward Specific Behaviour

Behavioural intentions	Attitudes	Lulworth β	Charmouth β
1. No climbing the cliffs	I am **_concern_**ed that people climb the cliffs Visitors should not be _allow_ed to climb the cliffs I think that it is _dangerous_ to climb the cliffs	0.292 0.171 0.149	0.268 0.249 0.234
Adjusted R²		**0.340**	**0.327**
2. No collecting the fossils from the cliffs	I am **_concern_**ed that people collect the fossils from the cliffs I think that visitors should _not be allowed_ to collect the fossils from the cliffs I think that it is _dangerous_ to collect the fossils from the cliffs I think that fossil collecting _helps one to learn_ about the fossils	0.289 0.259 0.133 - 0.115	0.164 0.263 0.306
Adjusted R²		**0.368**	**0.408**
3. Removing the beach litter	I think visitors **_should help remove_** beach litter I am _concern_ed that people dispose of beach litter I think picking up beach litter _will reduce_ the amount of water pollution	0.408 0.135 0.112	0.392 0.108
Adjusted R²		**0.249**	**0.215**

This finding supports the assumption of previous research that attitudes which are specifically related to a particular behaviour should be better predictors of that behaviour than general attitudes (Ajzen & Fishbein, 1980; Cottrell & Graefe, 1997; Hungerford & Volk, 1990). According to previous studies, they indicated that positive attitudes toward the environment do not necessarily lead to environmentally responsible behaviour and found a weak relationship between attitudes and behaviour (quoted in Baron & Byrne, 1987).

Therefore, this research agrees with the notion of Adams (2003) that especially strong specific and narrowly defined attitudes that have been acquired through direct experience and that influence the person's self-interest, have a strong influence on behaviour.

(2) Identifying the primary beliefs or emotional components of attitudes for target messages

With respect to the importance of identifying the primary beliefs or emotions of the visitors for target messages, this study attempted to identify the relative impacts of the three main types of beliefs toward a certain specific behaviour including the negative or the positive outcomes of particular behaviour and personal safety. The interesting findings showed that the most effective approach is to appeal to people's emotions and concern for personal safety associated with 'climbing the cliffs' and 'collecting fossils from the cliffs'.

For example, in the results of regression analysis, visitors' perceptions about the safety of 'climbing the cliffs' or 'collecting the fossils from the cliffs' (e.g. 'it is dangerous to climb the cliffs') had a stronger positive impact on their responsible behavioural intentions rather than their perception about environmental damage caused by those behaviour (e.g. climbing the cliffs will damage the environment', 'collecting fossils from the cliffs will damage the cliffs'). In addition, in the results of comparison between Group B and Group C divided by the experiences of the Visitor Centre, there were significant differences between the two groups on belief statements such as 'it is dangerous to climb the cliffs' and 'it is dangerous to collect the fossils from the cliffs'. Through explaining information about the continuing cliff erosion process and unstable landform at the Jurassic Coast through a wide range of interpretive techniques at the Visitor Centre, visitors with the interpretation experiences were more aware of the 'danger' of climbing the cliffs or collecting fossils from the cliffs than visitors who had not visited the Centre.

These findings support Manning's (2003) assumption that these types of messages may be warranted when applied to issues such as visitor safety and protection of critical and sensitive resources (Manning, 2003). That is, the visitors will always pay more attention when the basic human emotions of fear, anxiety and pity are aroused (McCool & Braithwaite 1992; Heylin, 1993).

These results might explain how visitors' beliefs influence specific behavioural intention through interpretation experiences based on the idea of the Theories of Reasoned Action/Planned Behaviour (Ajzen and Fishbein, 1980) or central route to persuasion (Roggenbuck, 1992). As explained by Bright *et al.* (1993), changing beliefs about performing a particular behaviour has an impact on changing attitudes toward that behaviour and subsequently, intentions to perform that behaviour. As mentioned earlier in the previous section (10.2.1 and 10.2.2), that is, visitors who had experienced interpretation on-site, changed their beliefs or feelings of concern regarding the negative outcomes of 'climbing the cliffs' and 'collecting fossils from the cliffs' and in turn, influenced their positive willingness not to engage in those types of specific problem behaviour. However, even though most respondents believed the protection of the environmental resources are very important, these beliefs did not significantly influence each type of specific responsible behaviour.

This finding also supports the viewpoint of Ballantyne and Hughes (2004) that the effectiveness of interpretation in influencing visitors' behaviour can be substantially improved by addressing specific messages targeting beliefs that are relevant and important to the target audience. Although this study focused only on limited types of beliefs about the negative or positive consequences of the particular behaviour and feelings of 'danger' or 'concern' about that behaviour, previously other researchers have identified several other types of beliefs for the effectiveness of belief target messages on behavioural change. They suggested that interventions should provide different information about the social acceptability of the behaviour, the ease with which the action can be done, and the different levels of moral development (e.g. fear of punishment, consideration for justice, social norms, fairness and self-respect) (Monroe, 2003; Christensen and Dustin, 1989) and emphasise emotional factors (Orams, 1997) in targeting visitors through different types of media (Manning,2003). Therefore, further study is needed to identify the different impacts of other types of beliefs and emotional factors depending upon the different types of behaviour and in what direction, as have been recommended by previous researchers (Ham and Krumpe, 1996; Lee and Balchin, 1995).

(3) Other factors

This research confirms the notion that specific attitudes toward a given behaviour had the greatest impact on site-specific behaviour. However, the non-significant relationships between other elements of attitudes and intentions were found in this study. In addition, the previous section (10.2.2) also reflects that the majority of visitors would not necessarily engage in environmental activism and 'removing beach litter' behaviour although they had strongly favourable environmental awareness and attitudes toward local environmental protection issues at the Jurassic Coast. In particular, with regards to behavioural intention toward 'removing beach litter', the positive link between attitudes toward 'coastal protection' and behavioural intention was weaker than the other two types of site-specific behaviour (i.g. the results of regression analysis for this behaviour explained 24% of variance at the Lulworth and 21% of variance at the Charmouth). These additional findings indicate that certain types of attitudes are not always the most important factor in influencing environmental behaviour in a particular situation. Many of the previous studies showed only a weak or non-existent link between attitude and behaviour (quoted in Uitto et al., 2004). The findings suggest that there might be a need to investigate the impacts of other psychological variables on long term conservation behaviour or the particular behaviour of 'removing beach litter' rather than only attitudes.

Various reasons are given why an obviously environmentally concerned person will not extend their concern and feelings to actual behaviour. In some cases it is because people do not realise the consequences of their actions on the environment, in other cases it is because people feel that they do not need to do anything or that their actions alone will not help to make a difference. Sometimes people are just unwilling to make the necessary sacrifices and thus inconvenience themselves or spend more money (Bell *et al.*, 2001). Another reason for this might be the lack of conviction about their own role and responsibility in these problems. Furthermore, the feedback about the effectiveness of the behaviour might help visitors to overcome several barriers related to specific behaviour (cited in Adams, 2003).

As reviewed in the literature, the complex relationships of several other factors have different influences depending on the types of behaviours. This might explain why interpretation failed sometimes in influencing certain types of behaviour due to the stronger impacts of other psychological and situational factors on behavioural changes. Other research has suggested the significant importance of 'locus of control' and 'responsibility' to influence environmentally responsible behaviour in the long term (Newhouse, 1990, Hwang *et al.*, 2000). This study also confirms the notion of Widner and Roggenbuck (2000) for the importance of a multiple approach in examining behaviour change research. Other researchers also indicated that no single strategy will likely effectively control all inappropriate behaviours in parks and therefore, researchers should draw from as many theories as possible in developing or evaluating successful interpretation programmes (Christensen & Dustin, 1989; Knopf & Dustin, 1992; Johnson and Vande Kamp, 1994). According to Widner and Roggenbuck (2000), the effectiveness of a single intervention strategy should be increased by incorporating multiple behaviour influence techniques. This means that "if norm appeals reach some people and attitude-change proposals can be used to influence others, a single intervention that includes both norm- and attitude-based approaches should be more effective overall than interventions based on any single approach" (p.4).

Discussion 4: How Do Characteristics of the Visitor Influence Specific Responsible Behavioural Intentions?

Cottrell and Graefe (1997) argued that socio-demographic variables influence a number of general environmental variables (knowledge, attitudes, behavioural intentions) and thus indirectly influence actual behaviour. Therefore, individual background characteristics are necessary to understand the process of responsible environmental behavioural change (Cottrell & Graefe, 1997; Hines *et al.*, 1986/87) as mentioned in the previous Chapter 6. Although weak and inconsistent relationships between socio-demographic factors and environmental attitudes or behaviour were found in previous researches, it is important to ask whether and how different segments of people differ regarding environmental attitudes and behaviour (Bell *et al.*, 2001; Adams 2003). With regard to this point, this section addresses how different characteristics of the visitors are associated with specific behavioural intentions. Additionally, the interesting findings provide a better understanding of how interpretation interacts with different individual characteristics in what situation. This may provide guidance to developing more effective programmes for the target audience.

10.3.3 Which Characterises of the Visitors are the Most Significant Contributors 5.1 (in Figure 10.1)

This study examined the relative impact of individual characteristics on behavioural intentions. Previous researchers have identified a wide range of social variables which have been linked to environmental action. They include age, gender, education, income and family type (Barr, 2003) as well as ethnicity, income and place of residence (Adams, 2003). In current study, the four most important contributors of visitor attributes were identified as follows: (1) gender, (2) age, (3) education, and (4) environmental involvement. Despite different influential contributing factors to the different types of behavioural intention at both case study sites, the highlighted findings showed that female, older people, people with lower levels of education, and people who had been involved in environmental organisations or activities had the higher levels of behavioural intentions in this current study. However, past experience of natural areas and this site and place of residence were not significantly related to all types of behavioural intentions. The findings of the study support the view that there were inconsistent and even contradictory relationships between socio-demographic factors and attitudes/behaviours (Adams, 2003; Barr, 2003). For example, stereotypically, previous research has provided evidence for higher levels of pro-environmental behaviour amongst younger, female, well-educated, wealthy individuals in nuclear families (Hines *et al.*, 1986/87). In this way, Fransson and Gärling (1999) suggest that such a view must be made with great caution. The relationships between each of the important contributors of visitor attributes and specific behavioural intention are discussed as follows:

(1)   Gender
The results of this study showed that gender was a moderate factor in influencing 'motivation to act' toward specific responsible behaviours at both sites. Another interesting finding indicated there were significant differences in behavioural intentions and attitudes between females and males. As

expected, females were more aware of and concerned about environmental issues and negative impacts of problem behaviours and this, in turn, led to higher levels of pro-environmental behavioural intentions than males. This supports the findings of other researchers that, generally, females appear to have more positive environmental attitudes than males (Brown 1999; Adams 2003).

However, other researchers suggested that one should beware of ambiguous results indicating an inconsistent direction of the relationship between gender and environmental variables. In some cases, there was no significant gender-gap in terms of environmental concern (Hayes, 2001; Lyons and Breakwell, 1994 quoted in Adam, 2003). According to Schahn and Holzer's (1990) findings, gender differences in the levels of environmental concern were dependent on the specific environmental issue under consideration. Scott and Willits (1994) supported the viewpoint that females were more likely to report environmentally pro-consumer behaviours, while men were more likely to participate in environmental political action. Another study of antecedents of climbing Uluru (Ayers Rock) behaviour in Central Australia by Brown (1999) also suggested that 'gender difference reflects the greater determination of males to be active, and their reduced concerns about the risks associated with the climb (p.691)'. That is, females were concerned more about the negative outcomes of climbing Ululu in terms of both cultural and environmental impacts and risk concerns related to personal safety, while males considered climbing the rock as a good activity to pursue.

These previous empirical studies indicated that significant gender differences were found when environmental attitudes focused on risk-related environmental issues such as the health and safety implications (Hayes, 2001). One of the several reasons was accounted for by different values and motivation between men and women (McKenzie, 2000; Fransson and Gärling, 1999). For example, the study of Knapp (1985) revealed that males valued their main domain with an emphasis on conquering the elements whereas women placed more value on "connection towards nature and the environment". (cited in Brown, 1999: 692).

As reviewed above, therefore, as this study focused on specific attitudes towards environmental issues related to personal safety of 'climbing the cliffs' or 'collecting the fossils from the cliffs', the different perceptions of the consequences of those particular behaviours between males and females might affect a significant gender-gap in terms of environmental attitudes and behavioural intentions. That is, this may be a result of more females perceiving less challenge in climbing the cliffs or being more concerned about personal safety than males. This suggests that different perception of target audiences regarding the type of behaviour can have different influences on the process of persuasive behavioural change.

(2)   Age

This study supports the notion that age is one of the moderating factors among socio-demographic variables in intention toward specific responsible behaviour (Bell *et al.*, 2001). Another interesting finding of this study indicated that older people (over 45 years old) were more concerned about environmental issues and had higher levels of willingness to engage in specific environmental behaviour than younger adults (18 to 35 years old). This study is inconsistent with the findings of other researchers into the relationships between age and environmental behaviour. Other researchers supported the idea that younger children (generally targeted children/school groups) have more favourable attitudes and behaviour than older children (Leeming *et al.* 1997) and older people (Fransson and Gärling, 1999).

However, this study focused on adult groups for target samples, mainly tourists in tourism settings, and it is difficult to compare it with findings of previous researchers investigating targeted children/school groups. This corresponds with the findings of Barr's (2003) study which examined the determinants of waste reduction behaviour through a case study in Exeter, UK. The two important factors of socio-demographic variables to environmental behaviour included gender and age. He found that females and older people were more likely to reduce their waste.

The contradictory and inconclusive findings of previous research and this current study can be explained by several reasons. One of the explanations of older people's increased environmental attitudes and behaviour might be that older people were also more aware of environmental issues through the media since the late 1980s (Howell and Laska, 1992, quoted in Fransson and Gärling, 1999).

For this study, another explanation of this finding might be considered, including different levels of participation in interpretive programmes during their visit to the sites and different perceptions of the consequences of a particular behaviour in target audiences. For example, at the Lulworth coastal area, older visitors appeared to have experienced the Visitor Centre more while younger people seemed to participate less in the Visitor Centre. Therefore, the higher levels of participation in the Visitor Centre by older people might help to increase their understanding and concern about the danger of 'climbing the cliffs' behaviour and in turn, be less interested in the challenge of 'climbing the cliffs', whereas younger people might be more interested in the challenge of that behaviour. The finding for the age differences by different levels of activities is consistent with those of Moscardo's (1999) study which indicated that younger people were more likely to engage in a wider range of the activities available on a reef day trip and so had less time to take and read a brochure related to the Great Barrier Reef, Australia.

This finding emphasised again the different responses to the interpretation by different types of visitors. Therefore, this study suggests that there is the need to develop special efforts to approach in different ways different targeted groups, especially younger male groups who are unlikely to use information on site through various types of interpretive programmes.

(3) Education

The results from this study also revealed that education was slightly but negatively associated with only one type of behavioural intention, toward 'not collecting fossils from the cliffs' at the Lulworth coastal area. One of these findings confirms the notion that education has good use as a determinant of environmental knowledge, concern and subsequent behaviour (Ostman & Parker, 1987, cited in Cottrell, 2003b; Van Liere & Dunlap, 1981). However, while other researchers argued that there was a positive correlation between education and environmental concern (Van Liere & Dunlap, 1981), this was not the case in this study. Inconsistent with the contention of previous research, this study indicated a negative significant association between education and, in particular, one type of behavioural intention. Therefore, it is noteworthy in that it needs to examine when and why the relationship between education and behaviours differs in a particular situation.

For example, with regards to attitude and behavioural intention toward 'not collecting fossils from the cliffs', the results demonstrated that people with university qualification had a higher level of specific belief toward positive outcomes of fossil collecting for learning while people with lower levels of qualifications were aware of and concerned about the negative impacts of fossil collecting (See Table 10.6). Subsequently, people with university qualifications tended to express less favourable intentions to 'not collecting fossils from the cliffs' than people with lower levels of educational qualifications.

One of the possible reasons for this finding might be accounted for by visitors' different interests and different beliefs about the consequences of fossil collecting activities between visitors with university qualifications and those with lower levels of qualifications. As the Jurassic Coast is considered as one of the coastal earth science heritage sites (Jurassic Coast Team, 2004a), special interest groups might already know about the scientific and geological importance of this site. Visitors with university qualifications might have a higher level of interest in geology and fossils. Their special interest might affect beliefs regarding the positive outcomes of fossil collecting activities as learning experiences. However, these positive beliefs about fossil collecting activities might mislead to inappropriate behaviour. This suggests that interpretation needs to have carefully designed belief-target messages to influence visitors' beliefs in order to change behaviours in targeted groups when the particular behaviours have either negative or positive outcomes.

Table 10.6 Comparison of Attitudes and Intentions toward Specific Behaviour by Different Levels of Education

	Lower levels of education (below college) (n=235)		The higher levels of education (university only) (n=186)
• **Attitude Statements** I think that visitors need to report to the Visitor Centre about the discovery of special fossils	*3.89*	<	*4.18*
I think that fossil collecting helps one to learn about the fossils	*3.47*	<	*3.73*
I think that collecting the fossils from the cliffs will damage the environment	**4.09**	<	**4.12**
I think that visitors should not be allowed to collect the fossils from the cliffs	3.77	>	3.64
I think that it is dangerous to collect the fossils from the cliffs	4.19	>	3.94
• **Behavioural Intention Statement** I will not collect the fossils	4.29	>	3.98

(4) Environmental Involvement

Several researchers have emphasised the role of pre-existing environmental involvement and interest in natural areas on pro-environmental attitudes and behaviour (Cable *et al.*, 1986; Beaumont 2001). For this study, variables regarding pre-existing environmental involvement and interest in natural areas included 'previous experiences of this site, 'previous experiences of natural areas', and 'pre-existing environmental involvement'.

Interestingly, through the results of the multiple regression analysis, this study revealed that the strong significant relationships between pre-existing environmental involvement and only one type of behavioural intention toward 'removing beach litter' were found at both sites in this study. However, there was no significant impact of environmental involvement on the other types of intentions of 'not climbing the cliffs' and 'not collecting the fossils'.

Specifically, as revealed in the previous section, compared to the other two types of site-specific minimal impact behaviours such as 'not climbing the cliffs' and 'not collecting fossils from the cliffs', those site-specific minimal impact behaviours appeared to be mainly dependent on demographic criteria (i.e. gender, age, and education) and interpretation experiences. Yet the particular behaviour regarding 'removing beach litter' was significantly associated with pre-existing environmental involvement.

Based on this finding, this study emphasised that the different types of behaviour were affected by different contributors of visitor characteristics. One of reasons might be explained from the findings of Dietz *et al*. (1998) that the influence of environmental involvement was associated with attitudes and was the most significant contributor to environmental activism. For example, through their environmental involvement experiences, individuals receive knowledge of particular environmental issues and how to participate effectively in activist behaviour and, in turn, this might convert into the commitment of individuals to engagement in environmentally responsible behaviour (Dietz *et al*., 1998; McFalane & Boxall, 2003; Brulle, 1996).

Therefore, the additional findings for different contributors to the visitor characteristics on different types of behaviour help to answer these questions such as how different target visitor groups modify the types of specific behavioural intentions in what situation and why site-specific interpretation failed in influencing 'removing beach litter behaviour to the target visitors.

10.3.4 The Inter-Relationships Between Interpretation and the Different Ranges of The Receiver   5.2 (in Figure 10.1)

Interestingly, the current study indicated that the relative impacts of interpretation with correlating the four main visitor characteristics factors were positively associated with behavioural intentions and attitudes. Although the relative impacts of different contributors varied widely depending on different types of behavioural intention, the interactive impacts of interpretation on behavioural intentions tended to be similarly positive between men and women, or between older and younger people, or between those with lower levels of educational qualifications and those with higher levels of educational qualifications.

This section presents an empirical evidence for the significant influences of interpretation on responsible environmental behavioural change across a wide range of visitor groups. This also provides the additional guidance as to why and when interpretation might or might not be an effective management tool for a particular behaviour.

Firstly, one of the findings supports the conclusion of Roggenbuck (1992) that the effectiveness of persuasion seems to depend largely on the type of impact, the behaviour involved and motives for the behaviour. The positive relative impacts of interpretation for a variety of visitor groups were significant on site-specific behaviours in relation to personal safety (i.e. 'not climbing the cliffs' and 'not collecting fossils from the cliffs'). For example, both female and male visitors, and both younger and older visitors increased their behavioural intentions through the levels of interpretation participation as seen in the results of the two-way ANOVA tests. Although significant gender or age differences in attitudes and behavioural intentions were found, information and interpretation influenced positively behavioural intentions of both females and males and both younger and older people.

The more interesting findings of this study demonstrated that the significant impacts of interpretation were found for different levels of education qualifications. It provided the beneficial evidence that interpretation plays an important role to change the dissonances between attitudes and behaviour in particular groups of visitors.

For example, Table 10.7 showed that when visitors had not experienced any interpretation, visitors who had the higher levels of educational qualification held less positively a strong willingness to 'not collect the fossils from the cliffs'. However, as visitors used more amounts of interpretive methods, visitors with university qualifications appeared to express the higher levels of positive behavioural intentions to 'not collecting the fossils from the cliffs' rather than visitors with lower levels of education qualification. This implies that the higher levels of interpretation participation clearly were clearly influential in increasing more positive behavioural intentions of visitors with university qualifications through converting their old beliefs or perceptions of the negative consequences of fossil collecting activities. According to central route persuasion model (Roggenbuck 1992), relevant beliefs of visitors are modified through delivery of substantive messages. As visitors' beliefs and attitudes have been changed by their experiences and information, these new or modified beliefs implant to alter appropriate behaviours (Manning, 2003). Therefore, this suggests that interpretive planners need to pay special attention to those groups with higher levels of interests in fossils and those with university qualifications.

Table 10.7 The Link between Levels of Interpretation Participation and Education on Behavioural Intention toward 'Not Collecting Fossils from the Cliffs'

Levels of interpretation participation	Education	
	Lower level (n=235)	Higher level (n=186)
None	**3.986** >	**3.793**
Lower level (1-2)	4.396 >	4.079
Higher level (3-5)	4.593 <	**4.800**

Dependent variable: Behavioural intention toward 'not collecting fossils from the cliffs'

Additionally, the alternative possible explanation for the role of pre-existing variables adds the question of why and when there were no effects of interpretation in influencing attitudes and behavioural intentions. As discussed in the previous section, previous environmental experiences and involvement seemed to diminish the effects of interpretation on attitude and behavioural changes due to a 'ceiling effect' (Dresner and Gill, 1994; Beaumont 2001). For example, the majority of visitors were repeat visitors (over 60%) and local residents from South coastal areas in England (i.e. Dorset, South-East, South-West).

These visitors might already have a high level of pre-existing knowledge regarding local environmental issues and appropriate behaviour for the protection of the geological environment at Jurassic costal areas. This confirms the finding of Thorn (1995) that area experience and repetition of messages seems to influence the high level of favourable attitudes and behavioural intention in all ranges of environmental issues and specific minimal impact behaviour. This 'ceiling effect' might mislead us regarding the failure of interpretation in influencing visitors' attitudes and behaviours. Therefore, it is important to examine visitors' existing levels of knowledge, interests, place of residence, and previous experiences of the site or other natural areas in order to distinguish whether behavioural changes result from the direct effects of interpretation or from the 'ceiling effects' of individual factors.

Finally, the strong link between environmental involvement and behavioural intentions regarding removing beach litter might show the limitation of interpretation effectiveness on long term conservation behaviour or responsibility-denial behaviour. This implies that it might require different strategies of interpretation in influencing the numbers and types of inappropriate behaviours.

According to typology of undesirable visitor behaviour summarised by Roggenbuck (1992), removing others' beach litter appears to be categorised into 'responsibility-denial' behaviour which occurs when people generally believe an action is wrong, but do not assume moral responsibility for the inappropriate act in a specific setting. By contrast, site-specific appropriate behaviour regarding 'not collecting fossils from the cliffs' and 'not climbing the cliffs' could be categorised into unintentional and uninformed actions which result from ignorance of the rules, and of the negative consequences of the action in question (Roggenbuck, 1992; Gramann and Vander Stoep, 1987). In this study, the results of factor analysis supported this category that the clean-up beach litter behaviour was an underlying factor labelled 'environmental activism' while both site-specific behaviours regarding 'not collecting fossils from the cliffs' and 'not climbing the cliffs' were in another underlying factor termed 'specific responsible behaviour'. Therefore, performing responsibility-denial behaviour regarding 'removing beach litter' for this study may be influenced by several other external factors including time, sacrifice of money and convenience, strong responsibility (Adams, 2003), as well as incentives (Roggenbuck, 1992).

On the other hand, unintentional and uninformed actions might require specific information about the consequences of the actions, the benefits of those consequences, and how easy to perform (Monroe, 2003; Roggenbuck 1992) which can be easily influenced by effective interpretive messages. The findings of this study provide the empirical evidence of this premise suggested by previous researchers.

For examples, the site-specific behaviour were influenced by the increased levels of awareness or feelings of the 'danger' or 'care' of the negative outcomes of the particular behaviour through relevant persuasive messages to the target audience. By contrast, although the majority of visitors to this site were more aware of all local environmental issues regarding 'coastal protection' and the negative impacts of beach litter issues, they were not yet engaged in removing beach litter and environmental activism behaviour. As mentioned earlier, the findings indicate that environmental involvement plays a more significant role in engagement in behavioural intentions regarding removing beach litter.

Unfortunately, this current study agrees with the assertion of Alessa *et al.* (2003) that it may be more difficult to influence those types of behaviours through current education/interpretation programmes based on the attitude-based theories or central route to persuasion perspective. However, several researchers showed that effective techniques or strategies can promote the clean-up litter behaviour. In particular, according to applied behaviour analysis (Roggenbuck, 1992), use of rewards or punishment by regulation might be more effective in some type of behaviours which are illegal or are lacking in responsibility, such as littering, vandalism, and picking-up litter. However, in the long term, interpretation can be effective in influencing 'removing beach litter' through conveying specific belief-targeted messages. Those belief-targeted message factors include visitors' responsibility for the clean-up of littered areas or role modelling of appropriate behaviour by the tour guides, reducing the barriers to the behaviour (i.e. inconvenience of time or money) (Adams, 2003), and signing a petition indicating support for litter-free parks (Clark *et al.*, 1972a,b; Roggenbuck, 1992).

Roggenbuck (1992) argued that the results of previous empirical studies investigating the effects of those variables have produced mixed results and, therefore, this study suggests that there is a need to investigate the existing level of responsibility, locus of control and other barriers in order to influence the particular behaviour regarding 'removing beach litter' in long-term approach. Therefore, the mixed behaviour change strategies of interpretation might be most successful in influencing the multiple types of behaviours in protected areas (Widner and Roggenbuck, 2000).

Overall, the relative impacts of interpretation and visitor characteristics depending on types of behaviour may be found to support the notion by Chandool (1997) that tourists are a very diverse group of people looking for diverse recreation experiences. This makes it difficult to develop persuasive messages to address the diversity of tourists in an effective manner. As a result, some messages have been unsuccessful as a management tool in achieving their goals. This study also confirms the conclusion of Moscardo (1998) that 'the key to quality interpretation is to keep visitors as the central focus' (p.11).

10.4 The Management Role of Interpretation in Achieving the Goals of Sustainable Tourism [6] (in Figure 10.1)

The previous section highlighted the successful outcomes of interpretation in promoting visitors' concern and support for conservation of geological environments at the Jurassic Coast. Empirical evidence for this fact also emphasises that effective interpretation can prompt tourists' site-specific responsible behaviour though a single short-term experience in a particular tourism setting.

In this way, a major lesson to be learnt from this study is that there is the possibility for interpretation to help achieve the goals of sustainable tourism management. This study supports the view that interpretation plays a vital central role in the development of sustainable tourism as well as visitor management and conservation (Moscardo, 1998; Barrow, 1996; Ham and Weiler, 2002; Tubb, 2003).

For example, this case study also emphasises the significant roles of interpretation as a visitor management tool in achieving the goals of sustainable tourism. It is worthwhile to reflect the main goals of the management plans and its implementation in achieving the management policy objectives at this site. In the case of the Jurassic Coast, in particular, long term conservation of cliff erosion and spectacular fossils is the priority of the management issues in this area (see Jurassic Coast Management Plan by JCWHSSG, 2003a,b). A number of management plans or the Jurassic Coast project by Dorset Coast governments and other local partnerships have been developed in order to achieve sustainable tourism on a holistic and integrated basis (Dorset Coast Forum, 1999; JCWHSSG, 2003a,b; Johnson, 2002). The main key aims of the management strategies have embraced the principles of sustainable tourism development in light of the different dimensions of sustainability by different stakeholders' perspectives.

With regards to environmental sustainability, management actions for the goals of conservation include managing human activities for minimal disturbance to natural coastal processes and the quality of the environment as well as promoting responsible behaviours in collecting fossils and other geological specimens (JCWHSSG, 2003a,b). Regarding economic sustainability, Dorset County Council is also attempting to use this unique earth science legacy to promote a new and sustainable niche market to 'out of season' tourist interests, particularly geo-tourism, as well as to extend visitor stay time and to maximize visitor satisfaction and economic benefit for the quality of life of the local communities (Johnson, 2002; JCWHSSG, 2003a,b).

In terms of the practical application of those policies to more sustainable approaches, interpretation has been employed by Dorset County Council at this site (Johnson, 2002). The current coastlink visitor centres have been developed and include a network of the 5 marine visitor centres at the Dorset Coast such as the Charmouth Heritage Coast Centre and the Lulworth Heritate Centre, along with the Jurassic Coast (Dorset Coast Strategy, 1999). Working papers have also highlighted new educational initiatives, an interpretation strategy and a marketing approach. Hose (1995) emphasised that interpretation has the potential to assist in conservation for both earth science heritage sites and marine coastal areas as well as the quality of visitor experiences. This supports the viewpoint that tourism can be a positive activity with the potential to benefit the local communities, tourists and the region (Johnson, 2002). This is consistent with the example of Tubb (2003) who indicated that Dartmoor National Park Authority (1991) also stated that environmental interpretation is a key strategy in the management of tourism development in environmentally sensitive places.

371

The current study clearly provides the empirical evidence to confirm the conclusion of Ham and Weiler (2002) that interpretation can facilitate environmental sustainability in ecological dimensions by minimising the negative impacts of tourists or promoting appropriate behaviour. Indeed, it has been suggested that such tourism activity may be ecologically beneficial when interpretation is used to educate visitors about conservation (Oram, 1996a). However, the results of this study suggest that there is the need to develop special efforts through the mixed strategies of interpretation techniques in promoting among tourists a conservation ethic for the long-term.

In addition, this study suggests that there might be required to do research about an additional role of interpretation on the other dimensions of sustainability in this area. As emphasised regarding the significant roles of interpretation on sustainable tourism by several researchers (Moscardo, 1997; Kuo,2002; Butler, 1991; Tubb, 2003; Ham and Weiler, 2002), interpretation can also contribute to economic sustainability by satisfying tourists' demand, and by creating local employment such as tour guides and interpreters (Ham and Weiler, 2002). Firstly, it has been argued that when visitors enjoy their visit, they are more likely to support management strategies (Orams, 1996b; Cooper *et al.*, 1998; Moscardo, 1999). In the long term, visitors' enjoyable experiences of sensitive resources may be beneficial to other resources, as their knowledge and awareness of the environment has been increased by their previous experiences (Schänzel and McIntosh, 2000, quoted in Kuo, 2002). For instance, at the Charmouth Coast, the positive effects of interpretation were found in visitors' enjoyable experiences related to learning about fossils or geology as well as their increased awareness of both the negative and positive outcomes of fossil collecting.

With regard to the social dimensions of sustainability, Johnson (2002) states that increasing the participation by local people and communities in voluntary efforts is currently helping to deliver sustainable tourism. Therefore, further study is needed to research the emphasis on social responsibility among local communities through interpretation or community education in order to achieve another key element of sustainability.Therefore, this study suggests that further research must be worthwhile in the other additional roles of interpretation as a key visitor management tool in order to achieve socio-economic sustainability.

Overall, this section highlights the contributions of interpretation as a visitor management strategy to the achievement of aspects of sustainability in the long-term. However, the issues in this study demand that it is important to choose specific targeted objectives of interpretation depending on the different dimensions of sustainability at the natural heritage sites or coastal areas. Therefore, it is necessary to apply appropriate implications of visitor management strategies depending on types of management problems in a particular setting. Regular and continued research and the evaluation of the effectiveness of interpretation might provide feedback in providing appropriate tourism policy and planning on the holistic and integrated perspectives by all stakeholders for different dimensions of sustainability.

CHAPTER

11

Chapter 11 Conclusions

11.1 Introduction

In this chapter, the conclusions will be presented. The chapter begins with an overview of the main findings. The second section examines the contributions of this study in terms of the methodological approaches and managerial implications. In the following section, the limitations of the study are outlined and then recommendations for future work are made.

11. 2 Summary of The Research

The purpose of this study was to examine the management role of interpretation in achieving the environmental goals of sustainable tourism by influencing the selected antecedents of responsible behaviour. The research questions were "is interpretation effective in promoting visitors' attitudes and behavioural intentions towards local environmental conservation and responsible behaviour?" and "how does interpretation influence relatively the types of specific behavioural intentions, along with the visitor attributes and attitude components?". The study provides the empirical evidence that interpretation makes significant contributions to sustainable tourism management at the Jurassic Coast by promoting visitors' awareness, concern and support for site-specific appropriate behaviour toward geological environmental conservation.

However, the results of the research highlight that the successful effectiveness of interpretation varies according to different aspects of responsible environmental behaviours and local conservation issues at the Jurassic Coast. In particular, the study examined the three main types of responsible environmental behaviours including site-specific behaviour (e.g. 'not climbing the cliffs', 'not collecting fossils from the cliffs'), general responsible behaviour (e.g. 'removing beach litter', 'following code of conduct'), and environmental activism behaviour (e.g. 'donation', 'volunteer work'). Local environmental conservation issues focused on three key topic areas: 'cliff erosion', 'fossil protection (fossil collecting)', and 'coastal protection (beach litter)'. The findings of the study reveal that the use of the current interpretation provision had significantly increased visitor awareness of the importance of Dorset's coastal geology and geomorphology environment and in turn, had fostered their support for management policies related to site-specific responsible behaviour for geological environmental conservation. By contrast, the weaknesses of site-based interpretation was also revealed in terms of the failure of strengthening visitors' support for engaging in environmental activism or 'removing beach litter'.

375

Additionally, the findings of the study emphasise that the strengths or weaknesses of interpretation on desired beneficial outcomes are dependent upon a number of variables associated with interpretive channels, belief- or emotion-targeted message content, and visitor characteristics. This finding was important in realising that interpretation could fail if planners do not have a better understanding of the needs, preferences, and perceptions of each target visitor group. Therefore, additional research monitoring the most important factors provides guidance in deciding 'when' and 'how' interpretation promotes responsible behaviour, which will help in targeting visitors in particular situations. Several important determinants for the success or failure of interpretation on three types of responsible behavioural intentions are identified as follows:

11.3 The Significant Findings

11.3.1 The Strengths of Interpretation and the Important Determinants Influencing Specific Responsible Behavioural Intentions

The Strengths of Interpretation at the Jurassic Coast
Interpretation was effective in promoting visitors' appropriate behaviour for geological environmental conservation (i.e. 'cliff erosion' and 'fossil protection') through increasing their awareness, concern, and support for site-specific responsible behaviour regarding 'not climbing the cliffs' and 'not collecting the fossils from the cliffs'.

The Important Determinants Influencing Specific Behavioural Intentions
(i.e. 'not climbing the cliffs' and 'not collecting the fossils from the cliffs')

(1) Interpretation Channel Variables
- Multiple use of interpretive methods can be more effective when delivering persuasive messages in reaching a different range of targeted receivers in order to influence specific responsible behavioural intentions for geological environment conservation.
- The majority of visitors used the Visitor Centres at both sites. The Visitor Centre plays a key role in increasing visitors' awareness of the negative or positive outcomes of the site-specific behaviour (i.e. fossil collecting activities) as well as enhancing visitors' enjoyable experiences. Yet, it had a small impact on behavioural intentions towards responsible environmental behaviour.
- Reading of the Code of Conduct brochure regarding the targeted behaviour (i.e. fossil collecting activities) was also effective in alerting visitors about responsible behaviour.

However, only a small number of visitors had actually read the brochure, particularly at the Lulworth coast site.

(2)   Attitudes of the Visitors in Relation to Message Content Variables

- There was a consistent relationship between attitudes and behavioural intentions in relation to those two conservation topics ('cliff erosion' and 'fossil protection'). In particular, belief- and emotion- targeted messages (i.e. safety and concern) related to those aspects of specific attitudes towards the consequences of a particular behaviour were more effective in influencing specific responsible behavioural intentions (i.e. 'not climbing the cliffs', 'not collecting fossils from the cliffs') than general attitudes toward the importance of geological environmental protection.

- The majority of visitors had a higher level of awareness about the consequences of site-specific problem behaviour (e.g. climbing the cliffs or collecting fossils from the cliffs) and support for the responsible behaviour. Yet, they had a moderate level of environmental concern regarding the two conservation issues and associated with problem behaviour.

- Visitors' beliefs related to ambiguous outcomes of the particular behaviour were significantly different between the Charmouth and Lulworth coastal areas as a result of interpretation experience (i.e. 'fossil collecting contributes to the positive economy of the local area' vs 'it is dangerous to collect fossils from the cliffs')

(3) Visitor Characteristic Variables

- Females, older people and visitors with lower levels of education qualifications had more environmentally supportive attitudes and behavioural intentions than males, younger people and visitors with higher levels of education as a result of interpretation experiences on-site.

- Visitors with university qualifications had significant changes in behavioural intentions with regard to 'not collecting fossils from the cliffs' as a result of their interpretation experiences, particularly, at the Lulworth coast site.

11.3.2 The Weaknesses of Interpretation and the Important Determinants Influencing Specific Behavioural Intentions

The Weaknesses of Interpretation at the Jurassic Coast

Interpretation was not effective either in strengthening behavioural intentions regarding 'removing beach litter', general responsible environmental behaviour, and environmental activism behaviour, nor in influencing general attitudes related to environmental protection and the 'beach litter' issue.

The Important Determinants Influencing Specific Behavioural Intentions

(i.e. 'removing beach litter')

(1)   Interpretation Method Variables

- Multiple use of interpretation was not effective in influencing environmental attitudes and behavioural intentions in relation to the 'beach litter' issue and 'removing beach litter'.
- The Visitor Centre had no effects on attitudes and behavioural intentions regarding 'removing beach litter'.
- Reading the Code of Conduct Brochure moderately influenced intentions regarding 'removing beach litter', only at the Charmouth coastal area.

(2)   Attitudes of the Visitors in Relation to Message Content Variables

- Belief and emotion components of specific attitudes regarding the consequences of a particular behaviour had a more significant impact on specific responsible behavioural intentions regarding 'removing beach litter' than general attitudes toward the importance of coastal environmental protection and concern about pollution by beach litter.
- However, there were the inconsistent relationships between general attitudes and specific behavioural intentions in relation to the 'beach litter' issue. That is, although the majority of visitors had extremely a high level of favourable attitudes toward 'coastal protection' and the 'beach litter' issue, they had a low level of positive intentions to engage in 'removing beach litter'.

(3) Visitor Characteristic Variables

- Pre-existing environmental involvement had a significant impact on behavioural intentions related to responsible-denial behaviour (i.e. 'removing beach litter').

378

- Previous experiences of natural areas, this sample site, and local residence appeared to influence favourable attitudes towards conservation issues. However, pro-environmental attitudes did not lead to fostering pro-environmental behavioural intentions toward conservation issues. Pre-existing favourable environmental attitudes from previous experiences seemed to diminish the direct effects of interpretation on the desired behavioural outcomes.

11.4 Contributions of the Research

11.4.1 Contributions to Theoretical and Methodological Approaches

Several contributions have been made in this research, as follows: multiple measurements of the main indicators, the conceptualisation of attitude and behaviour based on a site-specific approach, the relationships between the independent variables and specific behavioural intentions, and methodological issues.

The highlighted contributions of this study were to explore the multiple measurement of the effectiveness of interpretation from a number of perspectives. Previous research has reviewed the inconsistent findings of the beneficial effects of interpretation as a visitor management tool because of involving various factors. In response to this, multiple assessments were suggested by Madin and Fenton (2004). It could be useful to examine 'when' interpretation is effective upon which management policies or which types of behaviour rather than exploring whether or not interpretation is successful or unsuccessful in the particular situation. In this sense, this study identified the strengths and weaknesses of interpretation in the light of various site-specific conservation issues, different types of interpretive programmes, multidimensional attitudes, and multi-sets of behaviour.

First, the study attempted to determine which of the management policies associated with various local conservation issues might or might not be achieved by site-based interpretation in the specific tourism settings. The findings suggest that site-based interpretation could promote visitors' awareness, concern, and support for at least two key geological conservation topic areas including 'cliff erosion' and 'fossil collecting' at the Jurassic Coast. This multiple assessment of site-specific issues allowed us to identify how effectively the current site-based interpretation as a visitor management tool contributes to geological environmental conservation.

Secondly, the study supports the premise that the respondents' levels of interpretation participation can be critical in promoting different types of site-specific responsible behaviour. Consistent with the notion suggested by recent research (Manning, 2003; Madin and Fenton, 2004; Roggenbuck, 1992), the study empirically demonstrates that a multiple media approach to deliver persuasive messages can be useful to reach a wide range of the visitor groups in influencing appropriate behaviour rather than use of a single medium. In particular, the study contributes to a better understanding of visitors' preferences for types of media and their interest in available activities as well as their actual attention and readiness for the particular brochure through measurement of the effectiveness of both the levels of interpretation participation and each type of a single medium.

With regards to the multiple measurements of the concepts of environmental attitudes and behaviour, it is worth noting that this study attempted to explore the multidimensional aspects of the attitude and behaviour constructs from general aspects to specific aspects. More details, multidimensional attitudes are measured from general aspects of protection of the environment to specific aspects toward the particular action in relation to three main local conservation issues. The results indicate that interpretation was effective in influencing changes in specific attitudes toward the site-specific behaviour rather than general attitudes toward environmental protection.

Additionally, this study directly measured multi-act dimensions of responsible environmental behaviour including both site-specific appropriate behaviour and long-term conservation behaviour in order to examine the potential role of interpretation in achieving the ecological goals of sustainability in the protected heritage coast area, the Jurassic Coast. Previous research has focused on either inappropriate behaviour related to site-specific settings or general conservation behaviour. Not much has been studied to measure multi-act behaviour in the interpretation fields. This study revealed that site-based interpretation had a greater impact on a site-specific behaviour than on long-term conservation behaviour. Overall, the highlighted findings of this study show that the effects of interpretation varied depending on belief or feeling components of the attitude constructs and the types of behaviour. This multiple approach helps to examine 'when' interpretation influences different types of attitudes or behaviour in order to target visitors with a view to evaluating the impact of interpretation on the beneficial outcomes as a management tool.

This study also makes a significant theoretical and practical contribution to the design of priority messages or information more effectively through examining the relationships between multidimensional attitudes and specific behavioural intentions in relation to local conservation issues and responsible behaviour. In terms of developing persuasive message content in behavioural change research, the theory of reasoned action/planned behaviour has been the most commonly used in identifying the primary salient beliefs towards a particular behaviour in previous research. However, Widner and Roggenbuck (2000) suggested that the inconsistent and contradictory findings of the effectiveness of interpretation might be due to the way of examining behaviour change research based on the particular theory. They indicated that no one theory fully explained visitor behaviour and the influence of interpretive programmes since there are so many different types of behaviour and different ranges of visitor. In this sense, this study did not attempt to test or validate one theory. Instead of applying one particular theory to the conceptual and operational measurement of attitude and behaviour, this research attempted to integrate belief and feeling components of attitudes from different types of construct reviewed from the previous research.

The results show that specific attitudes towards the particular behaviour have a more significant impact on specific behavioural intentions than those impacts of general attitudes towards the types of issues or types of resource protection. The findings enabled the researcher to compare the relative influence of both the belief and feeling domains of specific attitudes on the types of specific behavioural intentions. Therefore, this research supports the idea that interpretation should provide different information regarding different types of salient beliefs based on different theoretical approaches such as the theory of reasoned action, central path to persuasion, and moral development theories as well as arousing emotions related to fear appeal, anxiety and pity in influencing undesirable or uninformed behaviour.

An additional contribution of this study to the improvement of effective interpretation techniques is that understanding of visitor characteristics is important in influencing a particular behaviour, particularly due to there being heterogeneous groups in tourism settings. The study provides a better understanding of how different segment of visitors differ regarding environmental attitudes and behaviour. For example, different attributes of the visitor characteristics have a moderate impact depending on the types of behaviour, particularly, between site-specific responsible behaviour and responsibility-denial behaviour (i.e. 'removing beach litter'). More details, demographic characteristics and interpretation experiences (e.g. gender, age, education, levels of interpretation) were the important determinants of site-specific behavioural intentions regarding 'not climbing the cliffs', 'not collecting fossils from the cliffs'). However, responsibility-denial behaviour was influenced by pre-existing environmental involvement. Therefore, this study confirms the view that different strategies of interpretation according to the types of behaviour need to be applied through tailoring the needs and perceptions of targeted audience groups as well as the barriers of particular behaviour.

With regards to the contributions of this study to methodological approaches, the research adopted comparisons between different groups according to their Visitor Centre experiences. Previous research has mostly been employed to compare two groups such as pre-visit and post-visit groups according to the respondents' experiences of the interpretive programmes. However, this method was considered to be limited due to the mediating effects of previous experience, motivation, and pre-existing knowledge on the effectiveness of interpretation. Therefore, this study divided the sample into three groups according to their Visitor Centre experiences, previous experiences of the Centre, and plans to visit the Centre. The findings demonstrate that the direct effects of the Visitor Centre were limited in their influence on attitudes and behavioural intentions.

Multiple regression analysis was employed to examine the relative contributions of the selected antecedents of the site-specific responsible behaviour (i.e. visitor characteristics, specific attitudes, the level of interpretation participation, and type of interpretation methods) on behavioural intentions associated with each specific responsible behaviour. Multiple regression analysis helps to understand the different explanatory power of the independent variables on each type of behavioural intention.

However, this study did not examine the mediating effects of each of the independent variables on behavioural intentions. Such additional findings may help managers to gain a more insightful and thorough understanding of how visitor attributes and interpretation channel variables are associated with different types of responsible behaviour in a site-specific situations.

11.4.2 Practical and Managerial Implications of Interpretation Research

The specific findings should be used with caution, as the sample on which they are based is not necessarily representative of all visitors to the Jurassic Coast or other heritage coastal areas. However, several practical implications are related to the findings of this research. The practical and managerial implications might help site managers gain a more insightful understanding of how best to design, evaluate, and implement interpretive programmes in the application to the other Jurassic Coast Sites which might have the similar management policies or in other coastal areas in general (See Table 11.1).

(1) Identify the main goals of interpretation as a visitor management tool

Managers need to be aware of the multiple roles of interpretation in managing the holistic and integrated balance between different stakeholders' needs and requirements for the longer-term. In order to achieve different aspects of sustainable tourism, managers need to target specific objectives of interpretation according to management policies associated with different impacts of tourism in particular settings. In the case of this study, the primary management goal of this site is to conserve the coastal and geological environment through managing human activities. In response to this primary management goal, interpretation should be designed to persuade visitors to adopt responsible behaviour with management policies rather than simply providing the factual information to increase visitors' appreciation and understanding of the natural environment related to geology, natural history of the coastal process, and fossils as well as enhancing visitors' experiences and enjoyment.

Table 11.1 Implications for Site-Specific interpretation at the Jurassic Coasts

Interpretation Strategies	The Research Objectives
1. Identify specific goals of interpretation for sustainable tourism in terms of different impacts, stakeholders, different policies, and particular objectives	• Environmental impacts by visitors • Interpretation or regulation? • Promoting visitors' responsible behaviour through effective interpretation
3. About What? The topics Identify **the main issues and problem behaviours related to tourism activities**	• Cliff erosion • ('not climbing the cliffs'/'keeping to the footpaths') • Fossil collecting • ('not collecting fossils from the cliffs'/ • 'reporting to the Centre about the discovery of special fossils') • Beach litter ('removing beach litter')
3. Type of message Identify **the target beliefs to the problem behaviours** for target message design	• Negative environmental impacts of the problem behaviour • Personal safety and support for the policy • Importance of protection of natural resources • Concern about the problems
4. Type of media Identify **the types of media regarding target audience**	• Use of the Visitor Centre • Reading Code of Conduct brochure • Levels of Interpretation Participation
5. Type of Barriers Identify **the barriers to reduce the inconsistency between attitudes and behaviour**	• The relationships between attitudes and behaviours • Is it true that favourable attitudes lead to pro-environmental behaviour through interpretation?
6. Target audience Identify **the target audience**	*Visitor characteristics* • Their preferences of media • Their previous experiences • Environmental involvement

(Source: Adapted from Ham & Krumpe, 1996)

(2) Identify the main issues and problem behaviours related to tourism activities

Site-specific management issues should be considered in order to discourage undesirable or uninformed low impact behaviour on a certain environment setting for effective interpretation to be successful. This study suggests that it is important to consider different policies at each site due to the particular environment and tourism activities although both sites were managed under the Jurassic Coast Project. In contrast with national parks or other natural sites, tourism at the Jurassic Coast Sites includes a variety of tourism activities; both leisure related and activities related to natural attractions, such as beach-based activities, fossil collecting, viewing natural attractions and walking on cliff paths. Managers need to identify the strengths and the weaknesses of interpretation on all various target site-specific appropriate behaviours from a number of perspectives.

(3) Identify the target beliefs or emotions in relation to the problem behaviours for target message design

Managers should target salient beliefs regarding management policies in a persuasive interpretation to effectively change different types of behaviours. The findings of this study suggest that it is important to identify which types of beliefs have a greater impact on the type of behaviour. Different visitor groups perceived and processed messages in different ways according to their interests, pre-existing knowledge, previous experiences and pre-existing attitudes. The content of a message should be developed by obtaining the beliefs which are most salient to the target visitors in promoting a particular behaviour. In order to influence uninformed behaviour, belief targeted messages in relation to the positive or negative outcomes of the particular behaviour appeared to be effective rather than an approach that targeted general attitudes towards environmental protection or issues. However, other types of beliefs regarding responsibility, locus of control, and social norms might need to be developed to promote responsibility-denial or long-term conservation behaviour. In addition, visitors' emotions regarding 'care', 'worry', 'danger' of climbing the cliffs or collecting the fossils can be very effective for females or older people.

(4) Identify the types of media regarding target audience

A multiple media approach should be considered due to different types of media used by visitors and the different ability of a single medium. In particular, an important consideration of further management is that the appropriate medium should be placed in the correct location in relation to the opportunity to perform the targeted behaviour in order to reach a wide range of visitors.

In the case of the Jurassic Coast, with regard to the visitors' use pattern of programmes, the majority of visitors had experienced the Visitor Centre which is located at the entrance near a car park and other facilities at the site. However, the particular Visitor Code brochure for fossil collecting was not effectively distributed to reach a wide range of the total visitor population although the Visitor Code brochure was very effective in alerting visitor responsible behaviour related to collecting fossils and other environmentally responsible behaviour at both sites. This indicates that managers need to consider that the influence of the particular Code brochure might be lost if the visitors have already made up their mind to climb the cliffs or to go to the beach without using it.

As most visitors appeared to use signs on-site, alternative methods might be considered maximising the effectiveness of signs. Mangers should identify the direct influence of signs on the outcomes or the right location of signs and need to examine the design of signs to attract visitors' attention and awareness as recommended by Espiner (1999). Therefore, brochures designed to promote responsible collecting of fossils or other media should be distributed in the right place at the right time, as well as using alternative on- and off-site methods to reach a wide range of visitors prior to their planning their trips.

In terms of the different ability of a single medium, the Visitor Centres at both sites play the multiple roles not only in increasing visitors' learning about and awareness of local environmental issues but also enhancing visitors' enjoyment and satisfaction. The influence of the Visitor Centre could, however, be less effective in prompting appropriate visitor behaviour due to many contributing factors. Therefore, managers might reconsider additional information such as the use of images of 'the cliff erosion' or the direct messages of appropriate behaviour in whatever location of the site those responsible behaviours might be required of the visitors in order to maximise the direct effects of the Visitor Centres.

(5) Identify the barriers reducing the inconsistency between attitudes and behaviour

This study helps to identify the weaknesses of the current interpretation in promoting various types of responsible environmental behaviour. Although the majority of visitors had favourable attitudes and behavioural intentions towards general environmental protection issues, their favourable attitudes did not lead to favourable behavioural intentions towards long-term conservation behaviour. This study suggests that the pre-existing environmental involvement of the visitors had a significant impact on those behaviours.

An appropriate interpretation strategy should promote long-term conservation or responsibility-denial behaviour in order to achieve the environmental goals of sustainable tourism for the longer-term. Managers need to develop targeted messages regarding visitors' personal responsibility or provide the opportunity for participation in conservation activities, such as picking up beach litter. To do so, it is also important to examine visitors' existing attitudes and the barriers to their performing responsible conservation behaviour.

(6) Identify the target audience

Managers need to understand who the major visitors to the site are because different visitor groups hold different motivations, beliefs, attitudes, and preferences for activities. Therefore, care needs to be taken in forming conclusions about the beneficial outcomes of interpretation due to the relative influence of visitor characteristic variables.

In this study, managers should focus particularly on younger male visitors (between 18 to 35 years old), special interest visitors who are interested in fossil collecting activities and have university qualifications, and the repeat and local resident groups who have higher levels of awareness and attitudes toward local environmental issues. For example, as mentioned earlier, younger male visitors (between 18 to 35 years old) appeared to hold a more positive attitude towards climbing or collecting fossils and to be less interested in participating in the interpretive programmes. In turn, it seemed to be difficult to change their attitudes and behavioural intentions towards site-specific responsible behaviour by the current interpretation.

In addition, visitors with university qualifications appeared to be more interested in fossil collecting activities rather than visitors with a lower level of education qualifications. However, when visitors with university qualifications had used more numbers of programmes, interpretation had changed their attitudes and behavioural intentions. To achieve maximum effectiveness of interpretation with those target groups, managers might need to deliver persuasive messages through different agents such as the information centre, accommodation and through off-site methods prior to their visits, like Internet. On-site, the volunteer or tour guides can be critical in their influence on younger male visitors or special interest groups for fossil collecting activities.

Moreover, the majority of visitors were local visitors and repeat visitors who already had higher levels of knowledge about local environmental issues. Therefore, updated and in depth information might need to be developed to target these groups through diverse topics and activities or community education for local residents.

11.5 Limitations of the Research

Despite the significant contributions of this study, it is important to recognise its limitations and the need for additional research. This study has strengths and weaknesses in its theoretical and methodological approaches as follows: behaviour indicator, selected antecedents variables of responsible environmental behaviour, response set bias, and sampling.

First of all, this study focused on behavioural intentions as behaviour indicators. Previous research has argued that there is a gap between behavioural intentions and actual behaviour due to situational factors (Hines et al., 1986). Therefore, it should be considered that favourable behavioural intentions do not automatically lead to actual behaviour on site. However, several researchers suggested that behavioural intention is an important indicator to create visitors' motivation for the longer term in the fields of interpretation and tourism (Cable et al., 1981; Orams, 1996). Moreover, several previous studies have supported the view that there is a significant relationship between intention and behaviour (i.e. Costarelli & Colloca, 2004). Previous studies have also demonstrated that individuals who express an intention to act in a pro-environmental manner are more likely to have engaged in environmental behaviour (Dimopoulos & Pantis, 2003).

Secondly, this study examined only selected independent variables as the important factors influencing site-specific behaviours. This study's approach was to demonstrate a thorough understanding of how interpretation influences behavioural intentions to the target visitor groups through enhancing attitudes in site-specific perspective.

In particular, in the data analysis process, this study focused on the relative influence of independent variables on only selected site-specific behavioural intentions in relation to the major undesirable or uninformed behaviour which can damage the geological environment at this site, and responsibility-denial behaviours which need to be promoted in the beach area. Therefore, only selected major variables such as socio-demographic factors, previous experience, attitudes, and interpretation channel factors were used rather than presenting a wider range of all antecedents of responsible environmental behaviour which have been identified in environmental studies. When interpretation or education aims to subsequently promote long-term conservation behaviour or to reduce vandalism behaviour, other factors might be considered including social norms, internal locus of control, responsibility, or other barriers (i.e. inconvenience of time or money) in further study.

Moreover, it is possible to look at the channel factors. In particular, this study examined the effects of the Visitor Centre and the particular brochure regarding the Code of Conduct for fossil collecting. Other channel variables such as signs and guided walks might relatively influence the direct effects of the Visitor Centre or the particular brochure on the management outcomes.

Another limitation is that response set biases were introduced by the measure, with regards to some of the items related to general attitudes and general responsible behaviour towards environmental protection, visitors might answer in a socially desirable manner while most visitors were aware of the environmental issues. It is important to consider this when looking to measure attitudes and behaviour

A further limitation is the use of non-probability sampling (convenience sample) and under-representation of non-English speaking and tour group visitors. Other limitations in sampling need to be considered such as timing of the data collection and the locations selected. In particular, this study used as the sample day visitors during summer time (June to August). With regard to informal interviews with the Centre staff prior to the research, they indicated that different visitor groups visited over the year. For example, family groups visited mostly during summer vacations while young couples visited during off-season. A survey incorporating a more diverse sample population needs to be conducted.

In terms of the locations selected, the coastlink visitor centres managed by the Jurassic Coast Project include a network of the 5 marine visitor centres at the Dorset Coast. This study investigated the two sample sites of the Charmouth Heritage Coast Centre at West-Dorset heritage coast, and the Lulworth Heritage Centre at East-Dorset heritage coast due to the similar theme objectives of interpretation and the environmental issues. While each site deals with different site-specific issues related to tourism activities or environmental cues under the Jurassic Coast Sites, the results of the present research need to be generalised only with caution when looking at the application of effective interpretation techniques at the other Jurassic Coast Sites. Yet, it is possible to apply the similar interpretation evaluation steps of the research in this implications section (see 11.4.2) at other coastal areas.

11.6 Recommendations for Future Research

In addition to the contributions and the limitations of this study outlined in the previous section, it is suggested that future research on the effectiveness of interpretation be undertaken utilising: behaviour indicators, measurement, and the identification of other factors,

As mentioned earlier in the limitations, the present research did not measure the actual behavioural change as behavioural indicator. Future study needs to examine the relationship between behavioural intentions and actual behaviour and to identify the barriers in performing the particular behaviour by comparing the visitor groups as a result of interpretation experiences. To do so, we may need to examine the effects of interpretation on conservation behaviour at home through a follow-up survey within 3 months or 6 months. This may help to diminish the criticism of the ineffectiveness of interpretation on behaviour change in the longer term.

In addition, the present research provided the conceptual pictures of the relative impacts of interpretation and the visitor attributes in modifying visitor behaviour. However, the lack of definitive evidence about what causes the variations in different outcomes may indicate a need for different lines of investigation. The way of measuring attitudes and other psychological variables, and the identification of other antecedents influencing each type of responsible environmental behaviour would be essential to maximise the effectiveness of interpretation in light of the appropriate selection of message content and media delivery to target recipients. For more detail, in terms of the measurement of multidimensional attitudes or other psychological variables for belief- or emotion- targeted messages, as suggested by recent research (Ballantyne and Hughes, 2004; Widner and Roggenbuck, 2000), further research is needed to approach either the relative effects of multiple-theory-based messages or the direct effects of single-theory-based messages in order to construct salient belief-targeted messages in influencing a wide range of responsible behaviour of the target groups.

Another area for future research in relation to the improvement of effective interpretation is to identify the antecedents of behavioural intentions or behaviour and examine how other antecedent factors (e.g. the visitor characteristics or situational variables) influence relatively each type of environmentally responsible behaviour along with different experiences of interpretation methods. Visitors' motivation, interest, and prior knowledge can be one of the important factors in influencing visitors' preferences of media, level of interpretation participation, and subsequently the effectiveness of interpretation. In this study, the majority of visitors who perceived the Centre educational had visited the Visitor Centre during their visits to the site and held higher levels of favourable attitudes and intentions towards environmental conservation. By contrast, visitors who perceived the Centre as a tourist information centre appeared to be less interested in participating in other interpretive programmes.

Alternatively, those groups that hold moderate levels of pro-environmental attitudes and behavioural intentions might look at signs or read a brochure when it is available for them on-site. Therefore, it is uncertain whether the different motivations of activities, different perceptions of the Visitor Centre and prior knowledge might influence their perceived persuasion by the media.

Further study may be needed to identify the relative influence of other factors related to interpretation (e.g. source factors, other types of message factors) on behavioural change. Moreover, the kinds of research questions or strategies developed for this study may be extended to other Jurassic Coast sites and adopt different environmental settings in future research.

This study has made some tentative but significant contributions to both interpretation and environmental behaviour research. It has demonstrated that managers and policy makers may gain a clearer understanding of pro-environmental attitudes and behaviour by considering three key elements in determining the effectiveness of interpretation. In this way, interpretation can play a management role in achieving the environmental goals of sustainable tourism in protected areas. However, there is much to be learned about the potential of interpretation in achieving other goals of sustainable tourism and this is a matter for future research. Figure 11.1 shows the relationships between the goals of sustainable tourism and the specific objectives of interpretation associated with each goal of sustainability.

In terms of additional roles of interpretation as a visitor management tool, effective interpretation can also enhance visitors' enjoyment and satisfaction and achieve economic benefits in the longer term. Alternatively, it could be that emotional responses to interpretive programmes such as enjoyment and satisfaction might also have possible impacts on such outcomes. Some studies have suggested that the impacts of emotional experiences of interpretation programmes can influence visitors' learning and behaviour (Howard, 2000; Moscardo, 1999).

390

Figure 11.1 The Significant Roles of Interpretation in Achieving the Goals of Sustainability

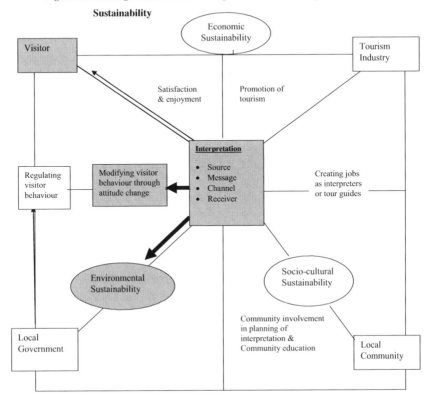

Note: The four areas with colouring with yellow are areas researched in this study.
This diagram was developed based on literature related to sustainability and stakeholders from Aronsson, 2000 & the role of interpretation (Moscardo, 1998; Ham & Weiler, 2002) by the author.

Therefore, future research may need to examine the relative impact of emotional responses and satisfaction on behavioural change. This might maximise the management roles of interpretation in achieving both environmental and economic goals of sustainability.

Finally, while less focused on the relationships between local communities and interpretation, further research might need to identify the potential roles of interpretation on volunteer work or tour guides in achieving socio-economic goals of sustainability. In this case, community involvement and community education must be considered in planning an interpretation strategy to promote appreciation of the environment and community stewardship of the site.

BIBLIOGRAPHY

Bibliography

Adams, W.J. (2003) *Promoting environmentally responsible behaviour: An evaluation of the global learning and observations to benefit the environment (GLOBE) programme*, Unpublished Master of Arts thesis, University of South Africa.

Aiello, R. (1998) Interpretation and the Marine Tourism Industry, Who needs it?: A case study of Great Adventures, Australia. *Journal of Tourism Studies*, 9(1), 51-61.

Aipanjiguly, S., Jacobson, S.K., Flamm, R. (2003) Conserving manatees: Knowledge, attitudes, and intentions of boaters in Tampa Bay, Florida. *Conservation Biology, 17*(4), 1098-1105.

Ajzen, I. (1988) *Attitudes, personality, and behaviour*, Buckingham, UK: Open University Press.

Ajzen, I. (1991) The theory of planned behaviour. *Organizational Behaviour and Human Decision Processes, 50*, 179-211.

Azjen, I. (1992) Persuasive Communication Theory in Social Psychology: A Historical Perspective, In M.J. Manfredo (ed) *Influencing human behaviour: Theory and Applications on Recreation, Tourism, and Natural Resources Management*, (pp.1-28), Champaign, Illinois: Sagamore Publishing Inc.

Ajzen, I. and Fishbein, M. (1977) Attitude-behaviour relations: A theoretical analysis and review of empirical research. *Psychological Bulletin, 84*, 888-918.

Ajzen, I., and Driver, B.L. (1992) Application of the Theory of Planned Behaviour to Leisure Choice. *Journal of Leisure Research, 24*(3), 207-224.

Ajzen, I., and Fishbein, M. (1980) *Understanding attitudes and predicting social behaviour*. Englewood Cliffs, NJ: Prentice-Hall.

Aldridge, D. (1989) How the ship of interpretation was blown off course in the tempest: Some philosophical thoughts. In D.L. Uzzell (ed.) *Heritage Interpretation. Volume 1: The Natural and Built Environment* (pp.64-87). London: Belhaven Press.

Aldridge, D. (1975) *Guide to Countryside Interpretation, Part one: Principles of Country side Interpretation and Interpretive Planning*, London: HMSO.

Alessa, L., Bennett, S.M., Kliskey, A.D. (2003) Effects of knowledge, personal attribution and perception of ecosystem health on depreciative behaviours in the intertidal zone of Pacific Rim National Park and Reserve. *Journal of Environmental Management, 68*, 207-218.

Arksey, H and Knight, P. (1999) *Interviewing for Social Scientists*. London: Sage publications.

Aronsson, L. (2000) *Development of Sustainable Tourism*, London: Continuum.

Asfeldt, M. (1992) *The impact of guided wilderness canoe trips on the participants' attitudes to, concerns for and behaviours toward the environment*. Unpublished masters thesis, University of Alberta, Edmonton.

Bagozzi, R.P., Gürhan-Canli, Z., Priester, J.R. (2002) *The social psychology of consumer behaviour*. Buckingham: Open University Press.

Ballantine, J.L. and Eagles, P.F.J. (1994) Defining Canadian ecotourists. *Journal of Sustainable Tourism, 2*(4), 210-214.

Ballantyne, R. and Hughes, K. (2004) Using front-end and formative evaluation to design and test persuasive bird feeding warning signs, *Tourism Management, Article in Press*.

Ballantyne, R. and Packer, J. (1996) Teaching and learning in environmental education: developing environmental conceptions, *Journal of Environmental Education, 27*(2), 25-32.

Ballantyne, R. and Packer, J. (2005) Promoting environmentally sustainable attitudes and behaviour through free-choice learning experiences: what is the state of the game? *Environmental Education Research, 11*(3), 281-295.

Ballantyne, R. and Uzzell, D.L. (1995) A Checklist for the Critical Evaluation of Information Environmental Learning Experiences, In W.D.S. Leal Fiho, Z. Murphy, and K. O'Loan (eds) *A Sourcebook for Environmental Education: A Practical Review based on the Belgrade Charter*, (pp. 166-181). Carnforth: Parthenon/ERTCEE, University of Bradford.

Ballantyne, R., Packer, J., and Beckmann, E. (1998) Targeted interpretation: Exploring relationships among visitors' motivations, activities, attitudes, information needs and preferences. *The Journal of Tourism Studies, 9*(2), 14-25.

Bamberg, S. (2002) Effects of implementation intentions on the actual performance of new environmentally friendly behaviours – results of two field experiments. Journal of *Environmental Psychology, 22*, 399-411.

Bamberg, S. (2003) How does environmental concern influence specific environmentally related behaviours? A new answer to an old question. *Journal of Environmental Psychology, 23*, 21-32.

Baron, R.A. and Byrne, D. (1987). *Social psychology: Understanding human interaction*. (5th ed.) Massachusetts: Allan and Bacon.
Barr, S. (2003) Strategies for sustainability: citizens and responsible environmental behaviour, *Area, 35*(3), 227-240.

Barrow, C.J. (1995) Sustainable development: concept, value and practice, *Third World Planning Review 17*(4), 369-386.

Barrow, G.C. (1996) *Environmental interpretation and sustainable tourism*. Manchester: Centre for Environmental Interpretation, Manchester Metropolitan University.

Beaumont, N.K. (1999) *Ecotourism: The contribution of educational nature experiences to environmental knowledge, attitudes, and behaviours*. Unpublished PhD thesis. Australian School of Environmental Studies, Griffith University: Nathan, Queensland.

Beaumont, N.K (2001) Ecotourism and the conservation ethic: Recruiting the uninitiated or preaching to the converted?. *Journal of Sustainable Tourism. 9*(4), 317-341.

Beckmann, E.A (1991) *Environmental interpretation for education and management in Australian national parks and other protected areas*, Unpublished PhD thesis, University of New England.

Beckmann, E.A. (1993) *Evaluating of DCNR Visitor Interpretation Programs with Emphasis on Night Walks and Rockpool Rambles Summer 1992/93*. Report for Department of Conservation and Natural Resources, Victoria.

Beckmann, E.A. (2002). *Communicating to the public about potentially dangerous wildlife in natural settings: A review of the research and management literature with an emphasis on the dingoes of Fraser Island*. Canberra: Beckmann and Associates.

Bell, P.A., Greene, T.C., Fisher, J.D. and Baum, A. (2001). *Environmental psychology*. (5th ed.). USA: Harcourt College Publishers.

Bengston, D.N., Fan, D.P., and Celarier, D.N. (1999) A new approach to monitoring the social environment for natural resource management and policy: The case of US national forest benefits and values. *Journal of Environmental Management, 56,* 181-193.

Bentler, P.M., and Speckart, G. (1979) *Models of attitude-behaviour relations. Psychological Review, 86,* 452-464.

Black, J.S., Stern, P.C. and Elworth, J.T. (1985) Personal and contextual influences on household energy adaptations. *Journal of Applied Psychology, 70,* 3-21.

Black, T.R. (1999) *Doing quantitative research in the social sciences: An integrated approach to research design, measurement and statistics*. London: Sage Publications.
Blaikie, N. (2000) *Designing Social Research: the logic of anticipation*. Oxford: Blackwell Publishers Ltd.

Blamey, R.K. (1995) *The Nature of Ecotourism*. Occasional Paper No. 21. Canberra: Bureau of Tourism Research.

Borden, R.J. and Francis, J.L. (1978). Who cares about ecology? Personality and sex differences in environmental concern. *Journal of Personality, 46,* 190-203.

Borrie, W.T., Freimund, W.A., and Davenport, M.A. (2002) Winter visitors to Yellowstone national park: Their value orientations and support for management actions. *Human Ecology Review, 9*(2), 41-48.

Boyd, S. (2000) Tourism, national parks and sustainability, In R.W. Butler & S.W. Boyd (ed.) *Tourism and National Parks: Issues and implications* (pp161-186) Chichester: John Wiley & Sons, LTD.

Brace, N., Kemp, R. and Snelgar, *R.* (2000*), SPSS for Psychologists: A Guide to Data Analysis using SPSS for Windows*, London: Palgrave.

Bramwell, B., and Lane, B. (1993), Sustainable Tourism, An evolving global approach, *Journal of Sustainable Tourism, 1*(1), 1-5.

Bramwell, B., Henry. J., Jackson, G., Prat, A.G., Richards, G., and Straaten, J., (1996) *Sustainable Tourism Management: Principles and Practice,* Tilburg University Press.

Brannen, J. (1992) Combining qualitative and qualitative approaches: an overview, In J.Brannen (ed.) *Mixing Methods: qualitative and quantitative research*. (pp.3-37) Aldershot: Avebury Ashgate Publishing Limited.

Bright, A.D., Manfredo, M.J., Fishbein, M., Bath, A. (1993) Application of the Theory of Reasoned Action to the National Park Service's Controlled Burn Policy, *Journal of Leisure Research*, 25(3), 263-280.

Britain Express (1996a), *Heritage Coast*, Available at (http://www.britainexpress.com/countryside/coast/index.htm), last accessed February, 2006.

Britain Express (1996b) *Purbeck Heritage Coast*, Available at (http://www.countryside.gov.uk/LAR/Landscape/DL/heritage_coasts/purbeck_wdorset.asp), last accessed February, 2006.

Britain Express (1996c) *West Dorset Heritage Coast*, Available at (http://www.britainexpress.com/countryside/coast/purbeck.htm), last accessed February, 2006.

Brown, T.J. (1999) Antecedents of culturally significant tourist behaviour. *Annals of Tourism Research*, 26(3), 676-700.

Brown, T.J. (2001) *Visitor characteristics influencing climbing Uluru: An investigation of culturally sensitive tourist behaviour*. Unpublished PhD thesis, Griffith University.

Brulle, R.J. (1996) Environmental discourse and social movement organisations: A historical and rhetorical perspective on the development of US environmental organisations. *Sociological Inquiry*, 66, 58-83.

Bryman, A. and Cramer, D. (1999) *Quantitative Data Analysis with SPSS Release 8 for Windows: A guide for social scientists*. London: Routledge.

Butler, R.W. (1991) Tourism, environment, and sustainable development. *Environmental Conservation*, 18 (1), 201-209.

Butler, R.W., (1993) Tourism – An evolutionary perspective. In J.G. Nelson, R.W. Butler and G. Wall (Eds) *Tourism and sustainable development: monitoring, planning, managing*, (pp27-43). Department of Geography Publication Series, No. 37 and Heritage Resources Centre Joint Publication No. 1, University of Waterloo, Waterloo, ON.

Butler, R. W. (1997), The Concept of Carrying Capacity for Tourism Destinations: Dead or Merely Buried? In Cooper, C. and Wanhill, S., *Tourism development – environmental and community issues*. (pp.11-21), John Wiley & Sons Ltd.

Butler, R.W. (1998) Sustainable tourism – looking backwards in order to progress?, In C. M. Hall and A. A. Lew (ed.) *Sustainable Tourism: a geographical perspective*, (pp.25-34), New York: Addison Wesley Longman Limited.

Butler, R.W., & Boyd, S.W. (2000) *Tourism and National Parks: Issues and implications*, Chichester: John Wiley & Sons, LTD.

Cable, T., Knudson, D.M., Udd, E., and Stewart, D.J. (1987) Attitude changes as a result of exposure to interpretive messages, *Journal of Park and Recreation Administration*, 5, 47-60.

Cable, T.T., Knudson, D.M., Theobald, W.F. (1986) The application of the Theory of Reasoned Action to the Evaluation of Interpretation, *Journal of Interpretation*, 2(1), 11-25.

Chandool, N. (1997) *Participation in park interpretive programmes and visitors' attitudes, norms, and behaviour about petrified wood theft*. Unpublished masters thesis. Department of Forestry, Virginia Polytechnic Institute and State University: Blacksburg, VA.

Charmouth Heritage Coast Centre (2006, last updated). Charmouth Heritage Coast Centre. Available at (http://www.charmouth.org/), Last accessed February, 2006.

Chawla, L. (1999), Life paths into effective environmental action, *Journal of Environmental Education, 31*(1), 15-26.

Christensen, H. and Cole, D.N. (2000) Leave No Trace practices: behaviours and preferences of wilderness visitors regarding use of cook stoves and camping away from lakes. In S.F. McCool, W.T. Borrie, J. O'Loughlin (eds.) *Wilderness Science in a Time of Change Conference Proceedings* May 23-27, 1999 (pp.77-85). Ogden, UT: Rocky Mountain Research Station.

Christensen, H.H., and Dustin, D.L. (1989) Reaching recreationists at different levels of moral development. *Journal of Park and Recreation Administration, 7*(4), 72-80.

Churchill, G.A. (1999) *Marketing Research Methodological Foundations*. London: Dryden.

Cialdini, R.B. (1996) Activating and aligning two kinds of norms in persuasive communications. *Journal of Interpretation Research, 1*(1), 3-10.

Clark, R.N., Burgess, R.L., Hendee, J.C. (1972a) *The development of anti-litter behaviour in a forest campground. Journal of Applied Behaviour Analysis. 5*, 1-6.

Clark, R.N., Hendee, J.C. and Burgess, R.L. (1972b) The experimental control of littering. *Journal of Environmental Education,* 4(2), 22-28.

Coakes, S.J. and Steed, L.G. (1997) *SPSS Analysis without anguish version 6.1 for IBM and Macintosh users*. Milton: Jacaranda Willey Ltd.

Cole, D.N. (1995) Wilderness management principles: Science, Logical thinking or personal opinion? *Trends 32*(1), 6-9.

Cole, D.N., Hammond, T.P. and McCool, S.F. (1997) Information quantity and communication effectiveness: Low-impact messages on wilderness trailside bulletin boards, *Leisure Sciences,* 19(1), 59-72.

Cooper, C., Fletcher, J., Gilbert, D., Wanhill, S. (1998) In R, Sheperd (ed) Tourism: Principles and Practices. (2nd). Harlow, Essex: Addison Wesley Longman.

Costarelli, S. and Colloca, P. (2004) The effects of attitudinal ambivalence on pro-environmental behavioural intentions. *Journal of Environmental Psychology, 24*, 279-288.

Cottrell, S. (2003a) Monitoring environmental behaviour among recreational boaters. *Environmental Papers Series: Vol 6*(2), Scotland: Glasgow Caledonian University.

Cottrell, S.P. (2003b) Influence of Sociodemographics and Environmental Attitudes on General Responsible Environmental Behaviour Among Recreational Boaters. *Environment and Behaviour, 35*(3), 347-375.

Cottrell, S.P., and Graefe, A.R. (1997). Testing a conceptual framework of responsible environmental behaviour. *Journal of Environmental Education, 29*(1), 17-27.

De Vaus, D.A., (1991) *Surveys in Social Research*. London: George Allen and Unwin.
Dietz, T., Stern, P.C., and Guagnano, G.A. (1998) Social structural and social psychological bases of environmental concern. *Environment and Behaviour, 30,* 450-471.

Dimopoulos, D.I. and Pantis, J.D. (2003) Knowledge and attitudes regarding sea turtles in elementary students on Zakynthos, Greece. *The Journal of Environmental Education, 34*(3), 30-38.

Dorset AONB Partnership (2004) *The Dorset AONB Management Plan*. Available at (http://www.dorsetaonb.org.uk/text01.asp?PageId=227), last accessed February, 2006.

Dorset Coast Forum (1998) *Dorset Coast Forum Christmas Meeting: The Launch of the Draft Dorset Coast Strategy*. Dorset Coast Forum.

Dorset Coast Forum (1999), *Dorset Coast Strategy*. Available at (http://www.dorsetcoast.com/index.jsp?articleid=21517), last accessed February, 2006.

Dorset Coastlink & Bournemouth University (1997a) *Dorset Coastlink*. Available at (http://csweb.bournemouth.ac.uk/oldcoastlink/index.htm), Last accessed February, 2006.

Dorset Coastlink & Bournemouth University, (1997b) *Lulworth Cove and Heritage Coast*, Available at (http://csweb.bournemouth.ac.uk/oldcoastlink/lulworth.htm), Last accessed February, 2006.

Dorset Coastlink and Bournemouth University (1997c) *the Visitor Seashore Code*, Available at (http://csweb.bournemouth.ac.uk/oldcoastlink/seashore.htm), Last accessed February, 2006.

Dorset Coastlink and Bournemouth University (1997d) *Charmouth Heritage Coast Centre* Available at (http://csweb.bournemouth.ac.uk/oldcoastlink/charmouth.htm),Last accessed February, 2006.

Dorset For You partnership (2005) *Dorset Tourism Facts*. Available at (http://www.dorsetforyou.com/index.jsp?articleid=332863), last accessed February, 2006.

Dorset Tourism Data Project (1998) *Dorset Tourism Facts,* Available at (http://apollo4.bournemouth.ac.uk/si/mrg/Dorset.htm.), Last accessed February, 2006.
Doucette, J.E. and Cole, D.N. (1993) *Wilderness visitor education: Information about alternative techniques*. US Department of Agriculture, Forest Service, Intermountain Research Station: Ogden, UT.

Dresner, M. and Gill, M. (1994) Environmental education at summer nature camp. *Journal of Environmental Education, 25*(3), 35-41.

Dunlap, R.E. and Van Liere, K.D. (1984) Commitment to the dominant social paradigm and concern for environmental quality. *Social Science Quarterly, 64,* 1013-1028.

Dunlap, R.E., and Jones, R.E. (2002) Environmental concern: conceptual and measurement issues. In R.E. Dunlap, and W. Michelson (eds.), *Handbook of environmental sociology*. Westport, CT: Greenwood Press.

Dunlap, R.E., and Jones, R.E. (2003) Environmental attitudes and values. In R. Fernandez Ballesteros, (ed.), *Encyclopedia of psychological assessment*, vol. I (pp.364-369). London: Sage.

Dunlap, R.E., and Van Liere, K.D. (1978) The new environmental paradigm. *Journal of Environmental Education, 9,* 10-19.

Dunlap, R.E., Van Liere, K., Mertign, A., and Jones, R.E. (2000). Measuring endorsement of the New Ecological Paradigm: A revised NEP scale. *Journal of Social Issues, 56,* 425-442.

Eagles, P.F.J. and Demare, P. (1995) Factors influencing children's environmental attitudes. Manuscript submitted for publication.

Eagles, P.F.J., McCool, S.F., and Haynes, C.D. (2002) *Sustainable Tourism in Protected Areas: Guidelines for Planning and Management, World Commission on Protected Areas (WCPA) Best Practice Protected Area Guidelines Series No.8,* Cambridge: IUCN Publications Services Unit.

Eagly, A.H. and Chaiken, S. (1993) *The psychology of attitudes*. Fort Worth, TX: Harcourt Brace Jovanovich.

English Nature (1998) *Geological Conservation*. Available at (http://www.english-nature.org.uk/special/geological/default.htm), Last accessed February, 2006.

Espiner, S.R. (1999) *The use and effect of hazard warning signs: Managing visitor safety at Franz Josef and Fox Glaciers,* Science for Conservation: 108, Wellington, NZ: Department of Conservation.

Ewert, A., and Baker, D. (2001) Standing for where you sit: An exploratory analysis of the relationship beteeen academic major and environmental beliefs. *Environment and Behaviour, 33*(5), 687-707.

Fabrigar, L.R., Smith, S.M., and Brannon, L.A. (1999) Applications of social cognition: Attitudes as cognitive structures. In F.T. Durso (ed.), *Handbook of applied cognition* (pp.173-206). Chichester: John Wiley & Sons Inc.

Falk, J.H., and Adelman, L.M. (2003) Investigating the impact of prior knowledge and interest on aquarium visitor learning, *Journal of Research In Science Teaching, 40*(2), 163-176.

Fallon, L.D., and Kriwoken, L.K. (2003) Community involvement in tourism infrastructure – the case of the Strahan Visitor Centre, Tasmania, *Tourism Management,* 24, 289-308.

Fazio, J. (1979) Agency literature as an aid to wilderness management. *Journal of Forestry, 77,* 97-98.

Fazio, R.H. and Zanna, M.P. (1981) Direct experience and attitude-behaviour consistency. In L. Berkowitz (ed.), *Advances in experimental social psychology,* Vol. 14. (pp.161-202). San Diego, CA: Academic Press.

Fishbein, M., and Manfredo, M.J. (1992) A theory of behaviour change. In M.J. Manfredo (ed.). *Influencing Human Behaviour: Theory and applications in recreation, tourism and natural resources management.* (pp.29-50). Champaign, Illinois: Sagamore Publishing.

Frankfort-Nachmias, C. and Nachmias, D. (1996) *Research Methods in the Social Sciences*. (5th edn.) London: Arnold, the Hodder Headline Group.

Fransson, N. and Gärling, T. (1999) Environmental concern: conceptual definitions, measurement methods, and research findings. *Journal of Environmental Psychology, 19*, 369-382.

Garrod, B. and Fyall, A. (1998) Beyond the rhetoric of sustainable tourism? *Tourism Management 19*, 199-212.

Geller, E.S. (1987) Applied behavioural analysis and environmental psychology: From strange bedfellows to a productive marriage. In: D. Stokols, and I. Altman, (eds.), *Handbook of environmental psychology. Vol. 1* (pp361-388). New York: John Wiley and Sons.

Gifford, R., Hay, R. and Boros, K. (1982/83) Individual differences in environmental attitudes. *Journal of Environmental Education, 14*(2), 19-23.

Gigliotti, L.M. (1992) Environmental attitudes: 20 years of change? *Journal of Environmental Education, 24*(1), 15-25.

Gilbert, A.H., Manning, R.E., Negra, C., Koenemann, E.J. (1996) Economic and social values of parks: An empirical approach. In C. Dawson (ed), *Proceedings of the 1995 Northeastern Recreation Research Symposium*, Gen. Tech. Report NE-218. (pp.141-147). Radnor, PA: U.S. Department of Agriculture, Forest service, Northeastern forest Experiment Station.

Gillett, D.P., Thomas, G.P., Skok, R.L. and McLaughlin, T.F. (1991) The effects of wilderness camping and hiking on the self-concept and the environmental attitudes and knowledge of twelfth graders. *Journal of Environmental Education, 22*(3), 33-44.

Goodey, B. (1994) Interpretative planning, in R. Harrison (ed.) *Manual of Heritage Management*, (pp.302-315), Oxford: Betterworth-Heinemann.

Gramann, J.H., and Vander Stoep, G. (1987) Prosocial behaviour theory and natural resource protection: A conceptual synthesis. *Journal of Environmental Management, 24*, 247-257.

Gudgion, T.J., and Thomas, M.P. (1991) Changing environmentally relevant behaviour, *Environmental Education and Information, 10*(2), 101-112.

Hair, F.H, Anderson, R.E., Tatham, R.L., and Blac, W.C., (1998) *Multivariate Data Analysis* (5th edn). London: Prentice-Hall Inc.

Hall, C.M., and McArthur, S. (1998). *Integrated Heritage Management: Principles and Practice*, London: The Stationery Office.

Hall, C.M., and Lew, A.A., (1998) *Sustainable Tourism: a geographical perspective*, New York: Addison Wesley Longman Limited.

Hall, C.M., and Page, S.J. (2006) *The geography of tourism and recreation: Environment, place and space* (3rd) London and New York: Routledge.

Hall, C.M., and McArthur, S. (1998) *Integrated Heritage Management: Principles and Practice*, London: The Stationery Office.

Ham, S. H. (1992) *Environmental Interpretation: A practical guide for people with big ideas and small budgets*. Colorado: North American Press.

Ham, S.H. and Krumpe, E.E. (1996) Identifying audiences and messages for nonformal environmental education: A theoretical framework for interpreters. *Journal of Interpretation Research, 1*(1), 11-23.

Ham, S.H., and Weiler, B. (2002) Interpretation as the centrepiece of sustainable wildlife tourism, In R. Harris, T. Griffin, and P. Williams, *Sustainable Tourism: A global perspective,*(pp.35-44). Oxford: Butterworth-Heinemann.

Hammond, S. (1995) Introduction to Multivariate Data Analysis. In G.M. Breakwell, S.Hammond, and C. Fife-Schaw (eds.), *Research Methods in Psychology* (pp.360-385). London: Sage Publication.

Hardy, A.L. and Beeton, R.J.S. (2001) Sustainable tourism or maintainable tourism: managing resources for more than average outcomes. *Journal of Sustainable Tourism 9*, 168-192.

Hardy, A., Beeton, R.J.S. and Pearson, L. (2002) Sustainable tourism: an overview of the concept and its position in relation to conceptualisations of tourism. *Journal of Sustainable Tourism 10*, 475-496.

Harris, R., Griffin, T., and Williams, P. (2002) *Sustainable Tourism: A Global Perspective*, Burlington: Butterworth-Heinemann.

Hayes, B.C. (2001) Gender, scientific knowledge, and attitudes toward the environment: A cross-national analysis. *Political Research Quarterly, 54*(3), 657-671.
Hein, G.E. (1998) *Learning in the museum*. London: Routledge.

Hendee, J.C., Stankey, G.H., and Lucas, R.C. (1990) *Wilderness management. (2nd ed.)* Golden, CO: North American Press, An Imprinted of Fulcrum Publishing.

Herbert, D.T. (1998) Does Interpretation Help? In D.T. Herbert, R.C. Prentice, C.J. Thomas (eds), *Heritage Sites: Strategies for Marketing and Development. (*pp. 191-230). Aldershot: Avebury.

Heylin, A. (1993) *Putting it across: The art of communicating, persuading and presenting*, Great Britain: Duncan Petersen Publishing.

Hines, J.M., Hungerford, H.R., and Tomera, A.N. (1986/87) Analysis and synthesis of research on responsible environmental behaviour: A meta-analysis. *Journal of Environmental Education, 18*(2), 1-8.

Hockett, K.S. (2000) The effectiveness of two interpretations on reducing deer feeding behaviour by park visitors. Unpublished masters thesis. Virginia Polytechnic Institute and State.

Holden, A. (2000) *Environment and Tourism*, London: Routledge.

Holden, A. (2003) Investigating trekkers' attitudes to the environment of Annapurna, Nepal. *Tourism management, 24*, 341-344.

Hopper, J.R. and Nielsen, J.M. (1991) Recycling as altruistic behaviour: Normative and behavioural strategies to expand participation in a community recycling program. *Environment and Behaviour, 23*, 195-220.

Hose, T. (1995) Selling the story of Britain's stone. *Environmental Interpretation, 10*(2), 16-17.

Hovland, C.I., Janis, I.L., and Kelley, H.H. (1953) *Communication and persuasion.* New Haven: Yale University Press.

Howard, J. (2000) Research in progress: Does environmental interpretation influence behaviour through knowledge or affect? *Australian Journal of Environmental Education* 15/16, 153-6.

Howard, J., Lipscombe, N., and Porter, A. (2001) The tourist, the dingo, and interpretation on Fraser Island Queensland, *Presented at 9th Annual Conference of Interpretation Australia Association,* Alice Springs:IAA.

Howell, S.E. and Laska, S.B. (1992) The changing face of the environmental coalition: A research note. *Environment and Behaviour, 24,* 134-144.

Howitt, D & Cramer, D. (1999) *A guide to computing statistics with SPSS release 8 for windows.* Harlow: Prentice Hall.

Hull, R.B. (1991) Mood as a product of leisure: Causes and consequences, In B.L. Driver, P.J. Brown, and G.L. Petersen (eds.), *Benefits of leisure,* State College, PA: Venture Publishing.

Hurbes, D., Ajzen, I., and Daigle, J. (2001) Predicting hunting intentions and behaviour: An application of the Theory of Planned Behaviour. *Leisure Sciences, 23,* 165-178.

Huffman, M.G., & Williams, D.R. (1987) The use of microcomputers for park trail information dissemination. *Journal of Park and Recreation Administration, 5,* 34-46.

Hungerford, H.R. and Volk, T.L. (1990). Changing learner behaviour through environmental education. *Journal of Environmental Education, 21*(3), 8-21.

Hunter, C. (1995) On the need to re-conceptualise sustainable tourism development. *Journal of Sustainable Tourism 3,* 155-65.

Hunter, C. (1997) Sustainable Tourism as an adaptive paradigm. *Annals of Tourism Research 24*(4), 850-67.

Hunter, C. (2002) Aspects of the sustainable tourism debate from a natural resource perspective in R. Harris, T. Griffin., & P. Williams (eds) *Sustainable Tourism: A Global Perspective,* (pp.3-23), Burlington: Butterworth-Heinemann.

Hunter, C. and Green, H. (1995) *Tourism and the Environment: A Sustainable Relationship?* London: Routledge.

Hutcheson, G.D. & Sofroniou, N. (1999) *The multivariate social scientist.* London: SAGE.

Hwang, Y-H., Kim, S-I., and Jeng, J-M. (2000) Examining the causal relationships among selected antecedents of responsible environmental behaviour. *Journal of Environmental Education, 31*(4), 19-25.

Iozzi, L.A. (1989) What research says to the educator. Part one: Environmental education and the affective domain. *Journal of Environmental Education, 20*(3), 3-9.

Iversen, G.R. and Norpoths, H. (1987) *Analysis of variance (2nd edn.)* Sage University Paper Series on Quantitative Applications in the Social Sciences, Series No. 07-001. Beverly Hills: Sage Publications.

Jacob, M (1994) Toward a methodological critique of sustainable development, *Journal of Developing Areas 28,* 237-252.

Jacobson, S.K. (1988) Media Effectiveness in a Malaysian Park System. *Journal of Environmental Education, 19,* 22-27.

Jennings, G. (2001) *Tourism Research.* Milton: John Willey & Sons, Australia.

Johnson, D. (2002) Towards sustainability: examples from the UK coast. In R. Harris, T. Griffin, and P. Williams (eds.) *Sustainable tourism: A global perspective.* (pp.166-179). Oxford: Butterworth-Heinemann.

Johnson, D.R., and Vande Kamp, M.E. (1994) An applied research approach to develop strategies to deter noncompliant visitor behaviour in the national parks. In D. Johnson, M.Vande Kamp, and T. Swearingen (eds.), *A survey of park managers' perceptions of noncompliant visitor behaviour causing resource damage in the National Park System.* Technical Report NPS/PNRUN/NRTR-92/07.

Jurassic Coast Team (2004a) *About the Jurassic Coast.* Available at (http://www.jurassiccoast.com/index.jsp?articleid=157198), last accessed February, 2006.

Jurassic Coast Team (2004b). *West Dorset: Charmouth,* Available at (http://www.jurassiccoast.com/index.jsp?articleid=159879), Last accessed February, 2006.

Jurassic Coast Team (2005), *News Archive: Jurassic Coast shortlisted in Tourism for Tomorrow Awards 2005 28/02/05,* Available at (http://www.jurassiccoast.com/index.jsp?articleid=334004), last accessed February, 2006.

Jurassic Coast World Heritage Steering Group (2003a) Jurassic Coast World Heritage Site Management Plan, Available at (http://www.jurassiccoast.com/media/pdf/World%20Heritage%20Site%20management%20Plan.pdf), last accessed February, 2006.

Jurassic Coast World Heritage Steering Group (2003b) *Jurassic Coast World Heritage Site Framework for Action.* In Jurassic Coast World Heritage Steering Group, Jurassic Coast World Heritage Site Management Plan (see Appendix 2), Available at (http://www.jurassiccoast.com/media/pdf/World%20Heritage%20Site%20management%20Plan.pdf), last accessed February, 2006.

Jurassic Coast World Heritage Steering Group (2005) *Jurassic Coast Interpretation Action Plan.* Jurassic Coast World Heritage Steering Group. Available at (http://www.jurassiccoast.com/media/pdf/a/2/JCWHSInterpretationActionPlanMarch2005_1.pdf), last accessed February, 2006.

Kaiser, F.G., Wölfing, S., Fuhrer, U. (1999) Environmental attitude and ecological behaviour. *Journal of Environmental Psychology, 19,* 1-19.

Kellert, S.R. (1985) Attitudes toward animals: Age-related development among children, *Journal of Environmental Education, 16*(3), 29-39.

Knapp, C.E. (1985) Escaping the gender trap: The ultimate challenge for experiential educators. *Journal of Experiential Education 8*(2), 16-19.

Knapp, D., & Volk, T. L. (1997) The identification of empirically derived goals for program development in environmental interpretation. *Journal of Environmental Education. 28*(3), 24-35.

Knopf, R.C., and Dustin, D.L. (1992) A multidisciplinary model for managing vandalism and depreciative behaviour in recreation settings, In M.J. Manfredo (ed) *Influencing human behaviour: Theory and Applications on Recreation, Tourism, and Natural Resources Management* (pp. 209-262), Champaign, Illinois: Sagamore Publishing Inc.

Knudson, D.M., Cable, T.T., Beck, L. (1995) *Interpretation of Cultural and Natural Resources,* State College, PA: Venture Publishing.

Kollmuss, A. and Agyeman, J. (2002) Mind the gap: why do people act environmentally and what are the barriers to pro-environmental behaviour? *Environmental Education Research, 8*(3), 239-260.

Kostka, M. (1976) Nature centre program impact. *Journal of Environmental Education, 8*(1), 53-64.

Kuhlemeier, H., Bergh, H.V.D., Lagerveij, N. (1999) Environmental knowledge, attitudes, and behaviour in Dutch secondary education. *Journal of Environmental Education, 30*(2), 4-14.

Kuo, I-L. (2002) The Effectiveness of environmental interpretation at resource-sensitive tourism destinations, *International Journal of Tourism Research 4,* 87-101.

Kuvan, Y. and Akan, P. (2004) Residents' attitudes toward general and forest-related impacts of tourism: the case of Belek, Antalya. *Tourism Management,* Article in Press.

Lane, B. (1994) Sustainable rural tourism strategies: A tool for development and conservation. Journal of Sustainable Tourism, 2(1&2), 102-111.

Lee, T. and Balchin, N. (1995) Learning and Attitude Change at British Nuclear Fuel's Sellafield Visitors Centre, *Journal of Environmental Psychology,* 15, 283-298.

Lee, T.R. (1998) Evaluating the effectiveness of heritage and environmental interpretation, In D. Uzzell, and R. Ballantyne (eds) *Contemporary issues in heritage and environmental interpretation,* (pp.203-231). London: The Stationery Office.

Lee, W.H., and Moscardo, G. (2005) Understanding the impact of ecotourism resort experiences on tourists' environmental attitudes and behavioural intentions. *Journal of Sustainable Tourism. 13*(6), 546-565.

Leeming, F.C., Porter, B.E., Dwyer, W.O., Cobern, M.K., and Oliver, D.P. (1997). Effects of participation in class activities on children's environmental attitudes and knowledge. *Journal of Environmental Education, 28*(2), 33-42.

Leung, Y-F., Marion, J.L., and Farrell, T.A. (2001) The Role of recreation ecology in sustainable tourism and ecotourism, In S.F. McCool and R.N. Moisey (eds) *Tourism Recreation and Sustainability – Linking Culture and the Environment,* (pp. 21-39) New York; CABI.

Lewis, W.S. (1980) *Interpreting for park visitors*, USA: Eastern Acorn Press.

Light, D. (1991) *Heritage places in Wales and their interpretation: a study in applied recreational geography*, Unpublished PhD thesis, University of Wales.

Liska, A.E. (1984) A critical examination of the causal structure of the Fishbein/Ajzen attitude-behaviour model. *Social Psychology Quarterly, 47*, 61-74.

Lisowski, M. and Disinger, J.F. (1991) The effect of field-based instruction on student understandings of ecological concepts. *Journal of Environmental Education, 23*(1), 19-23.

Littlefair, C.J. (2003) *The effectiveness of interpretation in reducing the impacts of visitors in national parks*. Unpublished PhD thesis, School of Environmental and Applied Sciences, Griffith University.

Loomis, R.J. (1996) How do we know what the visitor knows?: Learning from interpretation. *Journal of Interpretation Research, 1*(1), 35-47.

Lucas, R. (1981) Redistributing wilderness use through information supplied to visitors. *Res. Paper INT-277*. Ogden, UT: U.S. Department of Agriculture, Forest Service, Intermountain Forest and Range Experiment Station.

Lulworth Cove Online (2003) *Lulworth Online: about the area*. Available at (http://www.lulworthonline.co.uk/lulworth-cove-aboutthearea.php), Last accessed February, 2006.

Lumley, R. (ed) (1988) *The museum time machine*, London: Routledge.

Lyons, E. and Breakwell, G. (1994) Factors predicting environmental concern and indifference in 13- to 16- year olds. *Environment and Behaviour, 26*(2), 223-238.

Machlis, G.E., & Field, D.R. (1992) *On interpretation: sociology for interpreters of natural and cultural history*. Oregon: Oregon State University Press.

Mack, J.A., and Thompson, J.A. (1991) Visitor centre planning: Using visitor interests and available time. In G. Moscardo and K. Hughes (eds), *Visitor centres: Exploring new territory*. Townsville: James Cook University of North Queensland.

Madin, E.M.P. and Fenton, D.M. (2004) Environmental interpretation in the Great Barrier Reef Marine Park: An assessment of programme effectiveness. *Journal of Sustainable Tourism, 12*(2), 121-137.

Maloney, M.P. and Ward, M.P. (1973) Ecology: let's hear from the people. An objective scale for the measurement of ecological attitudes and knowledge. *American Psychologist, 28*, 583-586.

Maloney, M.P., Ward, M.P., and Braucht, G.N. (1975) Psychology in action: a revised scale for the measurement of ecological attitudes and knowledge. *American Psychologist, 30*, 787-790.

Manfredo, M.J., and Bright, A.D. (1991) A model for assessing the effects of communication on recreationists, *Journal of Leisure Research, 23*(1), 1-20.

Manfredo, M.J., Fishbein, M., Haas, G., and Watson, A. (1990) Attitudes toward prescribed fire policies. *Journal of Forestry, 88*(9), 19-23.

Manfredo, M.J., Yuan, S.M. and McGuire, F.A. (1992) The influence of attitude accessibility on attitude-behaviour relationships: Implications for recreation research. *Journal of Leisure Research, 24*, 157-170.

Manning, R.E. (2003) Emerging principles for using information/education in wilderness management. *International Journal of Wilderness*, 9(1), 20-27.

Markwell, K. (1996) Challenging the pedagogic basis of contemporary environmental interpretation. *Australian Journal of Environmental Education, 12*, 9-14.

Marsh, J.S. (1986) *Natural and Cultural Heritage Interpretation Evaluation*. Ottawa: Interpretation Canada.

Marshall, C. and Rossman, G.B. (1995) *Designing Qualitative Research*. (2nd edn.) California: Sage Publications.

Martin, B. and Taylor, D. (1981) *Informing backcountry visitors: A catalog of techniques*. A research report published by the Research Department, Appalachian Mountain Club, Gorham, New Hampshire.

Masberg, B.A., and Savige, M. (1996) Incorporating ecotourist needs data into the interpretive planning process. *Journal of Environmental Education, 27*(3), 34-40.

Mason, J. (1996) *Qualitative Research*, London: Sage.

Mason, P. (2003) *Tourism Impacts, Planning and Management*, Oxford: Butterworth-Heinemann.

Mathieson, A. and Wall, G. (1982) *Tourism: Economic, Physical and Social Impacts*, London: Longman.

McArthur, S. (1998) Introducing the undercapitalized world of interpretation. In K. Lindberg, M. Epler Wood and D. Engeldrum (eds) *Ecotourism: A Guide for Planners and Managers*, Vol. 2, (pp.63-85). North Bennington, VT: The Ecotourism Society.

McArthur, S. and Hall, C.M. (1993) Visitor management and interpretation at heritage sites. In C.M. Hall and S. McArthur (eds) *Heritage Management in New Zealand and Australia: Visitor Management, Interpretation and Marketing* (pp. 18-39). Auckland: Oxford University Press.

McArthur, S., and Hall, C.M. (1996) Interpretation: principles and practice, In C.M. Hall and S. McArthur (eds) *Heritage Management in Australia and New Zealand*, (pp.) Melbourne: Oxford University Press.

McAvoy, L.H., & Hamborg, R. (1984) Wilderness Visitor Knowledge of Regulations: A comparison of visitor contact methods. *Journal of Interpretation*. 9(1). 1-10.

McCarville, R.E., Driver, B.L., and Crompton, J.L. (1992) Persuasive communication and the pricing of public leisure services. In M.J. Manfredo (ed.), *Influencing Human Behaviour: Theory and applications in recreation, tourism and natural resources management*. (pp.77-101). Champaign, Illinois: Sagamore Publishing.

McCool, S.F, and Moisey R. N., (2001) *Tourism Recreation and Sustainability – Linking Culture and the Environment*, New York; CABI.

McCool, S.F. and Braithwaite, A.M. (1992) Persuasive messages and safety hazards in dispersed and natural recreation settings (pp.293-326), In M.J. Manfredo (ed) *Influencing human behaviour: Theory and Applications on Recreation, Tourism, and Natural Resources Management* (pp. 209-262), Champaign, Illinois: Sagamore Publishing Inc.

McDonough, M.H. (1986) Evaluation: The interpreter's dilemma. In G.E. Machlis (ed) *Interpretive views: opinions on evaluating interpretation in the National Parks Service* (pp.99-105). Washington, DC: National Parks Conservation Association.

McDougall, G.H.G. and Munro, H. (1994) Scaling and attitude measurement in travel and tourism research. In J.R.B. Ritchie and C.G. Goeldner (eds), *Travel, tourism, and hospitality research: A handbook for managers and researchers* (2nd ed.) (pp. 115-129), New York: John Wiley.

McFarlane, B.L. and Boxall, P.C. (2003) The role of social psychological and social structural variables in environmental activism: an example of the forest sector. *Journal of Environmental Psychology, 23,* 79-87.

McGuire, W.J. (1969) The nature of attitudes and attitude change. In G. Lindzey and E. Aronson (eds.), *The handbook of social psychology: Vol.3. The individual in a social context* (2nd ed.) (pp.136-314). Reading, MA: Addison-Wesley.

McIntosh, P.A., (1976) Signs and Labels, In G.W. Sharpe (ed) *Interpreting the Environment,*(pp.215-231) New York: John Willey & Sons, Inc.

McKenzie, M.D. (2000) How are adventure education program outcomes achieved?: A review of the literature. *Australian Journal of Outdoor Education, 5*(1), 19-28.

Milfont, T.L. and Duckitt, J. (2004) The structure of environmental attitudes: A first- and second-order confirmatory factor analysis. *Journal of Environmental Psychology, 24,* 289-303.

Miller, G. & Twining-Ward, L. (2005) *Monitoring for a sustainable tourism transition: The challenge of developing and using indicators,* Oxfordshire: CABI Publishing.

Milne, S.S. (1998) Sustainable tourism – looking backwards in order to progress?, In C. M. Hall and A. A. Lew (Eds.), *Sustainable Tourism: a geographical perspective,* (pp35-48). New York: Addison Wesley Longman Limited.

Monroe, M.C. (2003) Two avenues for encouraging conservation behaviours. *Human Ecology Review, 10*(2), 113-125.

Moscardo, G. (1996) Mindful visitors: heritage and tourism. *Annals of Tourism Research, 23* (2), 376-397.

Moscardo, G. (1998) Interpretation and Sustainable Tourism: Functions, examples and principles, *The Journal of Tourism Studies, 9*(1), 2-13.

Moscardo, G. (2000) Interpretation. In J. Jafari (ed.) *Encyclopedia of Tourism,* London: Routledge.

Moscardo, G., Pearce, P., and CRC-TREM. (1997) *Interpretation and sustainable tourism in the Wet Tropics World Heritage Area: A case study of Skyrail Visitors.* Townsville: James Cook University.

Moscardo, G., and Woods, B. (1998) Managing tourism and the experience of visitors on Skyrail. In E. Laws, B. Faulkner, and G. Moscardo (eds), *Embracing and managing change in tourism,* (pp.307-323). London: Routledge.

Moscordo, G. (1999) *Making Visitors Mindful: Principles for Creating Quality Sustainable Visitor Experiences through Effective Communication,* Champaign, IL: Sagamore.

Mowforth, M. & Munt, I. (2003) *Tourism and sustainability: Development and new tourism in the Third World* (2nd), London and New York: Routledge.

National Association for Interpretation. (1990) *Preparing for the 21st Century: Solving management problems through interpretation.* Ft. Collins, CO.

Natural History Museum, (2003). *the Natural History Museum Scoping Study on Interpretation Facilities.* Available at (http://www.jurassiccoast.com/media/pdf/l/l/JCWHSifiFinalreport.pdf), last accessed in February, 2006.

Negra, C. and Manning, R.E. (1997) Incorporating environmental behaviour, ethics, and values into nonformal environmental education programs, *Journal of Environmental Education, 28*(2), 10-22.

Newhouse, N. (1990) Implications of attitude and behaviour research for environmental conservation, *Journal of Environmental Education, 22*(1), 26-32.

Newman, W.L. (2000) *Social Research Methods: Qualitative and Quantitative approaches.* (4th edn.) Needham Heights: A Pearson Education Company.

Newsome, D., Moore, S.A., and Dowling, R.K., (2002) *Natural Area Tourism: Ecology, Impacts and Management,* Clevedon: Channel View Publications.

Nielsen, C., and Buchanan, T. (1986) A comparison of the effectiveness of two interpretive programs regarding fire ecology and fire management. *Journal of Interpretation, 2*(1), 1-10.

Norfolk Coast AONB (2006) *Tourism Benefits and Impacts Analysis in Norfolk Coast AONB: Executive Summary.* Available at (http://www.norfolkcoastaonb.org.uk/mediaps/pdfuploads/pd000319.pdf), last accessed July, 2006.

Norfolk Coast Partnership (1995) Visitor Management Strategy, Available at (http://www.norfolkcoastaonb.org.uk/pages/pspage.php?PageID=59), last accessed July, 2006.

O'Reilly, A.M. (1986) Tourism carrying capacity, *Tourism Management, 7* (4), 254-258.

Oliver, S.S., Roggenbuck, J.W. and Watson, A.E. (1985) Education to reduce impacts in forest campgrounds, *Journal of Forestry, 83*(4), 234-236.

Olli, E., Grendstad, G., and Wollebaek, D. (2001) Correlates of environmental behaviours: bringing back social context. *Environment and Behaviour, 33,* 181-208.

Olson, E.C., Bowman, M.L. and Roth, R.E. (1984) Interpretation and nonformal environmental education in natural resource management, *Journal of Environmental Education,* 15(4), 6-10.

Olson, J.M. and Zanna, M.P. (1993) Attitudes and attitude change. *Annual Review of Psychology, 44*, 117-154.

Olson, M.E., Lodwick, D.G. and Dunlap, R.E. (1992) *Viewing the world ecologically*. Boulder, CO: Westview Press.

Oppenheim, A.N. (1996) *Questionnaire Design, Interviewing and Attitude Measurement*. London: Continuum.

Orams, M.B. (1994) Creating effective interpretation for managing interaction between tourists and wildlife, *Australian Journal of Environmental Education, 10*, 21-34.

Orams, M.B. (1996a) Using interpretation to manage nature-based tourism, *Journal of Sustainable Tourism, 4*(2), 81-95.

Orams, M.B. (1996b) A conceptual model of tourist-wildlife interaction: the case study for education as a management strategy. *Australian Geographer, 27*(1), 39-51.

Orams, M.B. (1997). The effectiveness of environmental education: Can we turn tourists into greenies? *Progress in Tourism and Hospitality Research, 3*(4), 295-306.
Orams, M.B. (1999) *Marine Tourism: Development, Impacts and Management*, London: Routledge.

Orams, M.B., and Hill, G.J.E. (1998) Controlling the ecotourist in a wild dolphin feeding program: Is education the answer?, *Journal of Environmental Education, 29*(3), 33-39.

Ostman, R.E., and Parker, J.L. (1987) Impact of education, age, newspapers and television on environmental knowledge, concerns and behaviours. Journal *of Environmental Education, 19*(1), 3-9.

Page, S.J., & Dowling, R.K. (2002), *Ecotourism*. Essex: Pearson Education Limited.

Pallant, J. (2005), *SPSS Survival Manual*, Buckingham: Open University Press.

Palmer, J.A. (1993) Development of concern for the environment and formative experiences of educators. *Journal of Environmental Education, 24*(3), 26-30.

Parcel, G.S. (1984) Theoretical models for application in school health education research, *Journal of School Health, 54*(6), 39-49.

Pearce, D., Barbier, E. and Markandy, A. (1987) *Sustainable Development and Cost-Benefit Analysis,* London:vEnvironmental Economics Centre, Paper 88-01.

Pearce, P. (1991) Visitor centres and their function in the landscape of tourism. In G. Moscardo, and K. Hughes (eds.), *Visitor centres: Exploring new territory*. Paper presented at the national conference on visitor centres (pp. 7-15). Townsville, Australia: James Cook University.

Pearce, P.L. (1988). *The Ulysses factor: Evaluating visitors in tourist settings*. New York: Springer-Verlag.

Peart, B. (1986) Learning in informal environments, In J.S. Marsh (ed) *Natural and Cultural Heritage Interpretation Evaluation,*(pp.29-35). Ottawa: Interpretation Canada.

Petty, R.E. and Cacioppo, J.T. (1981) *Attitudes and persuasion: Classic and contemporary approaches*. Dubuque, IA:Wm. C. Brown.

Petty, R.E. and Cacioppo, J.T. (1986) The Elaboration Likelihood Model of persuasion. *Advances in Experimental Social Psychology, 19,* 123-205.

Petty, R.E., McMichael, S., Brannon, L. (1992) The elaboration likelihood model of persuasion: Applications in recreation and tourism, In M.J. Manfredo (ed) *Influencing human behaviour: Theory and Applications on Recreation, Tourism, and Natural Resources Management* (pp. 77-102) Champaign, Illinois: Sagamore Publishing Inc.

Plimmer, W.N. (1992) Managing for growth: regulation versus the market. In *Proceedings of the Conference on Ecotourism Business of the Pacific*. University of Auckland, Auckland.

Porter, A., and Howard, J.L. (2003) Warning visitors about the potential dangers of dingoes on Fraser Island, Queensland, Australia. *Journal of Interpretation Research, 7*(2), 51-63.

Puri, B.K. (1996) *Statistics in practice: an illustrated guide to SPSS*. London: Oxford University Press, Inc.

Rajecki, D.W. (1982) *Attitudes: themes and advances*. Sunderland, MA: Sinaver Associates.

Reid, S., and Marion, J.L. (2003) *The efficacy of visitor education programs*. Paper published online at the Leave No Trace Web Site (www.lnt.org/TeachingLNT/teachingpdffiles/Inteducationeffectivness.pdf), last accessed June, 2006.

Rogers, R.R., Prentice-Dunn, S. (1997). Protection motivation theory. In D.S. Gochman (ed), *Handbook of health behaviour research,* Vol. I (pp.113-132), New York: Plenum Press.

Roggenbuck, J.W and Berrier, D. (1982) A comparison of the effectiveness of two communication strategies in dispersing wilderness campers, *Journal of Leisure Research 14*(1), 77-89.

Roggenbuck, J.W. (1987) Park interpretation as a visitor management strategy. In *Proceedings of the Sixtieth Annual Conference of the Royal Australian Institute of Parks and Recreation*. Royal Australian Institute of Parks and Recreation, Canberra.

Roggenbuck, J.W. (1992) Use of Persuasion to reduce resource impacts and visitor conflicts. In M.J. Manfredo (ed), *Influencing Human Behaviour: Theory and Applications in Recreation Tourism, and Natural Resources* (pp. 149-208). Campaign, Illinois: Sagamore Publishing.

Roggenbuck, J.W. and Passineau, J. (1986) Use of the field experiment to assess the effectiveness of interpretation. In B. McDonald and H.K. Cordell (eds) *Proceedings Southeastern recreation research conference*. Recreation Technical Assistance Office, Institute of Community and Area Development, University of Georgia: Athens, GA.

Rokeach, M. (1973). *The Nature of Human Values*. New York: Free Press.

Rossi, A.N., and Armstrong, J.B. (1999). Theory of reasoned action vs. theory of planned behaviour: Testing the suitability and sufficiency of a popular behaviour model using hunting intentions. *Human Dimensions of Wildlife, 4,* 40-56.

Ryan, C. (1995) *Research Tourist Satisfaction: Issues, Concepts, Problem.* London: Routledge Publishers.

Schahn, J. and Holzer, E. (1990). Studies of individual environmental concern: Specification and test of the model. *Environment and Behaviour, 21,* 57-81.

Schänzel, H. (1998) *The effectiveness of environmental interpretation: Understanding the values gained from wildlife viewing tourism experiences.* A Publication of the Environmental Policy and management Research Centre, ISSN: 1172-4420.

Schänzel, H.A., and McIntosh, A. (2000) An insight into the personal and emotive context of wildlife viewing at the Penguin Place, Otago Peninsula, New Zealand. *Journal of Sustainable Tourism, 8*(1), 36-52.

Scott, D. and Willits, F.K. (1994) Environmental attitudes and behaviour: A Pennsylvania survey. *Environment and Behaviour, 26*(2), 239-260.

Schultz, P.W. (2000). Empathizing with nature: The effects of perspective taking on concern for environmental issues. *Journal of Social Issues, 56,* 391-406.

Schultz, P.W. (2001) The structure of environmental concern: Concern for self, other people, and the biosphere. *Journal of Environmental Psychology, 21,* 327-339.

Schultz, P.W., and Zelezney, L. (1999) Values as predictors of environmental attitudes: Evidence for consistency across 14 countries, *Journal of Environmental Psychology, 19,* 255-165.

Schultz, P.W., Shriver, C., Tabanico, J.J., and Khazian, A.M. (2004) Implicit connections with nature. *Journal of Environmental Psychology, 24,* 31-42.

Schwartz, S. (1992), Universals in the content and structures of values: Theoretical advances and empirical tests in 20 countries. In M. Zanna, (ed.), *Advances in experimental social psychology, Vol. 25.* (pp.1-65). Orlando, FL: Academic Press.

Schwartz, S.H. (1977) Normative influences on altruism In L. Berkowitz (ed.) *Advances in experimental social psychology Vol 10.* (pp.221-279), New York: Academic Press.

Sekaran, U. (2000) *Research Methods for Business: A skill-building approach.* (3rd edn.) New York: John Wiley & Sons, Inc.

Sharpe, G.W. (ed) (1976) *Interpreting the Environment,* New York: John Wiley & Sons, Inc.

Shepard, C.L. and Speelman, L.R. (1985/86) Affecting environmental attitudes through outdoor education, *Journal of Environmental Education, 17*(2), 20-23.

Sia, A.P., Hungerford, H.R., and Tomera, A.N. (1985/86) Selected predictors of responsible environmental behaviour: An analysis. *Journal of Environmental Education, 17*(2), 31-40.

Sivek, D.J., and Hungerford, H. (1989/1990) Predictors of responsible behaviour in members of three Wisconsin conservation organizations. *Journal of Environmental Education, 21*(2), 35-40.

South West Observatory / Environment (2006, last updated). South West Environment: Landscape Map, Available at (http://www.swenvo.org.uk/environment/landscape.asp), last accessed February, 2006.

Stern, P. and Dietz, T. (1994). The value basis of environmental concern. *Journal of Social Issues, 46,* 1-20.

Stern, P., Dietz, T., Kalof, L. and Guagnano, G. (1995) Values, beliefs, and proenvironmental action: attitude formation toward emergent attitude objects. *Journal of Applied Social Psychology, 25,* 1611-1636.

Stern, P.C., and Oskamp, S. (1987) Managing scarce environmental resources. In D. Stokols, and I. Altman (eds.), *Handbook of environmental psychology, Vol.2* (pp.1043-1088). New York: Wiley.

Stewart, E. J., Hayward, B. M., & Devlin, P. J. (1998) The "Place" of interpretation: a new approach to the evaluation of interpretation. *Tourism Management 19*(3), 257-266.

Sustainable Development, (1998) *Tourism – Towards sustainability* (A consultation paper on sustainable tourism in UK), Department for Culture, Media and Sport.

Swarbrooke, J., (1999) *Sustainable Tourism Management,* Wallingford: CABI.

Tabachnick, B. and Fidell, L.S. (1996) *Using multivariate statistics.* (3rd edn.) Northridge: Harper Collins College.

The Countryside Agency (2005a) *Designated Landscapes,* Available at (http://www.countryside.gov.uk/LAR/Landscape/DL/index.asp), last accessed February, 2006.

The Countryside Agency (2005b) *Heritage Coast,* Available at (http://www.countryside.gov.uk/LAR/Landscape/DL/heritage_coasts/index.asp), last accessed February, 2006.

The Lulworth Estate (2002) *Management Statement,* Available at (http://www.lulworth.com/education/management_statement.htm), Last accessed February, 2006.

The Lulworth Estate (2004a) *The Lulworth Coastline.* Available at (http://www.lulworth.com/education/coast.htm), Last accessed February, 2006.
The Lulworth Estate (2004b) Lulworth Cove World Heritage Site. Available at (http://www.lulworth.com/education/world_heritage.htm), Last accessed February, 2006.

The Lulworth Estate (2004c) *The Fossil Forest.* Available at (http://www.lulworth.com/education/fossil_forest.htm), Last accessed February, 2006.

The Lulworth Estate (2004d) *Lulworth Cove Heritage Centre.* Available at (http://www.lulworth.com/education/heritage_centre.htm), Last accessed February, 2006.

The Map of Dorset and East Devon World Heritage Site in the UK. Available at (http://www.great-britain.co.uk/world-heritage/devon-dorset-coast.htm), Last accessed August, 2006.

Thøgersen, J. (2004) A cognitive dissonance interpretation of consistencies and inconsistencies in environmentally responsible behaviour. *Journal of Environmental Psychology, 24,* 93-103.

Thom, V.M. (1980) Evaluating countryside interpretation: a critical look at the current situation, *Museums Journal*, 79(4), 179-185.

Thorn, T.F. (1995) *Teaching low-impact camping practices to wilderness backpackers: An evaluation of trailhead information signing and personal contact*. Unpublished masters thesis. Utah State University.

Thompson, S.C.G., and Barton, M.A. (1994) Ecocentric and anthropocentric attitudes toward the environment. *Journal of Environmental Psychology, 14*, 149-157.

Tilden, F. (1977) *Interpreting Our Heritage*. Chapel Hill: The University of North Carolina Press.

Triandis, H.C. (1977) *Interpersonal behaviour*. California: Brooks-Cole Publishing Co.

Tribe, J., Font, X., Griffiths, N., Vickery, R. and Yale, K. (2000) *Environmental Management for Rural Tourism and Recreation*. London: Cassell.

Tubb, K.N. (2003) An evaluation of the effectiveness of interpretation within Dartmoor National Park in reaching the goals of sustainable tourism development. *Journal of Sustainable Tourism, 11*(6), 476-498.

Tull, D.S. and Hawkins, D.I. (1990), *Marketing Research: Measurement and Method* (5th edition), New York: John Wiley and Sons Inc.

Turner, R.K., Pearce D. and Bateman, I., (1994) *Environmental Economics: An Elementary Introduction*, Hemel Hempstead: Harvester Wheatsheaf.

Twining-Ward, L., and Butler, R., (2002) Implementing STD on a Small Island: Development and Use of Sustainable Tourism Development Indicators in Samoa, *Journal of Sustainable Tourism, 10* (5), 363-387.

Uitto, A., Juuti, K., Lavonen, J. and Meisalo, V. (2004) Who is responsible for sustainable development? Attitudes to environmental challenges: A survey of Finnish 9th grade comprehensive school students. In A. Laine, J. Lavonen, and V. Meisalo (eds.), *Current research on mathematics and science education, Department of Applied Sciences of Education, Research Report 253.* (pp.80-102). University of Helsinki.

UK Fossils Network (2005a) *Lulworth Cove*, Available at (http://www.ukfossils.co.uk/Fossils-and-Geology/Lulworth-Cove/Introduction-to-Lulworth-Cove.htm), Last accessed February, 2006.

UK Fossils Network (2005b) *Charmouth*, Available at (http://www.charmouth.ukfossils.co.uk), Last accessed February, 2006.

United Nations Conference on Environment and Development (UNCED) (1992) *Agenda 21: A Report of the United Nations Conference on Environment and Development*. Rio de Janeiro: United Nations.

United Nations Environmental Programme (UNEP) and World Tourism Organisation (WTO) (2005) *Making Tourism More Sustainable: A Guide for Policy Makers*, UNEP and WTO.

Uysal, M., Jurowski, C., Noe, F.P. and McDonald, C.D. (1994) Environmental attitude by trip and visitor characteristics. *Tourism Management, 15*(4), 284-94.

413

Uzzell, D. (1998) Strategic considerations and practical approaches to the evaluation of heritage and environmental interpretation, In D. Uzzell, and R. Ballantyne (eds) *Contemporary issues in heritage and environmental interpretation,* (pp.185-202). London: The Stationery Office.

Uzzell, D. and Ballantyne, R. (1998) *Contemporary issues in heritage and environmental interpretation,* London: The Stationery Office.

Van Liere, K.D. and Dunlap, R.E. (1981) Environmental concern: does it make a difference how it's measured? *Environment and Behaviour, 13,* 651-676.

Vander Stoep, G.A., and Gramann, J.H. (1988) Use of interpretation as an indirect visitor management tool: An alternative to regulation and enforcement. In M. Legg, (ed) *National Association of Interpretation 1988 Research Monograph,* 47-55.

Veal, A.J. (1997) *Research methods for leisure and tourism: A practical guide.* (2nd edn.) London: Pearson Education Limited.

Verplanken, B. and Aarts, H. (1999) Habit, attitude, and planned behaviour: is habit an empty construct or an interesting case of automaticity? *European Review of Social Psychology, 10,* 101-134.

Vincent, M.A. and Fazio, R.H. (1992) Attitude accessibility and its consequences for judgement and behaviour. In M.J. Manfredo (ed.), *Influencing Human Behaviour: Theory and applications in recreation, tourism and natural resources management* (pp.51-76). Champaign, Illinois: Sagamore Publishing.

Wall, G. (1997) Sustainable tourism – unsustainable development. In S. Wahab, and J.J. Pigram (eds) *Tourism Development and Growth.* (pp. 33-49). London: Routledge.

WCED (World Council for Economic Development) (1987) *Our Common Future, World Commission on the Environment and Development.* Oxford: Oxford University Press.

Wearing, S. and Neil, J. (1999) *Ecotourism: Impact, potentials and possibilities,* Oxford: Butterworth-Heinemann.

Weigel, R.H. (1983) Environmental attitudes and the prediction of behaviour. In N.R. Feimer, and E.S. Geller (eds.), *Environmental psychology: directions and perspectives* (pp. 257-287). New York: Praeger Publishers.

Weigel, R.H., and Weigel, J. (1978). Environmental concern- the development of a measure. *Environment and Behaviour, 10,* 3-15.

Weigel, R.H., Vernon, D.T.A. and Tognacci, L.N. (1974) specificity of the attitude as a determinant of attitude-behaviour congruence. *Journal of Personality and Social Psychology, 30,* 724-728.

Weiler, B. (1992) Educating the tourist: who's responsible? In B. Weiler (ed) *Ecotourism incorporating the global classroom. 1991 International conference papers* (pp. 288-292), Canberra: Bureau of Tourism Research.

Widner, C.J. and Roggenbuck, J. (2000) Reducing theft of pertrified wood at Pertrified forest national park, *Journal of Interpretation Research, 5*(1), 1-18.

Wight, P. (1998) Tools for sustainability in planning and managing tourism and recreation. In C. M. Hall and A. A. Lew (eds.) *Sustainable Tourism: a geographical perspective*, New York: Addison Wesley Longman Limited.

Wiseman, M., and Bogner, F.X. (2003). A higher-order model of ecological values and its relationship to personality. *Personality and Individual Differences, 34*, 783-794.

World Tourism and Travel Council (WTTC) World Tourism Oraganisation (WTO) and Earth Council (1995) *Agenda 21 for the Travel and Tourism Industry: Towards Environmentally Sustainable Development*. London: WTTC.

Wydle, L. (1996) *Is interpretation an effective sales tool for visitor information centres*. Paper presented at the fifth annual conference of the interpretation Australian association, Interpretation in action (pp. 119-120). Bendigo, Australia: Interpretation Australia Association.

Yale, P. (1991) *From Tourist Attractions to Heritage Tourism*. Huntington: ELM Publications.

Zanna, M.P. and Rempel, J.K. (1988) Attitudes: A new look at an old concept. In D. BarTal and A.W. Kruglanski (eds), *The social psychology of knowledge* (pp.315-334). Cambridge: Cambridge University Press.

Appendices

Appendix 1 Fossil Collecting Code of Conduct Brochure

Help conserve our World Heritage Site by following these guidelines when you visit.

Rules about fossil collecting vary along the coast so make sure you read local signs. In West Dorset between Lyme Regis and Burton Bradstock there is a code of conduct.

The Fossil Collectors' Code of Conduct for the West Dorset Coast

Aims

* Promote responsible and safe fossil collecting
* Restrict in situ digging or prospecting for fossils in the cliffs
* Clarify ownership of fossils
* Promote better communication between all those with an interest in fossils from the West Dorset coast
* Promote the acquisition of key scientifically important fossils by registered museums.

If you find a special or rare fossil from the West Dorset Coast, please register it at Charmouth Heritage Coast Centre:
Tel: 01297 560772, e-mail: register@charmouth.org
Fossils found outside the area of the code can also be registered.

The Centre will simply take details for a data base.
To see the records visit: www.charmouth.org

Further details of the fossil code can be found at
www.jurassiccoast.com or contact the World Heritage Team.
Tel 01305 225101.

Fossil Collecting on the Jurassic Coast

A guide to enjoyable, safe and responsible collecting

JURASSICCOAST
DORSET AND EAST DEVON
WORLD HERITAGE SITE

DORSET County Council

ENGLISH NATURE

  Responsible and safe fossil collecting

* Always read and comply with local signs. Rules and guidelines vary along the coast.

* Fossil hunting is like beach combing, the best fossils are found amongst the pebbles and boulders on the beach.

* Stay away from the cliffs. Rock falls can occur at any time.

* Do not hammer or dig in the cliffs.

* Your eyes are your best tools for finding fossils. Look for fossils in loose material on the beach.

* Keep hammering to a minimum.

* Wear eye protection when hammering.

* Check the weather and tides before setting out. It is best to collect on a falling tide.

* Beware of mudflows, especially after wet weather.

* Let someone know where you are going and when you plan to return.

* Wear appropriate clothing and footwear.

* Take special care in rough weather, never underestimate the power of the sea and beware in particular of strong undertows.

417

Appendix 2 Informal Exploratory Interview for the Visitor Centre Staff

2.1 Introduction Letter to the Visitor Centre Staff e-mail addresses:

<u>Charmouth Heritage Coast Centre</u>
Meirel Whaites (Warden)
Enquiries@charmouth.org

Lulworth Heritage Coast Centre
Maddy Pfaff
maddy@lulworth.com

To Whom It May Concern:

I'm a PhD student who is currently studying Tourism Management at the University of Surrey, Guildford. I am doing research regarding the evaluation of the effects of interpretation in promoting visitors' attitude and behaviour in achieving the goals of sustainable tourism at Heritage Coastal areas. For the case study sites of my research, I selected Charmouth Heritage Coast Visitor Centre and Lulworth Cove Heritage Visitor Centre which are located within the Jurassic Coast World Heritage Site.

Now, I'm planning to develop and conduct a visitor questionnaire survey. Before conducting the survey, I would like to ask for your permission and some advice regarding the content of the questionnaire through an informal interview with you. In particular, I would like to ask whether I am examining effectively the main concepts and themes of interpretation provided at Charmouth (or Lulworth) Heritage Coast Visitor Centre.

The research findings are expected to help identify whether effective interpretation can play an important role as a visitor management tool in sustainable tourism management at a resource sensitive area. It is hoped that the findings of this study will contribute to improve visitor services and enhance their experiences of the Visitor Centre. Also, this will contribute to promote appropriate responsible environmental behaviour of visitors, thus achieving sustainable tourism and environmental conservation.

In addition, if you have any research about the effects of interpretation at the Charmouth or the Jurassic Coastal Areas related to questionnaire and visitor profile, can you provide me with the copies of these documents and articles?. It would be very helpful information for my research. I would greatly appreciate your kind assistance with this matter.

I am looking forward to hearing from you soon.

Thank you in advance for your kind help.

Yours Sincerely,

Aise KyoungJin Kim (PhD Researcher)
School of Management
University of Surrey
Guildford, Surrey GU2 7XH
E-mail: icekjkim@yahoo.co.uk
Telephone: (01483) 68 6378

Continued Appendix 2.1,

The Main Questions for Informal Interview will be follow:

1. *Visitor Management and Conservation Issues*
2. What are the major environmental conservation issues at this area?
3. What are the main problems of negative impacts of tourism on the environment?
4. What are the major problems for visitor management?
5. How do you encourage visitor responsible behaviour toward local environmental conservation issues?

6. *Tourism*
7. General information regarding visitor profiles, visitor numbers, seasonality, motivation of the visitor, visitor facilities
8. What are the major tourism attractions and activities?

9. *Interpretation*
10. What are the main theme and objectives of the Visitor Centre?
11. How is the visitor centre managed?
12. General information regarding the number of staff, facilities, private or public fund, guided activities, and other interpretation programmes.

Appendix 3. The Main Visitor Survey Questionnaire (Lulworth)

UNIVERSITY OF SURREY

SCHOOL OF MANAGEMENT

	Pre	Post

**INTERPRETATION
AT LULWORTH
HERITAGE VISITOR
CENTRE**

Thank you for visiting the Lulworth Coastal Area today. This site is participating in a study of the effectiveness of interpretive services at the Lulworth Heritage Visitor Centre. The work is being conducted by a PhD student under the supervision of the University of Surrey. This survey will take roughly **10 minutes** of your time. Your answers will help us to evaluate your visit. Results from this research will provide useful information to the Lulworth Heritage Visitor Centre managers and future visitors. Your help is greatly appreciated and all information collected will remain strictly confidential.

Please return this questionnaire to the researcher who gave it to you or the visitor centre

✉ **Aise K. KIM**
Research office
SOM
University of Surrey
Guildford, GU2 7XH
Tel:01483 68 6378
E-mail:
k.kim@surrey.ac.uk

THANK YOU VERY MUCH FOR YOUR TIME
☺

Part A: About Your Visit Today

Please tick (√) only the appropriate box or comment to indicate your answers.

1.   Have you visited the ***Lulworth Heritage Visitor Centre*** today?

(Tick one (√) only)

☐   Yes , I did (Please Go to Q.2)   ☐   No, I didn't (Please Go to Q 1.1)

1.1. If no, do you plan to visit the ***Lulworth Heritage Visitor Centre***?
☐   Yes   ☐   No

2.   Is this your first visit the **Lulworth** Coastal Area?

☐   Yes   ☐   No

3. Did the new World Heritage Site Status influence your decision to visit
   the **Lulworth** Costal Area?

☐   Yes   ☐   No   ☐   I didn't know it was one

4. Are you involved in any environmental conservation activities?
(Please tick (√) as many as appropriate)
☐   None
☐   Volunteer work for environmental conservation
☐   Regular reader of environment, nature or wildlife magazines
☐   Membership of a conservation organisation
    (e.g. National Trust, English Heritage)
☐   Other_____

5. How often do you visit any natural areas, on average?
   (e.g. national parks & coastal areas)

☐ Less than once   ☐ 1 to 2   ☐ 3 to 4   ☐ 5 to 10   ☐ More than 10 times
per year   per year

6. Which of the following was **the most important** in your decision to visit this site
   today?   (Please tick (√) one only)

☐   To spend a good time with my family/friends
☐   To learn about the need to protect this area
☐   To have a relaxing time
☐   To enjoy the beauty of nature
☐   Other (please specify _____)

7. Who are you with today? (Tick one (√) only)

☐   Alone   ☐   Friends
☐   Spouse/partner   ☐   Friends and Family
☐   Family including children   ☐   An organised tour group
☐   Other _____   ☐   With guided tour

8. Have you read the *'Code of Conduct'* **brochure** about fossil collecting today?

☐   Yes   ☐   No   ☐   I don't know

9. Which of the following information source did you use today on-site?
☞ (Please tick (✔) as many as appropriate)

❏   None   ❏   Signboard   ❏   Brochure
❏   Guided walks tour   ❏   Talked to the Centre staff ❏   Exhibition/displays
❏   Computer interaction   ❏   Film   ❏   Publications
❏   Others _____

10. Have you ever visited the ***Lulworth Heritage Visitor Centre*** before?

☐   Yes (Go to Q.11)   ☐   No (Go to Q.12)

11. How many times a year do you normally visit the ***Lulworth Heritage Visitor Centre***? (Please tick (√) one only)

☐ Rarely   ☐ Once   ☐ Twice   ☐ 3 to 4   ☐ 5 to 10   ☐ More than 10 times

12. Thinking of the role of visitor centres, please indicate the extent to which you agree or disagree with the following statements where 1= Strongly disagree, 5= Strongly agree.
(Please tick (√) one response on each line)

	Strongly disagree				Strongly agree
	1	2	3	4	5
Visitor centres are good places to <u>educate</u> people	☐	☐	☐	☐	☐
Visitor centres provides <u>entertainment</u>	☐	☐	☐	☐	☐
Visitor centres provide a good introduction to <u>local</u> attractions	☐	☐	☐	☐	☐
Visitor centres provide a useful source of <u>tourist</u> information about local facilities	☐	☐	☐	☐	☐
Visitor centres are designed to help people <u>understand</u> the local environment	☐	☐	☐	☐	☐

13. Overall, how serious do you think the threats to the environment are at the **Lulworth** Coastal Area? (Please tick (√) one only)

Not at all	1	2	3	4	5	Very much

14. With reference to the **Lulworth** Coastal Area, please indicate the extent to which you agree or disagree with the following statements, where 1= Strongly disagree, 5= Strongly agree. There is no correct or wrong answer. Please read carefully and express what you believe to be the closest to your feelings. (Please tick (√) one response on each line)

I think that …………..	Strongly disagree				Strongly agree
	1	2	3	4	5
It is important to protect the quality of the coastal area	☐	☐	☐	☐	☐
Visitors should report the discovery of special fossils, for example, to the *Lulworth Heritage Visitor Centre*	☐	☐	☐	☐	☐
It is safe to climb the cliffs	☐	☐	☐	☐	☐
It is important to protect fossils for future generations	☐	☐	☐	☐	☐
Collecting fossils from the cliffs will damage the cliffs	☐	☐	☐	☐	☐
Visitors should help to remove beach litter	☐	☐	☐	☐	☐
It is dangerous to climb the cliffs	☐	☐	☐	☐	☐
Fossil collecting helps in the progress of scientific research	☐	☐	☐	☐	☐
Visitors should be allowed to collect fossils from the cliffs	☐	☐	☐	☐	☐
Walking off the footpaths will not damage the cliffs	☐	☐	☐	☐	☐
Visitors do not need to remove beach litter	☐	☐	☐	☐	☐
It is important for visitors to behave in an environmentally responsible way	☐	☐	☐	☐	☐
Climbing cliffs will damage the environment	☐	☐	☐	☐	☐
It is dangerous to collect fossils from the cliffs	☐	☐	☐	☐	☐
It is important to keep cliff erosion to a minimum	☐	☐	☐	☐	☐
Visitors do not need to report special fossils to the *Lulworth Heritage Visitor Centre*	☐	☐	☐	☐	☐
Fossil collecting helps one to learn about fossils	☐	☐	☐	☐	☐
Picking up litter will reduce the amount of water pollution	☐	☐	☐	☐	☐
Visitors should not be allowed to climb the cliffs	☐	☐	☐	☐	☐
Beach litter does not contribute to water pollution	☐	☐	☐	☐	☐
It is safe to collect fossils from the cliffs	☐	☐	☐	☐	☐
Visitors should be allowed to climb the cliffs	☐	☐	☐	☐	☐

15. With references to the **Lulworth** Coastal Area, please indicate the extent which you agree with each of the following statements, where 1= Not seriously concerned at all, 5=Very seriously concerned. (Please tick (√) one response on each line)

I am concerned that...... Or I worry that.........	Not seriously at all			Very Seriously	
	1	2	3	4	5
People climb the cliffs	☐	☐	☐	☐	☐
The cliffs are eroding rapidly	☐	☐	☐	☐	☐
People collect the fossils from the cliffs	☐	☐	☐	☐	☐
There is too much litter on the beach	☐	☐	☐	☐	☐
Important fossils are damaged by visitors	☐	☐	☐	☐	☐
People do not keep to the footpaths on the cliffs	☐	☐	☐	☐	☐
People dispose of litter on the beach	☐	☐	☐	☐	☐
People take special fossils home	☐	☐	☐	☐	☐
Pollution on the coast is being increasing by beach litter	☐	☐	☐	☐	☐

16. We would like to know about your willingness to protect the **Lulworth** Coastal Area. Please indicate the extent to which you agree or disagree with the following statements, where 1= Strongly disagree, 5= Strongly agree. (Please tick (√) one response on each line)

	Strongly disagree			Strongly agree	
	1	2	3	4	5
I will keep to the footpaths on the cliffs	☐	☐	☐	☐	☐
I will inform the ***Lulworth Heritage Visitor Centre***, if I discover special fossils	☐	☐	☐	☐	☐
I intend to behave in a way that will not harm plants and animals	☐	☐	☐	☐	☐
I intend to become more involved in environmental issues	☐	☐	☐	☐	☐
I intend to make a donation to an environmental organisation	☐	☐	☐	☐	☐
I do not intend to disturb any marine life	☐	☐	☐	☐	☐
I will tell people about the importance of the geological environment in this area	☐	☐	☐	☐	☐
I will not climb the cliffs	☐	☐	☐	☐	☐
I will follow the Code of Conduct (e.g the countryside code, the fossil collecting code)	☐	☐	☐	☐	☐
I will pick up beach litter when I see it, even if it did not belong to me	☐	☐	☐	☐	☐
I will not collect fossils from the cliff	☐	☐	☐	☐	☐
I intend to become involved in volunteer work for environmental conservation activities	☐	☐	☐	☐	☐
I intend to become a member of an environmental organisation	☐	☐	☐	☐	☐

17. Thinking of your experience today, how satisfied were you with your visit to the
Lulworth Coastal Area?

(Tick (√) one only)

Not at all satisfied	1	2	3	4	5	Very satisfied

Part B: About You

Please tick (√) the appropriate box or comment to indicate your answers.

18. Are you?

    ❑   Male   ❑   Female

19. How old are you?

    ☐   18-25   ☐ 26 to 35   ☐ 36 to 45   ☐ 46 to 55   ☐ 56 to 65   ☐ Over 66

20. Do you have any educational qualifications? (Tick the highest one (√) only)

    ☐   No formal educational qualification   ☐ High school qualifications

    ☐   College/ professional qualification(s)   ☐ University/ Post-graduate degree(s)

21. Where do you live? (Tick one (√) only)

    ☐   Dorset Region   ☐   The South West of England

    ☐   The South East of England   ☐   Elsewhere in the UK
           (including London)

    ☐ Overseas   _____
    (If you are from overseas, **Please state your country of residence**)

The following section is to evaluate your experience to the *Lulworth Heritage Visitor Centre*.
✓ If you did not visit the centre today, please do not answer (☺ **Thank you very much for your time** ☒)

☞ **Please return this questionnaire to the researcher who gave it to you or the centre**

✓ **If you visited the centre today, please continue to the end of the questions**

---

22. Overall, what have you experienced **the most** from your visit to the **Lulworth** Coastal Area? (Please tick (√) one only)

☐	I simply had a good time with family/friends
☐	I learned the need to protect this area
☐	I had a relaxing time
☐	I enjoyed the beauty of nature
☐	I learned about the fossils

23. Of the following, which best describes your visit to the _**Lulworth Heritage Visitor Centre**_ today? (Please tick (√) one response on each line)

	1	2	3	4	5	
Uninspiring	☐	☐	☐	☐	☐	Inspiring
Not educational	☐	☐	☐	☐	☐	Educational
Not enjoyable	☐	☐	☐	☐	☐	Enjoyable
Boring	☐	☐	☐	☐	☐	Stimulating
Disappointing	☐	☐	☐	☐	☐	Fulfilling
Dull	☐	☐	☐	☐	☐	Exciting

24. Which one of the following do you feel you have learnt most about the **Lulworth** Coast Area? (Tick (√) one only)

☐ Geology of the coast   ☐ Marine life
☐ Fossils   ☐ Responsible environmental behaviour
☐ Conservation   ☐ History
☐ Other _____   ☐ None of them

25. To what extent has your understanding of this site been changed by your visit to the _**Lulworth Heritage Visitor Centre**_? (Tick (√) one only)

Not at all changed	1	2	3	4	5	A great deal

26. To what extent has the _**Lulworth Heritage Visitor Centre**_ helped you to increase your awareness of environmental conservation in the **Lulworth** Coastal area?   (Tick (√) one only)

Not at all	1	2	3	4	5	A great deal

27. To what extent has the _**Lulworth Heritage Visitor Centre**_ helped you to change your attitudes toward conservation issues in this area ? (Tick (√) one only)

Not at all	1	2	3	4	5	A great deal

28. Overall, how satisfied were you with the quality of the _**Lulworth Heritage Visitor Centre**_?

Not at all satisfied	1	2	3	4	5	Very satisfied

☺   Thank you very much for your time   ☺